Adobe®
Photoshop® CS2
VISUAL™
ENCYCLOPEDIA

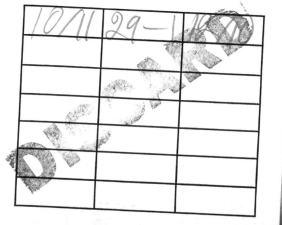

COLLECTION MANAGEMENT

Photoshop® CS2 Visual™ Encyclopedia

Published by
Wiley Publishing, Inc.
111 River Street
Hoboken, NJ 07030-5774

Published simultaneously in Canada

The Library of Congress Control Number is available
from the Library of Congress

ISBN-13: 978-0-7645-9860-9

ISBN-10: 0-7645-9860-0

Manufactured in the United States of America

10 9 8 7 6 5 4 3 2 1

Trademark Acknowledgments

Contact Us

For general information on our other products and
services please contact our Customer Care Department
within the U.S. at (800) 762-2974, outside the U.S. at
(317) 572-3993, or fax (317) 572-4002.

For technical support please visit
www.wiley.com/techsupport.

006.686

Romaniello, S.

WILEY

Wiley Publishing, Inc.

Sales

Contact Wiley at
(800) 762-2974 or
fax (317) 572-4002.

CREDITS

Project Editors
Sue Hobbs
Maureen Spears

Acquisitions Editor
Michael Roney

Product Development Manager
Lindsay Sandman

Technical Editors
Michael Cohen
David Herman

Editorial Manager
Robyn Siesky

Manufacturing
Allan Conley
Linda Cook
Paul Gilchrist
Jennifer Guynn

Screen Artists
Ronda David-Burroughs
Jill A. Proll

Illustrators
Kristin Corley
Rita Marley

Book Design
Kathie Rickard
LeAndra Hosier

Production Coordinator
Adrienne Martinez

Layout
Jennifer Heleine
LeAndra Hosier
Amanda Spagnuolo

Proofreader
Sossity R. Smith

Quality Control
Leeann Harney
Joe Niesen
Rob Springer

Indexer
Richard T. Evans

Additional Editorial Contributions
Elizabeth Cardenas-Nelson

**Vice President and Executive
Group Publisher**
Richard Swadley

Vice President and Publisher
Barry Pruett

Director of Composition Services
Debbie Stailey

ABOUT THE AUTHOR

Stephen Romaniello is an artist, educator, and writer. He began his career in graphics in 1980 as a production artist and typesetter; soon he was promoted to designer and then art director. In 1982, he became a partner in Armory Park Design Group. Three years later he founded Congress Street Design, a full-service design firm. In 1987, at the beginning of the digital revolution in graphics technology, he purchased his first computer. Stephen accepted a faculty position in 1990 in the Advertising Art program at Pima Community College in Tucson, Arizona, with the intention of developing a state-of-the-art digital graphics program. He served as department chair of the renamed Digital Arts Department for eight years.

Stephen has developed curriculum and training materials for many mainstream graphics programs and has offered seminars at the Maine Photographic Workshops, the League for Innovation, and the National Business Media. A certified instructor in Photoshop, he currently teaches digital art courses at Pima Community College in Arizona. He is the co-author of *Mastering Adobe GoLive 4* with Molly Holtschlag and the author of *Mastering Photoshop 6, Photoshop 7 Savvy, Photoshop CS Savvy,* and *Photoshop CS2 Savvy,* all published by Sybex. His column, "The Digital Eye," appears monthly in the magazine *Digital Graphics*. Romaniello is the founder of Gorilla Geeks, a company that offers onsite training and consulting throughout the country. His home and studio are in Tucson, Arizona.

DEDICATION

For Karen

ACKNOWLEDGMENTS

Writing a book of this kind is by no means a solitary venture. Many friends contributed their time, expertise, and support. Thanks are in order to David Fugate, my agent at Waterside Productions. Thanks and kudos to the production team at Wiley, including acquisitions editor Mike Roney, whose tenacity and foresight helped get this book going, and to development and copy editor Sue Hobbs, whose great sense of humor took the edge off the intense deadline pressure, and whose editing skills tightened up the material. Thanks to technical editor David Herman for his expertise and attention to detail.

Thanks is owed to contributors Allan Timmerman and Imo Baird, to my artist friends who provided images and inspiration including Andy Rush, Pasquale Maroni, Silvia Plant, Claude Bailey, Michael McNaulty, Doug Anderson, to my daughter Leah Romaniello for providing some wonderful images for this book, and to Michael Robinson and Katrina Munzar for keeping my computers running at optimal performance.

I want to thank my friends Margo Taylor, Randal Williams, Mark Williams, Charlotte Lowe Bailey, Molly Holtschlag, Seth Schindler, and especially Karen Brennan, whose support helped me through some tough moments.

My gratitude to my colleagues at Pima Community College, including Frank Pickard, Dennis Landry, Dave Wing, Patty Gardiner, Mary Leffler, Margo Burwell, and Jack Mertes, and of course to my students, who are the best teachers of all.

Many thanks to the Photoshop beta team for keeping me appraised of the many changes to the program during its development. Also, thanks to Image Stock, Corel, PhotoDisk, ImageIdeas, and Eclectic Collections for providing images from their CD libraries. Thanks to my brother, Chuck, and to my mom, Violetta, for their effusive enthusiasm.

Table of Contents

B

C

D

E

L

M

N

O

P

Q

INTRODUCTION

Since its first release in 1990, Photoshop has emerged as the standard in image manipulation software. It has revolutionized the way we view and create images. It has become the tool of choice of amateur and professional photographers, designers, artists, printers, and publishers. It is even used by scientists.

Photoshop's popularity is in part attributable to the fact that it empowers us to change the reality of pictures in many ways. From the simple auto color correction to full blown professional compositing, Photoshop's elegant graphic user interface places you in a virtual art studio, darkroom, print shop, or design loft with features that empower you to warp the reality of the image and publish to printable and electronic media. And after all, who can resist the temptation to change the nature of what we see?

Photoshop CS2 Visual Encyclopedia is a visual approach to a visual medium. It is designed as a companion reference to the art of digital image manipulation, but moreover it is a unique method of learning how to use and apply Photoshop's vast power. It is also designed to be a comprehensive visual reference to Photoshop's tools and techniques. Its sections have a description of each feature and a step-by-step demonstration of their potential for creating and editing images. Each section also contains tips that further extend the capabilities of the program.

Photoshop CS2 Visual Encyclopedia is organized so that you can easily access information about Photoshop's features. Its alphabetical listing of features includes descriptions and step-by-step modules that will make all aspects of the software more accessible and familiar. Photoshop has the capability to perform almost any imaginable imaging operation. When you consider the number of operations that Photoshop can execute, and how they might be combined, the image-editing possibilities become endless. Making this information comprehensible and interesting to you is the goal of this book. *Photoshop CS2 Visual Encyclopedia* takes the sting out of learning the program, because you can visually follow each illustrated step and apply these techniques to your own images. The book is for users on both the Mac and Windows platforms. Key commands are provided for both.

The primary content of *Photoshop CS2 Visual Encyclopedia* is divided into two parts. Part I details all of Photoshop's tools and demonstrates how they work and their potential applications. Part II is devoted to techniques, which range from menu items, palettes, interface operations, and multiple task processes. The book thoroughly covers the nuts and bolts of the basic operations but it also demonstrates the latest and greatest features of the software.

It gives me great pleasure to make the information I've gathered over the past 15 years available to you in this innovative visual format. I truly hope that *Photoshop CS2 Visual Encyclopedia* meets your needs, answers your questions, and inspires you to create brilliant images.

Stephen Romaniello
Tucson Arizona, 2005

Photoshop CS
Visual Encyclopedia

Part I: Tools

The Tools palette displays Photoshop's tools in the Photoshop workspace so that you can easily access them. Photoshop represents each tool with its own cursor icon. To use a tool, you select it from the Tools palette. You can then place the cursor where you want to affect the image and apply the effect by clicking or clicking and dragging the mouse (depending on the tool) over the image.

The Tools palette displays icons for 22 different tools. However, that is not the extent of the tools available to you. When you see a small black arrow in the right bottom corner of a tool icon, it means that you have additional variations of that tool available to you. To access those additional tools, click and hold the mouse

button and a pull-out menu appears from which you can make additional selections.

There are 58 tools available altogether. The Tools palette has ten general sections. From top to bottom, the categories are the Adobe On-Line access logo, selection tools, painting tools, editing tools, vector tools, and display tools. Below those sections are the foreground and background color swatches, Quick Mask options, display options, and at the very bottom of the palette, the Edit-In command.

When you select a tool, the Options bar at the top of the screen offers options unique to the tool you have selected. These options allow you to change the characteristics of the current tool.

ANNOTATIONS:
Attach a Note

At some point, you may need to attach a note within a document to remember specific settings or other particulars about the image. You may also want to make sure that a print operator, Web programmer, or another computer artist gets important instructions or information about an image as they process it. Photoshop provides several tools to do this. The Notes tool, the Audio Annotation tool, and the File Info palette can record and provide useful information within the image. Also accessible from Photoshop but outside of an image is information available via Adobe Bridge — a file management application included with Photoshop that uses

Metadata. The Notes tool works like an electronic post-it note. Just click somewhere on the image and a small window will appear so you can type reminders, warnings, or instructions. When you close the note, a small icon remains. When you want to open the note just click on the icon.

See also>>

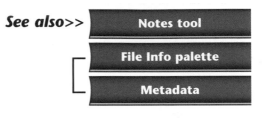

Notes tool

File Info palette

Metadata

---

① Click the Notes Annotations tool from the Notes tool pull-out menu in the Tools palette.

② In the Options bar, type your name in the Author text box.

The default name in the box is the registered owner of Photoshop.

③ Click the Color swatch and choose a color for the note that appears on the image.

④ Click the image where you want to place the note.

The Notes Annotations dialog box appears.

⑤ Type a reminder or instruction in the box.

● When you are finished you can close the note by clicking here.

Notice that a small icon remains after you close the note.

6 Click on the Notes Annotation icon.

The note reappears.

TIPS

Did You Know?

Even though you can see the notes icon on top of your image, it will not print or be visible in another application. In fact, unless you save the image as a Photoshop, TIF file, or PDF it will not be visible (available) in Photoshop.

Try This!

The Audio Annotations tool allows you to actually record an audio message and store it within your image file. Just click on the image and a dialog box appears giving you instructions on how to record your message.

Warning!

Do not use an Audio Annotation unless you really need to record a spoken message. Audio files require more disk space than text files. Attaching an audio annotation to a Photoshop image will not only increase the size of your document, but may also make Photoshop less efficient with its additional need for memory.

Apply It!

To discard an audio or note annotation, click the icon with the Move tool and then press Delete (Backspace). To clear all of the annotations from a document, click the Clear All button in the Options bar. A dialog box appears and asks you if you are sure that you want to omit the annotations. Click OK.

BACKGROUND COLOR:
Specify a Background Color

You can change the background color and apply it to a background layer or erase with it. You can think of a background as the distant environment in front of which you place the important elements of an image, or a board onto which you have pasted your image. If you cut a shape with an X-acto knife on the image and remove the resulting piece, you reveal the underlying pasteboard.

In Photoshop, the background is more than the cyclorama for the action. In fact, the term *background* applies to several items important to Photoshop's dynamic workflow. The *Background layer* is the default opaque layer at the bottom of the layer stack. You apply the *Background color* when you make a selection, move or cut the background layer.

The default background color is white, but you can change it using the Color Picker or Color palette. You also apply the background color when you drag the Eraser tool over the Background layer, when you fill an area with the Fill command, and when you increase the overall size of the image with the Canvas Size dialog box.

See also>>

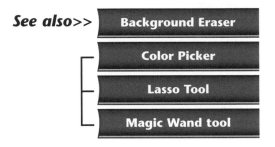

- Background Eraser
- Color Picker
- Lasso Tool
- Magic Wand tool

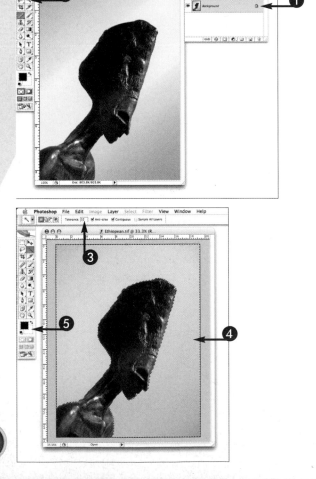

❶ Open an image that contains a background layer.

❷ Click the Magic Wand tool.

Alternatively, you can press W.

❸ Type a Tolerance value in the Options bar.

❹ Click the image to make a broad selection that contains similar colors.

❺ Click the Background Color Swatch in the Tools palette.

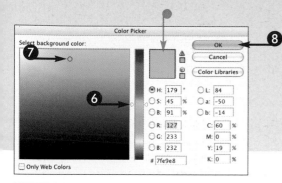

The Color Picker appears.

⑥ Click and drag the Hue slider to select a color range.

⑦ Click the color you want in the color field.

You can click and drag the circular color indicator left to lower the saturation, or right to increase the saturation; move it up to lighten the brightness, or down to darken the brightness.

● The color swatch changes to reflect the current color.

⑧ Click OK.

⑨ Press Delete (Backspace).

Photoshop fills the area with the specified color.

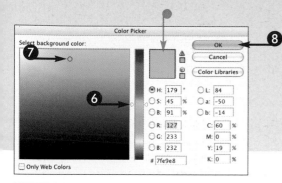

TIPS

Did You Know?
You can specify precise colors in the Color Picker by typing values in the HSB, RGB, LAB, or CMYK fields.

Try This!
Select the Move tool by pressing V. Place the Move tool inside the selection and drag. Photoshop replaces the selected area with the background color.

Try This!
You may switch between the background and foreground by simply pressing X.

Try This!
Click the Eraser tool. Select a brush from the Brush presets in the Options bar. As you drag across the image, the brush deposits a stroke of the background color.

BLUR TOOL:
Reduce Depth of Field

You can use the Blur tool to blend colors, soften edges, or reduce the focus of a background. The application of the Blur tool emphasizes elements in the foreground or background.

The manual counterpart of a set of Blur filters, the Blur tool softens the region where you apply it by decreasing the relative contrast values of adjacent pixels. Like all the tools that rely on brushes for their application, the effect can vary greatly depending on the brush shape and dynamics that you select from the Brushes palette.

You can apply the Blur tool directly to an image or to an Alpha channel, Quick mask, or Layer mask to soften all or part of a selection. Lower-resolution documents are affected more quickly than higher-resolution documents.

You can increase the intensity of the tool by adjusting its Strength setting in the Options bar from 1 to 100 percent. You achieve the illusion of depth of field by applying different variations in the Strength tool to various regions of the image.

See also>>
> **Filters: Blur**

> **Brushes palette**

❶ Open an image that has the same focus in the foreground and background areas.

❷ Click the Blur tool.

③ In the Options bar, select a brush tip.

④ Click here and select a Strength value.

This example uses a 100-point brush tip and a Strength of 100.

⑤ Drag over the area that you want to appear farthest back in the picture plane.

⑥ With a reduced Strength setting, drag over the areas that you want to appear slightly out of focus.

This example changed the Strength setting to 50.

⑦ Leave the closest areas untouched.

The selected area appears slightly out of focus.

TIPS

Warning!

The Blur tool requires a lot of memory to process its effects, especially on high-resolution documents. It may take some time for you to see the effect after you drag over an area. To maintain control, make a pass with the tool, release the mouse, and then pass over the area again until the desired results are achieved.

Try This!

To further control the effect, make multiple passes with the Blur tool at lower strengths.

Try This!

To blur larger areas, make a selection. Select the Gaussian Blur filter or any other of the blur filters and apply it to the selected area within the marquee.

BURN TOOL:
Darken an Area of a Photograph

Many photographers use Adobe Photoshop as an alternative to traditional darkroom techniques. In addition to a vast array of color correction and image adjustments that can restore and enhance overall image quality, Photoshop has two little tools that simulate what photographers once did with an enlarger in the darkroom. The Dodge and Burn tools are virtual knockoffs of traditional lightening and darkening techniques that required the use of the hand or a wand.

Photographers frequently use the Burn tool to underexpose or darken areas of an image. It does this by lowering the brightness values of pixels as you move it over the image. As with the Dodge tool, the Options bar lets you pick a range of pixels to affect by selecting Highlights, Midtones, or Shadows from the menu. Adjusting the exposure weakens or strengthens the effect.

You can use the Burn tool to push back or darken areas adjacent to elements you want to emphasize.

See also>> **Dodge tool**

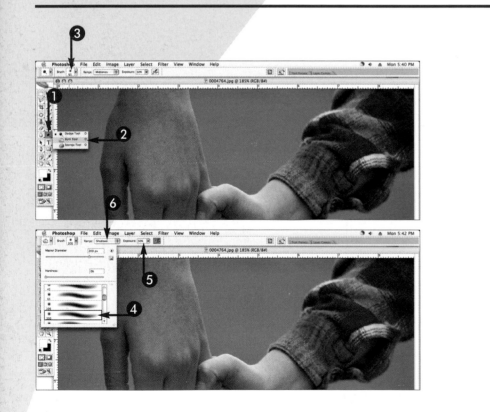

① Click and hold the Dodge tool.

② Click the Burn tool from the fly-out menu.

③ Click a brush size from the Options bar.

④ Click a shape from the Brushes presets in the Options bar.

⑤ Click here and set the Exposure value to a low value.

⑥ Click here and select the range of pixels that you want to affect.

This example uses an Exposure value of 17 percent and a Range of Shadows.

Note: *In all context menus, holding down shift while typing the tools letter cycles through the hidden tools.*

7 Place your cursor on a dark area of the image that you want to make even darker.

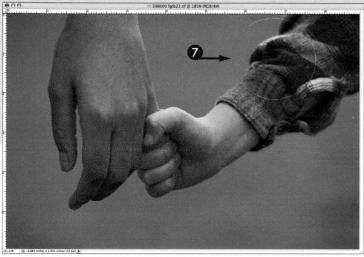

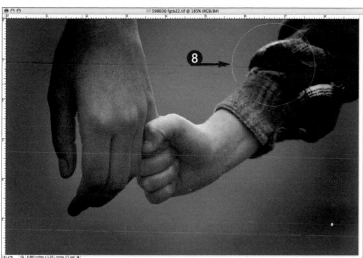

8 Click and drag over the area.

Continue to drag over the areas until the desired level of darkness is achieved.

TIPS

Caution!
High exposures can darken an area too quickly. Set the exposure low and make multiple passes for more control.

Try This!
The Burn tool can cause severe and undesirable color shifts on color images. To avoid this problem, copy the layer you want to burn and place it directly over the original layer. Assign a Luminosity Blending mode to the new layer and burn the target area.

Did You Know?
The Burn tool's strength depends on the resolution of the document. Higher-resolution documents are affected less by the same exposure than lower-resolution documents.

CLONE STAMP:
Replace Unwanted Elements

You can perform visual miracles with the Clone Stamp tool, which lets you replace pixels in one area by cloning pixels from another area of an image. You can therefore copy textures from one small area to another, or eliminate unwanted elements. The size of the brush determines the size of the sampled area.

The Aligned option in the Options bar is selected by default. This option locks the relative distance of the sampled point from the target point. As you paint with the Clone tool, the sample point changes. It is as if the sample and target point are connected by rigid cable — the two points move in tandem, always maintaining the same distance from each other. If you deselect the

Aligned option, the Clone tool samples pixels from only one designated point.

The following example illustrates a common use for the Clone tool. You can eliminate the utility cables marring an otherwise clear sky in a lovely picture. Because there is plenty of sky from which to sample, you can "paint" the sky over the cables.

See also>>

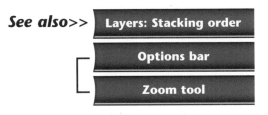

Layers: Stacking order

Options bar

Zoom tool

❶ Click the Clone Stamp tool from the Tools palette.

Alternatively, you can press S.

❷ Click an appropriate brush from the Brushes Preset menu on the Options bar.

Soft-edged brushes allow the new, cloned pixels to blend in more smoothly with the target area.

❸ Zoom in on the area you want to modify.

❹ Press Opt (Mac) or Alt (Win), and click the area which you want to serve as the sample point

The sample cursor appears.

❺ Release the mouse and move the cursor to the target area.

6 Click and drag your cursor.

The tool replaces the target pixels with the sampled pixels.

As you drag the brush across the image, a small cross indicates the area that is being copied.

The unwanted elements are gone from your image.

Caution!

When cloning a texture, sample frequently in different locations on the texture to make the cloned area unrecognizable.

Did You Know?

Other tools that copy pixels from one area to another are the Healing Brush, Patch tool, and Spot Healing Brush.

Try This!

On long, straight areas like electrical lines, sample the sky just below the wire. Choose a soft brush, one that is a little thicker than the wire. Click either end of the wire. Move the curser to the opposite end of the wire. Press Shift and click the mouse. The clone automatically fills in the distance between the two points.

COLOR REPLACEMENT TOOL:
Manually Change the Color of an Area

Similar to the options in the Hue/Saturation and the Replace color dialog boxes, the Color Replacement tool changes the relative color of pixels. This tool is unique, however, because it has the accessibility and accuracy of a manual tool with the versatility of features in the Brushes palette.

The Color Replacement tool swaps the existing color on an image with the foreground color. The default Mode setting in the Options bar is Color, and it maintains the luminosity and saturation of a color while replacing its hue. You can choose other modes from the Mode menu that apply other characteristics of the foreground color to the image.

The Sampling menu determines the method in which the colors that you want to alter are selected. Continuous samples colors continuously as you drag, coloring areas of different colors. Once affects only the color that you have sampled. You use this option to affect areas of solid color. Background Swatch colors areas that contain the current background color.

See also>>

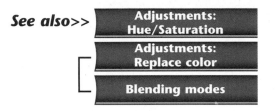

Adjustments: Hue/Saturation

Adjustments: Replace color

Blending modes

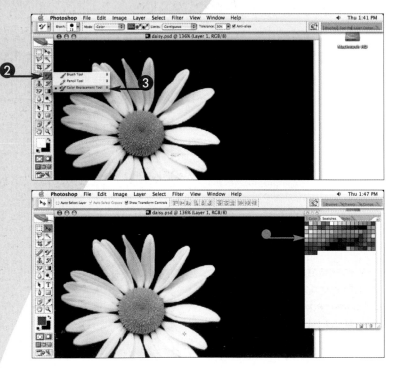

① Open a file in which you want to replace color.

② Click the Brush tool until the fly-out menu appears.

③ Click the Color Replacement tool.

● You can use the default settings in the Options bar.

Press F6 to display the Swatches Palette.

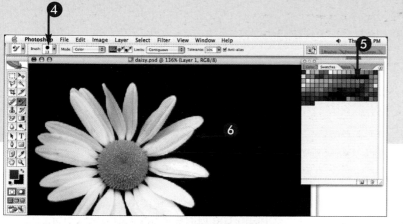

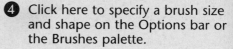

④ Click here to specify a brush size and shape on the Options bar or the Brushes palette.

⑤ Click a colored square in the Swatches palette to specify a foreground color.

⑥ Click and drag over the areas of the image.

The hue changes.

⑦ Continue painting until you cover all the areas you want to replace.

You can select a different color from the Swatches palette and drag over the additional areas as you experiment with the various properties of the Color Replacement tool.

TIPS

Did You Know?

Other features on the Color Replacement tool's Options bar control important aspects of the tool's performance. Limits control what pixels will be colored. Select Discontiguous to color all of the pixels within the Tolerance range on the entire layer.

Contiguous colors pixels of the sampled color that are adjacent to each other. Find Edges affects pixels of the sampled color that are adjacent to each other, but it better preserves the sharpness of the edge pixels of the remaining image.

Tolerance controls the range of colors to be altered. Low Tolerance affects colors that are similar to the sampled colors; Higher Tolerance affects colors that are more diverse in range.

CROP TOOL:
Eliminate Unwanted Edges

You can often salvage a photograph with an undesirable composition using the Crop tool, which allows you to focus on a section of an image and trim away the rest. When you define the area you want to keep, Photoshop places a translucent shadow on everything outside your crop box. You can then adjust the crop box's size using one of its corner handles, or you can rotate the mask in any direction.

The Crop tool can scale the image to a specific size and resolution. Besides allowing you to define a custom size, it has standard presets, which define the options and characteristics you normally set manually, such as Height, Width, and Resolution.

Once you set these options, the crop tool generates a rectangle with proportional dimensions, which remains the same as you position and size the area you want to crop. For example, if you set the crop tool for a 4 x 6 photo, even if you zoom in on a two-inch area, the crop tool generates a 2 by 3 image.

The Perspective option adjusts the corner anchor points of the bounding box independently. This feature is useful for distorting an image as you crop it or fit an image's content into a rectangular document of a specific size.

See also>> **Trim**

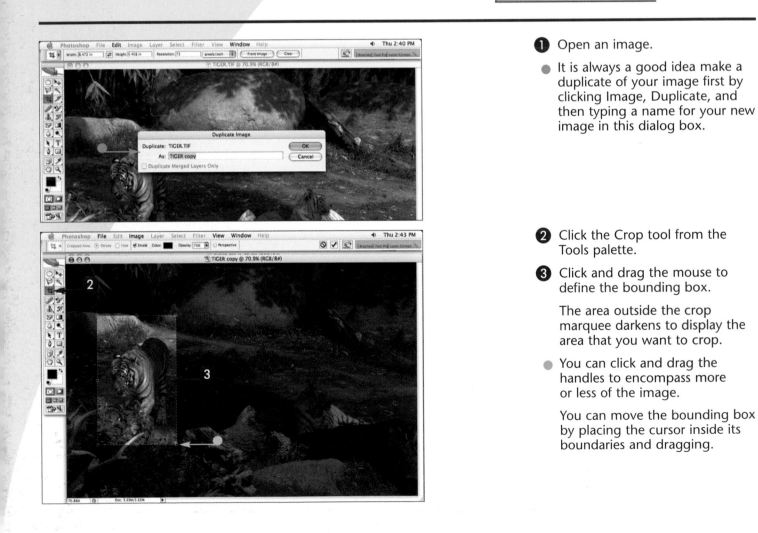

❶ Open an image.

● It is always a good idea make a duplicate of your image first by clicking Image, Duplicate, and then typing a name for your new image in this dialog box.

❷ Click the Crop tool from the Tools palette.

❸ Click and drag the mouse to define the bounding box.

The area outside the crop marquee darkens to display the area that you want to crop.

● You can click and drag the handles to encompass more or less of the image.

You can move the bounding box by placing the cursor inside its boundaries and dragging.

You can place the cursor outside one of the corners of the crop marquee until you see the Rotation icon and then click and drag the icon either clockwise or counterclockwise to rotate the image.

④ When the marquee is where you want it, click the Commit button (☑) in the Options bar or press Return (Enter).

● You can also double-click inside the cropping area to commit your crop.

Your cropping is complete.

Try This!

You can constrain the crop bounding box proportions by pressing Shift as you click and drag from a corner point. Press Opt (Alt) and drag from a corner point to generate the bounding box from the center point.

Did You Know?

You can use the Crop tool to increase the size of a cropped area if the height and width values you type are greater than the original size.

Try This!

You can turn the crop shield on and off by selecting or deselecting the Shield option (☑ changes to ☐) in the Crop tool Options bar. Select a color for the shielded area by clicking an appropriate swatch. You can select an opacity by selecting or typing a value.

COLOR PALETTE:
Choose a Color

You can quickly apply a new color to an image or a portion of an image using the Color palette, located in the same palette cluster as the Swatches and Styles palettes. Although the document's color model appears by default when you open the Color palette, you can also select RGB, HSB, Grayscale, CMYK, Lab, or Web Color models from the palette's Options menu. You can also use the swatches in the upper-left corner of the palette, to select a foreground or background color swatch.

You define the swatches' colors using the various sliders. For example, the RGB color model has sliders for R (red), G (green) and B (Blue). These sliders control the amount of each color to go into the swatch color, which in turn defines the color of any coloring tools. The sliders are dynamic, meaning that

a gradient bar displays the selected color component that corresponds to the position of the sliders. Adjusting the sliders changes the color of the color bars. The Tool and Color palette swatches also change as you adjust the slider. If you use a specific color library and know the values for the color you want, you can enter those values for each component.

See also>>

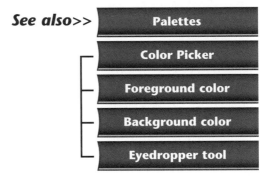

Palettes

Color Picker

Foreground color

Background color

Eyedropper tool

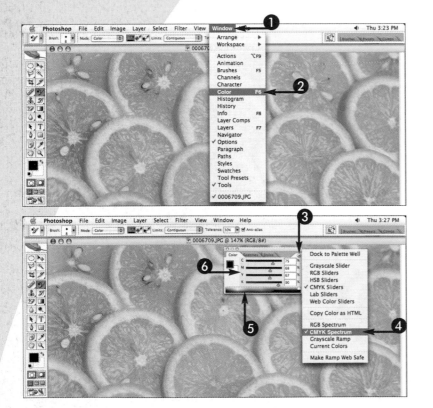

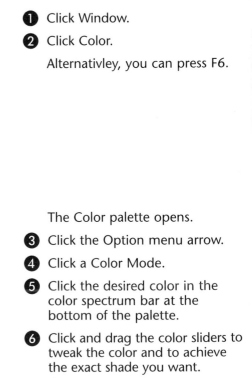

❶ Click Window.

❷ Click Color.

Alternativley, you can press F6.

The Color palette opens.

❸ Click the Option menu arrow.

❹ Click a Color Mode.

❺ Click the desired color in the color spectrum bar at the bottom of the palette.

❻ Click and drag the color sliders to tweak the color and to achieve the exact shade you want.

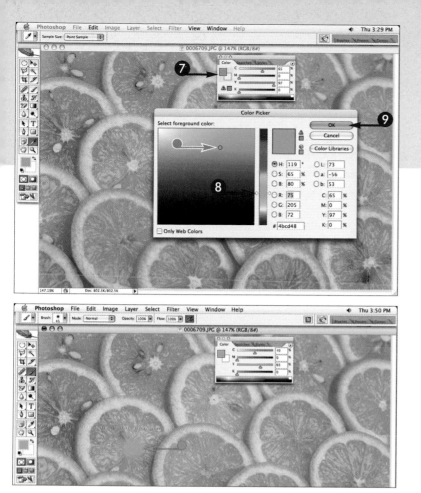

7 Click either the foreground or the background color swatch.

The Color Picker appears.

8 Click and drag the slider to further refine your color.

● Alternatively, you can click somewhere in the Select Background Color spectrum.

9 Click OK.

● You are now ready to use your new color.

COLOR PICKER:
Choose an HSB Color

The Color Picker is the most versatile color tool in Photoshop. All of the color models are displayed in a single dialog box. By default, the Color Picker opens in HSB mode with Hue as the active parameter. The slider represents the hues on the color wheel, and the field represents the saturation and brightness of the selected hue.

You can change the Color Picker to display four different color models: HSB (Hue Saturation Brightness), RGB (Red Green Blue), LAB (Lightness A and B), CMYK (Cyan Magenta Yellow Black), and Web Colors.

When you select a color model, the vertical bar represents the selected characteristic in the selected model. For example, when you select the B option, the active parameter of the Color Picker shifts to Brightness and the vertical bar becomes a Saturation slider. The color field displays hue and saturation variations. Moving the field to the left or right affects the hue; moving the field up or down affects the brightness.

See also>>

Foreground color

Background color

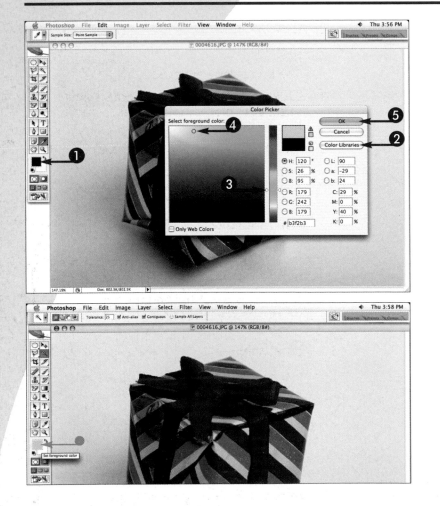

① Click the Foreground color swatch in the Tools palette.

The Color Picker opens.

② Click Color Library and select color model.

③ Click a color on the color ramp to select a hue.

④ Click the color field to select a saturation and brightness.

⑤ Click OK.

● The color appears as the foreground swatch.

COLOR SAMPLER TOOL:
Determine a Color Value

The Color Sampler tool marks an area so that you can compare before-and-after color adjustments. With this tool, the cursor deposits a marker, and the Info palette expands to display the numerical color values for the pixels underneath the sample. While you perform a color adjustment, the Info palette displays two numbers for each value, divided by a slash. The number on the left represents the original value of the sampled pixel prior to the adjustment. The number on the right represents the new values of the color after the adjustment. You can compare these values and, with a bit of practice, determine the effect the adjustment has on the targeted area.

You can sample up to four colors and record the information in the Info palette. You can change the color model of the sample by using the arrow next to the Eyedropper icon in the Info palette. Drag down to the desired color model in the pull-down list shown.

See also>>

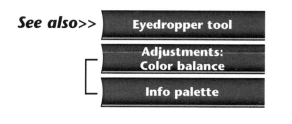

- Eyedropper tool
- Adjustments: Color balance
- Info palette

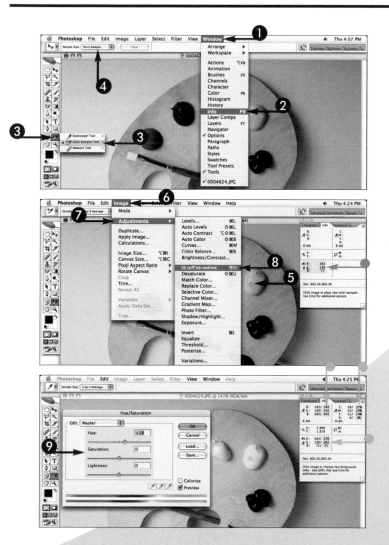

① Click Window.

② Click Info.

The Info palette appears.

③ Click and hold the Eyedropper tool and select the Color Sampler tool from the fly-out menu.

④ Click here and select a sample size.

Point Sample samples a single pixel; 3 by 3 average samples 9 pixels; 5 by 5 average samples 25 pixels.

Note: The center point is the sample point.

⑤ Click the areas of the image that you want to sample.

A marker is deposited and the Info palette displays the sampled color information.

⑥ Click Image.

⑦ Click Adjustments.

⑧ Click a color adjustment.

● A new column appears to the right of the sample color column.

⑨ Make adjustments in the dialog box that appears.

● As you make the adjustment, the color values in the right column of the Info palette change while the sampled color remains constant.

DODGE TOOL:
Lighten an Area of a Photograph

You can use the Dodge tool to enhance highlights, diminish shadows, or lighten areas you want to emphasize. *Dodging* is a traditional darkroom technique that overexposes or lightens specific areas of an image. Although you normally perform dodging with a cardboard wand and an enlarger in a darkroom, in Photoshop you use the Dodge tool — the functional opposite of the Burn tool.

The Dodge tool works by increasing the brightness values of pixels. You can focus on a specific range of tonality by specifying Highlights, Midtones, or Shadows from the Range menu in the Options bar.

Adjusting the exposure weakens or strengthens the effect.

Like all of the tools that require brushes, the ultimate dodge effect is dependant on the size, hardness, and dynamics of the selected brush. This tool works best when you apply it in multiple passes of smaller exposures because high-exposure passes (50 to 100 percent) can overwhelm the area and increase its brightness and decrease its contrast.

See also>>

| Dodge Tool |
| Burn Tool |

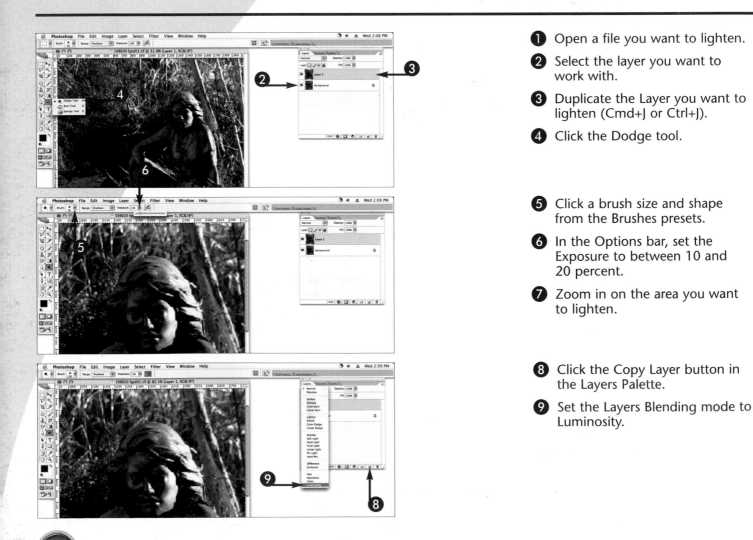

❶ Open a file you want to lighten.

❷ Select the layer you want to work with.

❸ Duplicate the Layer you want to lighten (Cmd+J or Ctrl+J).

❹ Click the Dodge tool.

❺ Click a brush size and shape from the Brushes presets.

❻ In the Options bar, set the Exposure to between 10 and 20 percent.

❼ Zoom in on the area you want to lighten.

❽ Click the Copy Layer button in the Layers Palette.

❾ Set the Layers Blending mode to Luminosity.

10 Click and "paint" the area you want to lighten.

The features of the face become more evident as Photoshop applies the Dodge effect.

11 Zoom out to view the entire Image.

12 Click and drag to apply the Dodge tool to any areas that need more definition.

The Dodge tool defines the area.

You can repeat step 11 as needed.

TIPS

Caution!

The key element in using the Dodge tool is subtlety. Be patient and apply it softly. Start out with a 15% exposure and a soft brush. An over exposed image is not any prettier than an underexposed one.

Try This!

Want to glamorize your Portraits? One way is to brighten teeth and the whites of eyes. You can also iron out some wrinkles. Use it gently and apply it in small increments so that the effect is realistic.

Did You Know?

The Dodge tool's strength depends on the resolution of the document. Higher-resolution documents are affected less by the same exposure than lower-resolution documents.

ERASER:
Omit Unwanted Areas

You can erase sections of an image using various eraser tools. These tools perform differently depending on whether you apply them to a background or to a layer. For a background, the Eraser tools replace the area you to which you apply them with the current background color in the Tools palette. For layers, the Eraser tool replaces the areas to which you apply it with transparency unless you lock the transparency option on the layer, in which case the pixels you erase are replaced with the background color.

The Eraser tools include three modes: Brush, Pencil, or Block. With the Brush or Pencil mode, you set characteristics such as size, roundness, or softness in the Brushes palette. The pencil option produces a hard-edged stroke while the brush produces a softer edge. The Block option creates a square stroke, the

size of which is dependent on the size and resolution of the image.

You can also "erase" by using the History Brush tool to return a section of the image to a previous state. The History Brush actually works like a selective "undo" option.

See also>>

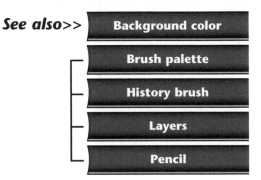

Background color

Brush palette

History brush

Layers

Pencil

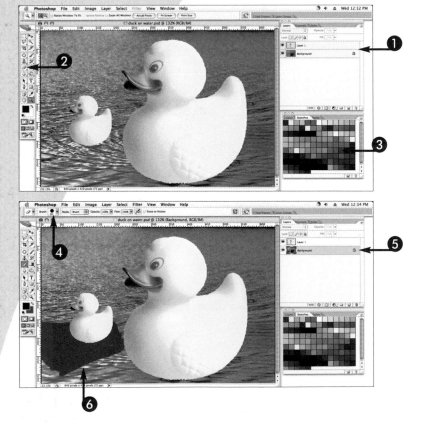

Apply the Eraser to a Background

① Open a document with Background layer and at least one other layer with content.

② Click the Eraser tool.

You can also press E.

If the Swatches palette is not visible, you can click Window and then Swatches.

③ Press Opt (Ctrl) and click a color from the Swatches palette.

Photoshop defines the background color.

④ Click here and select a brush from the Brush presets in the Options bar.

⑤ In the Layers palette, click the Background layer.

⑥ Click and drag the Eraser tool as if you were painting.

Photoshop erases the original background and applies the background color to the area.

Apply the Eraser to a Layer

1 Click the layer containing an object or objects you want to erase.

2 Click and drag the eraser tool over that object.

3 Continue erasing the object.

Photoshop erases the object and the background is revealed — that portion of the layer is now transparent.

TIPS

Try This!

You can change the Opacity setting of the Eraser tool to any value between 0 percent and 100 percent. The result is that the transparency of the pixels on a layer can run the gamut between full transparency to no transparency; the affect on the background is that the background color will run from "nothing" to tints of the color to full color.

Try This!

To erase along a straight line, click at one end of the area that you want to erase. Move the cursor to the other end of the area. Press Shift and click the mouse.

Try This!

To erase along a horizontal or vertical line, click the mouse once. Press Shift and drag the mouse in the direction you want the erasure.

ERASER, BACKGROUND:
Pick and Choose the Colors to Erase

You can use the Background Eraser tool to select a specific color that you want to remove from an image. You can then erase only that color and its variations The options associated with this tool allow you to set limits such as color range, so that you can limit the scope of erasure, and protect the areas you want to keep.

When you apply the Background Eraser to the Background layer, Photoshop automatically converts that layer to a normal layer that supports transparency. The tool erases directly to transparency on all other layers. The Limits menu in the Options bar specifies which pixels are erased. *Discontiguous* erases all of the pixels within the Tolerance range on the entire layer. *Contiguous* erases adjacent pixels of the sampled color.

Find Edges erases pixels of the sampled color that are adjacent to each other, but have more contrast to preserve the sharpness of the edges on the remaining image. *Tolerance* controls the range of colors to be erased. Low tolerance percentages erase fewer colors. High tolerance percentages erase more colors.

See also>>

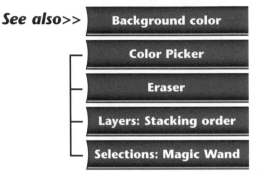

Background color
Color Picker
Eraser
Layers: Stacking order
Selections: Magic Wand

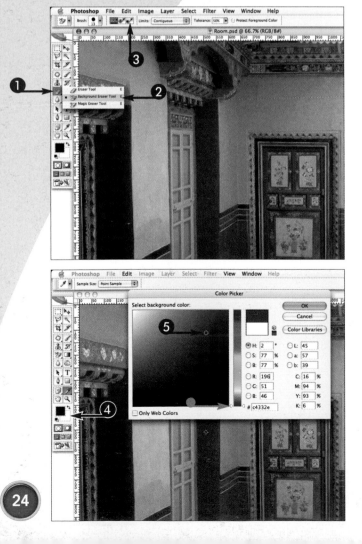

Using the Sampling Background button

① Click and hold the Eraser tool.

② Click the Background Eraser tool from the fly-out menu.

You can also press Shift+E until the Background Eraser tool appears in the palette.

③ On the Options bar, click the Sampling Background Swatch button.

This allows you set the color you want removed via the Background swatch in the menu.

④ Click the Background Swatch.

The Color Picker dialog box opens.

⑤ Click a color from the Color Picker.

● You can click and drag the Hue slider to select a different range of colors.

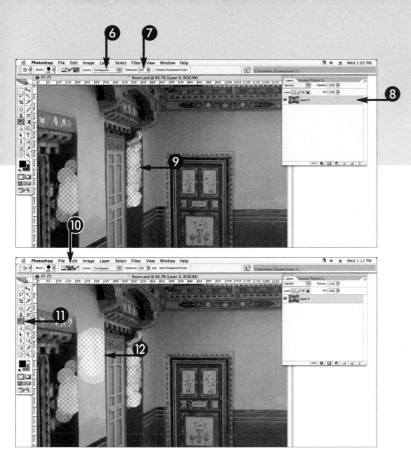

6 Click here and set the Limits to Contiguous.

7 Click here and set the Tolerance.

8 In the Layers palette, click the layer containing the color you want to erase.

9 Click and drag the Background Eraser tool back and forth as you might an eraser or a brush.

As you move the tool back and forth across the image, only the color you selected is erased.

Using the Sampling Once button

10 Click the Sampling: Once button.

11 Click the Background Eraser tool.

12 Click a different part of the image and start erasing.

Photoshop automatically changes the Background swatch to the color in the image where you click with the tool.

Did You Know?

You control the Background Eraser's behavior with the dynamics in the Brushes palette. Click a Sampling Option icon to determine how the colors are chosen. You select Contiguous to erase areas of different colors. You select Once to sample a color when you first click and then continue erasing only that color. Click Background Swatch to erase only areas of current background color.

Try This!

You can select the Protect Foreground Color option (☑ changes to ☐) in the Options bar to ensure that you do not erase areas of the foreground color.

ERASER, MAGIC:
Select and Erase a Range of Color

The Magic Eraser is a great tool for quickly eliminating areas of continuous color. It prevents the need to draw a selection marquee around an area of continuous color that you want to remove. The Magic Eraser does this by selecting all the colors within the tolerance range and deleting them with one click of the mouse.

If you apply the Magic Eraser to the Background, the Background automatically converts to a layer, and the area becomes transparent. If you apply the tool to any other layer, the selected areas become transparent. If you lock the transparency on the layer, it still erases, but only the background color.

If you select the Contiguous Option in the Options bar, the eraser tool erases only adjacent pixels on the current layer. If leave this option unselected, the tool erases all pixels throughout the image that match the selected color.

You can also specify a tolerance range to determine the range of colors you want to erase. Low tolerances erase colors that are the most similar to the sampled color. High tolerances erase a wider range of colors.

See also>> **Layers**

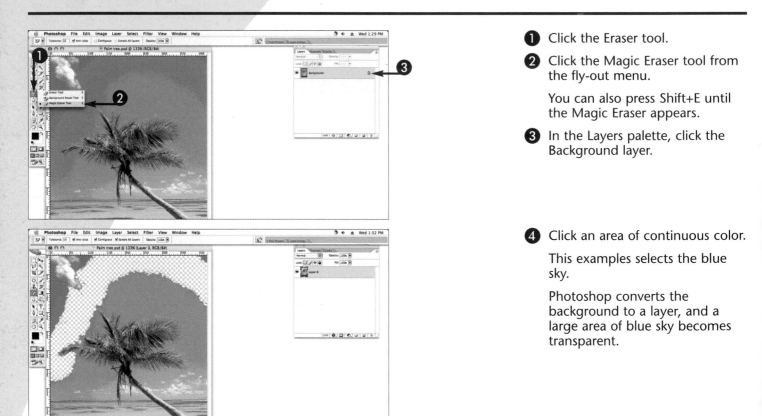

① Click the Eraser tool.

② Click the Magic Eraser tool from the fly-out menu.

You can also press Shift+E until the Magic Eraser appears.

③ In the Layers palette, click the Background layer.

④ Click an area of continuous color.

This examples selects the blue sky.

Photoshop converts the background to a layer, and a large area of blue sky becomes transparent.

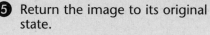

⑤ Return the image to its original state.

To return the image to its original state, you can click File, and then click Revert, and Photoshop will return the file to the last saved state.

⑥ Click here and type a different value for the Tolerance.

This example uses a Tolerance of 50%.

⑦ Click any part of the image that contains the color you want to remove.

By increasing the Tolerance level Photoshop becomes less specific about how close the colors are before it erases it.

A Tolerance value of 100% means that Photoshop selects and erases any pixels that are within the range of the specific color.

TIPS

Try This!
You can adjust the opacity of the Magic Eraser in the Options bar to control the strength of the erasure. A lower opacity produces a translucent effect.

Did You Know?
The Anti-aliased option creates a smoother appearance along the edges of the erased areas so that it blends seamlessly with the adjacent background color or the colors on the layer beneath it.

Try This!
You can select the Sample All Layers option (○ changes to ◉) in the Options bar to simultaneously erase areas of similar color on multiple layers.

THE EYEDROPPER TOOL:
Select a Color from the Image

The Eyedropper tool allows you to select a color from an image so that you can create a color swatch for use immediately with the brush or other tools used to apply color. It is most useful when you want to match a color exactly.

You can select colors from outside the image window — including any visible areas outside of the Photoshop window. To do so, you click and hold the right mouse button and you move the Eyedropper tool to anywhere around your monitor. As you do this, the color changes in the Foreground Swatch in the Tools palette. When you find the color you want, release the button and the color becomes the default Foreground color.

In the Eyedropper Options bar you can configure the Eyedropper tool to sample a point (1 pixel), a 3-x-3 average (9 pixels) or a 5-x-5-pixel average (25 pixels). You generallyget the best results with the 3-x-3 average; however, on high-resolution images greater than 300 pixels per inch, you may want to try the 5-x-5 option.

See also>>

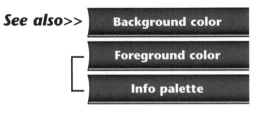

Background color

Foreground color

Info palette

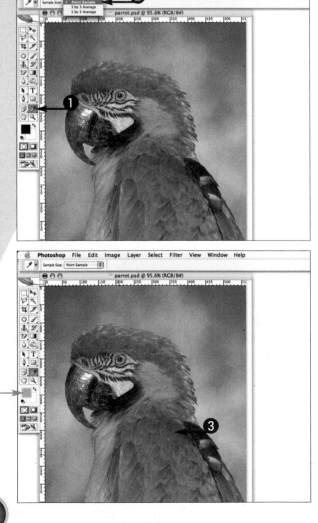

① Click the Eyedropper tool in the Tools palette.

You can also press I.

② Click here and select a sample size.

③ Click the image and drag the mouse.

● As the cursor moves across the image, the foreground color changes to reflect the new color that the Eyedropper is currently sampling.

④ Release the mouse.

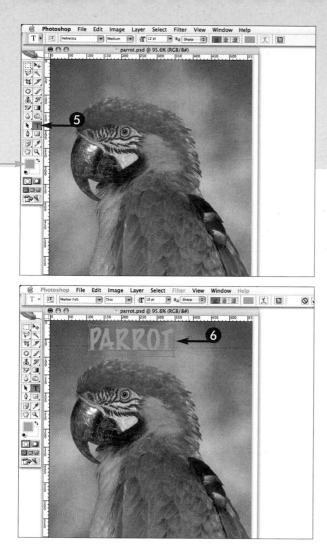

● The sampled color becomes the new foreground color.

⑤ Click the Text Tool.

⑥ Click somewhere on your image and type a word.

The color of the text is the sampled color from your image.

TIPS

Try This!
Press Opt (Alt) as you drag to sample a background color. When you release the mouse, the sampled color appears as the background swatch in the Tools palette.

Did You Know?
As you drag the Eyedropper across the image, the numerical values of the sampled colors appear in the Info palette.

Try This!
As you are applying color with the Brush, Pencil, Erasers, Gradient, or Paint Bucket tools, press and hold Opt (Alt). The tool changes to the Eyedropper. Release the key and continue painting to apply the new sampled color.

FOREGROUND COLOR:
Fill an Area with Foreground Color

You can apply foreground color with the Brush tool, Paint Bucket, Fill and Stroke commands, the Gradient tool, and Solid Color fill layers. You can also apply the foreground (and background) colors with some of the Artistic, Sketch, Stylize, and Render filters. You can fill a selection, a layer, or a background.

You can select a foreground color from the Color palette, Swatches palette, or the Color Picker. You can also use the Eyedropper tool to sample a foreground color from the image.

You can switch between the foreground color and the background color via the arrow next to the two color swatches in the Tools palette. You can restore the

foreground color to the default via the Default button under the color swatches.

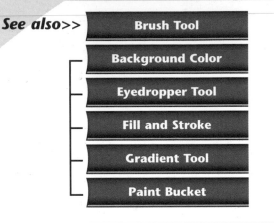

See also>>

| Brush Tool |
| Background Color |
| Eyedropper Tool |
| Fill and Stroke |
| Gradient Tool |
| Paint Bucket |

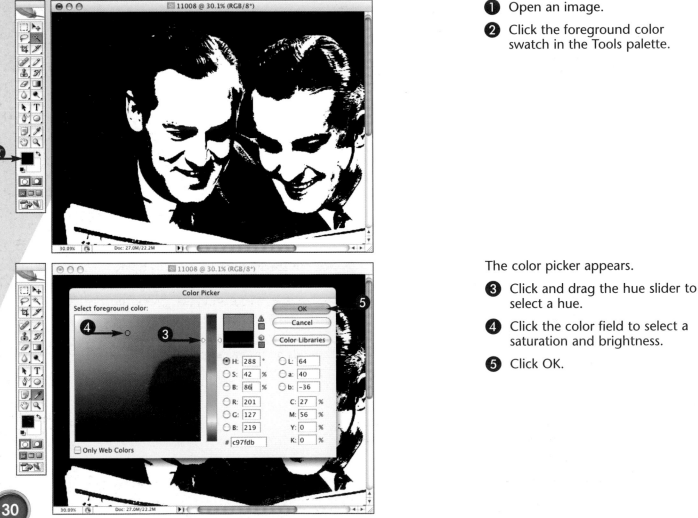

① Open an image.

② Click the foreground color swatch in the Tools palette.

The color picker appears.

③ Click and drag the hue slider to select a hue.

④ Click the color field to select a saturation and brightness.

⑤ Click OK.

● The color appears as the foreground swatch.

⑥ Click a Selection tool and make a selection on the area you want to fill.

⑦ Press Opt+Delete (Alt+Backspace).

● Depending on whether the selection is feathered or not, the area fills with 100 percent of the foreground color.

TIPS

Did You Know?
The foreground color is greatly affected by the blending mode specified in the Options bar of the current tool or the Mode menu in the dialog boxes when you paint or fill an area with it.

Did You Know?
By default, the foreground color is black and the background color is white; however, on an Alpha channel, the default foreground is white and the background is black.

Try This!
You can specify a precise color, by typing numerical values in the Color Picker's or Color palette's HSB, RGB, LAB, CMYK, or Web color fields. The actual output when printed or published to the Web, however, depends on several factors involving color management.

GRADIENT:
Apply a Smooth Multicolored Blend

You can apply a gradient to an image to blend multiple colors into each other or into transparency over a specified distance. When you select the Gradient tool in the Tools palette, the Options bar displays a gradient swatch.

The default gradient creates a fill that blends from the current foreground color to the current background color. You can select other gradients presets via the gradient swatch on the Options bar.

To the right of the gradient swatch are five gradient types that control how Photoshop distributes the color for the gradient. These include the Linear

option, which applies a gradient over a specified distance; the Radial option, which radiates colors from a center point to an endpoint; the Angle option, which radiates the colors clockwise around a center point; the Reflected option, which creates two linear gradients on each side of the central color; and the Diamond option, which radiates colors from a center point into a diamond-shaped blend.

See also>>

Gradient Editor

Fill layers

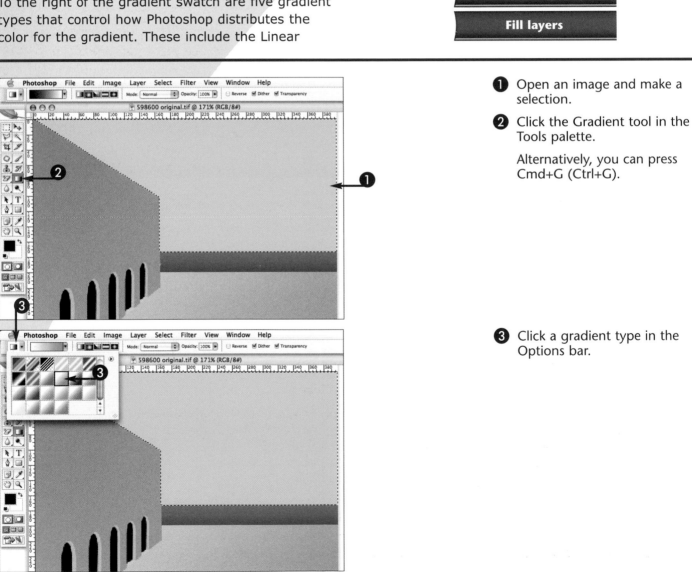

① Open an image and make a selection.

② Click the Gradient tool in the Tools palette.

Alternatively, you can press Cmd+G (Ctrl+G).

③ Click a gradient type in the Options bar.

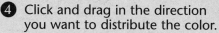

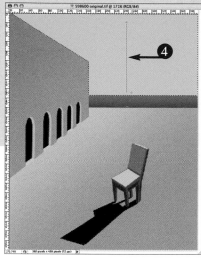

4 Click and drag in the direction you want to distribute the color.

The length and direction of the line you drag determines how the gradient colors are distributed.

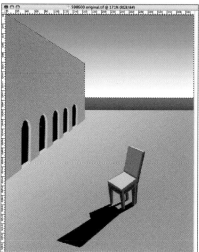

Photoshop applies the gradient.

This example here used the CYAN (color range white to cyan) gradient type that is included with Photoshop.

TIPS

Did You Know?
The length of the line you drag with the Gradient tool affects the distribution of color. If the line is relatively short, the gradient is compressed to a small area. A longer line produces a wider distribution of color. You can even drag outside of the Image window for a super-wide color distribution.

Try This!
Adjust the opacity of the gradient in the Options bar and then apply it to create a translucent or vaporous effect.

Try This!
You can press Shift while dragging to constrain the direction of gradient to a vertical, horizontal, or 45-degree angle.

GRID:
Display and Customize a Grid

You can use grids to view vertical and horizontal relationships between aligned elements on a design field. This is helpful when you want to precisely move and place objects within an illustration. In Photoshop, the grid is a visual matrix of equidistant horizontal and vertical lines. Grids consist of heavy gridlines and softer appearing subdivision lines. They differ from guides in their number; you generally have numerous grids, but only one or two guides to position elements.

By default, any element that you move — including layer content or an active selection — snaps to the grid whether or not you have the grid visible. You can easily turn the gridline feature on and off via the View menu.

After you turn on a grid, you can modify the gridlines' color and style to distinguish them from the image's color. You can select grid colors via the color swatch in the Preferences dialog box. The color swatch displays the Color Picker, where you can select any color you desire. You can also select a specific line style from the Style menu. Choices for gridlines and subdivisions include dashed or solid line, or dots.

See also>>

Alignment

Guides

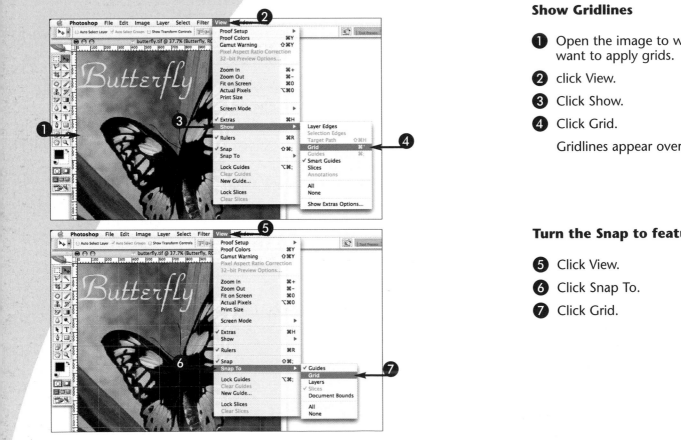

Show Gridlines

➊ Open the image to which you want to apply grids.

➋ click View.

➌ Click Show.

➍ Click Grid.

Gridlines appear over the image.

Turn the Snap to feature on

➎ Click View.

➏ Click Snap To.

➐ Click Grid.

The Snap To feature is turned on.

● You can now snap elements to the grids by clicking the appropriate layer in the Layers palette, clicking the Move tool and clicking and dragging the element to the area in the grid that you want.

⑧ Click Photoshop (Edit).

⑨ Click Preferences.

⑩ Click Guides, Grids & Slices.

The Preferences dialog box appears.

⑪ Click here and select gridline color.

● Alternatively, you can select a grid color from the color swatch.

⑫ Click here and select a line style.

● The grid properties change as you select options.

⑬ Click OK.

The new grid lines now appear more prominent.

TIPS

Did You Know?
A Grid in combination with the Snap To option gives you more control over the Pen tool. As you click with the Pen tool, the lines you create automatically snaps to grid points.

Did You Know?
Design-wise, it is usually a good idea to keep elements visually aligned on an invisible grid. The grid can help guide the viewer's eye to move fluidly across the page.

Did You Know?
Used properly, a grid can help contain elements and aid in the visual cohesiveness of the design field.

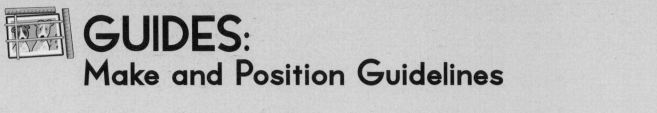

GUIDES:
Make and Position Guidelines

Designers and illustrators frequently use guides to assure the accurate placement and alignment of image elements. Photoshop has guide features to enable you to carefully place elements. Guides differ from grids in their number; you generally have numerous gridlines, but only one or two guides to position elements.

By default, floating elements or elements on independent layers snap to an invisible grid or to an existing guide when use the Move tool to position them. You can turn this feature on or off via the View menu. Guides float on the surface of the image and do not print. By default, guides are light blue. However, if your image contains too much of this default color, you can change it in the Preferences dialog box.

Photoshop generates horizontal and vertical guides from the ruler at the left or top of the image window. You can reposition your guides to the right or down from any point on the ruler. You can also reposition an existing guide using the Move tool to move it to a new location.

See also>>

> **Grids**
>
> **Guides: Smart Guides**
>
> **Rulers**

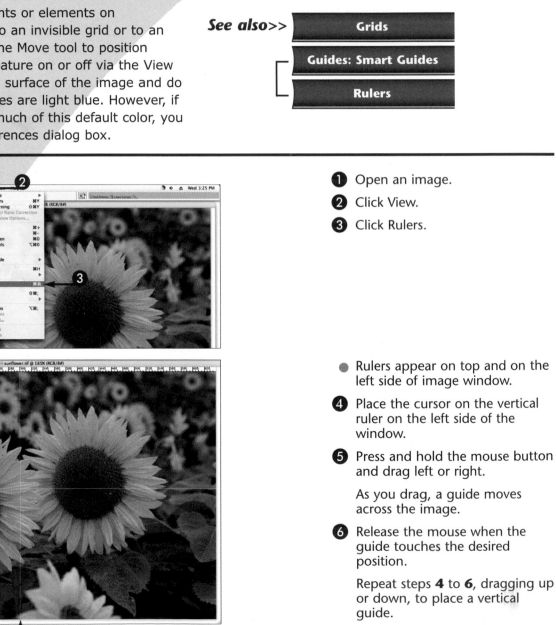

❶ Open an image.

❷ Click View.

❸ Click Rulers.

● Rulers appear on top and on the left side of image window.

❹ Place the cursor on the vertical ruler on the left side of the window.

❺ Press and hold the mouse button and drag left or right.

As you drag, a guide moves across the image.

❻ Release the mouse when the guide touches the desired position.

Repeat steps **4** to **6**, dragging up or down, to place a vertical guide.

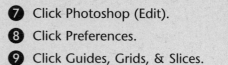

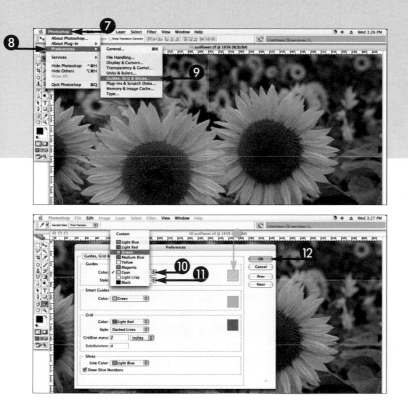

⑦ Click Photoshop (Edit).

⑧ Click Preferences.

⑨ Click Guides, Grids, & Slices.

The Preferences dialog box appears.

⑩ Click here and select a preset color.

● Alternatively, you can click the color swatch to display the Color Picker, where you can select a color.

⑪ Click a line style from the Guides Style menu.

The guides change as you select options so that you can preview the change before you confirm your choices.

⑫ Click OK.

Photoshop changes the properties of your guides.

TIPS

Did You Know?

To reposition guides when you are using tools other than the Move tool, press Cmd (Ctrl), and click and drag.

Try This!

To toggle guides on and off press Cmd+; (Ctrl+;). To toggle lock/unlock guides, press Cmd+Opt+; (Ctrl+Alt+;). Clear guides by Clicking View and then Clear Guides.

Try This!

Change the Rulers units of measure by right-clicking anywhere on the rulers. A menu appears from which you can select among seven units of measure. You can also double-click anywhere inside the rulers to access the Units and Rulers Preferences dialog box offering you additional options. To change grid or guide options, double-click a guide. The Guides, Grids, and Slices Preferences dialog box appears.

GUIDES, SMART:
Automatically Make Guides as You Place Elements

Smart Guides are horizontal or vertical lines that indicate the edge or midpoint of a shape, selection, or slice. You can use Smart Guides to help align shapes, slices, and selections. After you activate Smart Guides, they appear automatically as you drag a shape to align it or create a selection or slice. You may find Smart Guides useful for positioning an element on a top-most layer or floating element because they indicate the position of the center or midpoint of the element underneath.

You can change the color or style of Smart Guides to any color. This is particularly useful if the default color of the guides is too similar to the colors in an image. You do this via the Photoshop Preferences dialog box, which contains a menu with preset colors, a color swatch, which activates the Color Picker, and a Style menu, where you can change the style of your Smart Guide.

To illustrate how Smart Guides work, the example uses an image that has several layers with objects that are to align with other objects.

See also>>

Grids

Guides

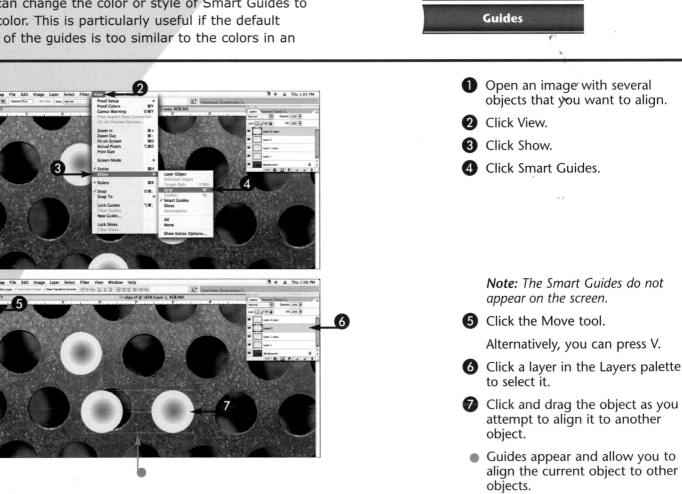

① Open an image with several objects that you want to align.

② Click View.

③ Click Show.

④ Click Smart Guides.

Note: The Smart Guides do not appear on the screen.

⑤ Click the Move tool.

Alternatively, you can press V.

⑥ Click a layer in the Layers palette to select it.

⑦ Click and drag the object as you attempt to align it to another object.

● Guides appear and allow you to align the current object to other objects.

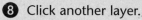

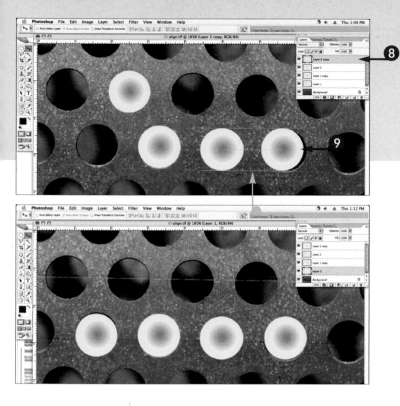

8 Click another layer.

9 Click and drag those objects to stack them all in a line.

● As you drag, Smart Guides appear and change as the moving object nears another object.

The objects align with the help of smart guides.

G

TIPS

Did You Know?
If Smart Guides are activated, they also appear when you use any of the transformation operations. You can select transformation operations by clicking Edit, and then Transform, or by selecting the Show Transform Controls option in the Move tool's Options bar.

Did You Know?
You can change the color of Smart Guides in the Smart Guides Preference menu. You can access the Preference menu by clicking Photoshop (Edit), then Preferences, and then Guides, Grids, & Slices. See the section "Guides: Make and Position Guidelines" for more on this dialog box.

Try This!
You can hide Smart Guides by clicking View, then Show, and then Smart Guides.

HAND TOOL:
Navigate Quickly

You can use the Hand tool to access sections of an image that are beyond the current view. Sections of an image may be beyond your view because you may have zoomed into a particular section of an image. You may need to magnify a particular section so that you can more precisely edit or check it, but this may also mean that other parts of that image become out of view and therefore out of reach. The Hand tool allows you to access those out of reach parts.

To reposition an image, you simply use the Hand tool to drag the image in any direction. If you are using

another tool or dialog box and need to see a different area of an image, you can access the Hand tool through its keyboard shortcut. This shortcut allows you to toggle back to whatever tool or dialog box you are using. The only tool that does not allow you to access the Hand tool in this manner is the Text tool.

See also>>
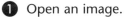

| Navigator |
| Zoom tool |

Using the Hand tool

① Open an image.

② Click the Zoom tool.

③ Click and drag the area you want to magnify.

The area fills your screen.

④ Click the Hand tool.

⑤ Click and move in any direction.

Photoshop changes the view as if your image is being moved underneath the screen.

Using the Hand tool with another tool

1 Open an image.

2 Zoom in on a section of your image.

3 Click another tool.

This example uses the Paint tool.

4 With the other tool still selected, press and hold the Spacebar.

The other tool's cursor changes to a Hand cursor.

● You can now use the Hand tool to readjust the position of your image.

When you release the Spacebar, the cursor changes back to the other tool's cursor and you can continue using this tool.

H

TIPS

Did You Know?

To scroll, you also can use the scroll bars to the right and bottom of the image. Click and drag a scroll thumb, or click an arrow at the end of a scroll bar. Click in the scroll bar section above or below the scroll thumb to jump a full screen view up or down.

Did You Know?

You can also scroll using these key commands:

Scroll	Mac Keyboard	Mac Extended Keyboard	Windows Keyboard
Up	Ctrl -K	PgUp	PgUp
Up slightly	Shift-Ctrl-K	Shift-PgUp	Shift-PgUp
Down	Ctrl-L	PgDn	PgDn
Down slightly	Shift-Ctrl-L	Shift-PgDn	Shift-PgDn
Left	Ctrl-K	Cmd-PgUp	Ctrl-PgUp
Left slightly	Shift-Cmd-Ctrl-K	Shift-Cmd-PgUp	Shift-Ctrl-PgUp
Right	CM-Ctrl l-L	Cmd-PgDn	Ctrl-PgDn
Right slightly	Shift-Cmd-Ctrl-L	Shift-Cmd-PgDn	Shift-Ctrl-PgDn

HEALING BRUSH:
Retouch a Scratch

You can use the Healing Brush to suture areas of texture that are scratched or torn. You start the process by sampling an area and then painting over the scratched area with the sample. When you apply the sampled area to the scratch, the tool "senses" the areas adjacent to the scratch and blends the edges to match, creating a seamless edit.

The appearance of the healed areas depends on several factors, including brush size and hardness, and blending mode. These characteristics can be specified in the tool's Options bar.

To apply a texture to a healed area, you use the Pattern button in the Options bar to select a pattern.

When the Aligned box appears in the Options bar, the initial sample point aligns to the distance of the brush. After you apply the brush the first time, you can continue to paint, which locks the sample point in an equidistant position from the brush. When you deselect the Aligned option, the brush starts sampling from the original point each time you paint.

See also>>

Clone tool

Healing Brush:
Spot Healing Brush

Zoom tool

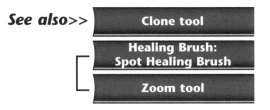

① Open an image that has a scratch.

② Click the Healing Brush.

③ Click an appropriate brush size from the Brush presets menu.

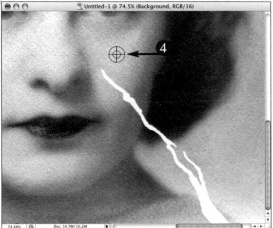

④ Press Opt (Alt) and then click in the area above the scratch to sample it.

You can use the Zoom tool to zoom in on the area that you want to repair.

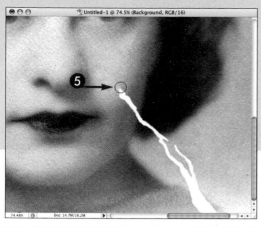

⑤ Release Opt (Alt), and move the cursor onto the scratch and drag the mouse.

⑥ Release the mouse.

The sample blends seamlessly into the surrounding pixels.

You can repeat steps **4** to **6** to repair the entire scratch area.

TIPS

Try This!
Select the All Layers option in the Options bar to sample the content of all the visible layers in the document. Deselect it to sample only the currently targeted layer.

Caution!
If an area adjacent to the scratch is of different tonal value, you may produce a darkening or lightening on part of the healed surface. You can always repair small areas with the Clone tool.

Did You Know?
You may need to sample several times to perfectly blend colors and textures.

HEALING BRUSH, SPOT:
Automatically Repair Blemishes

You can use the Spot Healing Brush tool to remove blemishes and small scratches or flaws in your image. The Spot Healing Brush is similar to the Healing Brush, but unlike the Healing Brush, the Spot Healing Brush does not require you to sample pixels from another area. Because it automatically samples the pixels around the area that you want to retouch, you can best use it in areas where there is consistency in texture and color.

The settings in the Options bar determine the Spot Healing Brush tool's behavior. The Proximity Match option samples the pixels at the edge of your brush and "mimics" those pixels to repair the area where the brush is being applied. The Create Texture option combines characteristics of all the pixels in the brush

area to create a texture. Photoshop then applies this texture to the area that you are repairing. The result is a softer look similar to adding a soft filter to a photograph.

Like other Photoshop tools, the affects of the Spot Healing Brush you can modify the final effect using blending modes, which you can access in the Options bar.

See also>>

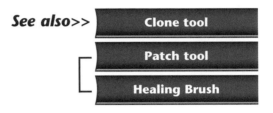

1 Open an image with a minor flaw.

This example has a pen mark that mars the forehead.

2 Click and hold the Healing Brush tool.

3 Click the Spot Healing Brush in the pull-down menu.

You can also press Shift+J to cycle through all the options available via this icon.

You can Zoom in on the area you want to repair.

4 On the Options bar, click the Brush Option icon.

5 Click options so that you have a brush that is slightly larger than the area you want to repair.

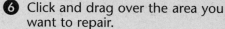

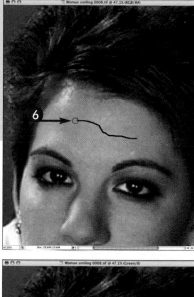

H

6 Click and drag over the area you want to repair.

Remember to use small passes as you click and drag.

7 Repeat steps **4** to **6** as needed to correct the mark.

The mark disappears.

Try This!

If you have an image where the subject's face has too much shine on the forehead or nose, use the Spot Healing Brush like you would a powder puff. Select the Create Texture option and apply the brush to soften the shine. You may need to experiment with different sizes to achieve the effect you want.

Caution!

The Spot Healing Brush is not intended for extensive repair. It works best when you use it to remove small scratches and to blend and soften color. Extensive repairs require more extensive techniques.

Caution!

Apply the Spot Healing Brush with care. Subtlety and patience should guide your brush. If you overuse the brush, not only do the repairs look unattractive, but you also lose detail and depth.

HISTOGRAM PALETTE:
View Brightness Values

You can use the Histogram Palette in Photoshop to determine if the range of brightness in an image is distributed uniformly. A *histogram* is a graph composed of lines that show the distribution of tonal values within an image.

The more lines in the histogram, the greater the tonal range. The height and position of a line on the graph represents the relative quantity of pixels of a specific brightness with taller lines representing more pixels of brightness. The lines are usually clustered close together and create a mountainous shape. Lines representing dark pixels, or shadows, are located on the left side of the graph; the lines for light pixels, or highlights, are on the right. The midtone lines are located in the central areas of the graph.

Ideally the tonal values of the pixels found in between the shadows and the highlights should form a bell shape. When this does not occur, it may be an indication that your image needs some tonal manipulation.

See also>> 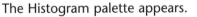 **Levels**

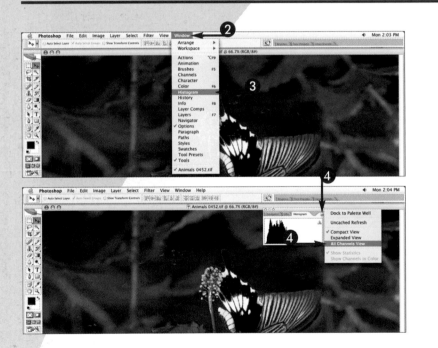

① Open an image that you want to evaluate.

② Click Window.

③ Click Histogram.

The Histogram palette appears.

④ Click here and then click All Channels View.

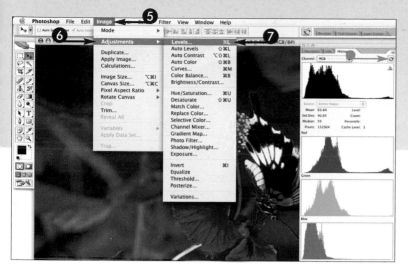

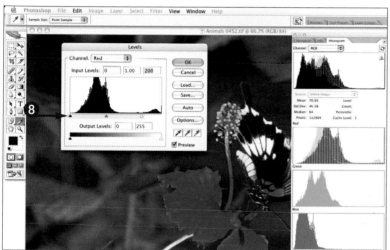

The palette expands and you can to view the histogram of each channel individually.

● You can click here and click Show Channels in Color to display the histogram of each channel in its corresponding color.

⑤ Click Image.

⑥ Click Adjustments.

⑦ Click Levels.

The Levels dialog box appears.

⑧ Click and drag the sliders to adjust color.

The graphs in the Histogram palette change as you move the sliders.

TIPS

Did You Know?
If the Histogram of your image is not a perfect "bell" curve, it does not mean that there is anything wrong with it. Extreme lighting conditions or stark colors adjacent to each other may cause the bell to skew. Trust your eyes!

Did You Know?
If you have taken several pictures with the same camera, it may be that all the images have a common brightness problem. Once you determine the correction for one image you can use information the Histogram provides to apply the same correction to the rest of your images.

HISTORY BRUSH:
Restore an Area to a Former State

The History Brush tool enables you to return an image to a former state by "painting" over the current effect and replacing it with a previous one. Photoshop automatically records every edit, operation, or technique that you apply to an image in its History palette. As you work, each event, or *state* is listed: paint strokes, filters, color corrections, or any other operation.

You can save a particular state as a snapshot. A snapshot is a series of steps that you can group as if it were one state. The History brush can then reestablish portions or all of a snapshot without having to recreate the whole environment. The

Source column at the far left of the History palette tells Photoshop the point to which you want to return.

Suppose you paint brush strokes on an image. As you continue to work, each time you perform an operation, Photoshop adds a new state. If you later decide that you want to retain only half of the original brush strokes, you can remove the undersired portion by painting to a former state with the History brush.

See also>> **History palette**

① Open an image.

② Click Window.

③ Click History.

The History palette appears.

This palette allows you to see the each change you make to the image.

④ Click a tool that or effect that you want to apply to your image.

This example uses the Brush tool.

⑤ Apply the tool to your image to change its appearance.

This example outlines the flower petals and fills the petals with a slightly different color.

● The History palette changes as you apply your tool or effect.

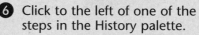

⑥ Click to the left of one of the steps in the History palette.

This establishes the point after which you can reverse any changes that you make with the History brush.

⑦ Click the History brush.

⑧ Apply more changes to your image using a tool or effect.

The only portions of your image affected are those below where you established a limit.

TIPS

Try This!

If you do not select the Allow Non-Linear History option, you must target the last state in the history to avoid losing the intervening states. Select Allow Non-Linear History from the History palette options menu to alter a state without losing the subsequent states.

Did You Know?

The History palette defaults to a limit of 50 history states. If you increase this number (maximum of 1,000), click Photoshop Preferences and then click General. Next, type the number in the History States box. Keep in mind that the larger the number of history states that Photoshop maintains, the more memory it will require.

Warning!

If you change the size or dimensions of pixels in your image (crop or image resize), the History brush becomes unavailable.

H

KEYBOARD SHORTCUTS:
Customize Your Keyboard

Keyboard shortcuts can save you time by eliminating superfluous mouse movements and menu searches. You can use Photoshop's default keyboard shortcuts for commands and tools, or you can customize the keyboard with your own shortcuts. You can define a set of shortcuts specific to your needs and change individual shortcuts within a set. Use the Keyboard Shortcuts and Menus dialog box to customize your shortcuts.

You can create shortcuts for application menus, palette menus, and tools. A list of keyboard sets appears when you select one of these broad categories. You can access the specific items within the set via the arrow to the left of the set's name. You can then program a new shortcut by assigning it a new name. An alert informs you if the keyboard shortcut is already assigned to another command or tool. If an item already has a shortcut, you can reprogram it by entering a new sequence of characters.

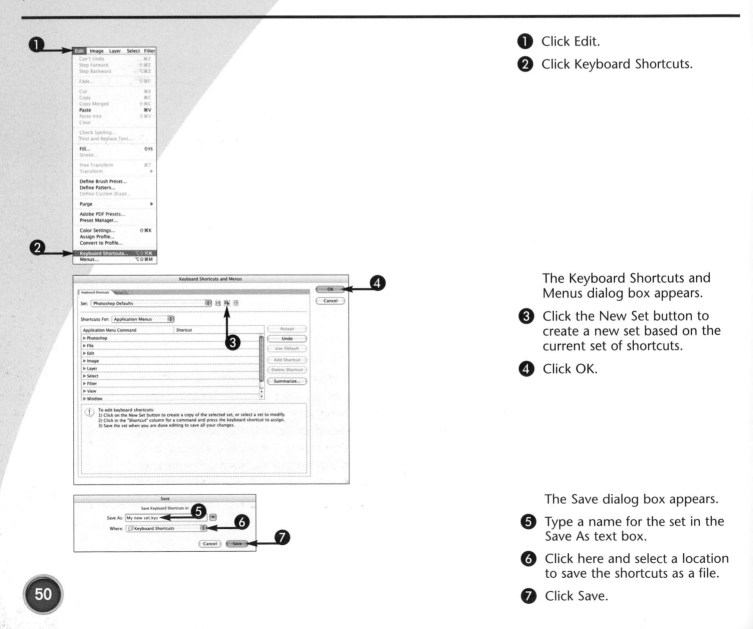

① Click Edit.

② Click Keyboard Shortcuts.

The Keyboard Shortcuts and Menus dialog box appears.

③ Click the New Set button to create a new set based on the current set of shortcuts.

④ Click OK.

The Save dialog box appears.

⑤ Type a name for the set in the Save As text box.

⑥ Click here and select a location to save the shortcuts as a file.

⑦ Click Save.

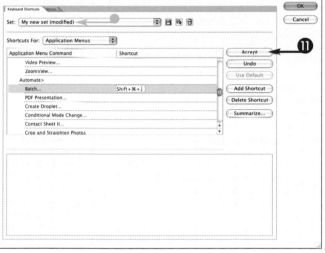

● The new key set appears in the Set fly-out menu.

⑧ Click here and select a shortcut type.

You can select types such as Application Menus, Palette Menus, or Tools.

⑨ In the Shortcut column of the list, select the shortcut you want to modify.

⑩ Type a new shortcut, or modify an existing one in the Set menu.

Note: If you specify a shortcut that is currently used, a caution will appear in a box at the bottom.

● After you make changes, the name in the Set menu is suffixed with (modified).

⑪ Click Accept.

Photoshop assigns the shortcut.

Try This!

To create a new set before you change default shortcuts, click New Set prior to typing in the shortcuts. To create a new set that includes any modifications you make, click New Set after you make the modifications.

Did You Know?

You can delete individual keyboard shortcuts from a set. Click the command or tool name of the shortcut you want to delete; then click Delete Shortcut. You can also delete an entire set of shortcuts. In the Set fly-out menu, click the shortcut set that you want to delete, and click Delete Set. Click OK to exit the dialog box.

K

MEASURE TOOL:
Determine the Distance Between Pixels

You can measure precise distances between pixels with Photoshop's Measure tool. Taking accurate measurements is necessary for almost any project. The Measure tool enables you to precisely determine the distance between any two points within the image window. When you measure from one point to another, a straight line is drawn that connects the two points. You can have only one active measure line per document.

When you activate the Measure tool, a number of values appear in the Options bar and the Info palette. The X and Y values are the vertical (X) and

the horizontal (Y) coordinates of the beginning of the line. The H and W values represent the horizontal (H) and vertical (W) distances from the X and Y axes. The A value is the angle of the line measured relative to the X axis; D1 is the total distance of the line, (D1 and D2) are the two distances if you calculate them with a protractor.

The measurements appear in the current units set in the Units & Rulers Preferences dialog box with the exception of the angle, which is displayed in degrees.

See also>> **Rulers**

① Click the Eyedropper tool and hold the mouse button to display the fly-out menu.

② Click the Measure tool.

Alternatively, press Shift+I until the Measure tool appears.

③ Click the point on the image from where you want to measure.

④ Drag to the point to which you want to measure.

The new measurements appear in the Options bar.

You can click and drag either point to reposition the start or endpoint, or click and drag the line to reposition the entire line.

The new measurements appear in the Options bar.

MOVE TOOL:
Move, Size, Rotate, and Distort the Contents of a Selection or Layer

You can use the Move tool as a shortcut to transform images on the fly. The Move tool replaces many of the Transform and Free Transform features — commands that you must access from the Edit menu. When you click the Move tool, the Show Transform Controls option appears on the Options bar. This option activates the Move tool's transformation features and surrounds the selection or the contents of the layer with a bounding box.

You can move, scale, rotate, or distort the contents of the bounding box depending on how you move your cursor over the bounding box.

See also>> **Free Transform**

Transform

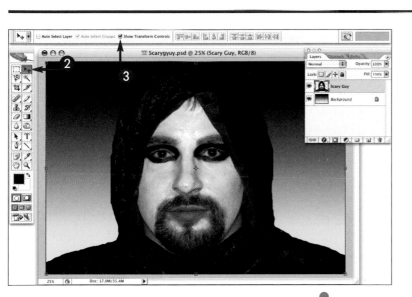

① Open a file and make a selection.

② Click the Move tool.

③ Select the Show Transform Controls check box in the Options bar.

   The bounding box appears.

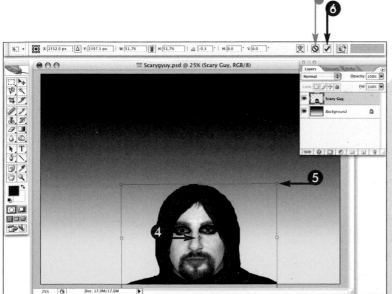

④ Click and drag inside the bounding box to move the image.

⑤ To scale the image, click and drag a corner point or middle point of the bounding box; drag inward to decrease and outward to increase the size of the image.

   You can rotate the image by placing the cursor outside the image, clicking and dragging clockwise or counterclockwise.

   You can distort the contents of a bounding box by pressing ⌘ (Ctrl) and clicking and dragging one of the corner points.

⑥ Click the Commit button in the Options bar to commit the transformation.

● You can also click the Cancel button to cancel the transformation.

NOTES TOOL:
Write an Annotation

At some point, you may want to attach a note within a document to remember specific settings or other particulars about an image. You may also want to make sure that a print operator, Web programmer, or another computer artist gets important instructions or information about an image as they process it. Photoshop provides tools to do exactly this.

The Notes tool, the Audio Annotation tool, and the File Info palette can record and provide useful information accessible within an image.

Also accessible from Photoshop but stored outside of an image is information available via Adobe Bridge — a file management application included with Photoshop that uses Metadata.

The Notes tool works like an electronic post-it note. A small window appears into which you can type reminders, warnings, or instructions. When you close the note, a small icon remains. You can open this icon to view or edit the contents.

See also>>
Audio Annotations Too
File Info
Metadata

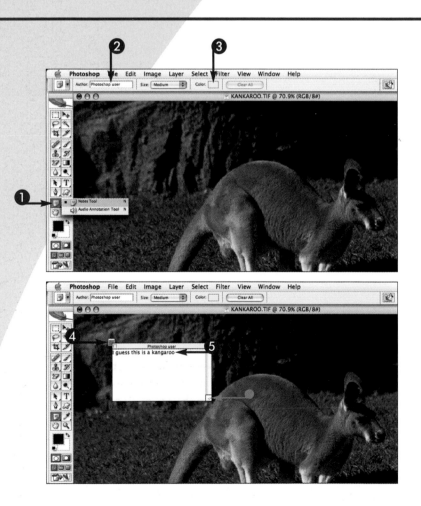

① Click the Notes Annotations tool from the Notes tool fly-out menu in the Tools palette.

② In the Options bar, type your name in the Author text box.

The default name in the box is the registered owner of Photoshop.

③ Click here and select a color for the note that appears on the image.

④ Click the image where you want to place the note.

The text box named in Step **2** appears as a window.

⑤ Type a reminder or instruction in the box.

● When you finish you can close the note by clicking here.

● A small icon remains after you close the note.

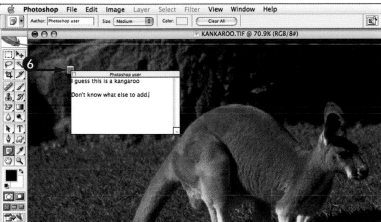

6 Double click the icon.

The note reappears.

TIPS

Did You Know?
Even though you can see the notes icon on top of your image, it will not print or be visible in another application. In fact, unless you save the image as Photoshop, PDF or TIF file, it will not be visible (available) in Photoshop.

Apply It!
To discard an audio or note annotation, select the Move tool, click the annotation icon and then press Delete (Backspace). To clear all annotations in a file, click the Clear All button in the Options bar. A dialog box appears and asks you if you are sure that you want to delete the annotations. Click OK.

OPTIONS BAR:
Set Tool Specifications

The Options bar gives you the power to control the behavior of tools. By default, Photoshop CS2 displays the Options bar at the top of the screen when you launch the program. Tool-specific options become visible in the Options bar when you click a tool, and you can determine the behavioral characteristics of the tool by setting values in the appropriate fields for the tools characteristics. For example, when you select the Brush tool, you can set its size, opacity, blending mode, and flow.

You can reposition this convenient element by using the far-left border. If you need more on-screen real estate, you can easily conceal or reveal the Options bar via the Window menu.

Because each tool's characteristics are quite different, the Options bar changes appearance when you select a different tool. The performance of a tool can vary considerably with different options, so pay attention to the Options bar settings before you apply the tool to the image.

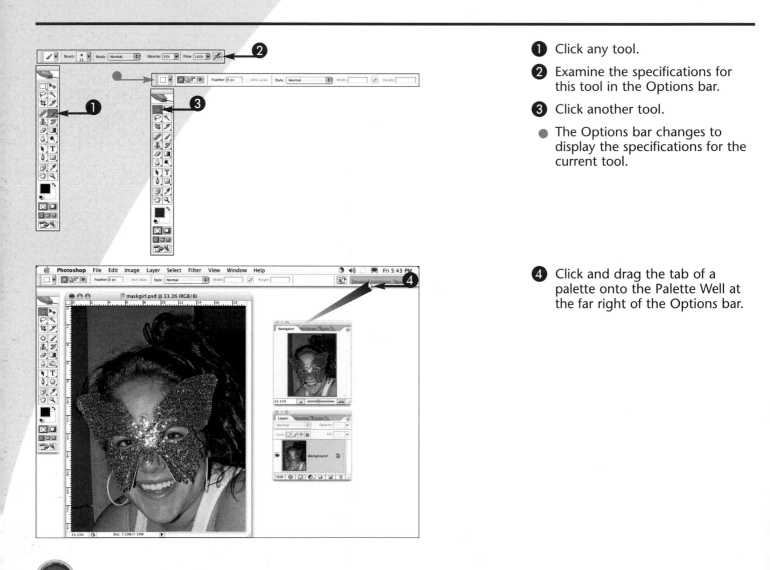

① Click any tool.

② Examine the specifications for this tool in the Options bar.

③ Click another tool.

● The Options bar changes to display the specifications for the current tool.

④ Click and drag the tab of a palette onto the Palette Well at the far right of the Options bar.

⑤ Click the tab in the Well.

The palette appears.

⑥ Double-click the gripper on the far left of the Options bar.

The palette collapses.

You can click again to expand it.

TIPS

Did You Know?

If you need more onscreen real estate, you can conceal or reveal the Options bar by Window and then Options. To conceal all palettes, including the Options bar, press Tab.

Did You Know?

The tool options you specify in the Options bar remain in effect until you quit the program or restore the preferences.

PAINT BUCKET:
Fill an Area with a Color

You can use the Paint Bucket tool, which is a handy combination of a simplified Color Replacement tool, to quickly replace color in an image. When you select areas of your image, the Paint Bucket tool selects pixels similar in color to the pixels you just clicked. It then replaces the color of those pixels with the color currently in the Foreground swatch in the Tools palette.

How much of an area the Paint Bucket tool affects depends on how similar in color the target pixels are to your selected pixels. You control this by setting a tolerance value from 0 to 255: 0 selects identical color pixels; 255 selects all pixels of any color.

By default, the Paint Bucket selects and fills adjacent pixels. You can, however, deselect the Contiguous option in the Options bar so that all matching pixels are selected — no matter where they are located in the image.

Photoshop also defaults the fill to the Foreground color, but you can fill the selected area with a pattern. These options are available in the Options bar.

See also>>

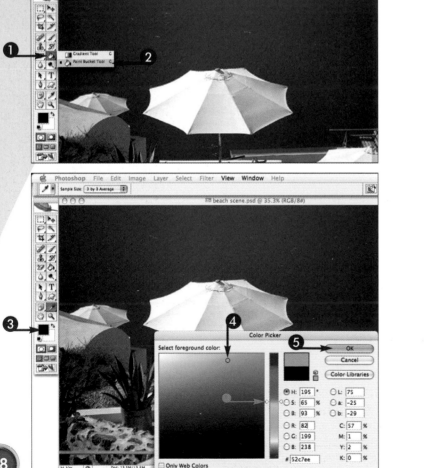

❶ Click and hold the Gradient tool.

❷ Click the Paint Bucket option.

The Gradient tool icon changes to the Paint Bucket icon.

❸ Click the Foreground swatch.

The Color Picker appears

❹ Click a color.

● You can click and drag the Hue slider to select a different color group.

❺ Click OK.

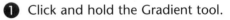

58

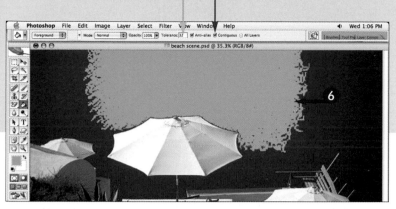

6 Click an area that is representative of the color you want to replace.

Photoshop replaces the color.

You can press ⌘ (Ctrl)+Z if you did not replace the color of all the area you wanted to replace.

● You can type a higher Tolerance Value to replace a wider range of pixels.

● To include more than the adjacent pixels, you can deselect the Contiguous option.

To have Photoshop measure the tolerance and apply the fill through multiple layers, you can click All Layers.

7 Place the cursor on the area you want to affect, and click the mouse.

The target area fills with the new color.

TIPS

Did You Know?
When you apply the Paint Bucket, the selected area is filled with a flat color and you lose all the texture and tonal variety in that area. If you want to retain some of the characteristics of the original pixels, you might want to experiment with Opacity values or a blend Mode. For example, if you select luminosity, your changes only affect the lightness of pixels and do not affect the hue and saturation.

Try This!
You can fill an entire document, a layer, or a selection with the foreground color by pressing Opt+Delete (Alt+Backspace). To fill with a background color, press Cmd+Delete (Ctrl+Backspace).

PATCH:
Repair a Scratch

Like the Clone tool, Healing brush, and Spot Healing brush, the Patch tool lets you repair an area with pixels sampled from another area of an image. The Patch tool is unique, however, in that it does not function like a brush, rather, it requires you to draw around the area that needs repair and then to find another area from which you can create a patch.

The whole process is similar to repairing a pair of jeans. You first determine what size and shape patch you need by making an initial selection with either the Patch tool or a selection tool. You then search for a piece of material that is similar in color and large enough to cover the hole — in this case by dragging your selection other areas of the image until you find a suitable "patch."

If you leave the Patch tool options to default, it does a fairly good job of blending the patch into the destination area. However, if you want to tweak the settings, you can experiment with the various options on the Options bar.

See also>>

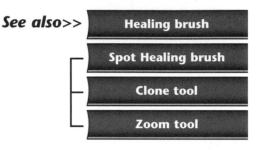

Healing brush

Spot Healing brush

Clone tool

Zoom tool

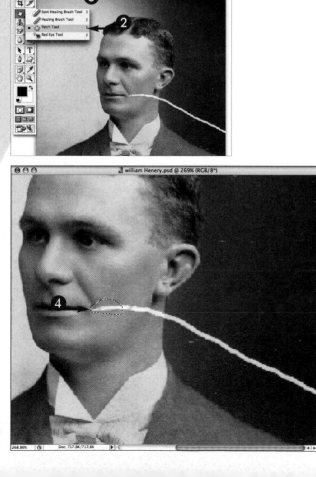

① Open a file in need of repair.

② Click the Patch tool.

③ Click the Source Option in the Options bar.

You can zoom in on the area you want to repair.

④ Click and drag the mouse to define the destination area — the area you want to repair.

If the damaged area is extensive, apply the Patch tool a little at a time.

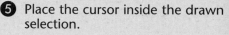

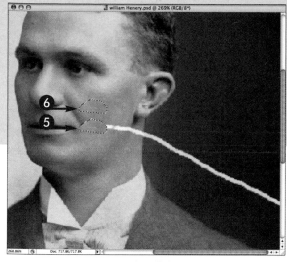

5 Place the cursor inside the drawn selection.

6 Click and drag the selected shape to an area suitable for sampling — this is your source area.

The destination area gives you a preview as you drag the shape.

7 Continue to sample by following step **6** until you are satisfied with the result.

8 Release the mouse.

Photoshop applies the patch using the last sampled area.

You can repeat steps **4** to **8** as needed until the image is repaired.

Try This!
Select the Transparent option (☐ changes to ☑) in the Options bar to better blend the sampled area with the underlying area.

Try This!
You can click Use Pattern and select a pattern from the list to blend the pattern with the initial selection.

Did You Know?
You can reverse the action of the Patch tool. Just click and activate the Destination button (the Source button is activated by default). Then you can select a patch area and use it to repair the damaged area.

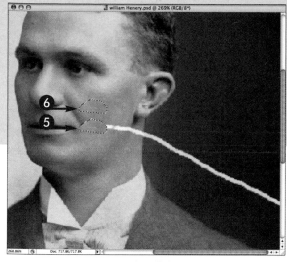

PATH EDITING TOOLS:
Add and Convert Anchor Points

You can create and edit a path to make a very precise mask. Photoshop provides several ways to create outline shapes — or *paths*. Paths are a combination of lines and curves (segments) joined by (anchor) points, which define a shape. In defining a precise path, you may need add, delete, or move these segments and anchor points.

You use the Pen tool to make a path. To add an anchor point to a path, use the Add Anchor Point tool and click somewhere on a segment of the path where it should be added. A new anchor point appears. To delete an anchor point, use the Delete Anchor Point tool and click an anchor point. The two segments once joined by the anchor point become one.

Smooth points connect curved or straight paths that flow into each other. *Corner points* connect paths that change direction abruptly. You can convert an anchor point from corner to smooth or smooth to corner by using the Convert Point tool. Clicking a smooth point converts it into a corner point; clicking a corner point and dragging convert it into a smooth point.

See also>>

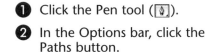

Pen tool

Path palette

Path Selection tools

Zoom tool

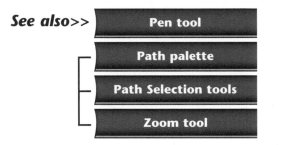

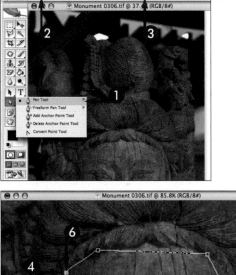

Create a Path

❶ Click the Pen tool (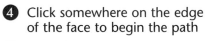).

❷ In the Options bar, click the Paths button.

❸ Click the Auto Add/Delete option (☑ changes to ☐).

❹ Click somewhere on the edge of the face to begin the path

❺ Position your cursor and continue clicking everywhere you want a point.

❻ Click on the first anchor point to close the path.

Convert Anchor Points

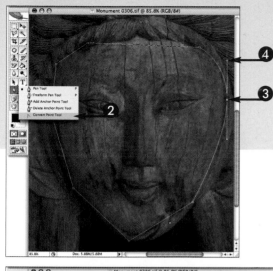

1 Zoom in on the area containing the path.

2 Click and hold on the Pen tool and select the Convert Anchor Point tool.

3 Move the cursor to the first point you want to convert and click.

The corner point is now an arc and two "handles" appear.

4 Click and drag the handle points to change the shape of the curved line segments to match the shape you are trying to create.

Dragging a handle "bends" the curves on both sides so the curves of the line between the handle ends serve as the bisector as the anchor point, which is the point of inflection.

Add or Delete Anchor Points

1 Open an image that has a path.

2 Click and hold the Pen tool and select the Add Anchor Point tool.

3 Click on a point in a segment where you want to add an anchor point.

Photoshop adds a point.

● You can drag the new point(s) or the handles that appear to new positions.

Note: The Pen tool converts to a selection tool as you hover over an anchor point.

● You can click and hold the Pen tool and select the Delete Anchor Point tool, then click an anchor point to delete it.

P

TIPS

Try This!
You can crate a Vector Mask with the Pen tool. With the Pen tool selected, click the Shape Layers button on the Options bar. Instead of a path, you create a filled shape, which Photoshop converts into a layer mask.

Did You Know?
You can draw straight or curved lines without changing the Pen tool. Click once to draw a straight line; click and drag to draw curves. As you drag, your Pen tool temporarily turns into a selection tool dragging a handle.

PATH/DIRECT
Selection Tools

You can use the Path Selection and Direct Selection tools to modify paths. The Path Selection tool can move a path in its entirety while the Direct Selection tool modifies individual segments and points on a path.

When you select a path with the Path Selection tool, all the anchor points appear as small, solid squares, which you can then move to another section of the image while retaining the image's original shape.

The Direct Selection tool changes your path's shape. You can stretch anchor points and change the shape of selected segments.

Unlike selection tools in other Adobe programs, the Path Selection tools in Photoshop only work with paths, which are vector shapes or lines that you usually create with the Pen tool, the Rectangle or

other Basic shapes, or paths imported from Illustrator. You cannot use Selection tools to modify type or other objects in Photoshop.

See also>>

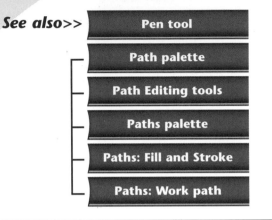

| Pen tool |
| Path palette |
| Path Editing tools |
| Paths palette |
| Paths: Fill and Stroke |
| Paths: Work path |

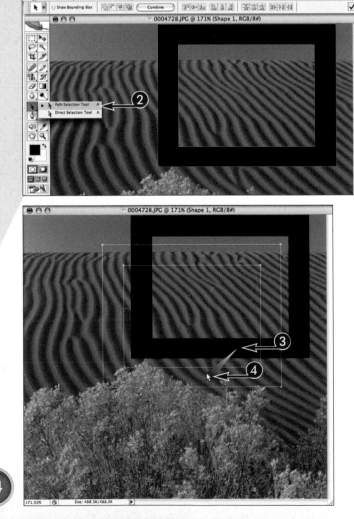

① Open an image that contains a path or vector shape.

② Click the Path Selection tool.

Alternatively, you can press A.

③ Click anywhere on a path.

④ Drag the path to a new location.

⑤ Release the mouse.

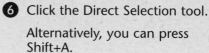

6 Click the Direct Selection tool.

Alternatively, you can press Shift+A.

7 Click and drag an anchor point.

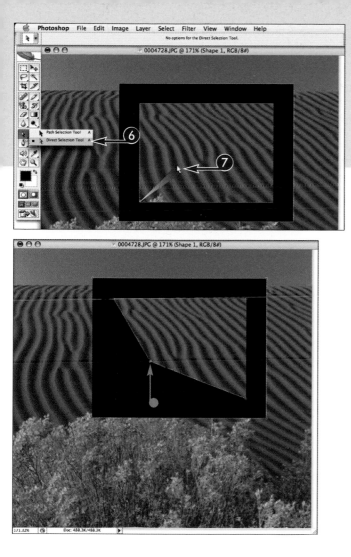

● The shape of the object changes.

TIPS

Did You Know?

When you select a path with the Path Selection tool, you must first deselect it by clicking off of it before you can select it with the Direct Selection tool.

Try This!

Another method of selecting a path is to use the Path Selection tool to click and drag a marquee that touches any part of the path. All of the anchor points appear solid, indicating that the entire path is selected.

PATTERN STAMP:
Paint with a Pattern

You can use the Pattern Stamp tool to paint an area with a repeating pattern or texture. You can choose a pattern provided by Photoshop or one that you have previously created. You can find these patterns in the Pattern fly-out menu on the Options bar.

The Aligned option works in the same manner with the Pattern Stamp as it does with the Clone Stamp. You select the Aligned option to maintain the alignment of the Pattern Stamp brush with the original painted pattern. When you paint, the alignment produces a tiled effect. Each time you release the mouse, move the brush, and resume

painting, the alignment persists, depending on where the brush is in relationship to the original painted pattern. If Aligned is not selected, each time you resume painting, the pattern begins again. You can control the opacity, blending mode, and flow, variables that can potentially produce an infinite variety of effects.

See also>>

Clone Stamp tool

Patterns

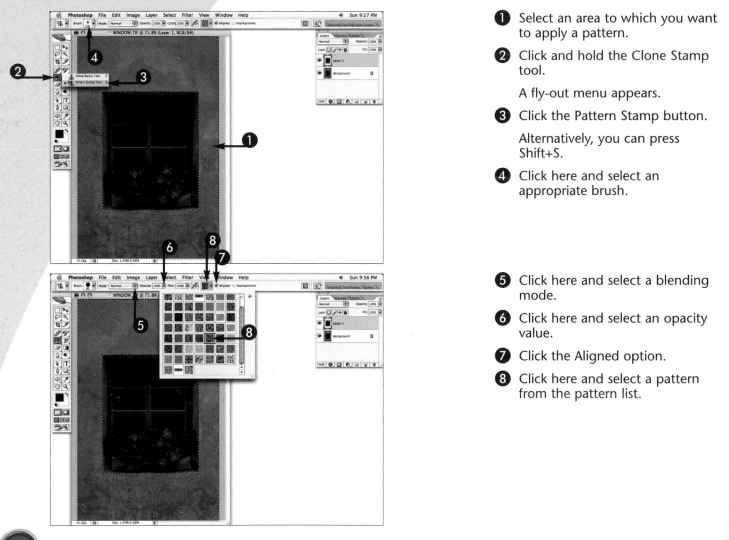

① Select an area to which you want to apply a pattern.

② Click and hold the Clone Stamp tool.

A fly-out menu appears.

③ Click the Pattern Stamp button.

Alternatively, you can press Shift+S.

④ Click here and select an appropriate brush.

⑤ Click here and select a blending mode.

⑥ Click here and select an opacity value.

⑦ Click the Aligned option.

⑧ Click here and select a pattern from the pattern list.

66

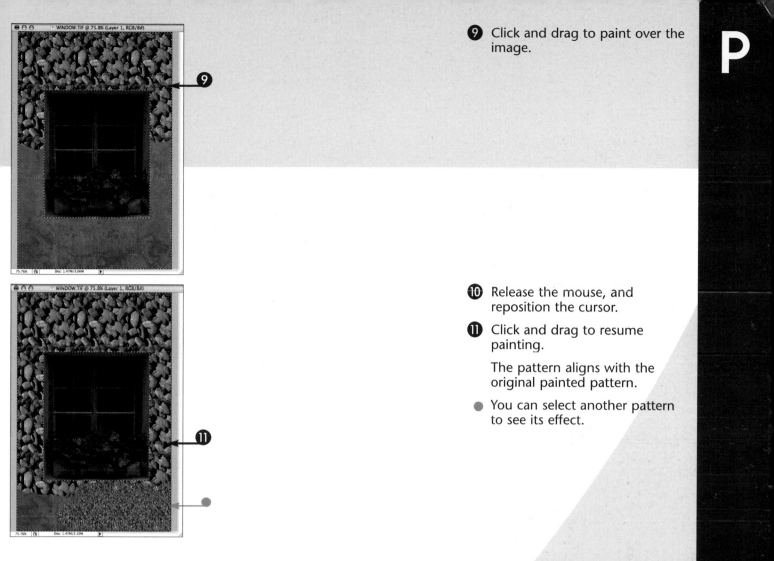

9 Click and drag to paint over the image.

10 Release the mouse, and reposition the cursor.

11 Click and drag to resume painting.

The pattern aligns with the original painted pattern.

● You can select another pattern to see its effect.

TIPS

Try This!
You can create interesting impressionist strokes by clicking the Impressionist box and using a large, soft brush.

Try This!
If you have a large area to fill, click Edit, and then click Fill. From the Fill dialog box, select Pattern and then click on a pattern sample from the list.

PEN TOOL:
Draw Combination Paths

You can draw complex paths using the Pen tool. Complex paths require you to change curve directions and type of anchor points. You may even need to extract or add sections to your shape. This is when the Path editing tools and Options bar choices come in handy.

The Path editing tools allow you to edit paths by converting, adding, or deleting anchor points. The Selection tools allow you to select and move segments or shapes. The Path Area buttons allow you to work with one or more shapes. Together all these options help you create a precise outline or filled shape.

This example outlines an object that has a combination of curved and straight lines.

See also>>

> Path Editing tools
>
> Path Selection tool; Direct Selection
>
> Pen tool
>
> Path Selection tool
>
> Pen tool, Free Form
>
> Pen tool, Magnetic option

Create a Curved Line

❶ Click the Pen tool.

❷ Click where you want to begin the path.

❸ Click and Drag to create a curved line.

❹ Opt (Alt) + click on the last point you created to end the last curve.

● You can click and drag to create a mirror image of the last curve.

Create a Straight Line

❺ Click at the next point to create a straight line.

❻ Continue creating curved or straight segments until you finish outlining the object.

Fix Mistakes

7 Click to select the Direct Selection tool.

8 Click the anchor point or segment you want to change.

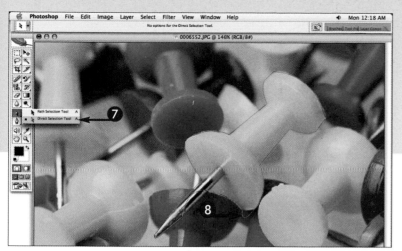

Using the Path Editing Tools

9 Click and choose one of the Path editing tools.

You can switch from an editing tool to a Selection tool at any time by pressing the Opt (Alt) key.

10 Continue editing until your shape is perfect.

TIPS

Try This!
To create a donut shape (a hole within a round shape) start with the Ellipse tool and create a round shape — if you want a perfectly round shape, press and hold the Shift key while dragging to create a round shape. Click the Exclude Overlapping path area button. Now draw a smaller round shape within the larger shape.

Did You Know?
To locate a smaller circle in the exact middle of a larger circle, select both paths with the Selection tool and then click the Align Vertical centers and the Align Horizontal centers buttons.

Try This!
To ensure that you are dragging a handle or segment in a straight line, hold down the Shift key as you drag.

PEN TOOL:
Draw Straight and Curved Paths

The Pen tool allows you to create paths consisting of points and line segments with which you can create working paths or shape layers.

You can make paths as simple as a line with two end points or as complex as a collection of points, with lines and curves defining the shape of a complicated object. Open-ended paths are point and line segments, which have joined end points. Closed-ended paths outline shapes and have joined endpoints. You can fill close-ended paths with a color, stroke them with an outline of a specific color and width, or store them in the Paths palette or the Shape menu for later use.

You can convert a path into a selection, to which you can apply any Photoshop action or command.

The simplest path consists of two anchor points joined by a straight-line segment. You can add additional

segments and you can have the segments change direction, making the connected straight paths zigzag. A curved path consists of two anchor points connected by a curved segment. *Direction handles* determine the position and shape of the line segment.

See also>>

Path Editing tools
Path Selection tool; Direct Selection
Pen tool
Path Selection tool
Pen tool, Free Form
Pen tool, Magnetic option

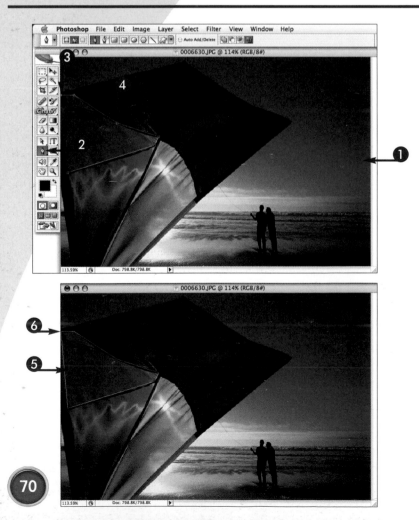

Draw a Straight Path

① Open an image.

② Click the Pen tool.

③ Click the image where you want to begin the path.

An anchor point appears.

④ Click at the two end points

A straight-line segment with another anchor point appears between the two points.

⑤ Continue to move and click your mouse to produce a series of straight line segments connected to each other by corner anchor points.

⑥ After you encircle the shape, close the path by clicking the first anchor point.

You have created a straight path box that can be filled with a color or pattern.

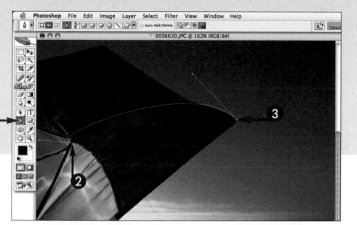

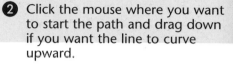

Draw a Curved Path

① Click the Pen tool.

You can zoom in on the area where you want to create the curve.

② Click the mouse where you want to start the path and drag down if you want the line to curve upward.

An anchor point and two direction handles appears.

③ Without releasing the mouse button, drag the handle up or down to increase or decrease the depth of the curve.

④ Repeat steps **2** and **3** to continue your segment.

Your curved line appears on your canvas.

● To close the path with a straight line segment, you can hold the Opt (Alt) key as you click the last point you created.

TIP

Try This!

You can create a custom shape with the Pen tool. You can then save this custom shape and use it again on another image. To create a custom shape, first draw a closed path shape per the steps in this section. Next, click Edit, and then click Define Custom Shape. In the Shape Name dialog box that appears, type a name for your shape, and then click OK. Your new shape now appears as a choice in the Shape menu on the Options menu.

PEN TOOL, FREEFORM:
Draw a Freehand Path

You can use the Freeform Pen tool, which acts similarly to the Lasso tool, to draw paths that conform to the movement of the mouse. If you then select the path with one of the Path Selection tools, the Freeform tool creates anchor points and segments as it moves around a shape. The Magnetic option works best when you need to create a path around or inside a shape that has marked color boundaries — that is a dark object set against a stark white background.

The Freeform Pen tool does not draw curves as accurately as the Pen tool. How closely the path follows the shape you draw depends not on your dexterity with a mouse or a stylus, but on the software drivers of that device. In addition, the Freeform Pen may produce more anchor points than

you really need, which may cause Photoshop to create a path that is less smooth than you want. Because of this effect, the Freeform Pen paths require some editing — usually removal of extra points. However, by selecting the Magnetic option in the Options Bar, you can increase the Freeform Pen's accuracy.

See also>>

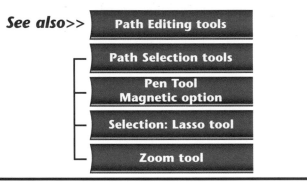

| Path Editing tools |
| Path Selection tools |
| Pen Tool Magnetic option |
| Selection: Lasso tool |
| Zoom tool |

Draw a Freeform Path

① Click and hold the Pen tool.

② Click the Freeform Pen tool.

Alternatively, you can press Shift + P until you see the Freeform Pen icon appear in the Tools palette.

You can zoom in on the are where you will be working.

③ Click at the start of the path you want to create and drag around the edge of a shape.

④ Release the mouse when you reach the starting point.

Your path, which contains extra anchoir points, is complete.

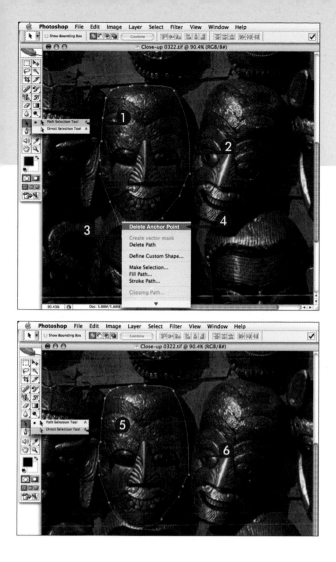

Delete Anchor Points

1 Click the Path Selection tool.

2 Click the path you created.

The path and all the anchor points display.

3 Right click a point you want to delete.

4 Click Delete Anchor Point.

Alternatively you can click the Delete Anchor Point tool (⬚), or press Shift+P until you see the Delete Anchor Point icon in the Tools palette.

5 Click the Direct Selection tool (⬚).

6 Click and drag along the path where you need to make adjustments.

Your path is devoid of unnecessary anchor points.

TIPS

Did You Know?
You can draw a Vector shape by clicking the Shape Layers button on the Freeform Pen tool's Options bar. Photoshop then creates a new layer which can serves as a Vector Mask.

Try This!
To toggle from drawing a freehand path to a straight path, click the mouse and drag to produce a free-form path. Press and hold Opt (Alt) and release the mouse. Drag in the desired direction. Release Opt (Alt) while clicking and holding the mouse to continue drawing the freehand path.

PEN TOOL, FREEFORM:
Magnetic Freeform Pen Option

You can use the Magnetic option to trace a shape on an image whose edges are well defined by contrasting colors. For example, you can best use this option on a black box set against a white background. You find the Magnetic option as one of the options of the Freeform Pen. This option's characteristics are similar in performance to the Magnetic Lasso tool. The Magnetic option automatically snaps to areas of high color contrast within an image as you drag around it. Once you define the area, the selection edges convert to a path.

To convert the Freeform Pen tool into a Magnetic Freeform Pen, you first select the Freeform Pen in the toolbar, then you activate the Magnetic option in the Options bar.

See also>>

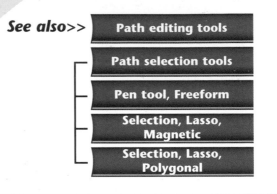

| Path editing tools |
| Path selection tools |
| Pen tool, Freeform |
| Selection, Lasso, Magnetic |
| Selection, Lasso, Polygonal |

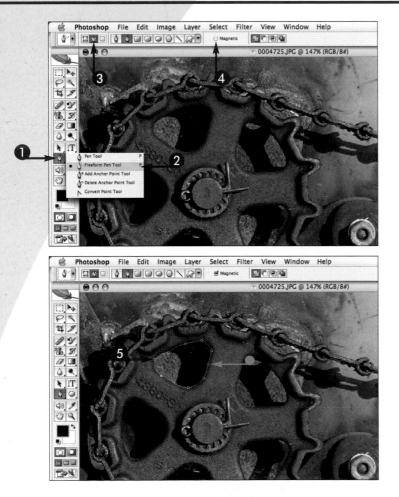

1 Click and hold the Pen tool.

2 Click the Freeform Pen tool.

Alternatively, you can press Shift + P until you see the Freeform Pen icon appear in the Tools palette.

3 Click the Paths Option.

4 Click the Magnetic option on the Options bar (☑ changes to ☐).

5 Click the image to set the first point.

Be sure to click near an edge of relatively high contrast.

6 Release the mouse button and drag slowly.

● A path is created as you trace the contour of the shape you want to create.

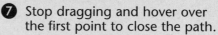

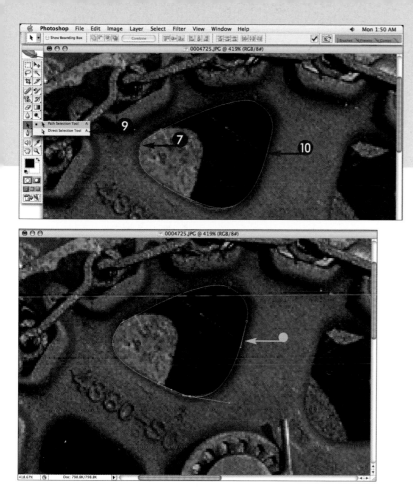

7 Stop dragging and hover over the first point to close the path.

8 Release the mouse.

You can release the mouse when you see a small circle over the first anchor point.

The path snaps to the image.

9 Click the Direct Selection tool.

10 Click the path you just created.

● The path and all the anchor points display.

TIP

Did You Know?

While using the Freeform Pen tool with the Magnetic option you can click a point to force the tool to follow a particular path. You may find this helpful when you have an area where the color boundary of a shape is indistinct. At any point thereafter you can return to using the magnetic option.

PENCIL TOOL:
Draw an Aliased Line

You can create the most crisp, clean lines that a Raster tool can create using the Pencil tool. The Pencil tool is like the Brush tool in that it applies color to image, however, it always produces a hard-edged stroke. Pixels still define this hard-edged stroke, which means that though the strokes it produces may be anti-aliased, they are not the pure Vector strokes that the Pen tool produces.

With the exception of Hardness, you can apply most of the same dynamics to the Pencil tool as the Brush tool. You can adjust the opacity (translucense) of a stroke by adjusting the Opacity slider anywhere within a range of 0 percent to 100 percent; you can also use all the Modes available to the Brush tool; and you can vary the size and texture of a Pencil tool stroke.

By default, the Pencil deposits the color that you have in the Foreground color swatch, but you can force it to deposit the Background color by selecting the Auto Erase option in the Options bar and have the foreground color beneath the cursor's center when you start the drag.

See also>>

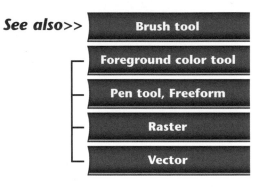

- **Brush tool**
- **Foreground color tool**
- **Pen tool, Freeform**
- **Raster**
- **Vector**

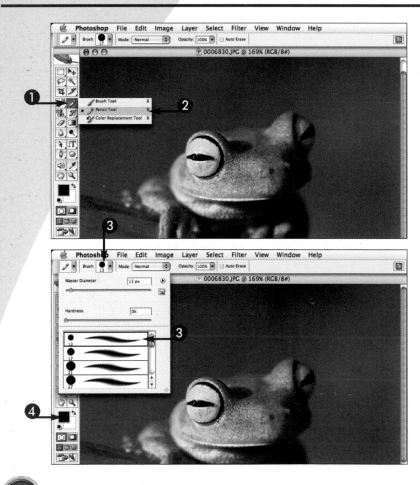

① Click and hold the Brush tool.

② Click the Pencil tool.

Alternatively, you can press Shift+B to select the tool.

③ Click here and select a brush.

④ Click the Foreground swatch.

The Color Picker appears.

5 Click a color.

● You can click and drag the slider to select a different Hue.

You can also select a color from the Swatches or Color palette.

6 Click and drag the cursor the length of the stroke you want to make.

7 Release the mouse.

The Pencil deposits the color in an aliased freehand stroke.

TIP

Try This!

You can hold the Shift key while dragging the pencil tool. The Pencil tool deposits a straight line. If, instead of dragging, you click a spot on the image, the Pencil tool creates a straight line which connects that spot with the stroke you are creating.

RED EYE TOOL:
Eliminate Red Eye on a Portrait

You can quickly eliminate the red eye effect on a portrait with Photoshop's new Red Eye tool. The Red Eye tool automatically removes red eye in photographs taken with a camera's flash attachment. Red eye appears as a red spot on the eye on photographs of people and as a white, blue or green spot on photos of animals. It is caused by the subject's retina reflecting the camera's flash.

When you select the Red Eye tool with the default settings, Photoshop searches for typical pixel configurations that red eye produces and a window appears informing you of the search results. If you apply the appropriate correction, and find that the correction is inadequate, you can undo the correction and change the settings in the Options bar to refine the effect. The Darken Pupil option reduces the brightness value of the pupil. Size increases or decreases the diameter of the effect.

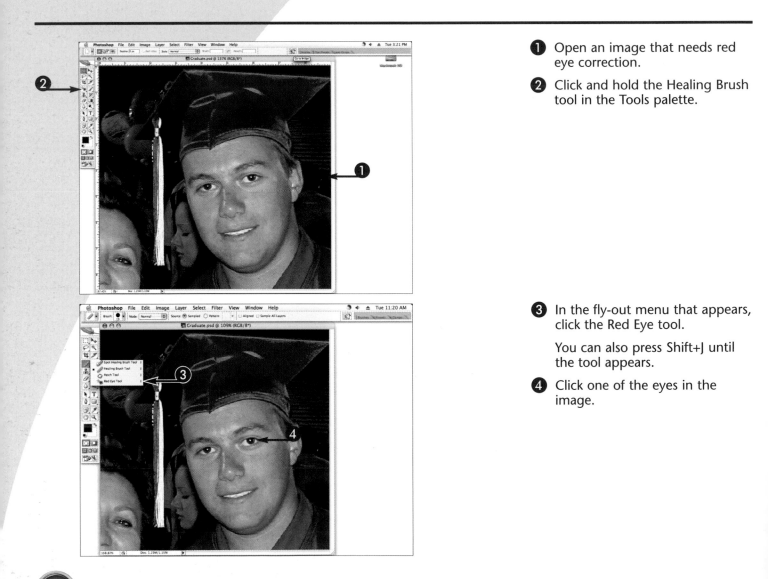

1 Open an image that needs red eye correction.

2 Click and hold the Healing Brush tool in the Tools palette.

3 In the fly-out menu that appears, click the Red Eye tool.

You can also press Shift+J until the tool appears.

4 Click one of the eyes in the image.

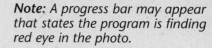

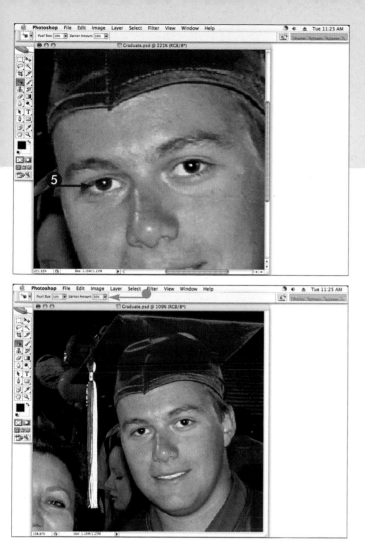

Note: *A progress bar may appear that states the program is finding red eye in the photo.*

⑤ Click the other eye in the image to correct it.

Photoshop corrects the red eyes in the image

● If the correction is not sufficient, you can experiment with the Pupil Size and Darken Amount settings in the Options bar and try again.

TIPS

Did You Know?

You see red eye more often when you take pictures in a darkened room. This is because the subject's irises are wider and more of the reflective area of the eye is exposed. To prevent this phenomenon, consider moving your subjects to a room with more light.

Try This!

Many cameras have a red eye reduction feature. To avoid red eye, turn on this feature before taking the picture. You can also use a detached flash unit or strobe that you place farther away from the camera's lens.

RULERS:
Set Ruler Units, Establish a Point of Origin

Rulers enable you to measure horizontal and vertical distances on your image. When you open a file in Photoshop, rulers are not visible. However, you can display them, and when you do, they appear at the top and left side of the image window.

By default, rulers display inches. However, you can change ruler units to pixels, millimeters, centimeters, points, picas, and percent in the Units and Ruler Preferences dialog box. By default, the point of origin

is in the upper-left corner of the image window, but you can change its position so you can more easily calculate distances within the image. You also use rulers to generate guides, which is a dotted line that travels across the image.

See also>>

Guides

Measure tool

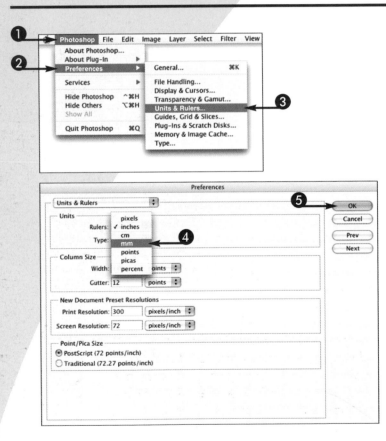

Change Ruler Preferences

❶ Click Photoshop (Edit)

❷ Click Preferences.

❸ Click Units & Rulers (Units & Rulers).

Note: If the Rulers are invisible, double click in a ruler to bring up the dialog box.

The Units & Rulers Preference dialog box appears.

❹ Click Rulers and select the desired unit of measurement.

❺ Click OK.

The ruler around your image changes with your new settings.

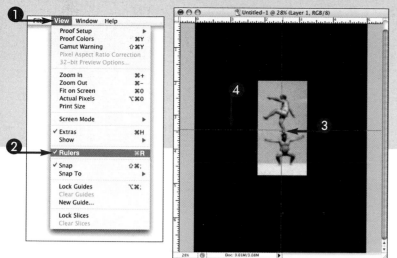

Change the Point of Origin

① Click View.

② Click Rulers.

Alternatively, you can press Cmd+R (Ctrl+R).

Horizontal and vertical rulers appear.

③ Place the cursor on where the two zero points of the rulers intersect.

④ Click and hold the mouse, and drag to the right and down until the dashed lines touch the desired horizontal vertical ruler marks.

⑤ Release the mouse.

● The new zero point of origin is now established.

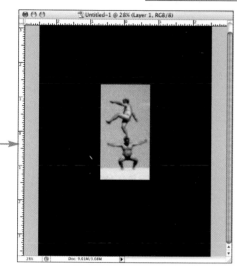

TIPS

Try This!

Want to reset the point of origin back to the default upper-left corner of your image? You can double-click the upper-left corner of your window where the two rulers originally intersected.

Try This!

Want a guide that snaps to the ruler tics? Press and hold down Shift and drag from the horizontal or vertical ruler. Your guide will be precisely aligned to a tic on the ruler.

Did You Know?

To quickly change units of measure on a Mac, hold the Control key and click anywhere within your ruler — a pop-up menu appears and allows you to select one of seven units of measure.

SELECTION, ELLIPTICAL MARQUEE:
Make an Elliptical Selection

Located in the Marquee tool menu, the Elliptical Marquee tool is one of eight selection tools in Photoshop.

The Options bar associated with the Marquee tools offers choices that enable you to customize selections. For example, with a click of a button, you can add to or subtract from a previous selection. You can feather a selection, which softens the edge. In the Styles menu, you can select one of three marquee styles to control the behavior of the tool. Normal lets you determine the size and proportion of the marquee. Fixed Aspect Ratio allows you set the proportion of your marquee. Fixed Size controls

the size of the marquee in pixels or any other specified unit.

Please note that it is difficult to create a perfect selection with the Elliptical Marquee. For this reason, this section illustrates both how to create a selection and how to reposition your selection.

The Elliptical and Rectangular Marquees are identical in their behavior. When you learn how to use one, you know how to use the other.

See also>>
Selection: Rectangular Marquee tool

Techniques, Select: Feather

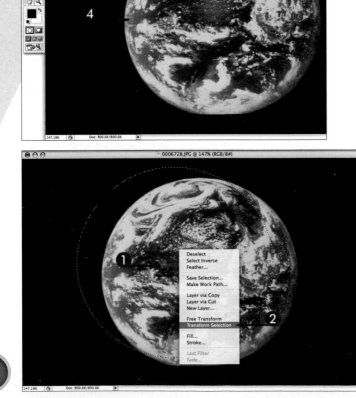

Select the object

1. With a circular object open, click and hold the Rectangle Marquee tool.

2. Click the Elliptical Marquee tool.

3. Click the New Selection icon in the Options bar.

4. Click and drag in your image to make a selection.

   You can press Shift as you drag to constrain your selection to a perfect circle.

Reposition or Scale the Selection

1. Right-click inside your selection.

2. Click Transform selection.

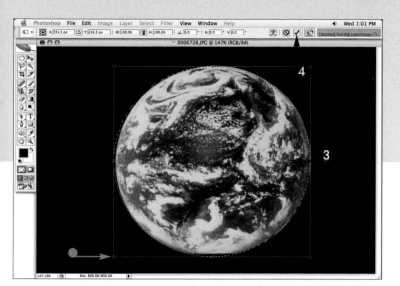

A bounding box appears around your selection.

③ Click inside the box to move the selection.

● You can click any of the corners to resize the selection.

④ Click the Commit Button.

Alternatively, you can press the Return (Enter) key.

The area is now isolated for editing.

TIP

Did You Know?

The following table gives keyboard commands or techniques, which control the behavior of the Elliptical and Rectangular Marquee tools. You can combining any of these commands.

Keyboard command	Result
Press Shift while drawing	Constrains a rectangle marquee to a square and an elliptical marquee to a circle
Click Opt (Alt)-drag in center of an area	Radiates the marquee from a center point
Hold Spacebar while dragging a marquee	Moves the selection while you draw
Click the tool and then the New Selection icon. Click and drag in the marquee	Moves the marquee after you have drawn it

SHAPE SELECTION BUTTONS:
Add, Subtract, Intersect, and Make New Selections

Whenever you select one of the eight selection tools, you are presented with four option buttons that help you edit and refine your final selection These buttons determine the function of the Selection tool: New Selection, Add to selection, Subtract from selection, and Intersect with selection.

The New Selection button creates a standard selection. Unusually, making a second selection means that you lose the first, but not if you selected Add to selection because Photoshop adds the selection to the previously selected area. Likewise, the Subtract button removes from the selected area; the Intersect button deletes any area(s) that the

previous and new selection do not share, leaving only the area they have in common.

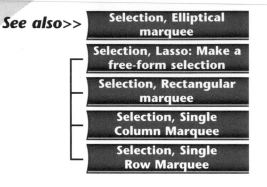

See also>>

| Selection, Elliptical marquee |
| Selection, Lasso: Make a free-form selection |
| Selection, Rectangular marquee |
| Selection, Single Column Marquee |
| Selection, Single Row Marquee |

Add to a selection

1. Click one of the Marquee tools.

   The New Selection, Add, Subtract, and Intersection icons appear at the top of the Option menu.

2. Click the New Selection icon.

3. Click and drag the Marquee tool on the image to make a selection.

4. Click the Add to Selection icon.

5. Click and drag the Marquee tool to create another selection.

Subtract from a Selection

   Photoshop adds the selection to the original selection.

6. Click the Subtract from Selection icon.

7. Click another Marquee tool.

8. Click and drag the Marquee tool somewhere in the selection to remove a section.

84

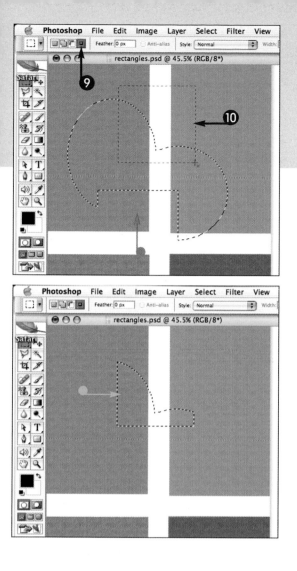

Intersection a Selection

● The area disappears from the image.

9 Click the Intersection icon.

10 Click and drag the Marquee tool somewhere in the image so that it overlaps a portion of the selection

● Only the intersection of the two selections remains.

![TIPS]

Did You Know?
When the Add icon is highlighted, a plus sign (+) appears next to your cursor, a minus sign (-) appears for the Subtract icon, and an X appears for the Intersect icon.

Try This!
To temporarily switch your cursor from Add to Subtract (and vice versa), press and hold Opt (Alt) key.

SELECTION, LASSO:
Make a Free-Form Selection

You can use the Lasso to select irregular shapes — that is, not rectangular or elliptical. It is ideal for organic shapes. You are not going to make a perfect selection every time, so you need to begin by making a quick and general selection around the object you want to isolate. You can then add or subtract sections to make the selection more precise. The Lasso tool is great to use in combination with other selection tools.

The most straightforward of the selection tools, the Lasso tool functions like a pencil on tracing paper; you drag the Lasso tool around the edge of an object while pressing the mouse. If you have a stylus

instead of a mouse, you may find it easier to outline an object, because it acts and feels more like a pencil. Like all the selection tools, the Lasso tool provides an option bar, which offers the New, Add, Subtract, and Intersect buttons. You can also feather or apply anti-aliasing to your selection.

See also>>

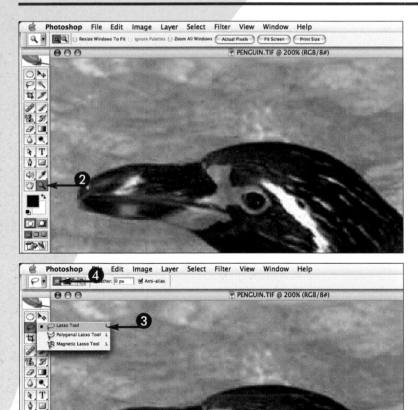

1 Open an image.

2 Click the Zoom tool to zoom in on your object's edges.

You can also press Cmd (Ctrl)+ +(Plus symbol) to zoom in.

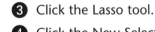

3 Click the Lasso tool.

4 Click the New Selection icon.

5 Click the edge of the object to select and trace the outline.

6 Close the marquee by placing the cursor on your starting point.

The selection is ready for editing.

TIPS

Try This!
You can toggle between the Lasso and Polygonal Lasso by pressing Opt (Alt). Remember that you cannot have the Opt (Alt) button down when switching to Polygon and the Opt (Alt) button must be down when switching to Lasso.

Did You Know?
Using the Lasso tool requires a bit of hand-eye coordination. It's much easier to use the Lasso tools if you have a stylus and tablet. Drawing and outlining shapes is quite natural with an implement that is more like a pen than with a mouse.

SELECTION, LASSO, MAGNETIC:
Make an Automatic Selection

The Magnetic Lasso is the ideal tool for selecting objects with complex edges set against a high-contrast background. The Magnetic Lasso, like all other selection tools, provides an option bar which offers the New, Add, Subtract, and Intersect options as well as the Feather option, which blurs the edge of your selection, and the Anti-aliased option, which creates a soft edge so you can blend pixels into whatever background you move or copy the selection.

The Magnetic Lasso also has options that are uniquely its own. The Width box determines how far the cursor "looks" to locate an edge; the Edge Contrast box sets the amount of contrast required for Photoshop to consider something an edge. The

Frequency box determines the distance (in pixels) between anchor points.

As you use the Magnetic Lasso, Photoshop creates points and segments that snap like a magnet between areas of great contrast. As always, no selection you initially make is perfect, so you may need to edit your selection.

See also>>

| Tools, Selection Lasso |
| Tools, Selection Lasso, Polygonal |
| Tools, Selection Icons |

① Open an image with a well-defined subject.

② Click Magnetic Lasso tool from the Lasso Tool fly-out.

Alternatively, you can press Shift+L until the Magnetic Lasso tool appears in the Tools palette.

③ Click the New Selection icon in the Options bar.

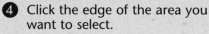

④ Click the edge of the area you want to select.

⑤ Drag around the area.

The outline snaps to the contrasted edge.

● You can add anchor points to force the Magnetic Lasso to snap to a particular point at any time by clicking the mouse.

⑥ Close the marquee by double-clicking your starting point.

The selection you made follows the contour of the irregularly shaped object closely.

TIPS

Try This!
To temporarily switch to the Lasso tool, press and hold Opt (Alt) while dragging the cursor and pressing the mouse button. Release and click to return to the Magnetic Lasso. To temporarily switch to the Polygonal Lasso tool, press and hold Opt (Alt) while clicking the object's edge.

Caution!
You can erase a selection by pressing Opt (Alt) and dragging toward the part of the selection you already made. Double-click to locate the anchor point, press Delete and begin again.

Did You Know?
You can increase or decrease the value in the Edge field (Options bar). Press the right bracket ( ]) to add or the left bracket ([ ) to subtract 1 pixel to the Edge value.

SELECTION LASSO, POLYGONAL:
Make Straight Edge Selections

You can use the Polygonal Lasso tool when the object you want to select has straight edges but is not a rectangle. To use the Polygonal Lasso select a starting point, then select another point on the edge of your object. Photoshop creates a straight line to connect the two points.

You can use the Shift key with the Polygonal Lasso to force the next line segment into a straight horizontal line.

As with other selection tools, you can modify the Polygonal Lasso tool's actions using the Options bar. You can use the New, Add, Subtract, and Intersect

buttons as you would with another selection tool. To make your selection better for blending into other images, you can also use the Feather or Anti-aliased option.

See also>>

Selection Lasso tool
Selection Lasso, Magnetic
Selection Icons: Add, Subtract, Intersect, New
Zoom tool

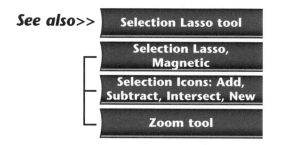

① Open an image with straight-edged elements.

② Click the Polygonal Lasso tool from the Lasso fly-out menu.

③ Click the New Selection icon in the Options bar.

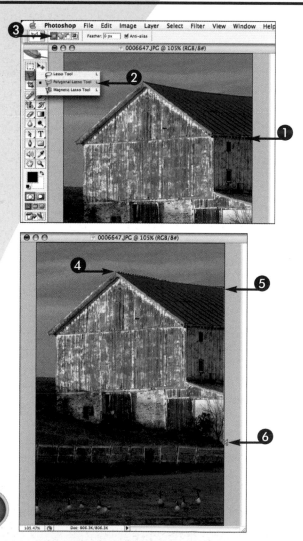

④ Click a corner of the object.

⑤ Move the cursor to the next corner and click again.

⑥ Repeat step **5** until you encounter an area that is not straight.

7 Press and hold the Opt (Alt) key to temporarily invoke the Lasso tool.

8 Drag along the edge of the object.

9 Release the Opt (Alt) key and continue to use the Polygonal Lasso.

When you return to the starting point, a closed circle appears next to the cursor.

Photoshop closes the selection outline with the last straight segment and your path becomes a selection outline of marching ants.

TIPS

Try This!

To finish a selection, double-click the last point you created. Photoshop closes the selection by creating a line between your current location and your starting point.

Did You Know!

To move to another section of your image while using the Magnetic Lasso, you can press the Spacebar at any point to switch to the Hand tool. Release the Spacebar to return to the Magnetic Lasso. This is particularly helpful, when you must zoom in on an area and you cannot see all parts of your image.

SELECTIONS, RECTANGULAR MARQUEE:
Select a Rectangular Area

You can make square or rectangular selections with the Rectangular Marquee tool. The Rectangular Marquee is one of eight selection tools in Photoshop and is the default Marquee tool in the Tools palette.

Depending on which button you select, you can create a new selection, add to or subtract from that selection, or isolate the intersection of two selections. Additional settings let you feather a selection, turn anti-alias on or off, and establish a Style.

The Styles fly-out menu lets you select one of three options. Normal lets you determines the dimensions of the marquee by dragging the Rectangular Marquee. Fixed Aspect Ratio allows you to set a height-to-width relationship — for example, setting the height to be twice the width. Fixed Size lets you assign specific values for the height and width.

See also>>

Selection Icons

Selection: Elliptical Marquee

---

① Click the Rectangular Marquee from the Tools palette.

You can press Cmd (Ctrl)+R to display rulers and use them to verify the size of your selection.

② Click the New Selection icon.

③ Click here and select Fixed Size.

④ Type a value for the selection width and height.

⑤ Click once and Photoshop automatically creates a selection with the size defined by your values.

To reposition your selection border, you can click inside the marquee and drag.

● You can click here to swap height and width.

⑥ Click the image to create a selection.

⑦ Click here and select Normal.

The width and height fields are not available.

⑧ Click and drag to create a selection.

Note that there are no proportion or size constraints.

● You can click here to Add to your selection.

Because you are still in Normal Style, you determine the size and shape of the selection.

Your new selection is created.

The example shows a combination of two selections.

You can reposition a selection as you create by depressing the mouse button, holding down the spacebar, and dragging; you can release the spacebar when you have the selection where you want it.

TIP

Did You Know?

You can use these keyboard commands or actions for the Rectangular and Elliptical Marquee tools to control their behavior. You can also combine any of these commands. For example, you can Shift+click and drag to constrain the image to a circle or square. Or, while dragging, you can press Opt (Alt) to radiate it from its center point.

Keyboard command	Action
Shift+drag	Constrains a Rectangular Marquee to a square and an Elliptical Marquee to a circle
place your cursor in the center of the area and Opt (Alt)+drag	Allows you to draw from the marquee's center
While dragging, press and hold the Spacebar	Repositions the marquee while you draw
While using the Marquee tool, place the cursor inside the marquee and drag to reposition it	Repositions the marquee after you have drawn it

SELECTION, MAGIC WAND TOOL:
Select an Area of Similar Color

The Magic Wand tool lets you make a selection of consistently colored pixels. You can control the number of selected pixels by using settings on the Options bar. As with other selection tools, you have the New, Add, Subtract, and Intersect buttons that help you change the shape of your selection. You can also set a value for Tolerance — a setting whose value determines how closely related in color pixels must be. The values can range from 0 to 255. The higher the value the broader range of pixels that Photoshop will select.

If you accept a default Tolerance value of 32, for example, and select a pixel that has a value of 128, or mid-gray, the selection includes all the pixels that are 32 steps lighter and all the pixels that are 32 steps darker than the sampled pixel — that is, Photoshop selects all adjacent pixels with brightness values between 96 and 160.

If you select the Contiguous option the Magic Wand selects only pixels in adjacent areas; if you do not select this option, all pixels throughout the image are selected. Sample all Layers includes pixels from all layers in a selection.

① Click the Magic Wand tool in the Tools palette.

Alternatively, you can press W.

② Deselect the Contiguous option in the Options bar.

③ Click the area of the image that you want to select.

A selection outline appears around the area that is within the tolerance range.

To deselect the area, press Cmd+D (Ctrl+D).

Alternatively, you can click another are of the image — as long as you have the New Selection button selected, the new area is selected, the old one is deselected.

④ Increase the Tolerance level in the Options bar.

⑤ Click again to make a selection.

6 Click the Add to selection button.

7 Click in the area(s) you want to add to your selection.

8 Repeat step **7** as needed.

Similar colors are selected in your image.

To select the reverse of what is selected, you can press Cmd(Ctrl)+Shift+I.

Did You Know?

When selecting RGB color images with the Magic Wand tool, the range is determined by each of the red, green, and blue values of the sampled pixel.

Warning!

You cannot use the Magic Wand to select pixels in Bitmap image or on a 32-bits-per-channel image.

SELECTION: SINGLE COLUMN/ROW MARQUEE:
Select a Single Column or Row of Pixels

Photoshop provides an easy method to select just a 1-pixel-wide column or row. This is an easy way to know for sure that you are selecting the smallest increment that one can select in Photoshop. It is especially helpful if you want to create a fine line of color. The Single Column Marquee and Single Row Marquee tools are both located in the Rectangular Marquee tool fly-out menu.

As with any selection, it is always a good idea to magnify the area where you want to select a 1-pixel-wide column or row. Use the Single Column Marquee tool for vertical selections or the Single Row Marquee tool for horizontal selections.

The only options available for the Single Column/Row Marquee tool are the New, Add, Subtract, or Intersect Buttons.

By default, the marquee extends the length or width of your image. If you do not want this, you can easily move the marquee left or right, up or down simply by dragging. By default, the Single Column and Single Row tools produce aliased selections.

See also>>   Selection, Elliptical Marquee

Selection, Rectangular Marquee

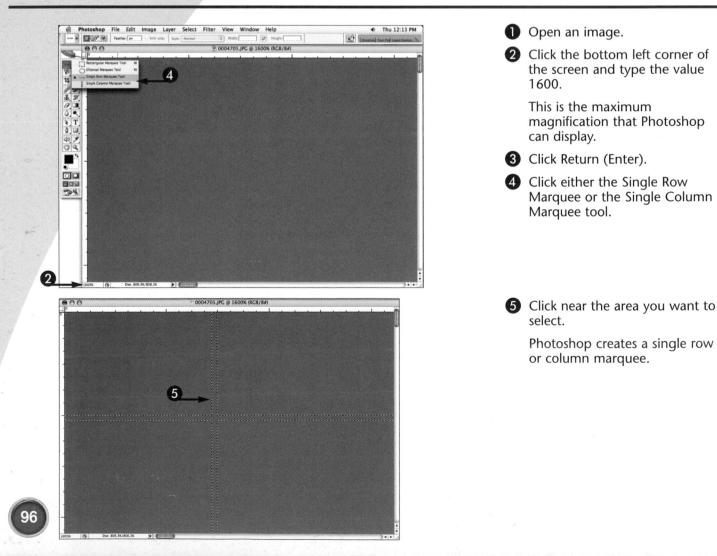

❶ Open an image.

❷ Click the bottom left corner of the screen and type the value 1600.

This is the maximum magnification that Photoshop can display.

❸ Click Return (Enter).

❹ Click either the Single Row Marquee or the Single Column Marquee tool.

❺ Click near the area you want to select.

Photoshop creates a single row or column marquee.

SHARPEN:
Bring an Area Into Focus

Sharpen tool focuses blurred images by increasing the contrast of adjacent pixles. It is ideal for correcting slightly out-of-focus images. It does not, however, improve badly-out-of–focus images.

The Sharpen tool increases the relative contrast among adjacent pixels thereby making edges more prominent. The more you apply this tool, the more contrast and diversity of color you achieve. The effect is especially pronounced where the image has high contrast between adjoining pixels.

Like all tools that rely on brushes for their application, the effect can vary greatly depending on the brush shape and dynamics that you select in the Brushes palette. You can increase the intensity of the sharpening effect by adjusting the Strength setting in the Options bar from 1 percent to 100 percent.

See also>>

Filter: Sharpen

Brushes palette

Filter: Sharpen: Sharpen for Print

① Open an image with a subject that needs sharpening.

② Click and hold the Blur tool.

③ In the fly-out menu, click the Sharpen tool.

④ Click here to select a brush, a blending mode of Luminosity, and a Strength.

This example decrease the Strength to 25 percent.

⑤ Click and drag over the area you want to sharpen.

Photoshop sharpens the image.

You can repeat step **5** until your subject is sharpened to your satisfaction.

SHAPE TOOL, CUSTOM:
Draw a Custom Shape

Photoshop provides several shape libraries that you can load via the Basic Shapes Option bar. However, if you need a unique shape that you anticipate using many times, you can create one from scratch and add it to your own shapes library.

After you create a custom shape, it is listed in the Shape menu in the Options bar. Like other Basic Shapes, custom shapes are vector objects. You use vector tool to create and edit them.

The option buttons you select from the Option bar determines what type of object Photoshop generates. The Shape layers button creates a vector mask on a separate layer; the Paths button creates a working path which you can save a selection or path; the Fill pixels button creates a filled shape to which you can apply Blend modes or adjust Opacity.

See also>>

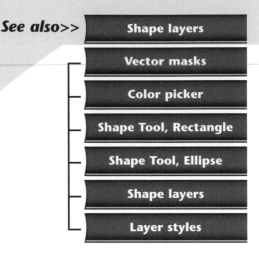

Shape layers

Vector masks

Color picker

Shape Tool, Rectangle

Shape Tool, Ellipse

Shape layers

Layer styles

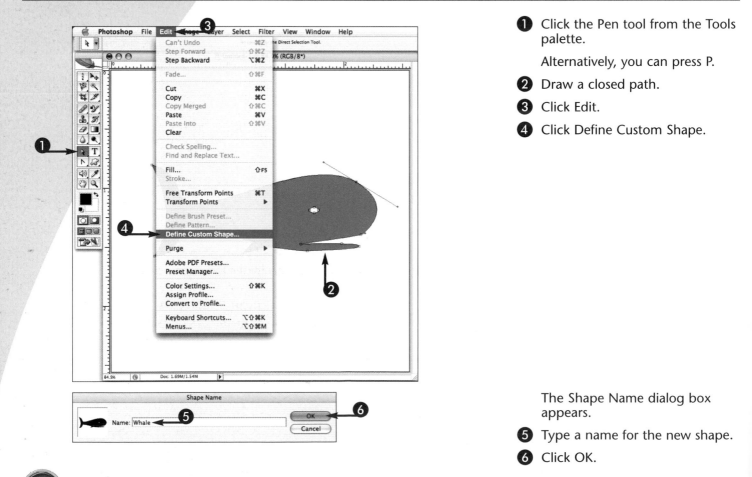

① Click the Pen tool from the Tools palette.

Alternatively, you can press P.

② Draw a closed path.

③ Click Edit.

④ Click Define Custom Shape.

The Shape Name dialog box appears.

⑤ Type a name for the new shape.

⑥ Click OK.

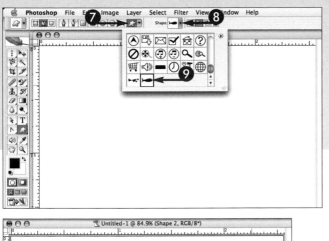

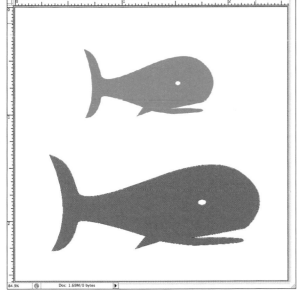

7 In a new document, click the Custom Shape tool from the Options bar.

You can also press Shift+U until the icon appears.

8 Click the Shape list in the Options bar.

Your shape appears at the bottom of the list.

9 Click your shape and select a shape option from the three icons — Shape layer (⬚), Path (⬚) or Fill (⬚) on the Options bar.

10 Place the cursor on the image; then click and drag the shape.

Photoshop create your custom shape automatically.

You can press Shift as you drag to change its size.

S

SHAPE TOOL, ELLIPSE:
Create an Elliptical Shape and Apply a Style to It.

You can create elliptical circular vector shapes with the Elliptical Shape tool. The Option bar for this tool has similar action buttons as the Marquee tool. You can use the New, Add, Subtract, Intersect, or Exclude buttons to modify your shape. Like all other vector objects, you can manipulate Elliptical objects by using path-editing tools.

You can use the arrow to the right of the last Shape tool in the Options bar to access a menu that offers addition controls: the default is Unconstrained; Circle radiates a perfect circle from the center; if you need a particular size you can enter values in Fixed

Size fields; Proportional maintains a ratio which you enter; From Center allow you to create a ellipse — not necessarily a perfect circle — that radiates from the center. You can also apply a Layer Style to a shape if it is on a Shape layer by selecting a style from the menu in the Options bar or creating your own.

See also>>

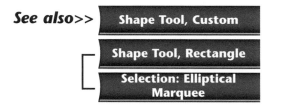

| Shape Tool, Custom |
| Shape Tool, Rectangle |
| Selection: Elliptical Marquee |

---

① Open or Create a blank document.

② Click and hold the Shape tool and select the Ellipse tool.

Alternatively, you can press Shift+U until the tool appears.

③ Click the Shape Layers icon in the Options bar.

④ Click here and select a fill style.

⑤ Click and drag an Ellipse.

⑥ Click and drag to create another ellipse.

⑦ Repeat step **4** to create another fill style from the Style menu.

Photoshop creates an ellipse with the characteristics you selected.

100

SHAPE, LINE:
Draw a Vector Line

You can draw a straight vector line with the Line tool. Like the other shapes, you can draw a line as a Shape layer, a path (vectors), or as fill pixels. When you generate a line as a vector, it is editable with the path-editing tools. When you draw a line as fill pixels, it draws in the current layer in the color selected in the Options bar.

The Line tool's Options bar enables you to choose a weight, color, and layer style. You can select one of the four icons to add to, subtract from, intersect with, or exclude an overlapping area of an existing path. The options in the Line Options

panel in the Options bar determine what type of arrowhead appears at either end of the line. You can select the Start or End options, or both, to produce an arrowhead at the beginning and/or end of the line. You can also enter values for the width, length, and concavity of the arrowhead.

See also>>

Shape layers

Vector masks

Color Picker

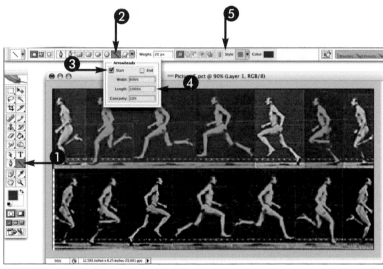

❶ Click the Line tool from the Rectangle tool fly-out menu.

❷ Click the Line tool in the Options bar.

❸ Click the option to determine whether your line will start or end with an arrowhead.

❹ Type values for an arrowhead.

❺ In the Options bar, click to select a shape, a weight, a style, and a color for your arrow.

❻ Click the image and drag from left to right the length of the desired arrow.

An arrow appears on your image.

SHAPE, POLYGON:
Draw an Equal-Sided Polygon or Star

You can draw perfect, regular polygons and stars with the Polygon tool. Similar to the other Shape tools, you can draw a polygon as a shape layer, a path, or as fill pixels. When you draw a polygon as a Shape layer or as a path, its sides are editable with the path-editing tools. When you draw it as fill pixels, Photoshop applies it to the current layer in the color selected in the Options bar.

The Polygon tool's Options bar has a number of options to control the number of sides, color, and layer style. You also have five buttons that allow you to add to, subtract from, intersect with, or exclude an

overlapping area from an existing path. Options in the Polygons Options panel in the Options bar determine the characteristics of the polygon. Radius determines a corner radius for a round-cornered polygon. The Star option indents the sides inward. Indent By is a percentage that determines the shape of the star. Smooth Indents rounds the indents of the star.

See also>>

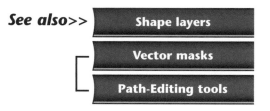

Shape layers

Vector masks

Path-Editing tools

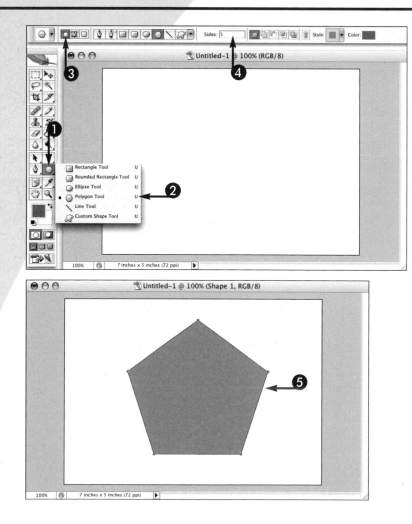

Create a Polygon

1 Click and hold the Shape tool.

2 Select the Polygon tool.

Alternatively, you can press Shift+U until the Polygon tool appears.

You can also choose it from the Options bar.

3 Click the Shape Layer icon in the Options bar.

4 In the Options bar, type the number of sides you want.

5 Click and drag on the canvas to create the polygon to the size you want.

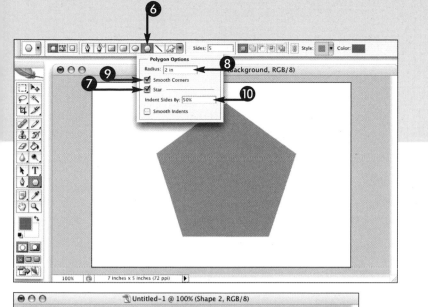

Create a Star

6 Click the Polygon tool options.

7 Click the Star option.

8 Type a corner radius.

9 Click the Smooth Corner option.

10 Type an indent percentage.

11 Click and drag to create a star shape of the desired size.

Your polygon and star shape are complete.

TIPS

Try This!
You can rotate the polygon or star into position by dragging the cursor in a circular motion as you draw it. You can reposition the polygon or star as you draw it by pressing the Spacebar.

Try This!
While dragging your shape, press the mouse button and at the same time press the Spacebar. You can then reposition the shape without exiting the tool mode. Release the Spacebar (but not the mouse button) to return to creating your shape.

SLICE/SLICE SELECT TOOL:
Prepare an Image for the Web

The Slice tool's function is strictly related to the creation of Web content in Photoshop and Image Ready. It lets you divide an image, which you can make as complex as a Web page layout, into smaller components . This makes images more efficient for loading onto a Web page and also allows you to assign specific functions, like menu buttons, to each part.

Photoshop can save the slices for Web use and create the HTML code for a Web page. You can slice the image with the Slice tool in Photoshop or its

companion Web program, ImageReady. By default, the image has one slice, but you can create more. You can select and edit a slice with the Select Slice tool in the Tools palette in Photoshop or ImageReady. You can also use the Save For Web command in Photoshop, and edit individual parts in other applications.

See also>>

Techniques: ImageReady

Techniques: Save for Web

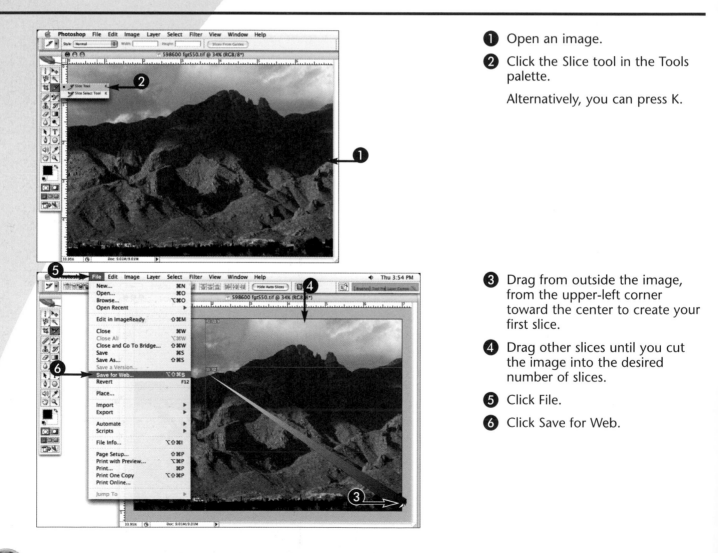

① Open an image.

② Click the Slice tool in the Tools palette.

Alternatively, you can press K.

③ Drag from outside the image, from the upper-left corner toward the center to create your first slice.

④ Drag other slices until you cut the image into the desired number of slices.

⑤ Click File.

⑥ Click Save for Web.

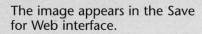

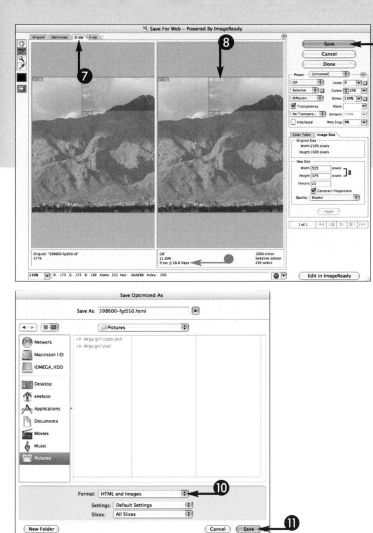

The image appears in the Save for Web interface.

7 Click the 2-Up tab.

Side-by-side versions of the image appear with the left side being the original and the right side the optimized version.

● At the bottom of the right window, Photoshop tells you how long the image will take to load.

8 Click on the right side of the window.

9 Click Save.

The Save Optimized As dialog box appears.

10 Click HTML and Images from the Format palette.

11 Click Save.

Photoshop saves your image as sliced components and HTML code.

TIPS

Caution!
Slices can only butt up against each other or butt up against the top, bottom, or sides of the image. You cannot cut a slice out of the center of the image because it creates new slices that are adjacent to it.

Did You Know?
By default, when you click the Slice tool, you see that the image is really one slice. The number 1 appears in the upper-left corner of the slice. Each time you create a slice, a new sequential number is assigned to it.

Try This!
The Slice tool's Option bar has a button called Divide that allows you to divide your image into evenly spaced vertical or horizontal slices (or both). Click Divide and in the dialog box that appears select the orientation and type values for number and size of slices. Click OK to accept your changes.

S

SMUDGE TOOL:
Produce Charcoal and Pastel Effects

You can use the Smudge tool to produces an effect like finger painting. In fact the tool looks like a hand with an extended finger. Located in the Blur tool fly-out menu, the tool acts like a finger dragging across a powdery or wet-painted surface. As you drag with the tool, you pick up colors from the starting point and blend them with colors that are situated in the direction of the stroke.

The Options bar provides many ways to customize the Smudge tool. You can start by picking a brush tip and size. You have a choice of seven blending modes

that change the method of mixing color. You can specify the strength of the effect in the Strength box. By default, the Smudge tool only uses color data from the active layer. The Sample All Layers option blends colors from all visible layers. By selecting the Finger Painting option, you can add your current foreground color to the mix at the beginning of each stroke.

See also>> **Color Picker**

① Open an image.

② Click and hold the Blur tool and select the Smudge tool.

③ Click here and select a brush size.

④ Click here and select a color mode.

⑤ Click here and select a strength.

⑥ Click and drag multiple times over your image to smudge the paint.

⑦ Click the Finger Painting option.

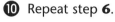

8 Double-click the Foreground Color set box in the Tools palette.

The Color Picker appears.

9 Click a foreground color from the Color Picker.

10 Repeat step **6**.

The Foreground color mixes with the colors from the original image as you drag.

TIPS

Try This!
Press and hold Opt (Alt) while dragging the Smudge tool and the finger-painting option is engaged. Instead of just mixing the existing colors on the image, the tool blends whatever color is displayed on the Foreground swatch.

Warning!
Be patient when using the Smudge tool. There is a delayed effect when you use this tool, so you may be tempted to overuse it when you do not see the effect taking place.

Try This!
For horizontal and vertical lines, press Shift as you drag up or down, left or right.

STATUS BAR:
Find Image Information

You can use the Status bar at the bottom of each document to help you gauge key information about your image. Two main concerns with Photoshop are the amount of memory and disk space that a user has on his or her computer. Adding layers, filters, and affects creates larger files that in turn may cause the system to crash or become unreliable. The Status bar provides information such as magnification, document dimensions, and a fly-out menu with 32-bit exposure, scratch size, efficiency, timing, and current tool information.

In the magnification field, you can enter values between 1 to 1600%. To its right is the field that displays the document file size. It contains two numbers divided by a slash with the left number being the amount of uncompressed space that the file consumes on your hard drive and the second number showing the size of the image with the addition of any layers, paths, channels, or annotations. This second number is the most accurate representation of the actual file size.

See also>>

Image size

Memory

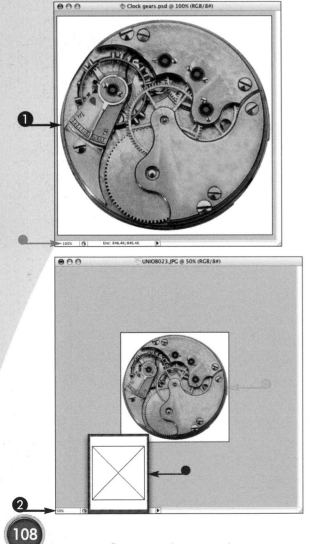

① Open an image.

● The view size appears here in the Status bar.

② Type a new size value.

③ Press Enter.

● The image appears at half the size.

④ Click the Status bar.

● A box appears that shows the dimensions of your image and how it will fit on the paper.

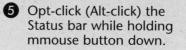

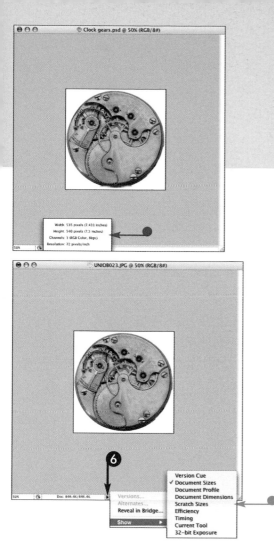

⑤ Opt-click (Alt-click) the Status bar while holding mmouse button down.

● A list of appears showing the image resolution, color mode, and dimensions.

⑥ Click the black arrow.

A fly-out menu appears.

● You can click show option to display it in the Status bar.

Version Cue
✓ Document Sizes
Document Profile
Document Dimensions
Scratch Sizes
Efficiency
Timing
Current Tool
32-bit Exposure

Versions...
Alternates...
Reveal in Bridge...

Show ▶

Did You Know?

The Status bar fly-out menu contains the following information:

Item	Description
Version Cue	The work group status of your image
Document Sizes	Print size/Image size with Layers, Channels, Paths, and/or Annotations
Document Profile	The name of the document's embedded color profile
Document Dimensions	The height, width, and resolution of the document
Scratch Sizes	Amount of RAM that the program currently uses /Amount of RAM available for image processing
Efficiency	Percentage of time spent performing an operation
Timing	Time spent performing the last operation
Current Tool	The name of the active tool
32 Bit Exposure	A slider for adjusting High Dynamic Range images

SWATCH PALETTE:
Create and Save a Custom Color

You can select a color and save it to the Swatches palette. Along with the Color Picker, the Color palette, and the Eyedropper tool, the Swatches palette is a device for selecting, creating and saving color swatches in Photoshop. You can display the Swatches palette via the Window menu, or you can click the Swatches palette tab in the Color/Swatches/Styles palette cluster.

The Foreground and Background color swatches in the tools menu determine where and when a color is applied. You can control the color that this swatch displays by selecting colors from thee Color Picker or

swatch libraries. You can also add or delete colors to create a custom swatch or a swatch library. Creating libraries of swatches can help you organize and streamline your workflow. It can also help to control palette size and avoid clutter. The Swatches palette provides access to many color libraries such as Pantone or Web-safe color libraries as well as additional library management tools.

See also>>

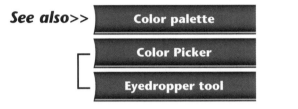

Color palette

Color Picker

Eyedropper tool

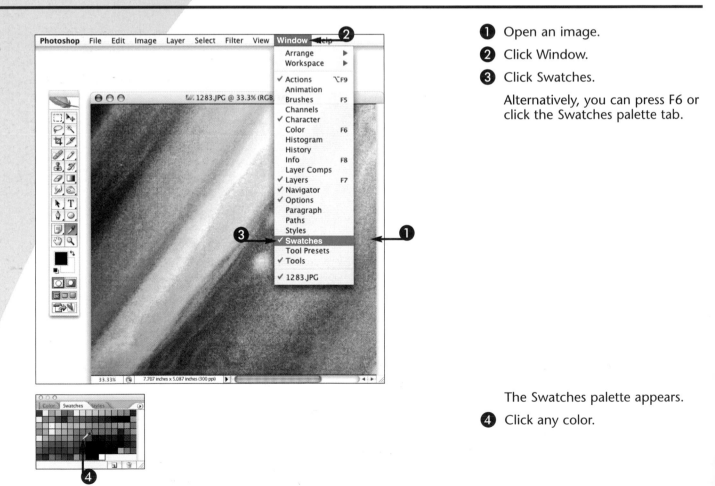

1 Open an image.

2 Click Window.

3 Click Swatches.

Alternatively, you can press F6 or click the Swatches palette tab.

The Swatches palette appears.

4 Click any color.

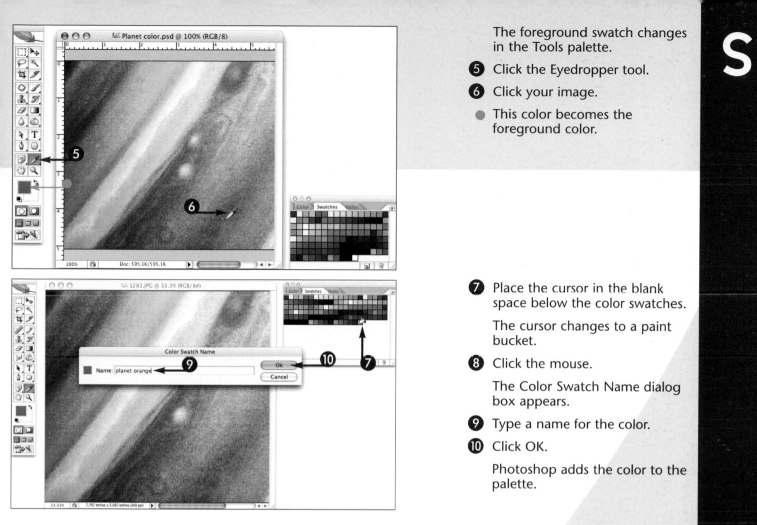

The foreground swatch changes in the Tools palette.

5 Click the Eyedropper tool.

6 Click your image.

● This color becomes the foreground color.

7 Place the cursor in the blank space below the color swatches.

The cursor changes to a paint bucket.

8 Click the mouse.

The Color Swatch Name dialog box appears.

9 Type a name for the color.

10 Click OK.

Photoshop adds the color to the palette.

TIPS

Try This!
You can position the cursor over a color in the Swatches palette to display its name.

Warning!
Photoshop saves the new swatches you create in the preferences file. If anything happens to preferences — for example if it becomes corrupt, or is recreated — your will lose your swatches unless you save them to a library.

Did You Know?
You can create a new swatch from the Foreground color by clicking an empty space in the library palette to which you want to add it.

Did You Know?
You can share solid swatches — that is not gradient, pattern, or registration swatches — with other Adobe applications. After creating a swatch library, select Save Swatches For Exchange from the Swatches palette menu. You can then load the swatches into the Swatches palette of the other Adobe applications. The Swatches palette Options menu offers these choices:

Item	Description
Save Swatches	Saves the swatch palette
Load Swatches	Opens a saved swatches set
Reset Swatches	Resets your swatches to their default colors

TYPE TOOL HORIZONTAL/VERTICAL:
Create Editable Type on a Layer

To add effects to your text, you can generate horizontal or vertical type on layers. The default Horizontal Type tool generates horizontally oriented text and the Vertical Type tool generates a column of vertical characters. You can preprogram the Type tool prior to entering text by setting values in the Options bar or in the Character or Paragraph palettes. You can also highlight the text afterward and modify its specifications.

The Type tool Options bar displays type characteristics. The Orientation icon toggles between horizontal and vertical orientation. The Font menu specifies the typeface, and the Styles menu specifies weight or italics. By default, the size is measured in points. Anti-Alias determines how the type blends into its

background. Alignment generates flush-left, centered, or flush-right text. You can change the text color using the Color Picker. The Warp icon enables you to bend or twist the type. The Character/Paragraph icon displays basic type characteristics in two palettes.

See also>>

Type, Character palette

Text, Box: Generate Type in a box

Text, Find/Change: Locate and change text

Text, Point Text: Generate type along a point

Text, Path Text: Generate type on a path

Create Horizontal Text

1. Click the Horizontal Type tool in the Tools palette.

   Alternatively, you can press T.

2. In the Options bar, click a font.

3. Type or select the font size.

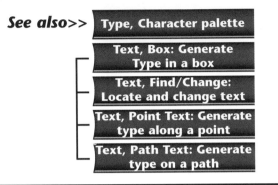

● You can align your text by clicking the Left Alignment (▤), Center Alignment (▤) or Right Alignment (▤) buttons.

● You can click here to select a color in the Color Picker that appears.

● You can click here to set anti-aliasing.

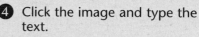

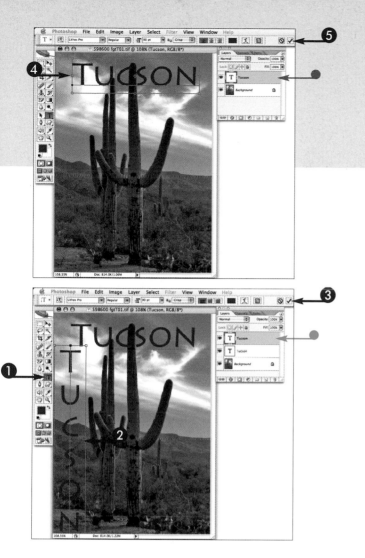

④ Click the image and type the text.

You can press Return (Enter) at the end of each line if you want to produce more than one line of type.

⑤ Click the Commit button.

● Photoshop produces a new Type layer in the Layers palette and automatically names the layer with the first few words of the type that you entered.

Create Vertical Text

① Click the Vertical Type tool.

Alternatively, you can press Shift+T.

② Click the image and type the text.

Photoshop enters the type vertically.

③ Click the Commit button.

● Photoshop creates A new Type layer in the Layers palette.

Did You Know?
When the type is horizontally oriented, the left, center, or right edge of the type aligns to the insertion point. When the type is vertically oriented, the top, center, or bottom of the text aligns to the insertion point.

Caution!
When you select or format text on a Type layer, the Type tool shifts into Edit mode. Before you can perform other operations, you must first click the Commit button in the Options bar or press Return (Enter) to commit the changes. You can cancel by clicking the Cancel symbol (▣) or pressing Esc.

Try This!
Use these mouse actions to select type that you have already entered.

Command	What Happens
Click and drag over text	Highlights text for editing
Double-click text	Selects a word
Triple-click text	Selects a line of text
Quadruple-click the box	Selects all characters in the bounding box

TYPE, WARP:
Bend, Twist, and Shape Type

You can bend, warp, and twist type into almost any curved shape. After you generate the text, you can use the Warp dialog box, which you access via the Warp Text icon on the Options bar, to select from one of 15 different warp styles, each with its own set of precision controls.

You can alter the amount and direction of the bend and the magnitude of the horizontal and vertical distortions using the sliders in the dialog box. This operation is similar to the New Warp Transformation feature that warps images. The difference is that the Warp Text feature works exclusively on text layers and text masks. The combinations of distortions can produce a practically infinite variety of text shapes. Experiment with settings, sizes, and fonts so you are familiar with some of the wild, twisted type effects that you can create. Combined with your choice of

font, layer styles, and the application of color or texture, you can produce some really eye-popping type effects.

See also>>

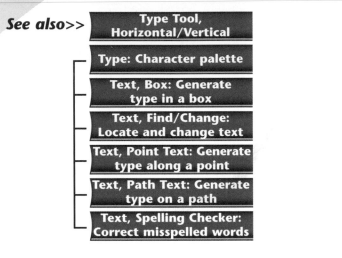

Type Tool, Horizontal/Vertical
Type: Character palette
Text, Box: Generate type in a box
Text, Find/Change: Locate and change text
Text, Point Text: Generate type along a point
Text, Path Text: Generate type on a path
Text, Spelling Checker: Correct misspelled words

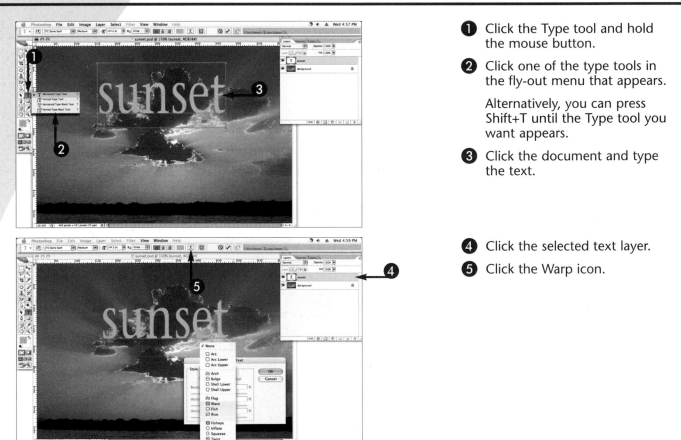

① Click the Type tool and hold the mouse button.

② Click one of the type tools in the fly-out menu that appears.

Alternatively, you can press Shift+T until the Type tool you want appears.

③ Click the document and type the text.

④ Click the selected text layer.

⑤ Click the Warp icon.

The Warp Text dialog box appears.

⑥ Click here and select various Warp options until you find one that you like.

Photoshop allows you to preview the effect before you accept it.

⑦ Click either the Horizontal or Vertical option depending on the text you want to warp.

⑧ Click and drag the sliders to produce the effect you want.

⑨ Click OK.

Photoshop warps the text as you specified.

This example shows the Arc Upper style.

To remove an unwanted text effect, you can follow steps **1**, **2**, **4**, and **5**, and then select the "None" style in the Warp Text dialog box.

TIPS

Did You Know?

As you warp the text, it may distort out of position, but you can rectify this situation. While in the Text Warp dialog box, place your cursor on the text, click, and drag it into position.

Try This!

It you want to warp the text using a grid of control points, rasterize it first. Click Rasterize. Click Layers and then click Type. Click Edit, Transform, and then Warp. Adjust the points on the grid. When you are satisfied with the adjustment, click the Commit button in the Options bar to commit, or press Return (Enter).

TYPE, CHARACTER/ PARAGRAPH PALETTE:
Set Type Specifications

The Character and Paragraph palettes attributes are combined in a floating palette with two tabs so that you can quickly make changes. You can access the Character/Paragraph palette either through the Window menu or via the Type tool.

On the Character palette, you can designate the type font and weight, size, and leading in points, pixels or millimeters, kerning, tracking, horizontal and vertical scale, baseline shift, color, style, language, and anti-alias. Additional choices including options to apply faux styles, text rotation and

orientation, case, ligatures, and ornamental styles can also be designated.

Options in the Paragraph palette include alignment — flush left, centered, flush right — and four justification options. You can also designate indentation and space before and after specifications. In the Paragraph menu, you can apply a hanging indent, compositional features, hyphenation, and justification options.

You can reset all the specifications to Photoshop defaults from either of these two palettes.

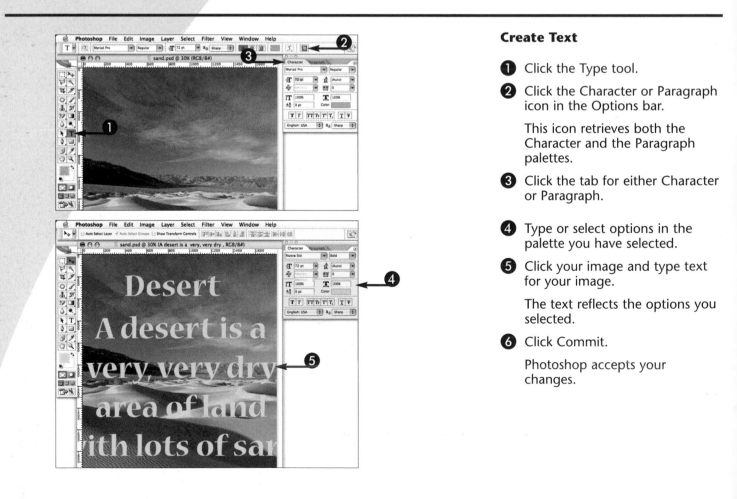

Create Text

① Click the Type tool.

② Click the Character or Paragraph icon in the Options bar.

This icon retrieves both the Character and the Paragraph palettes.

③ Click the tab for either Character or Paragraph.

④ Type or select options in the palette you have selected.

⑤ Click your image and type text for your image.

The text reflects the options you selected.

⑥ Click Commit.

Photoshop accepts your changes.

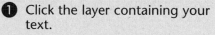

1 Click the layer containing your text.

2 Change any option in the Character palette or Paragraph palette.

As soon as you select an option the transformation takes place.

TIPS

Did You Know?

Every single character in a sentence can have a different attribute. Instead of simply selecting the layer, select a character in the text with the Type tool. With that character highlighted change size or font or anything else found in the Character Palette.

Try This!

You can apply attributes to selected text in a text layer by selecting the layer and with the Text tool:

Select	Use This Technique
A single character	Click and drag to the end of the character
A single word	Double click on the word
A single paragraph	Triple click between any two characters in a paragraph
Multiple paragraphs	Click at the beginning of a paragraph and drag to highlight the text range of the paragraphs you want to select

ZOOM TOOL:
Take a Close Look at the Image

With the Zoom tool, you can view your image at different magnifications. Photoshop's editing capabilities enable you to edit areas as large as the whole picture, or as small as a single pixel. To efficiently produce seamless edits, you need to zoom in and out of the image quickly and efficiently. Using the Zoom tool also enables you to observe the results of your work with a more critical eye.

Photoshop provides several methods of magnifying areas, from menu commands, tools, and keyboard commands, to a thumbnail "map" of the image. All produce similar results — they move you closer to or

farther from the work area. As with many Photoshop features, the method you choose depends on your personal preference, but the tool most commonly used for magnification is the Zoom tool. When you select an area with the Zoom tool, you get a closer look. Zooming does not affect the file's physical size, only how it is displayed.

See also>>

Navigator

View menu

1 Click the Zoom tool in the Tools palette.

Alternatively, you can press Z.

2 Place the cursor on the image.

The cursor appears as a small magnifying glass with a plus sign in its center.

3 Click the mouse.

The image appears larger.

You can also press and hold Opt (Alt) and click to see more of the image.

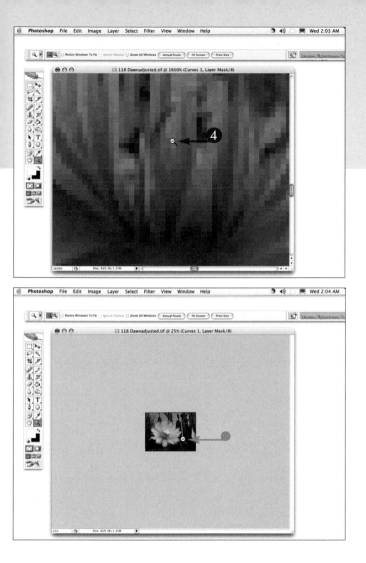

4 Continue clicking.

The image increases to a maximum zoom ratio of 1600 percent.

At this size you can discern the mosaic of pixels that comprise the image.

5 Press Opt (Alt).

The symbol on the cursor changes to a minus sign.

6 Continue clicking or pressing Opt (Alt).

● The image reduces to a tiny rectangle or one screen pixel.

TIPS

Did You Know?

If you double-click the Zoom tool in the Tools palette, the image is displayed at 100 percent.

Try This!

Select the Zoom tool and place your cursor on the image. Click the mouse button and drag. The area encircled by the marquee fills the image window.

Caution!

The size of the image displayed at 100 percent may not be its physical size. The resolution of the image compared to the resolution of the monitor determines the display ratio. For example, if the monitor is 72 screen pixels per inch and the image is 72 ppi, the ratio appears at 1:1, or actual size at 100 percent. If the image is 144 ppi (2 x 72), the image appears twice its physical size on-screen.

Photoshop CS
Visual Encyclopedia

Part II: Techniques

Photoshop has many features that automatically alter image content. You can find these commands and operations in the menus and palettes, and you can apply them to a selected area, a layer, or to the entire image. Photoshop has two types of commands. Commands with ellipses after them (...) present you with a dialog box when you select them. Often the dialog box contains a set of precision controls. As you adjust the values in the dialog boxes, you can usually preview the image as it changes. You cannot perform any other tasks with the exception of navigation and color sampling while you have a dialog box open. Commands without the ellipse simply implement the specified task without controls.

Photoshop's interface also has palettes that act as command centers. These palettes enable you perform tasks, make color choices, or access information. The palettes float on the workspace and you can reposition, collapse, or dock them. Photoshop also utilizes several plug-ins. Sometimes these are self-contained programs that provide a complete interface and that you use to perform specialized tasks. Other plug-ins may work behind the scenes to provide functionality to Photoshop.

When you work in Photoshop, you generally perform a sequence of procedures. You collect images from a scanner, digital camera, or other source. Perhaps you duplicate the image to preserve the original source file. You isolate areas using one of the many selection or layer techniques and apply effects, adjustments, filters, or other operations to the selected areas. Ultimately, you save the image to one of the numerous formats that Photoshop supports, depending on how you intend to publish or print it.

ADOBE BRIDGE:
Open and Preview and Open Files

You can use Adobe Bridge to browse, locate, and open images and folders as well as to display information about an image in the form of metadata. This new file and folder management program is bundled with Photoshop CS2 and is now a separate program that you use with other Adobe products such as Illustrator, GoLive, or InDesign.

Bridge also gives you access to tools — like Batch rename, Contact Sheet, and so on. You can preview an image before opening it; you can organize

images; you can label, color code, sort, and rate images by an assigned level of importance; you can move images from one folder to another, duplicate, and discard images — all packaged in one elegant interface.

In addition, Adobe Bridge offers automation and color management features which are discussed in later chapters. This new program from Adobe saves you time and labor as you utilize it to manage and open your images.

1 In Photoshop click File.

2 Click Browse.

● Alternatively you can click the Bridge icon.

Adobe Bridge opens.

3 Click the Folders tab.

4 Scroll down to the folder where the desired document is located.

5 Click the folder

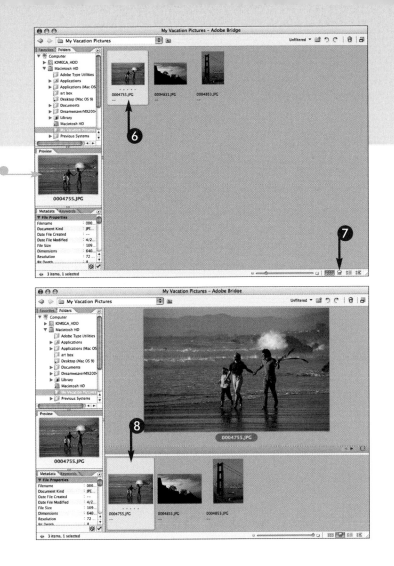

6 Click the thumbnail document.

● The thumbnail image appears in the Preview field.

You can click and drag the borders of the Preview field to the right and up, or down, to enlarge the thumbnail.

7 Click the Filmstrip view icon.

The right pane divides into two sections: the top section shows a preview of the thumbnail selected in the bottom section.

8 Double-click the thumbnail.

The image opens in Photoshop.

Alternatively, you can right-click (control-click) the thumbnail and select a different application in which to open the file.

Did You Know?

You can select a range of images by clicking the first image in the range, pressing the Shift key, and clicking the last image in the range. Select discontinuous multiple images by pressing Cmd (Ctrl) and clicking the images.

Try This!

To discard an image, select the thumbnail of the image or images and then click the Trash icon at the top right of the window.

Try This!

To rotate an image, click the image; then click the clockwise or counter-clockwise icons in top-right of the window.

ADOBE BRIDGE:
Find an Image

In addition to being a superb image browser, Adobe Bridge offers additional features that let you perform simple tasks prior to opening your images. If you need information about the image, you can look at its Metadata. You can easily drag files from one folder to another or create new folders without leaving the program. If you forget where the image is located, Bridge has an excellent Find command that automatically searches by a choice of several different criteria.

You can color-code an image or rate the image to assign a priority level. You can permanently discard an image directly from the browser window. Bridge can display your files in several different views and alternate versions. The Bridge window is expandable and enables you to simultaneously see several image previews. You can use the slider at the bottom of the window to enlarge or reduce the size of thumbnails or previews.

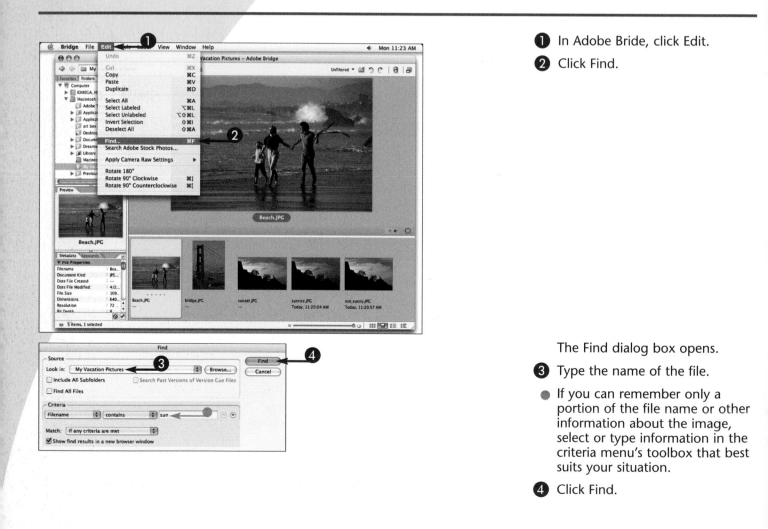

① In Adobe Bride, click Edit.

② Click Find.

The Find dialog box opens.

③ Type the name of the file.

● If you can remember only a portion of the file name or other information about the image, select or type information in the criteria menu's toolbox that best suits your situation.

④ Click Find.

The file appears in a new Bridge window.

● Bridge creates a collection of the files that meet the Find criteria.

● You can click Save As Collection and save the search criteria to retrieve the same set of files again.

You can copy or move the files to a different folder.

You can press Cmd(Ctrl)+A to select all the found files.

5 Double-click any of the files.

Bridge opens the files in Photoshop.

TIPS

Did You Know?
To view embedded image information, select the image and then click the Metadata tab. This panel lists File properties, camera data, History date, and IPTC data. Various programs recognize IPTC data — which includes name of creator, address, and e-mail address.

Try It!
By default, Photoshop places browsed folders under the Favorites tab, but you can designate frequently viewed items manually by clicking the Favorites tab, clicking the item you want to designate as a Favorite, and dragging the thumbnail to the Favorites panel.

Try It!
To assign a label, rating, or color code to an image, select the appropriate item under the Bridge Label menu. Select the image, click Label, and then scroll down to the desired label and click.

ACTIONS:
Record an Action

You can automate almost any set of commands, effects, or menu options as an Action. This is ideal when you want to repeatedly apply a process to a number of images. You record actions by activating the record function in the Actions palette, performing the commands or options, and turning off the record function when you are finished.

Before you record an action, determine what result you want, list the series of techniques or commands to achieve it, and finally, perform the actual keystrokes and actions. If the result is what you expect, you can repeat the step after you activate the record function in the Actions palette.

Photoshop organizes all actions by prompting you for a Name and Set in which the actions will be contained. Think of a set as a folder where you can

store several actions. Besides assigning a name and set, the New Action dialog box also lets you color code and assign a Function key to your action. To reuse an action, you must save it. You can then load and use actions as needed — both ones you create as well as several general actions provided by Photoshop. When you play an action, Photoshop performs the commands in the sequence listed in the Actions palette.

See also>>

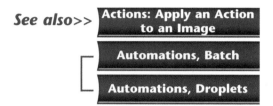

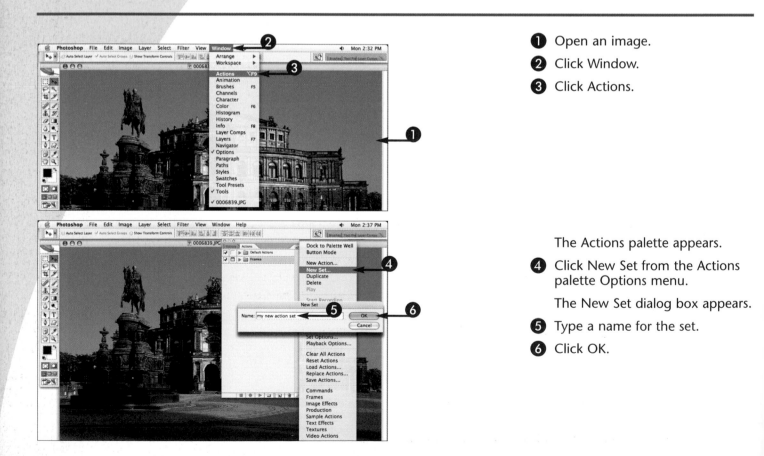

① Open an image.

② Click Window.

③ Click Actions.

The Actions palette appears.

④ Click New Set from the Actions palette Options menu.

The New Set dialog box appears.

⑤ Type a name for the set.

⑥ Click OK.

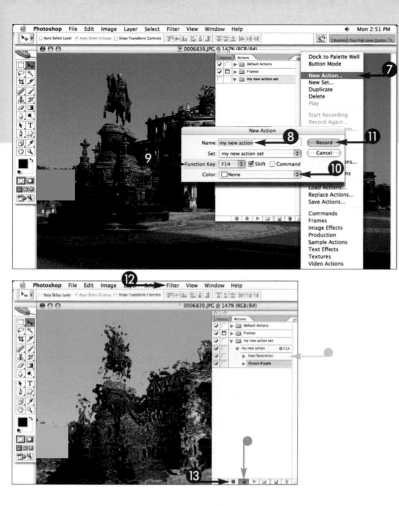

⑦ From the Options menu, click New Action.

The New Action dialog box appears.

⑧ Type a name for the action.

⑨ Click here and select a function key.

⑩ Click here and select a color.

⑪ Click Record.

● The dialog box closes and the begin recording button on the Actions palette turns red to remind you that your commands will be recorded.

⑫ Select commands and options in the order in which you want to apply them to the image.

You can apply operations, such as filters and effects.

⑬ Click the Stop button.

The action stops recording.

● The list of actions appears in the Actions palette.

TIPS

Did You Know?
By default Photoshop selects every item in an action to be performed. You can deselect items in an Action list (☐ changes to ☑) to prevent Photoshop from performing them.

Caution!
Actions record almost everything you do. If the image does not appear the way you want it to, or if you make a mistake, stop recording, drag the action or set to the Action palette Trash icon (🗑) and then rerecord the action. You can also select individual Action items and click 🗑 .

Caution!
Photoshop does not record some tool operations — particularly the Brush, Pen, and Shape tools. You can record the selection of the Brush tool, for example, but not the brushstroke you make with the Brush. You can record many menu commands, but you cannot record program preference settings.

ACTIONS:
Apply an Action to an Image

You can apply actions to images so you do not have to repeat a set of steps. Actions are a set of recorded steps that you can apply to an image with a click of a button. The Actions palette displays a set of actions that Photoshop includes, called Default Actions. The Palette Options menu contains additional sets that you can load. You can also record your own actions and save them via the Palette Options menu.

When you play an action, Photoshop applies the steps in the action sequence from top to bottom. You can avoid playing a particular step simply by

deselecting it. If you want to "see" the steps of an action as Photoshop plays it, you can select the Step by Step Option in the Playback Options dialog box. Also, the Dialog On/Off box feature causes the action to pause and display a dialog box so that you can change the settings.

See also>>   **Actions: Record an Action**

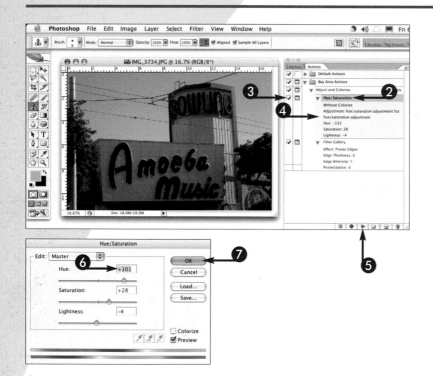

① Open an image.

② In the Actions palette, click an action that has an adjustment such as Hue/Saturation.

③ Click the Dialog On/Off icons next to the action you want to adjust.

④ Click the action you want to perform.

⑤ Click the Play button.

The Play button turns green and as the action runs, the action's related dialog boxes appears.

⑥ Type new values where necessary.

⑦ Click OK.

The new values are applied and the action continues to play.

ADJUSTMENTS:
Auto Color, Auto Levels, Auto Contrast

You can make quick overall adjustments to improve slight problems with your image using the Auto Levels, Auto Contrast, and Auto Color commands. These commands apply automatic color correction using default values. They correct common images that need small adjustment. However, you should not use them when the images contain complicated compositions, where lighting and color are exaggerated for artistic effect, or where image problems that require unique corrections. When you apply these commands, you have no options or settings to worry about — Photoshop does it all.

Auto Levels increase contrast in an image by adjusting the black and white points so that the lightest pixel in each channel converts to white, and the darkest pixel to black. The intermediate pixels are redistributed proportionally. Auto Contrast also adjusts the contrast of an image by adjusting the black and white points, but instead of adjusting each channel, as Auto Level does, it maps the lightest and darkest pixels without changing color balance. Auto Color goes one step further by mapping the black and white pixels and then attempting to neutralize any color casts in the remaining pixels.

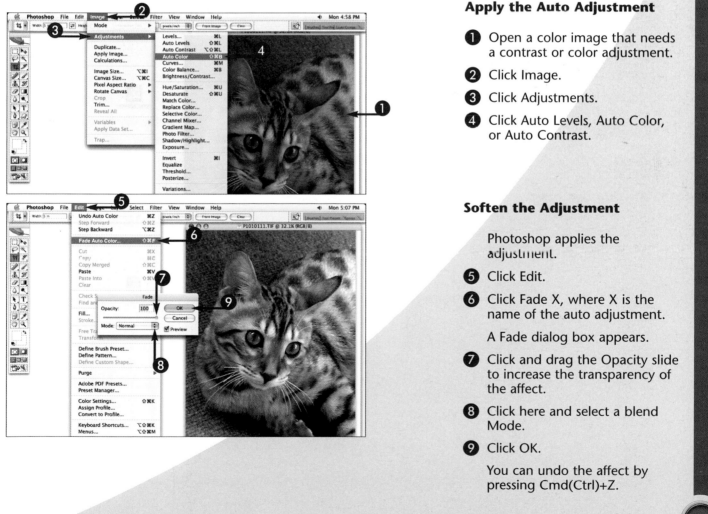

Apply the Auto Adjustment

1 Open a color image that needs a contrast or color adjustment.

2 Click Image.

3 Click Adjustments.

4 Click Auto Levels, Auto Color, or Auto Contrast.

Soften the Adjustment

Photoshop applies the adjustment.

5 Click Edit.

6 Click Fade X, where X is the name of the auto adjustment.

A Fade dialog box appears.

7 Click and drag the Opacity slide to increase the transparency of the affect.

8 Click here and select a blend Mode.

9 Click OK.

You can undo the affect by pressing Cmd(Ctrl)+Z.

ADJUSTMENTS:
Brightness/Contrast

The Adjustments–Brightness/Contrast command allows you to make basic adjustment to the tonal value of an image. You can drag sliders to adjust brightness and contrast or you can enter values ranging from –100 to +100. The Brightness slider makes overall pixels brighter or darker; the Contrast slider decreases or increases pixel contrast. By selecting the Preview option, you can view adjustments as you make them.

If you prefer, you can enter values in the appropriate fields. Positive numbers move the sliders to the right; negative entries move sliders to the left. You can

enter numbers from –100 to +100. Although the Brightness/Contrast adjustments are easy to use and provide a quick fix for low contrast or badly lit images, the Levels and Curves adjustments provide better results if you take the time to learn how to use them.

See also>>

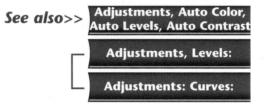

Adjustments, Auto Color, Auto Levels, Auto Contrast

Adjustments, Levels:

Adjustments: Curves:

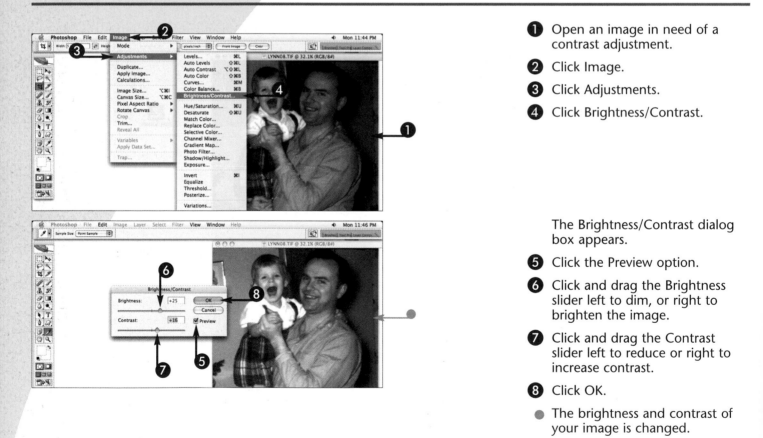

1 Open an image in need of a contrast adjustment.

2 Click Image.

3 Click Adjustments.

4 Click Brightness/Contrast.

The Brightness/Contrast dialog box appears.

5 Click the Preview option.

6 Click and drag the Brightness slider left to dim, or right to brighten the image.

7 Click and drag the Contrast slider left to reduce or right to increase contrast.

8 Click OK.

● The brightness and contrast of your image is changed.

ADJUSTMENTS:
Color Balance: Eliminate a Color-Cast

You can neutralize color casts with the Color Balance command by adjusting the overall mixture of colors in an image. To use the Color Balance command, be sure that you have the composite channel selected in the Channels palette; select a range of color that you want to neutralize — Highlights, the lightest areas; Midtones, the midrange of color; or Shadows, the darker colors.

Three sliders control the distribution of color. From top to bottom of the dialog box, the sliders are Cyan-Red, Magenta-Green, and Yellow-Blue. You

adjust the color of an image or selection by dragging the slider in the opposite direction of the color you want to neutralize. At each end of the sliders are colors that neutralize each other. For example, by moving the slider toward blue you decrease a yellow color cast and by moving a slider toward magenta, you decrease a green color cast. When you move a slider toward red, you decrease a red color cast. If you prefer, you can also enter values instead of using the sliders — the values can range from +100 to –100.

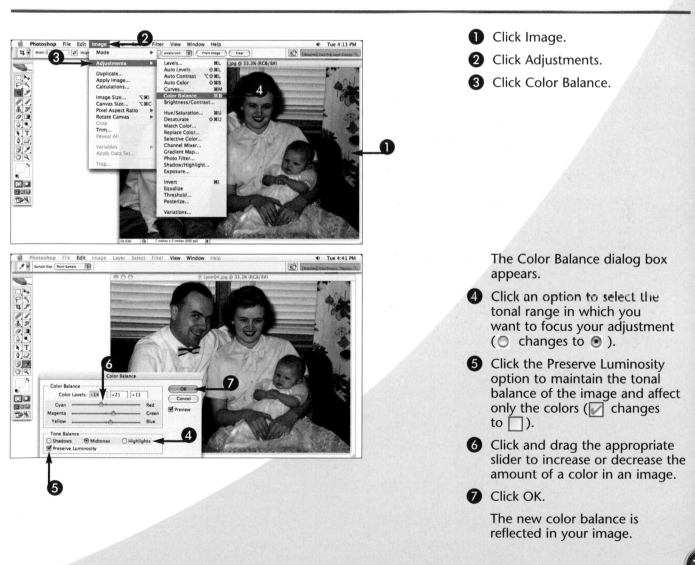

1 Click Image.

2 Click Adjustments.

3 Click Color Balance.

The Color Balance dialog box appears.

4 Click an option to select the tonal range in which you want to focus your adjustment (⚪ changes to ⦿).

5 Click the Preserve Luminosity option to maintain the tonal balance of the image and affect only the colors (☑ changes to ☐).

6 Click and drag the appropriate slider to increase or decrease the amount of a color in an image.

7 Click OK.

The new color balance is reflected in your image.

ADJUSTMENTS:
Channel Mixer: Make a Perfect Monochrome

You can use the Channel Mixer command to create a high-quality monochrome or grayscale image. You can select and swap tonal values from each channel to create the best monochrome representation in a targeted channel using the Channel Mixer. Converting a color image to grayscale was once a hit-or-miss deal. With the Channel Mixer, you can achieve more predictable results.

The Channels in an image are generally not of equal quality. Because Channel Mixer does not use color information and instead sees each channel as grayscale, it can make creative adjustments by combining different percent distributions from each channel with those of a target channel. The effect is similar to copying a crisp Red channel, for example, and pasting it on an unfocused Blue channel — the overall affect of the composite is an improvement over the original.

The Channel Mixer gives you additional control by allowing you to vary the degree of the effect.

The example in this section shows two copies of the same image with the top image converted to Grayscale using the Image, Mode, and the bottom image being adjusted using the Channel Mixer.

See also>> **Mode: Grayscale**

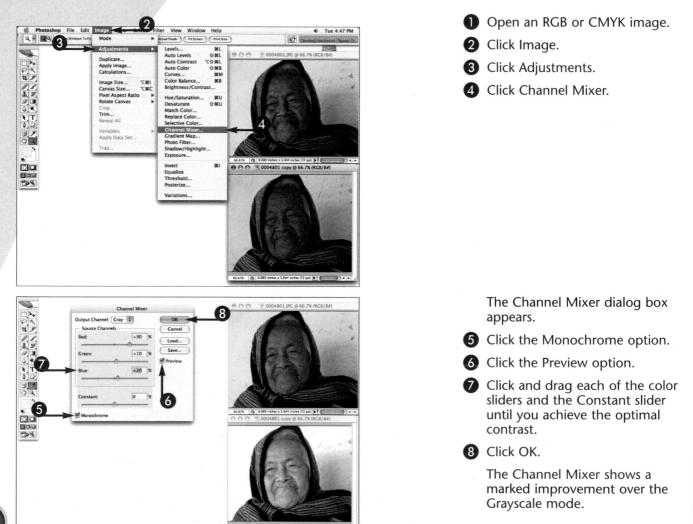

① Open an RGB or CMYK image.

② Click Image.

③ Click Adjustments.

④ Click Channel Mixer.

The Channel Mixer dialog box appears.

⑤ Click the Monochrome option.

⑥ Click the Preview option.

⑦ Click and drag each of the color sliders and the Constant slider until you achieve the optimal contrast.

⑧ Click OK.

The Channel Mixer shows a marked improvement over the Grayscale mode.

ADJUSTMENTS:
Curves: Adjust the Contrast of a Photo

You can use the Curves command, one of Photoshop's most powerful color adjustment tools, to target and map the entire tonal range of an image — not just the black/white and neutral points. You can adjust an image's brightness curve to lighten or darken an image, improve its contrast, or even create wild solarization affects.

The default Curves dialog box contains a 16-cell grid with a diagonal line running from the lower left to upper right. The horizontal axis of the graph represents the *input* levels, or the colors of the image before the adjustment. The vertical axis represents the *output* levels, or the color of the Image after you adjust it. By default, for RGB

images, the lower-left corner of the graph represents dark colors, while the upper-right corner represents light colors.

The diagonal line from lower left to upper right represents the brightness levels of the image. You make adjustments to the image by changing the shape of this line. The horizontal brightness bar below the graph represents the direction of the values of the graph.

See also>>

> **Adjustments: Levels**
>
> **Color Modes: Duotones**

---

① Open an RGB image that needs a tonal adjustment.

② Click Image.

③ Click Adjustments.

④ Click Curves.

The Curves dialog box appears.

⑤ Click the Preview option.

⑥ Press Opt (Alt) and click the grid to display the 100-cell grid.

⑦ Click the Expand icon to expand the dialog box.

⑧ Click and drag the center diagonal line upward to lighten an image, or downward to darken.

You can add additional anchor points by clicking the curve and dragging them up or down until specific ranges of color change to suite the image.

⑨ Click OK.

Photoshop applies the tonal adjustments to the image.

ADJUSTMENTS, CURVES, ANCHOR POINTS:
Adjusting a Narrow Range of Color

You can narrow color balance adjustments to a defined range of color by placing anchor points on the curve in the Curves dialog box. The tonal range of an image is represented graphically in the Curves dialog box by a straight diagonal line. Each end point represents the darkest and lightest pixels. In between is the area representing the full color range of the image. Bending line affects the color balance of the whole image, unless you place anchor points on the line. By placing anchor points representing the lightest and darkest points you limit the adjustment to the segment delimited by these anchor points.

If an image has a color cast problem — that is, one color that overwhelms the image, you can also limit adjustments to just that color by selecting a particular color channel from the Channels menu at the top of the dialog box. And because it is not unusual for a set of images that come from the same source to share the same color cast problems, you can save the curve adjustments and load them to correct other images.

See also>>   **Adjustment Layers**

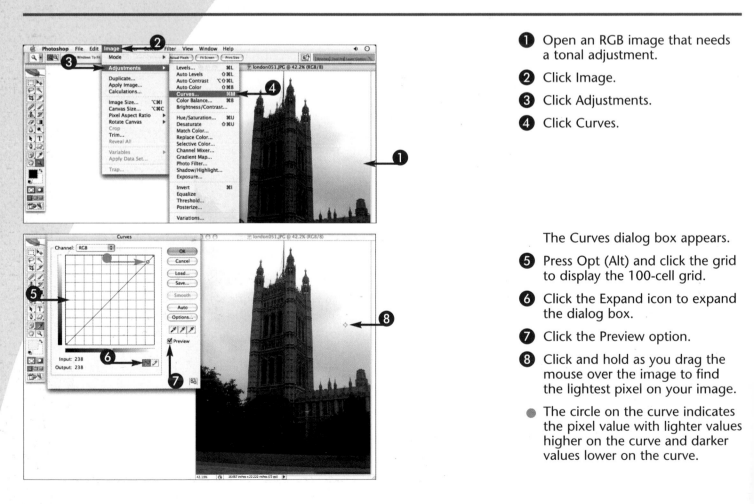

① Open an RGB image that needs a tonal adjustment.

② Click Image.

③ Click Adjustments.

④ Click Curves.

The Curves dialog box appears.

⑤ Press Opt (Alt) and click the grid to display the 100-cell grid.

⑥ Click the Expand icon to expand the dialog box.

⑦ Click the Preview option.

⑧ Click and hold as you drag the mouse over the image to find the lightest pixel on your image.

● The circle on the curve indicates the pixel value with lighter values higher on the curve and darker values lower on the curve.

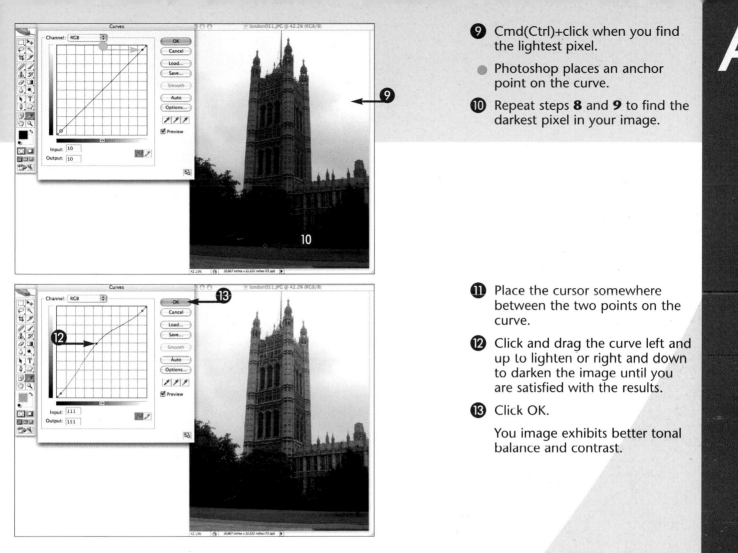

9 Cmd(Ctrl)+click when you find the lightest pixel.

● Photoshop places an anchor point on the curve.

10 Repeat steps **8** and **9** to find the darkest pixel in your image.

11 Place the cursor somewhere between the two points on the curve.

12 Click and drag the curve left and up to lighten or right and down to darken the image until you are satisfied with the results.

13 Click OK.

You image exhibits better tonal balance and contrast.

A

TIPS

Warning!

Because you depend on your monitor to determine the results of any color adjustments you make to an image, consider learning how to calibrate your monitor. Various specialized and costly products do this, but you also have tools at your disposal. Your monitor's product manual, however minimal, probably provides tools to calibrate your particular monitor. You can also use Adobe Gamma, ICC profiles, and the latest printer drivers — all free from Adobe and your printer manufacturer.

Warning?

Unless you want dramatic affects, go easy on adjustments and apply them in small increments with the Preview option activated (☑ changes to ☐). Trust your eyes and do not randomly enter values. Ultimately, only you can judge which and how much of an adjustment your image needs.

ADJUSTMENTS, EQUALIZE:
Apply an Automatic Contrast Adjustment

You can use the Equalize command to balance the brightness values in a image. Instead of looking at each color channel, the Equalize command evaluates the composite information and, using a normalization algorithm, redistributes brightness throughout an image. The darkest pixels in the image are converted to the equivalent of no light; the lightest pixels are converted to the brightest equivalent of light. Although our eyes interpret this as assigning the white/black colors to the pixels, it is actually assigning a brightness factor which ranges from

0 to 255. The Equalize command may not produce a much higher contrast image, but redistributing the brightness values will result in a lighter image.

The Equalize command has no settings or options, so when you select the command from the Adjustments menu, it immediately applies the effect. However, if you have an active selection in your image, a dialog box appears and gives you the option of equalizing the selected area only or equalizing the entire image.

1. Open an image.

2. Make a selection with one of the selection tools.

3. Click Image.

4. Click Adjustments.

5. Click Equalize.

   The Equalize dialog box appears.

6. Click to select what area you want to apply the Equalize command to.

7. Click OK.

   Photoshop applies the adjustment.

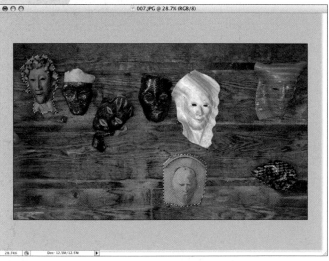

ADJUSTMENTS, EXPOSURE:
Correct an Over-Exposed Image

You can correct under- or over-exposed images with Photoshop's new Exposure adjustment. The Exposure adjustment is designed for making tonal adjustments to High Dynamic Range (HDR) images, but it works just as well with 8- and 16-bit images. The Exposure dialog box presents you with three sliders. The Exposure slider adjusts the highlights and has very little effect in the darkest shadows. The Offset slider darkens the shadows and midtones with little affect on the highlights. The Gamma slider adjusts midtones.

You can use the eyedroppers on the lower-right corner of the Exposure dialog box to adjust the image's brightness values, while leaving the hue and saturation unaffected. The Black eyedropper sets the offset, remapping the sampled pixel's value to zero or black and remaps all the other colors accordingly. The White eyedropper sets the exposure, shifting the pixel you select to a lighter range of the color. The Midtone eyedropper sets the Gamma, converting the sampled pixel's mid range value and remapping all the other colors in the image accordingly.

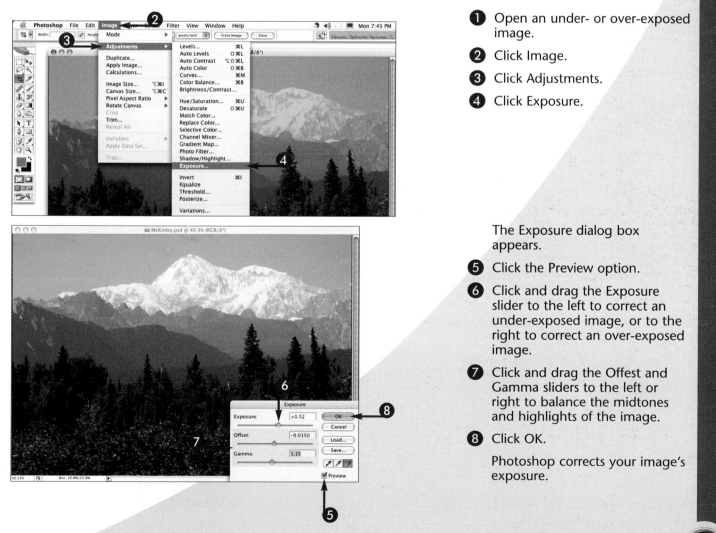

① Open an under- or over-exposed image.

② Click Image.

③ Click Adjustments.

④ Click Exposure.

The Exposure dialog box appears.

⑤ Click the Preview option.

⑥ Click and drag the Exposure slider to the left to correct an under-exposed image, or to the right to correct an over-exposed image.

⑦ Click and drag the Offest and Gamma sliders to the left or right to balance the midtones and highlights of the image.

⑧ Click OK.

Photoshop corrects your image's exposure.

ADJUSTMENTS, GRADIENT MAP:
Apply Colors Based on a Gradient

The Gradient map plots the equivalent tonal range of an image's grayscale mode to the colors of a specified gradient fill. When you map an image to a white-to-black gradient fill, the map plots the lightest pixels to the white end of the gradient. Likewise, it maps the darkest shadows to black. The Gradient map plots all the other values in between to the midsection of the gradient. In fact, Professionals sometimes use this method to convert a color image to grayscale.

You can choose from many gradient swatches and libraries using the Gradient Editor dialog box's menu. If you do not find what you need, you can also create custom swatches and add it to a library by opening the Gradient Editor. In addition, you can choose to turn on/off two options: Reverse switches the gradient colors mapping dark to light and light to dark; Dither adds random pixels to make transitions between colors smoother.

See also>> **Adjustment Layers**

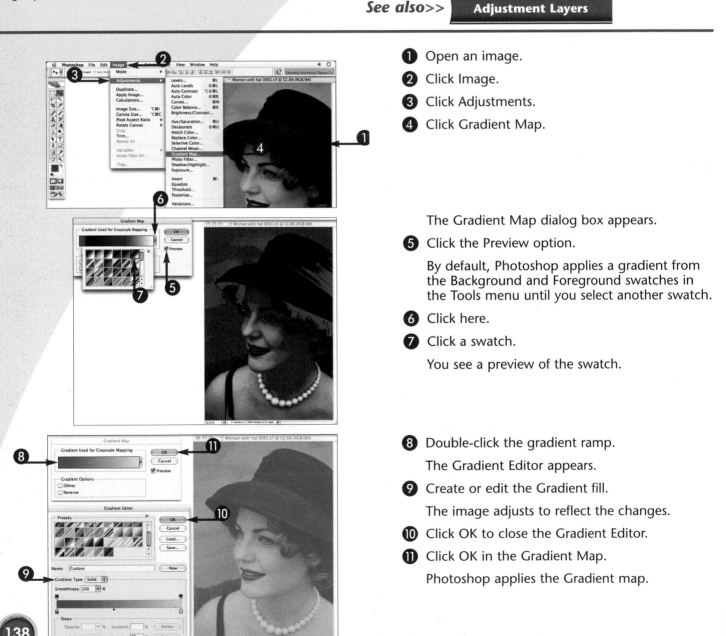

① Open an image.

② Click Image.

③ Click Adjustments.

④ Click Gradient Map.

The Gradient Map dialog box appears.

⑤ Click the Preview option.

By default, Photoshop applies a gradient from the Background and Foreground swatches in the Tools menu until you select another swatch.

⑥ Click here.

⑦ Click a swatch.

You see a preview of the swatch.

⑧ Double-click the gradient ramp.

The Gradient Editor appears.

⑨ Create or edit the Gradient fill.

The image adjusts to reflect the changes.

⑩ Click OK to close the Gradient Editor.

⑪ Click OK in the Gradient Map.

Photoshop applies the Gradient map.

ADJUSTMENTS, HUE SATURATION:
Recolor an Image

The Hue/Saturation command lets you alter the basic color characteristics of an image. When you choose the Hue/Saturation command, the Hue/Saturation dialog box appears and displays three sliders: Hue, Saturation, and Lightness.

Adjusting the Hue slider to the right and left is the equivalent of going around a color wheel, but instead of going around, you adjust the slider to the right or left. The values in the Hue field are based on the color's position on a color wheel, expressed in degrees, thus 360 total values.

You control color intensity by adjusting the Saturation slider to the right, up to +100% where

the affected colors are fully saturated, or to the left, to –100% where the colors are completely desaturated or gray.

You can control the brightness values of an image by adjusting the Lightness slider towards the left to darken the image or to the right to lighten it.

This example makes a selection with one of the selection tools in the center of the image. This allows you to compare the affect of various adjustments to the original pixels.

See also>> **Adjustments: Hue Saturation: Colorize**

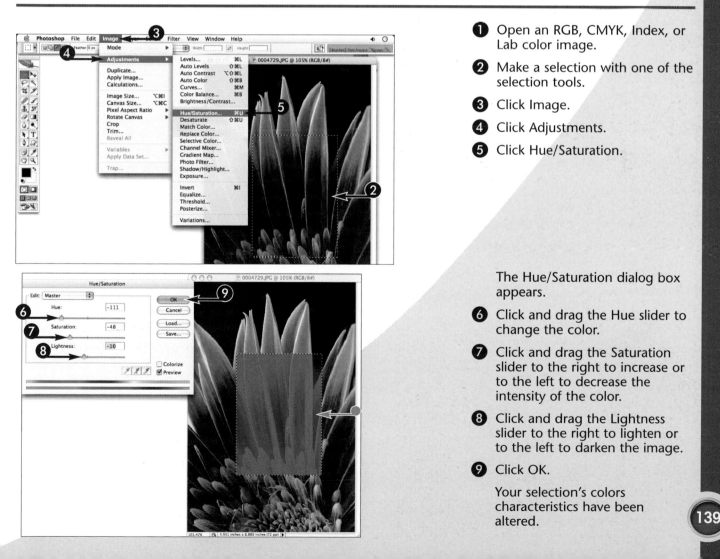

① Open an RGB, CMYK, Index, or Lab color image.

② Make a selection with one of the selection tools.

③ Click Image.

④ Click Adjustments.

⑤ Click Hue/Saturation.

The Hue/Saturation dialog box appears.

⑥ Click and drag the Hue slider to change the color.

⑦ Click and drag the Saturation slider to the right to increase or to the left to decrease the intensity of the color.

⑧ Click and drag the Lightness slider to the right to lighten or to the left to darken the image.

⑨ Click OK.

Your selection's colors characteristics have been altered.

ADJUSTMENTS, HUE SATURATION:
Colorize a Grayscale Image

The Hue/Saturation command allows you to change the color of an image via the Colorize option. Although you can use this option to color any image, it is most helpful and affective when you apply it to a grayscale image. The great advantage of the Hue/Saturation command is that pixels retain all characteristics, including shadows and highlights, with the exception of color resulting in colors that look natural and not flat.

Before you add color to a grayscale image, you must convert the mode to RGB, CMYK, Lab, or Index. No visible change occurs, but your image is now prepared to take on color. You can now make any color adjustments via the Hue/Saturation dialog box. The Colorize button applies whatever color you have currently displayed in the Foreground swatch in the

Tools palette. To change this color, you can adjust the Hue, Saturation, and Lightness sliders.

You can change the Saturation between values from 0% to 100%. Moving the Saturation slider to the right increases, while moving it left decreases, color intensity. You can adjust the Lightness values between –100 to +100, by moving the slider left to black color, or moving it right for whiter colors.

See also>>

- Adjustments: Hue/Saturation
- Adjustments: Replace Color
- Adjustment layers
- Tools: Color Picker

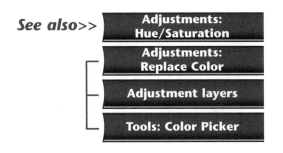

① Open a grayscale image.

② Make a selection with one of the selection tools, or target a layer with the content you want to affect.

③ Click Image.

④ Click Mode.

⑤ Click RGB, CMYK Index, or Lab.

⑥ Click Image.

⑦ Click Adjustments.

⑧ Click Hue/Saturation.

The Hue/Saturation dialog box appears.

9 Click Colorize

10 Click Preview.

The image is colored using the current foreground hue.

11 Click and drag the Hue, Saturation, and Lightness sliders to change the color, color intensity, and lightness of the image.

Clicking and dragging the sliders to the right increases the effect of these sliders, while clicking and dragging to the left decreases them.

12 Click OK.

You can repeat steps **9** to **12** to apply color to another area.

You can apply only one color at a time.

Photoshop colorizes your grayscale image to your specifications.

TIPS

Did You Know?
You can apply the Hue/Saturation command to an Adjustment layer. You can then make color changes without affecting the underlying image.

Try This!
You can reset any slider changes that you do not like by pressing Opt (Alt). All options and settings return to default values, and you can begin fresh.

Did You Know?
The Hue/Saturation command does not work well with an image's darkest areas. You must first lighten these areas to see the color. Because you do not actually apply an opaque layer of paint to your image, the underlying characteristics of the pixels remain. You see the darkest pixels in any color as black. Likewise, you see the lightest pixels in an image as white. Adding the smallest amount of gray helps you perceive color.

ADJUSTMENTS, INVERT:
Make a Negative

The Invert command converts pixel values to their inverse. If you think of an image as having values ranging from 0 to 255, the invert command changes a value of 255 to 0; a value of 5 to 250; a value of 10 to 245 and so on. This is similar to the strips of negatives you get from a photo lab, which show inverted color.

Although negative strips illustrate the concept of invert very well, the Invert cannot convert scans of color film negatives efficiently because it omits the colored tint called an *orange mask* — an important

component of color negatives. If you have a scanner that supports film negative, let the scanner do the conversion before you process it in Photoshop.

Like many other adjustments, you can apply the Invert command as an Adjustment layer, leaving your image intact. You can also limit the effect of the Invert command by making a selection before you invoke the command.

To illustrate how the Invert command changes an image, this example shows two identical images and which the Invert command is applied to one.

① Open an image in Grayscale, RGB, CMYK, Index, or Lab color mode.

② If desired, make a selection with one of the selection tools, or click a layer with the content you want to affect.

③ Click Image.

④ Click Adjustments.

⑤ Click Invert.

Photoshop inverts the image pixels or the selected area pixels.

ADJUSTMENTS, LEVELS:
Correct the Contrast of a Photograph

The Levels command displays an image histogram that you can use as a visual guide to adjust the image's tonal range. The black slider on the left of the graph adjusts the image's darkest pixel in the shadow areas, called the *black point.* The white slider on the right adjusts the lightest pixel in the highlight area, called the *white point.* When you adjust either slider, the midtone pixels are redistributed accordingly. You can adjust the midtone to change the Input levels of the shadow and highlight extremes of the image. The middle or Gamma slider determines the median value between the black and white points. Decreasing

the median value makes all values lower than the median darker, while increasing the value makes all values higher than the median lighter.

Where Input Levels increase contrast, Output Levels decrease contrast. You can adjust the white slider to the left and the black slider to the right to reduce the range of contrast in an image to eliminate the extremes of the highlight and shadow in an image.

See also>>   **Adjustment Layers**

① Open an image that needs a contrast adjustment.

② Click Image.

③ Click Adjustments.

④ Click Levels.

The Levels dialog box appears.

The graph shows deficiencies in the highlight and shadow areas of the image; short lines indicate few pixels.

⑤ Click and drag the white slider toward the center until it is aligned with the lines on the right of the graph.

⑥ Click and drag the black slider toward the center until it is aligned with the lines on the left of the graph.

● If necessary, you can click and drag the gray slider to the left to lighten or to the right to darken the image's midtones.

⑦ Click OK.

Your photograph now has the contrast you want.

ADJUSTMENTS, LEVELS:
Determine White and Black Points

You can improve the contrast and brightness of your image using the Levels command. This command makes your image's histogram look more like a bell curve by allowing you to adjust the white and black levels in your image.

You can apply Levels adjustments to a composite image or to each of the color channels individually. A menu lets you select which channel you want to work on. It is not unusual, especially when you have a color cast, for only one channel to need adjustment.

When you adjust Levels, adjust the white and black in the image either by dragging the appropriate slider or by determining the points by sampling with the appropriate eyedropper. To sample colors, you have three Eyedropper icons, one for the darkest, one for the midrange, and one for the lightest values. For example, to select the black point, you select an area on your image with the Black Point eyedropper. When you sample for the white point, use the lightest area

and not an isolated pure white. You should make the black point area the darkest area that contains detail and not an isolated absolute black.

See also>>

| Adjustments Levels |
| Adjustment Layers |
| Color Settings |
| Histogram |
| Tools: Color Sampler Tool |
| Tools: Eyedropper Tool |
| Techniques: Channels Palette |
| Tools: Info |

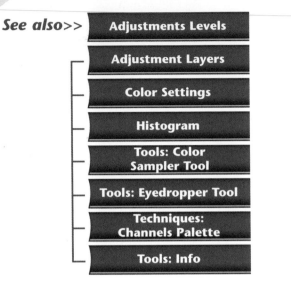

① Open an RGB image in need of a color and contrast adjustment.

② Click the Eyedropper tool in the Tools palette.

③ In the Option bar, set the Eyedropper tool to 3 by 3 Average.

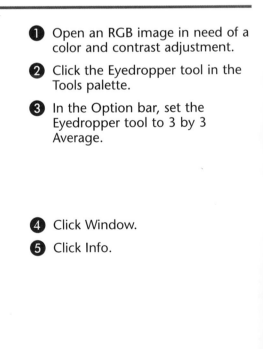

④ Click Window.

⑤ Click Info.

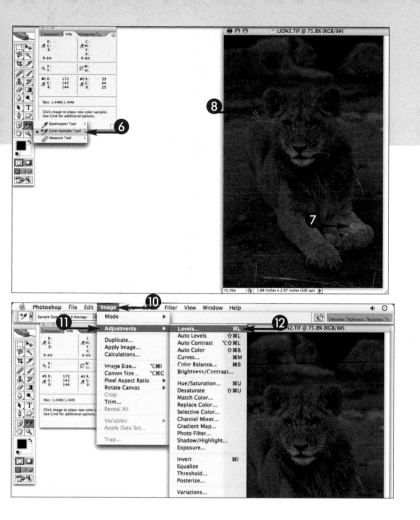

The Info palette appears.

⑥ Click and hold the Eyedropper tool and select the Color Sampler tool.

⑦ Place the cursor on the lightest area that you observed in the Levels high contrast preview.

⑧ Drag the mouse until you find the area that displays the highest numbers in the Info palette and then click.

The number 1 marker is deposited and a read-out for the marker displays in the Info palette.

⑨ Repeat step **8** for the Shadow areas, find the lowest numbers, but not black (0, 0, 0).

⑩ Click Image.

⑪ Click Adjustments.

⑫ Click Levels.

TIPS

Did You Know?

Prepress professionals frequently determine CMYK values for highlight and shadow areas based on the characteristics of their printing presses.

Warning?

If you use the eyedroppers, Photoshop resets any adjustments you made in the Levels or Curves dialog boxes. If you are going to use an eyedropper, use it first and then fine-tune your adjustments with the sliders.

The white point and black point values you use will vary depending on the image's color profile, but a good place to start is 240 red, 240 green, and 240 blue for the white point, and 20 red, 20 green, and 20 blue for the black point.

ADJUSTMENTS, LEVELS:
Determine White and Black Points (Continued)

You can use the Levels command to determine the black point and white point. The Levels command in Threshold mode locates the highlight and shadow areas of an image. You can then assign the specific values to those points to redistribute all of the other pixel values between those values. Be sure that you select the composite RGB channel from the Channels palette.

In the Levels dialog box, adjust the white point Input Level slider to the left to remove all shadows from the image and to make it all white. Next, adjust the left slider to the far right, to make the image pure black, then slowly adjust the slider toward the center until some white areas appear. These are the lightest part of the image. You then repeat the process with the right slider, adjusting it to the far right to identify the darkest areas of the image. Remember the approximate locations of the preview and then locate the exact area with the Color Sampler tool and the Info palette.

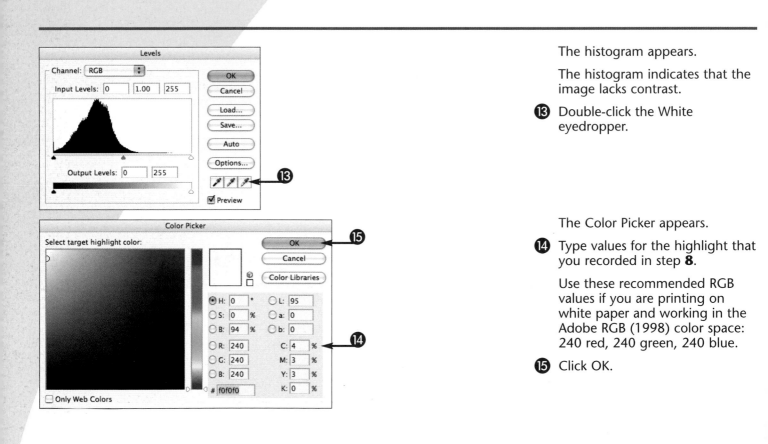

The histogram appears.

The histogram indicates that the image lacks contrast.

⑬ Double-click the White eyedropper.

The Color Picker appears.

⑭ Type values for the highlight that you recorded in step **8**.

Use these recommended RGB values if you are printing on white paper and working in the Adobe RGB (1998) color space: 240 red, 240 green, 240 blue.

⑮ Click OK.

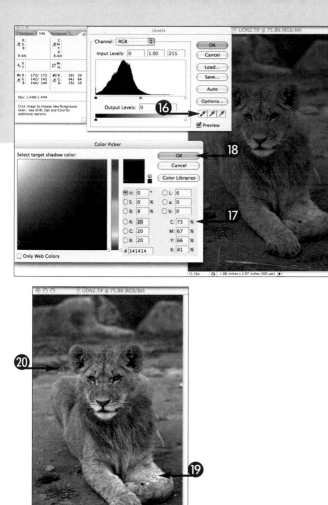

16 Double-click the Black eyedropper.

The Color Picker appears again.

17 Type RGB values for the shadow that you recorded in step **9**.

Use these recommended values if you are printing on white paper and working in the Adobe RGB (1998) color space: 20 red, 20 green, 20 blue.

18 Click OK.

19 Click the number 1 sample point.

The image becomes lighter.

20 Click the number 2 sample point.

The contrast of the image is substantially improved and color casts are eliminated.

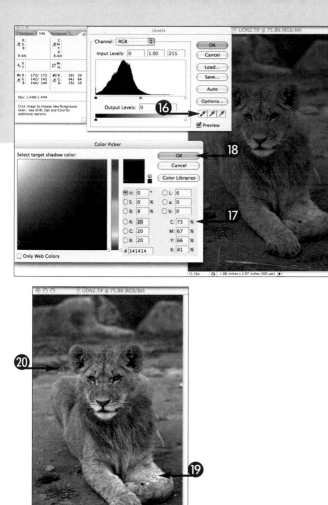

TIPS

Did You Know?

The RGB values vary, depending on the RGB color space you are working in. Adobe RGB 1998 works well for images destined for the four color process printing. sRGBIEC611966-2.1 is best for images destined for the Web.

Did You Know?

The Levels dialog box allows you save your settings so that you can load and reapply them to other images.

Try It!

If the image is in CMYK mode, or you plan on converting it to CMYK, you can type values in the CMYK percentage fields. The total of all ink coverage should not exceed 300%. You should type values that maintain the equality of the RGB values to assure neutrality.

ADJUSTMENTS, MATCH COLOR:
Match Color From One Image to Another

Photoshop's Match Color command matches colors in one image with those in another image. You want to match colors to create uniformity between a set of images that you plan to use together, even if they come from different devices, such as digital cameras, scanners, or downloaded files. For this reason, matching is also very important for creating professional pieces.

The Match Color dialog box contains the Destination image and the Image Statistics fields. The Destination field lists the target, or active, image by name. If you have an active selection on the target image, you can ignore it and apply the color to the entire image using the Ignore Selection when Applying Adjustment option.

The Image Options subfield contains control sliders that let you adjust the color relationships on the target image.

You select an image as a source of color in the Image Statistics field. Its thumbnail appears in the box to the right of the menu. You can also target a specific layer as a color source. If a selection is active on the source image, two options enable you to designate the colors within the selection as the source colors.

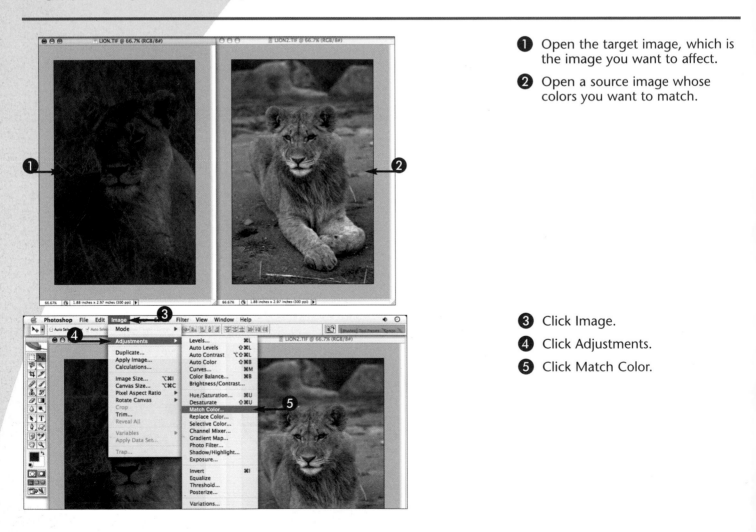

❶ Open the target image, which is the image you want to affect.

❷ Open a source image whose colors you want to match.

❸ Click Image.

❹ Click Adjustments.

❺ Click Match Color.

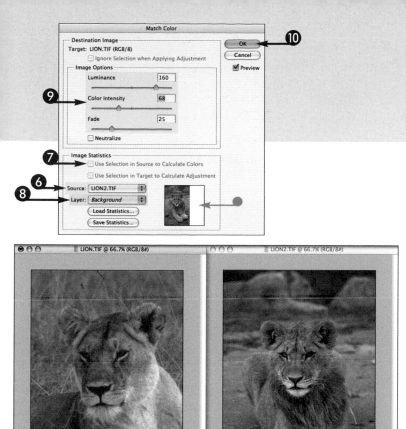

The Match Color dialog box appears.

⑥ Click here and select the name of the source Image.

● A thumbnbail appears in the box to the right of the menu.

⑦ If the image has more than one layer, click the layer in the Layers menu.

⑧ Click and drag the sliders in the Image Options section of the dialog box until you are satisfied with the image.

⑨ Click OK.

Photoshop matches the color from one image to the other.

A

TIPS

Did You Know?
After you complete the match, but before you click OK, you can save the statistics from the operation. Click Save Statistics and then select a location. You can load the statistics and apply them to another image.

Warning!
RGB and CMYK are device-dependent color models — that is, they vary depending on software, monitors, printers, scanners, paper, and so on, that you use. The only way to get consistent color results is to calibrate devices often. For professionals, there are also various Color Systems available — Pantone is a common one — that define colors as formulas. These colors have coded names, so it does not matter what color is visible on your monitor as long as you provide the printer with the right name.

ADJUSTMENTS, PHOTO FILTER:
Warm or Cool an Image

The Photo Filter adjustment lets you apply the effects of traditional photographic filters to an image. This adjustment warms or cools the colors of an image, and can reduce glare and simulate atmospheric conditions in a similar manner to a lens filter. In the Photo Filter dialog box, you can select a specific colored filter from the Filters menu in the Use section, that offers 20 filter choices, or you can specify a specific color from a swatch in the Color Picker.

You control the intensity of the effect with the density slider, which can be adjusted to values between 1 and 100 percent. The Preserve Luminosity option, when selected, maintains the brightness values of the image. The Photo filter works on RGB, CMYK, and Lab images; however, it does not work on Bitmap, Index, or Grayscale images. If you want to apply it to a black and white photo, convert the Grayscale to RGB first.

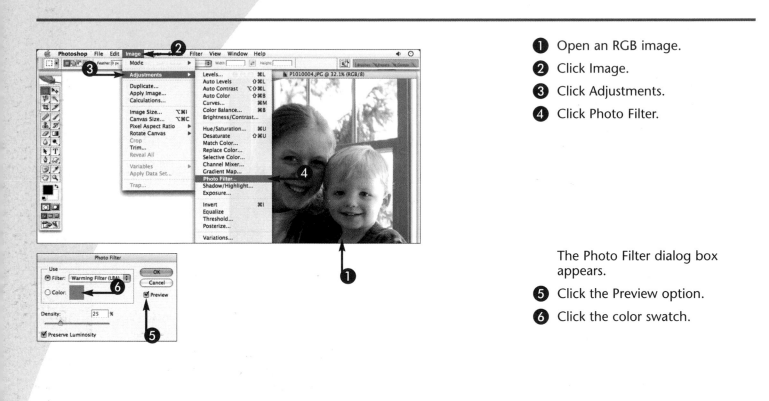

① Open an RGB image.

② Click Image.

③ Click Adjustments.

④ Click Photo Filter.

The Photo Filter dialog box appears.

⑤ Click the Preview option.

⑥ Click the color swatch.

The Color Picker appears.

7 Click a color.

8 Click OK.

● Alternatively, instead of performing steps **7** and **8**, you can click here and select a filter depending on whether you want to warm or cool the image.

9 Click and drag the Density slider to increase or decrease the intensity of the effect.

10 Click OK.

Your image is warmed or cooled, depending on your adjustments.

TIPS

Did You Know?
Photo filters can add depth to an image and can eliminate color casts. You can select a complementary color to neutralize the color cast.

Try This!
The Density slider controls the strength of the filter. Click and drag the slider slowly to the right to increase the density of the filter or to the left to decrease it. Observe the image as it changes.

Try This!
If you want to soften the effect of the Photo Filter, click Edit, and then click Fade Photo Filter. You must do this immediately after applying the filter. A Fade dialog box allows you to decrease the Opacity or you can select a blend Mode from the fly-out menu.

ADJUSTMENTS:
Posterize: Create a Serigraph Effect

You can use the Posterize command to specify the number of tonal values for each color channel in an image. This results in an interesting image that has fewer colors. Reducing colors creates patches of solid color with no shading. You may not always like the results because the outcome is not predictable.

You can enter any value from 2 to 255 in the Levels field of the Posterize dialog box. A 255 value has little affect on your image because it is the maximum values you can have in a normal file. A value of 3, however, reduces your image to three colors with

three values to each channel. For example, an RGB image, which has three color channels, will actually have nine colors.

One predictable use of the Posterize command is creating an image that looks like a serigraph, which has a specific number of colors. You can enter the number of colors you want in the Posterize dialog box, apply the command, and convert the image back to a color mode. You can then select each gray color and replace it with colors of your choice.

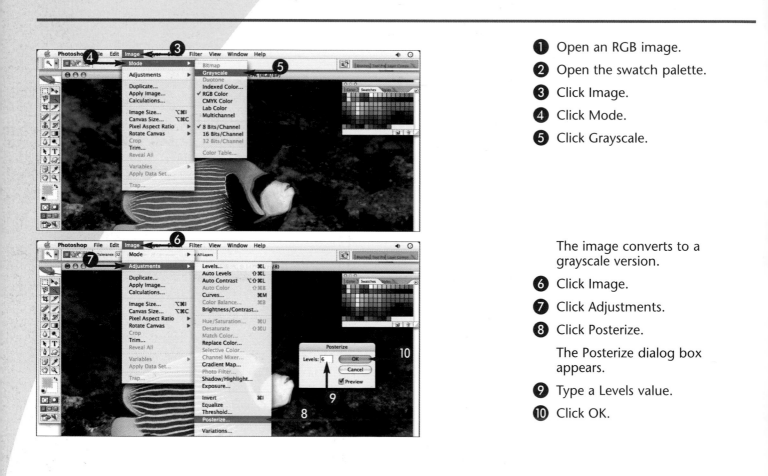

1. Open an RGB image.
2. Open the swatch palette.
3. Click Image.
4. Click Mode.
5. Click Grayscale.

The image converts to a grayscale version.

6. Click Image.
7. Click Adjustments.
8. Click Posterize.

The Posterize dialog box appears.

9. Type a Levels value.
10. Click OK.

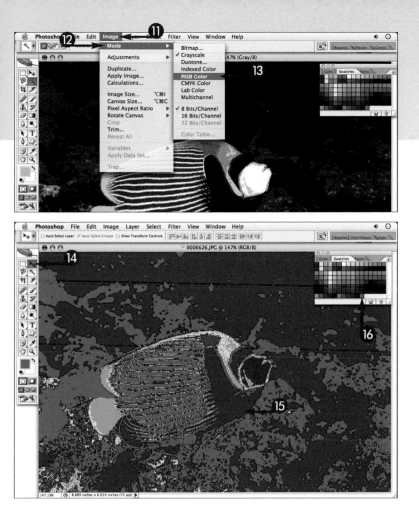

The image is now divided into shades of gray.

⑪ Click Image.

⑫ Click Mode.

⑬ Click RGB.

The image reverts back to RGB so it can support the color you want to apply to it.

⑭ Click the Magic Wand tool.

⑮ Click an area of black to select all of the black in the image.

⑯ Click a dark color from the Swatches palette.

⑰ Press Opt + Delete (Alt + Backspace).

The selected areas fill with color.

You can repeat steps **9** through **17** on the each area of gray choosing a color with a comparable value to replace each gray shade.

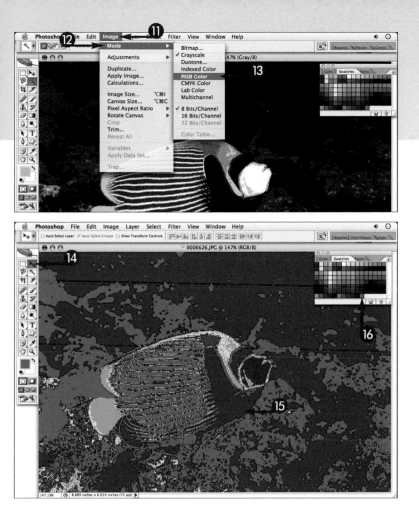

TIPS

Did You Know?

Spot colors are specially mixed inks that you can add to an image. Because a printing company must create additional printing plates in addition to four CMYK plates to produce spot colors, you can isolate the parts of your image where you want to apply a spot color. Posterization can help you identify and select blocks of pixels to which you want to apply a spot color making it easy for you to create an additional channel for this color. You can then use the channel to create a printing plate.

Try It!

Photoshop has a filter called Poster Edges. In addition to posterizing an image, it finds the edges of color blocks and outlines them in black. To access this filter click Filters, click Artistic, and then click Poster Edges.

ADJUSTMENTS, REPLACE COLOR:
Replace Color in an Image

You can sample a specific range of colors and automatically replace it with a different range of color. You can use this feature when you need to change similar colors that are scattered throughout an image. The Replace Color dialog box is a combination of the Hue/Saturation command and the Color Range command. The Color Range command makes selections based on colors you sample in the image. The Hue/Saturation command changes the key characteristics of color.

The default Replace Color dialog box displays a black mask over the image. There are three Eyedropper buttons. As you drag one of the Eyedroppers over

the image white areas appear which represent the colors being sampled. If you select the first Eyedropper, you sample a single color. If you select the Plus Eyedropper, you add colors to your selection. If you select the Minus Eyedropper, you remove the colors being sampled from the selection. The range of color sampled also depends on the sample size of the Eyedropper tool set in the Options bar.

See also>>

Eyedropper tool
Adjustments, Hue saturation
Selections, Color Range

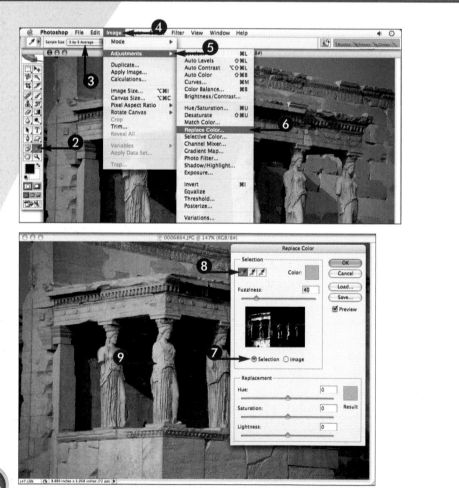

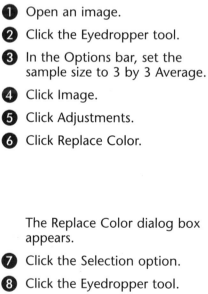

❶ Open an image.

❷ Click the Eyedropper tool.

❸ In the Options bar, set the sample size to 3 by 3 Average.

❹ Click Image.

❺ Click Adjustments.

❻ Click Replace Color.

The Replace Color dialog box appears.

❼ Click the Selection option.

❽ Click the Eyedropper tool.

❾ Click a color on the image to sample it.

The mask in the preview window changes to include the sampled areas.

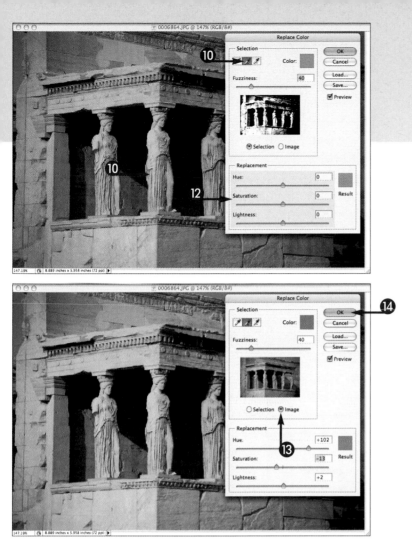

⓿ Click the Plus eyedropper to add areas which you want to be a part of the selection, but that you did not select because of exceptional brightness or shadow.

⓫ Click and drag over any additional areas of the image that did not get included in the first sampling.

Be careful not to touch the surrounding colors.

⓬ Click and drag the Hue, Saturation, and Lightness sliders to change the colors.

⓭ Click the Image option to compare before and after versions.

The preview pane in the Replace color shows the before version; the image window shows the after.

⓮ Click OK.

Replace Color replaces the selected areas with your color.

TIPS

Try This!
Instead of dragging the Hue, Saturation, and Lightness sliders, you can directly select a color by clicking the Result swatch and clicking a color from the Color Picker that appears.

Did you know?
You can limit color replacement to a particular area of your image by selecting that area before invoking the Replace Color command.

Try It!
If you have significant portions of the selection in the original color range, drag over them with the Plus eyedropper. If you include too many colors, drag over the unwanted colors with the Minus eyedropper to remove them. To expand the color to adjacent pixels, click and drag the Fuzziness slider to the right.

ADJUSTMENTS, SHADOW HIGHLIGHT:
Correct a Backlit Image

The Shadow/Highlight command enables you to correct poorly exposed areas of an image. Shadow/Highlights uses the luminance of the neighboring pixels to calculate the adjustment. You can enhance image contrast in the shadows or highlights without compromising contrast in the other tonal areas and bring out detail in over-exposed or backlit images.

The Amount slider setting determines how much the pixels are affected. Larger values provide greater lightening of shadows, or greater darkening of highlights. This slider controls the strength of the adjustment to each pixel.

The Show More Options option lets you view additional controls in the Shadows and Highlights fields. The Tonal Width slider sets how much modification is applied to the different tonal regions. When correcting shadows, small values of Tonal Width place most of the emphasis on the darker regions of the image; larger values include more of the midtones and highlights. The Radius slider determines the neighborhood in which the pixels are affected. The larger the radius is, the larger the extent over which the neighborhood luminance is averaged.

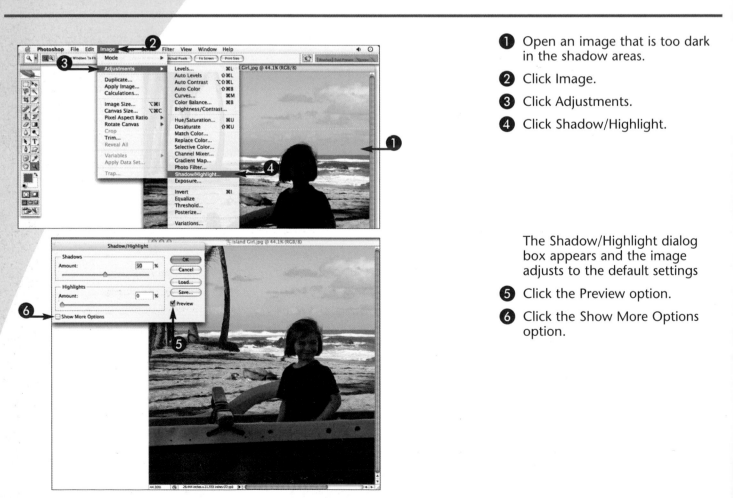

1 Open an image that is too dark in the shadow areas.

2 Click Image.

3 Click Adjustments.

4 Click Shadow/Highlight.

The Shadow/Highlight dialog box appears and the image adjusts to the default settings

5 Click the Preview option.

6 Click the Show More Options option.

The dialog box expands to show more options.

7 In the Shadows and Highlights sections of the dialog box, click and drag the sliders to improve the overall tonality.

● If the image has acquired a color cast, you can click and drag the Color Correction slider to correct it.

● If necessary, you can balance the contrast of the midtones by clicking and dragging with the Midtone Contrast slider.

8 Click OK.

The image's backlighting is enhanced and corrected.

A

Did You Know?

The Black clip and White clip percentage fields enable you to type an amount that absolute black and specular white are modified. By typing a value of **5%,** for example, the value of 95% black is increased to 100%. All the other colors in the image are remapped accordingly so the image appears darker.

Warning!

There is no magical formula to follow when making image corrections — that is, no single technique corrects common image problems. You should not depend on just one command or filter. You may need to use Levels or Curves, for example, to tweak the corrections made with the Shadow/Highlight command. That being said, you can save the settings that you use to correct an image, and load them for another image as a starting point.

ADJUSTMENTS:
Selective Color Balance CMYK

The Selective Color command allows you to adjust the amount of a particular color in an image without affecting other colors. It works with CMYK colors, but you can also use it to correct RGB images.

CMYK, the most commonly used color model for printing, represents the primary colors that create other colors — (C)yan, (M)agenta, (Y)ellow, and Blac(K). Each color also represents one printing plate in the printing process. You create different colors by adding different intensities of each primary color.

The Selective Color command targets one of these primary colors so that you can add or subtract from its value without changing the composition of the

other colors. For example, you can use Selective Color to dramatically increase the cyan in the blue component of an image while leaving the magenta, yellow, and black unchanged.

The Selective Color command offers you two options to change the value. The Relative option changes the existing quantity of process color as a percentage; the Absolute option adds color in absolute values.

See also>> **Info: Determine the Numerical Value of Pixels**

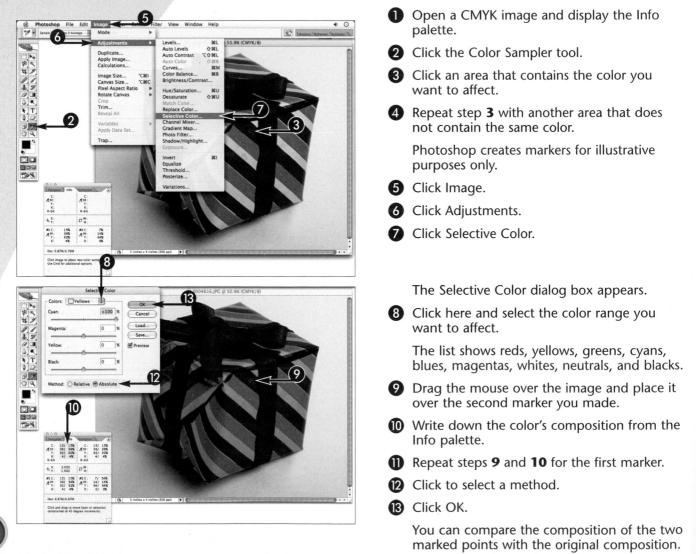

① Open a CMYK image and display the Info palette.

② Click the Color Sampler tool.

③ Click an area that contains the color you want to affect.

④ Repeat step **3** with another area that does not contain the same color.

Photoshop creates markers for illustrative purposes only.

⑤ Click Image.

⑥ Click Adjustments.

⑦ Click Selective Color.

The Selective Color dialog box appears.

⑧ Click here and select the color range you want to affect.

The list shows reds, yellows, greens, cyans, blues, magentas, whites, neutrals, and blacks.

⑨ Drag the mouse over the image and place it over the second marker you made.

⑩ Write down the color's composition from the Info palette.

⑪ Repeat steps **9** and **10** for the first marker.

⑫ Click to select a method.

⑬ Click OK.

You can compare the composition of the two marked points with the original composition.

ADJUSTMENTS, THRESHOLD:
Create Line-Art from a Photograph

You can use the Threshold command to convert grayscale or color images to high-contrast, black and white images. You control which pixels to convert to black or white by establishing a target value. Photoshop evaluates all the pixels in the image and any pixels with a lighter value than the target value convert to white; pixels with a darker value change to black.

The Threshold dialog box has three options: Preview, a Threshold Level field into which you can input a threshold value, and a Histogram,

which is a visual representation of the pixel distribution in your image, with a slider.

You can enter a value in the Threshold Level field or you can establish the threshold level visually using the slider. As you adjust the slider, the threshold value changes and so does you image, if you have activated the Preview option. Adjusting the slider to the left makes the image darker. Adjusting the slider to the right makes the image brighter. Extreme movement to either side reduces detail.

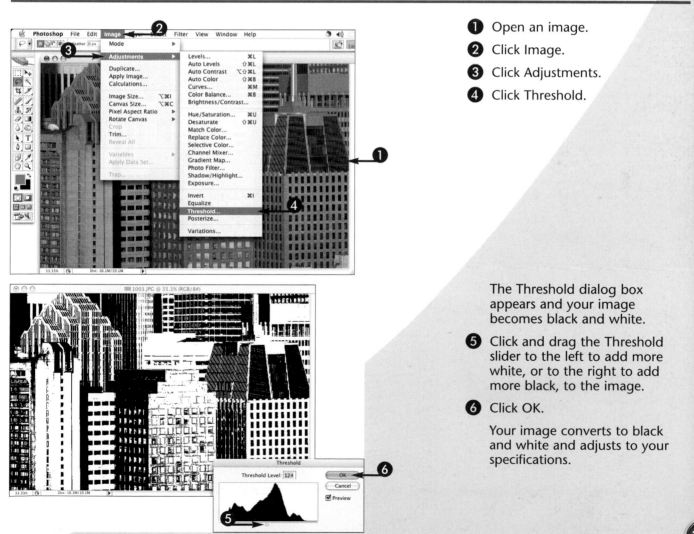

❶ Open an image.

❷ Click Image.

❸ Click Adjustments.

❹ Click Threshold.

The Threshold dialog box appears and your image becomes black and white.

❺ Click and drag the Threshold slider to the left to add more white, or to the right to add more black, to the image.

❻ Click OK.

Your image converts to black and white and adjusts to your specifications.

ADJUSTMENTS, VARIATIONS:
Use Variations to Predict Adjustment Results

The Variations command lets you adjust color balance, saturation, and contrast visually and is ideal for correcting images that do not require more precise tonal adjustments.

The Variations dialog box helps you visually select representations of the adjustments you want to make. Identical thumbnails at the top of the box give before and after views of your image. Just below this are thumbnails representing possible actions you can apply to your image. For CMYK and RGB images, you have six such thumbnails, with the center one, Current Pick, changing as you select any one of the

color thumbnails. To the right of this panel, another panel contains three thumbnails — Lighter, Darker, and Current pick.

The top right of the box has several settings and buttons that help you control shadows, midtones, highlights and saturation. The Fine/Coarse slider controls the amount of the adjustment, as you move to the right the intensity of the adjustment increases. Like most adjustments, Variations lets you save your settings so that you can load and reuse them on other images.

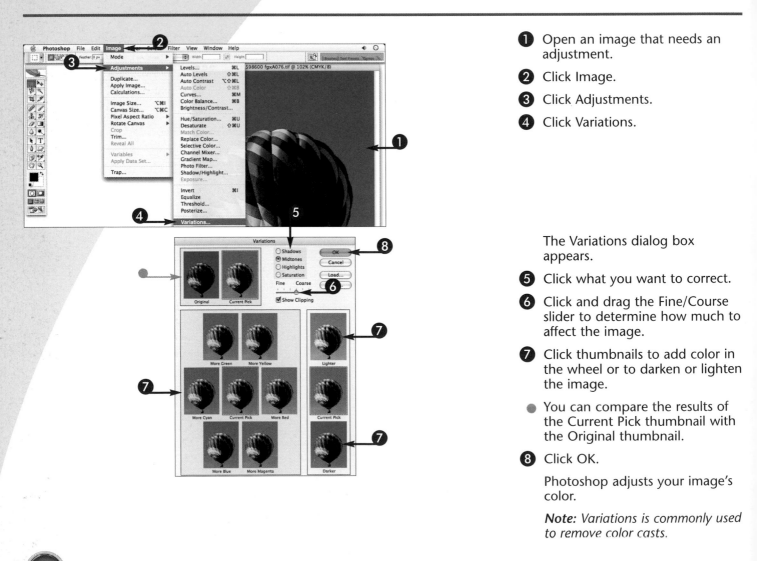

① Open an image that needs an adjustment.

② Click Image.

③ Click Adjustments.

④ Click Variations.

The Variations dialog box appears.

⑤ Click what you want to correct.

⑥ Click and drag the Fine/Course slider to determine how much to affect the image.

⑦ Click thumbnails to add color in the wheel or to darken or lighten the image.

● You can compare the results of the Current Pick thumbnail with the Original thumbnail.

⑧ Click OK.

Photoshop adjusts your image's color.

Note: *Variations is commonly used to remove color casts.*

ALIGN:
Align Layer Content

To activate the alignment buttons on the Options bar, you must either have the Move tool selected or employ the Align command in the Layer menu.

Either way, you can select from two sets of buttons representing different alignment options. The first set enables you to align top edges; align right edges, or align horizontal centers. The second set of buttons allows you to align left edges, align bottom edges; or align vertical centers.

To align multiple layers, select two or more layers in the Layers palette and apply the align buttons. You can also align a group of layers by selecting the group folder.

To align the content of one or more layers to a selection marquee, you can make a selection in the image and then select one or more layers from the Layers palette. Use this technique to align layers to a particular point on an image.

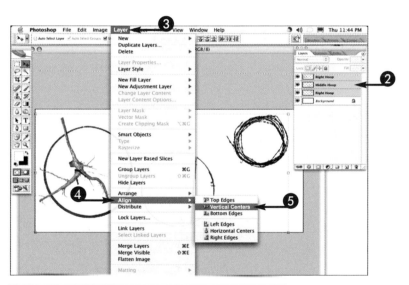

① Open an image with multiple layers.

② Click the first layer you want to align in the Layers palette.

You can press Shift and click additional layers.

③ Click Layer.

④ Click Align.

⑤ Click an alignment option.

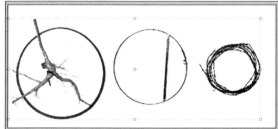

Photoshop aligns your layers per your specifications.

APPLY IMAGE:
Superimpose Two Images

The Apply Image command allows you to blend a layer or channel from a source image with a layer or channel of a current, or target image. You must have both the source and target images and the pixel dimensions of the images must match.

Although some of the tools available in the Apply Image command are similar to their counterparts in the Layers palette, this older method of compositing still remains useful. For example, you can apply elements of an image to itself, which allows you to heighten contrast, enhance a specific color channel, or combine colors.

The Apply Image dialog box offers set options to enhance the blended composite: An on/off Invert option, a set of blending modes, an Opacity field, and a Preserve Transparency option. Most of these options work as they do in other command dialog boxes, but, with the exception of Calculation, there are two Apply Image blending modes not available to other commands — Add and Subtract.

See also>>

Calculations

Layers Palette

1 Open two files with the exact same physical dimensions and resolution.

2 Click the image that you want as your target.

3 Click Image.

4 Click Apply Image.

The Apply Image dialog box appears.

5 Click the source file.

6 Set the opacity to the desired amount.

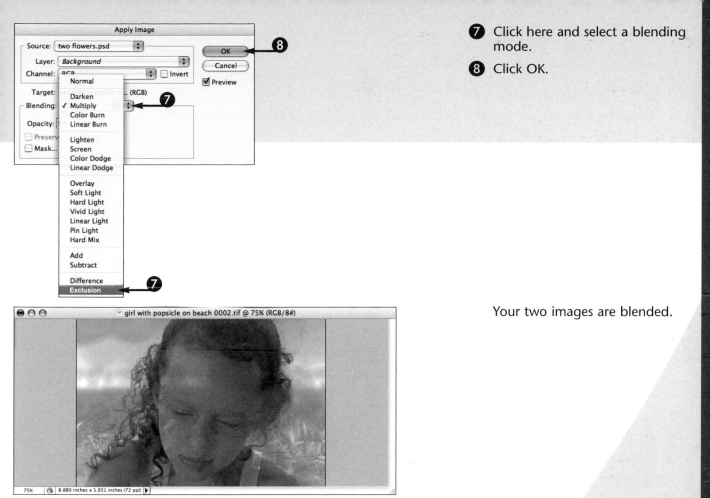

7 Click here and select a blending mode.

8 Click OK.

Your two images are blended.

ARRANGE:
Reposition Layers in the Stack

You can use the Arrange command in the Layers menu to change the order of layers in the Layers palette. To use the command, you need at least two layers. You can move layers to the front, the very top of the stack, forward, one layer up, backward, one layer down, back, or to the bottom of the stack. You can also reverse two adjacent layers to have them swap positions.

Although you can manually drag a layer to a new position, the Arrange layer feature is useful when you have an image with a large number of layers. The

Arrange command works on content layers, fill layers, adjustment layers, and layer groups. You can also select multiple consecutive or non-consecutive layers in the Layers palette and simultaneously move them forward or backward with the Arrange command.

See also>>

Layers Palette

Layers, Stacking Order

Arrange a Layer

① Click a layer near the top of the stack.

② Press Cmd (Mac) Ctrl (Win) and click another layer.

③ Click Layer.

④ Click Arrange.

⑤ Click an arrange command.

The layer moves within the stack.

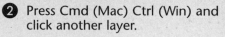

Reverse Layers

1. Click a layer.

2. Press Cmd (Mac) Ctrl (Win) and click another layer.

3. Click Layer.

4. Click Arrange.

5. Click Reverse.

The Layers exchange positions.

TIPS

Did You Know?

If you have a file with just a few layers, you may find it easier to just drag the layers to a new position instead of using the Arrange command.

Caution!

If you move a layer just below an expanded group of layers, it may inadvertly become part of the group. It is best to collapse all group layers before you do any rearranging of layers.

Caution!

When you rearrange a layer that is part of a clipping mask, the clipping mask becomes deactivated because it is dependant on the stacking order of consecutive layers. Actually, moving any adjustment layer can produce unexpected results because adjustments are based on one layer's relationship to lower adjacent layer(s).

AUTOMATIONS, BATCH:
Apply an Action to Multiple Images

You can apply an action or actions to several documents by using Photoshop's Automation Batch command. The dialog box lets you select Actions that are part of a set. You identify the files to which you want an action applied by making a selection from the Source pull-down menu.

Once you identify the files, you can override the open action commands. You can also apply actions to all subfolders, so long as you select a source folder. You can also suppress file open option dialog boxes or suppress color profile warnings — which means that the action does not stop to warn you or ask for additional information as it opens files.

You can save and close the processed file or you can save it to another folder. To save to a processed file,

you can also bypass entering options in the Save As dialog box.

Import applies the action to images from a scanner or digital camera. Opened Files plays the action on images open in Photoshop. Folder plays the action on all of the images within a selected folder. Bridge applies the action to images currently selected in Adobe Bridge. The Destination menu lets you pick a place to save your files.

See also>>   **Techniques, Actions**

Techniques Adobe Bridge

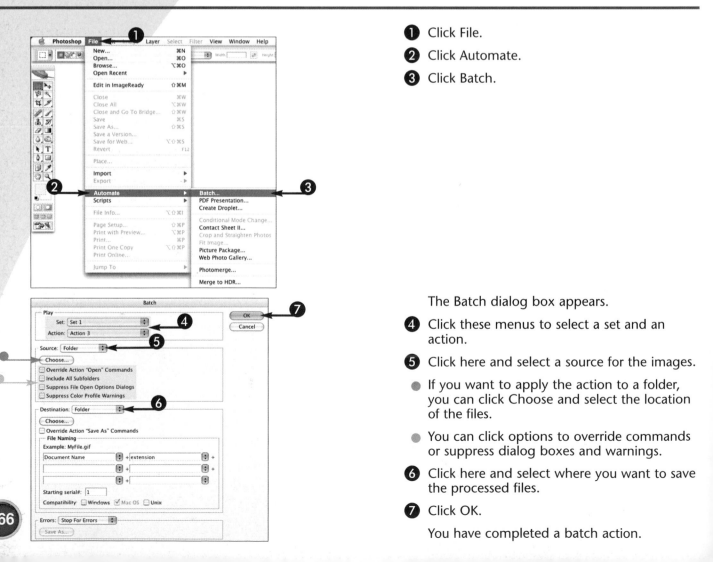

❶ Click File.

❷ Click Automate.

❸ Click Batch.

The Batch dialog box appears.

❹ Click these menus to select a set and an action.

❺ Click here and select a source for the images.

● If you want to apply the action to a folder, you can click Choose and select the location of the files.

● You can click options to override commands or suppress dialog boxes and warnings.

❻ Click here and select where you want to save the processed files.

❼ Click OK.

You have completed a batch action.

166

AUTOMATIONS:
Crop and Straighten: Create Multiple Documents from Scanned Images

If you scan several pictures in one operation, Photoshop imports them as one document. You can extract the individual images from the document, straighten them, and save them as individual files. The Crop and Straighten command can do all this. It recognizes the edges of images, eliminates white space, and straightens images that you may have scanned at an imprecise angle.

You can use the Crop and Straighten Automation technique on a single open image to automatically remove the background and straighten the image.

It recognizes the edges of each image as you scan them, so long as you place the hard copies on the scanner at least one-eighth of an inch apart and have a solid color background, which is not a problem with most scanners as they usually have a cover with a solid white or black color. The Crop and Straighten command works on RGB, CMYK, Grayscale, and Lab images. If you apply this command to a document with layers, you must select a visible and unlocked layer. Because the command is completely automated, there is no dialog box.

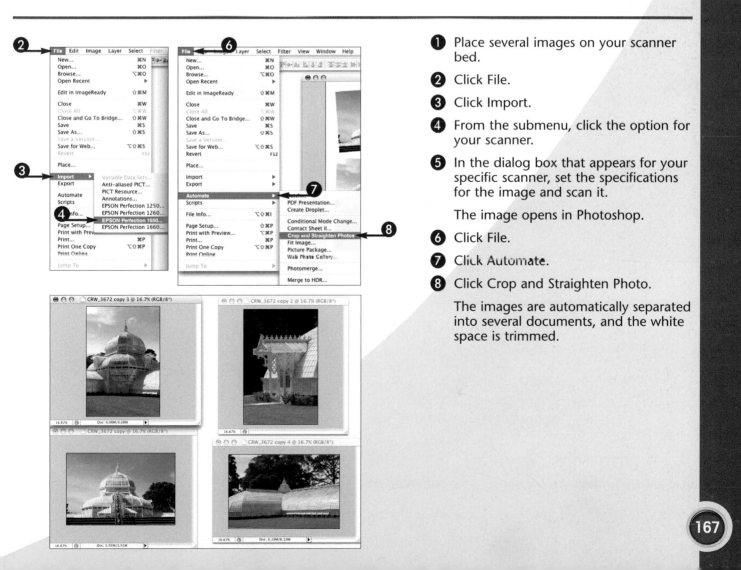

① Place several images on your scanner bed.

② Click File.

③ Click Import.

④ From the submenu, click the option for your scanner.

⑤ In the dialog box that appears for your specific scanner, set the specifications for the image and scan it.

The image opens in Photoshop.

⑥ Click File.

⑦ Click Automate.

⑧ Click Crop and Straighten Photo.

The images are automatically separated into several documents, and the white space is trimmed.

AUTOMATIONS, CONTACT SHEET:
Make a Grid of Thumbnail Images

You can create a new document called a contact sheet composed of reduced-size versions of images called thumbnails. Depending on the size of the document and the size of the thumbnails — both options you make — Photoshop may create several contact sheets.

The Contact Sheet dialog box, has several panes and options which allow you to determine what images to include, the size and layout of the contact sheet,

and what information to include with the thumbnails. The Source Images field lets you select the source for the images and their location; the Document pane lets you select the size of your contact sheet; the Thumbnails pane lets you design the layout; and the file name and caption lets you select whether to include the name of the file as a caption as well as the font and font size of the caption.

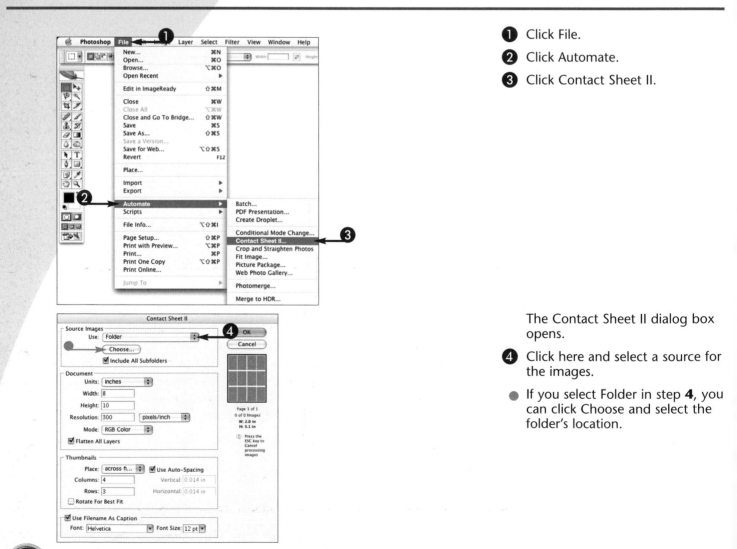

① Click File.

② Click Automate.

③ Click Contact Sheet II.

The Contact Sheet II dialog box opens.

④ Click here and select a source for the images.

● If you select Folder in step **4**, you can click Choose and select the folder's location.

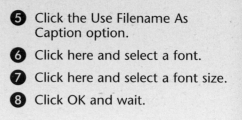

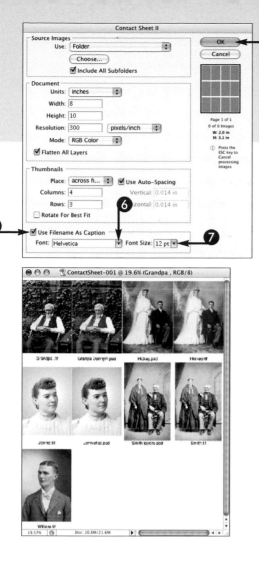

⑤ Click the Use Filename As Caption option.

⑥ Click here and select a font.

⑦ Click here and select a font size.

⑧ Click OK and wait.

Each image appears onscreen, diminishes in size, and is placed on the contact sheet.

TIPS

Caution!
When you select the Use Filename as Caption option (☑ changes to ☐), Photoshop creates a caption from the entire file name including the extension. Unless you change the font size, the thumbnails may be smaller than you expect to accommodate extra long names.

Try This!
To place the images on separate layers, you can deselect the Flatten All Layers option (☐ changes to ☑)

Caution!
When you select the Rotate For Best Fit option (☑ changes to ☐), Photoshop optimizes the use of space in a contact sheet by not only rotating, but making the size of the thumbnails as uniform as possible. This is good for saving paper, but it may be bad for judging the actual size and orientation of an image relative to other images.

AUTOMATIONS, DROPLET:
Run an Action from Your Desktop

You can convert Photoshop Actions into independent applications called Droplets. For example, you can create an Action that opens, adjusts, resizes, and saves a file after which you can convert the Action into a self-contained Droplet to store on your desktop.

You must save your Action as part of a set because Photoshop does not save individual Actions. This is important because the Create Droplet dialog box asks for both Set and Action to identify the process to that you want to save a Droplet.

Although a Droplet acts like an independent program, it is not independent of Photoshop. You must have Photoshop installed on your computer to run Droplets.

When you have a Droplet on your desktop, you can simply drag files into it to perform the sequence of commands. If Photoshop is not open, the Droplet opens Photoshop.

You create a droplet via the Create Droplet dialog box, where you select a location for the Droplet, the Action you want it to run, and where you want the droplet to place files once the process is complete. Other options include command overrides, and file naming and saving designations.

See also>> **Automation, Batch**

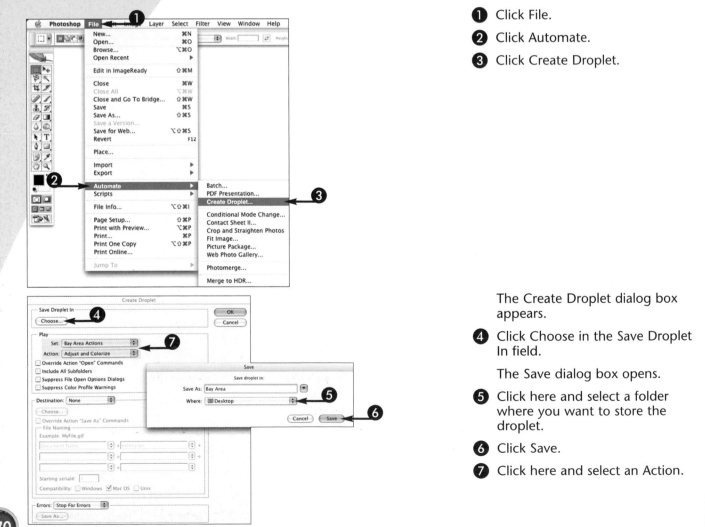

① Click File.

② Click Automate.

③ Click Create Droplet.

The Create Droplet dialog box appears.

④ Click Choose in the Save Droplet In field.

The Save dialog box opens.

⑤ Click here and select a folder where you want to store the droplet.

⑥ Click Save.

⑦ Click here and select an Action.

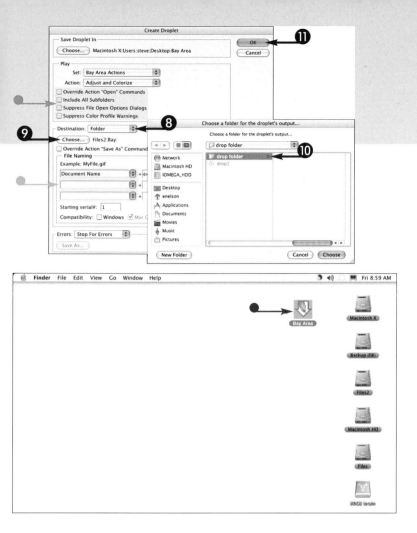

- To override any commands or suppress dialog boxes and warnings, you can click these options.

8 Click here to select the destination folder for your files.

9 Click Choose.

10 In the subsequent dialog box, click the folder.

- You can click here and select file naming conventions.

11 Click OK.

- The droplet appears in the specified location.

TIPS

Did You Know?
In the Destination menu, click None to open the file and leave it unsaved in the workspace. Click Folder to save it to a location. Click Save and Close to alter the source file.

Try This!
You can save a droplet you frequently use directly to your desktop. That way you do not have to search for the Droplet to run it. Just drag the image directly onto it to run the automated process.

Did You Know?
If you want to change specifications of any operation in a droplet, click the Toggle dialog box on/off icon for that action before you save it as a droplet.

AUTOMATE, FIT IMAGE:
Automatically Resize an Image

You can use the Fit Image command to resize an image to a specified width or height without changing its aspect ratio. The Fit Image dialog box displays the current image's width and height in pixels. When you enter new values in the Width and Height boxes in the Constrain Within field, the command takes the smaller of the two numbers and uses this number to calculate how to resize the image, constraining the proportion of the larger number to fit.

Keep in mind that this operation requires that your image be resampled. That is the operation changes the amount of data in the image by adding or

subtracting pixels. You can specify an Interpolation algorithm in the General preferences dialog box that controls how the image is resampled.

You can apply the Fit Image automation only to an image that is currently opened and active in the workspace. This automation's only advantage lies in the fact that it is a quick fix. It is not a replacement for the Image Size command, which offers considerably more control.

See also>> **Techniques: Image Size**

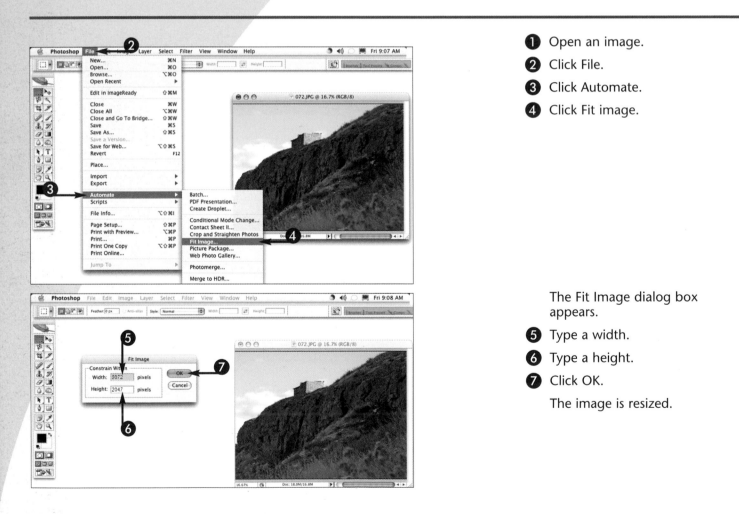

① Open an image.
② Click File.
③ Click Automate.
④ Click Fit image.

The Fit Image dialog box appears.
⑤ Type a width.
⑥ Type a height.
⑦ Click OK.
The image is resized.

AUTOMATIONS:
Photomerge: Create a Panorama

You can merge a series of images into a single, panoramic image. You do this in two Photomerge dialog boxes. In the first dialog box, you select the files that you want to place together into a panoramic image. The second Photomerge dialog box is where you stitch images into place.

If you have Photomerge merge automatically, the results appear in the main panel. If Photomerge cannot match the images well enough Photomerge will displays a message to that affect and present thumbnails of the images — just as it does when you choose to merge manually. You can then drag

the images to the panorama working pane and match them manually. The display shows transparency where the images overlap so that you can align them precisely. You can utilize the Tools palette tools to position and rotate the images, or create a common vanishing point.

You can preview your results using the Preview button in the Composition Settings pane. When you are satisfied with it, Photomerge then returns you to Photoshop and creates the new composite image. You may need to additionally edit your image to seamlessly blend the images together.

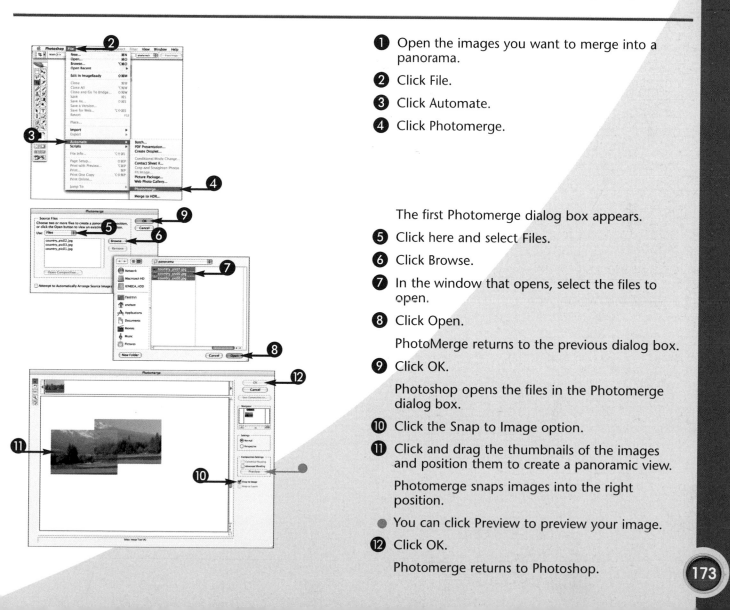

① Open the images you want to merge into a panorama.

② Click File.

③ Click Automate.

④ Click Photomerge.

The first Photomerge dialog box appears.

⑤ Click here and select Files.

⑥ Click Browse.

⑦ In the window that opens, select the files to open.

⑧ Click Open.

PhotoMerge returns to the previous dialog box.

⑨ Click OK.

Photoshop opens the files in the Photomerge dialog box.

⑩ Click the Snap to Image option.

⑪ Click and drag the thumbnails of the images and position them to create a panoramic view.

Photomerge snaps images into the right position.

● You can click Preview to preview your image.

⑫ Click OK.

Photomerge returns to Photoshop.

AUTOMATIONS:
PDF PRESENTATION:
Make a Slide Show or a Multipage Document

The PDF Presentation command collects and organizes images into one file that Adobe Reader can view. The PDF Presentation dialog box offers two options for saving and viewing your images; as a multiple page Portable Document File (PDF), or as an automated PDF slide presentation complete with time intervals and graphic transitions.

In the Source field of the PDF Presentation dialog box, you can select files for your PDF document via the Open dialog box. If you select the Add Open Files

option, the name and location of open Photoshop documents appears in the source list. The Output Options field lets you choose between a multipage document or a presentation. Both options create a PDF file that opens in Adobe Acrobat reader. If you select Presentation, the Presentation options activate, and you can select transitions from the menu and enter an Advance interval. The loop option creates a continually running slideshow.

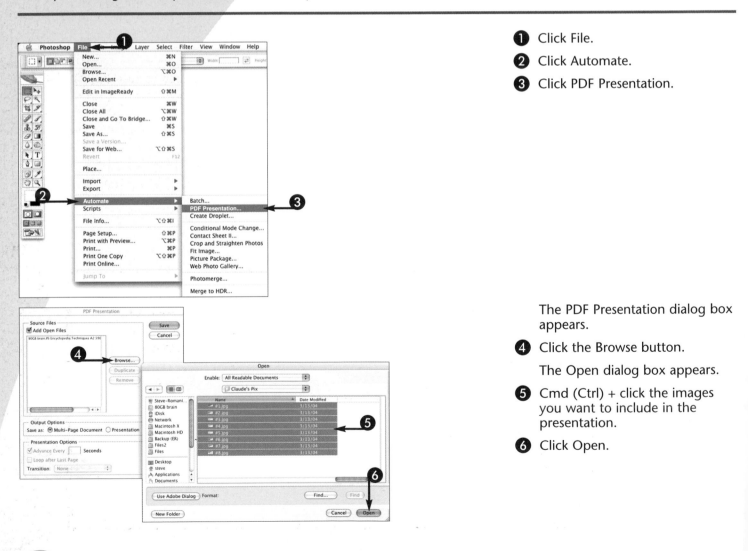

① Click File.

② Click Automate.

③ Click PDF Presentation.

The PDF Presentation dialog box appears.

④ Click the Browse button.

The Open dialog box appears.

⑤ Cmd (Ctrl) + click the images you want to include in the presentation.

⑥ Click Open.

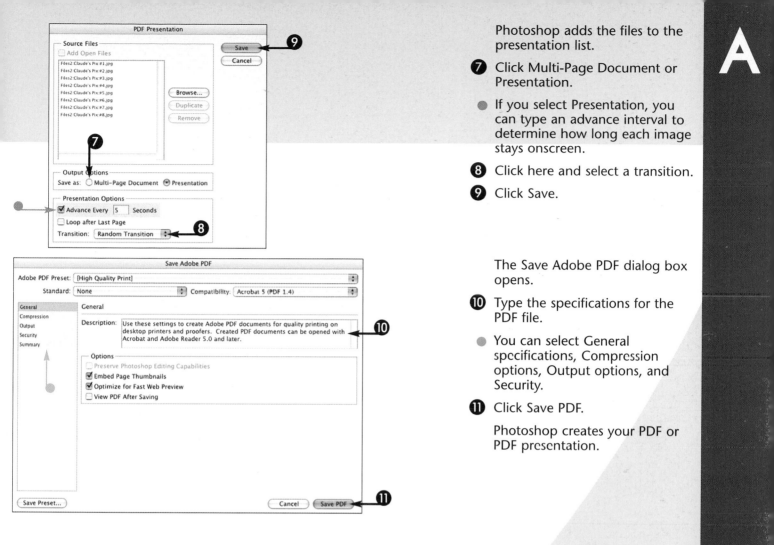

Photoshop adds the files to the presentation list.

7 Click Multi-Page Document or Presentation.

● If you select Presentation, you can type an advance interval to determine how long each image stays onscreen.

8 Click here and select a transition.

9 Click Save.

The Save Adobe PDF dialog box opens.

10 Type the specifications for the PDF file.

● You can select General specifications, Compression options, Output options, and Security.

11 Click Save PDF.

Photoshop creates your PDF or PDF presentation.

Try This!

With the Presentation option, you can select from a variety transitions that "fade" one image into another. You can also click Random Transition, which arbitrarily attaches a different transition to each image as it appears onscreen.

Try This!

To display an image more than once in your presentation, click the image's filename in the Source pane of the PDF Presentation dialog box. Click Duplicate. Click and drag the duplicate image to the appropriate location.

Did You Know?

The PDF Presentation command creates a new and separate document independent of the images from which it was created. When you double-click the PDF document's icon, Acrobat Reader opens and runs the Presentation slide show.

AUTOMATIONS: PICTURE PACKAGE:
Create a Single Page with Multiple Copies of an Image

You can use the Picture Package command to create a single-page document with multiple images on a single page — similar what a portrait studio offers. Photoshop defaults arranging multiple copies of the same image using a standard layout. However, you can substitute any image on the layout with another file.

The Picture Package dialog box lets you choose a source image within a folder, from selected images in Adobe Bridge, or the current document in the Photoshop workspace. You can specify page size and

layout, and color mode. You can also specify a resolution value. Photoshop creates a separate Layer for each of the document components. If you do not want layers, you can flatten them to produce a smaller file. You can designate a label and the labels appearance for each object in the Picture Package document, but they print over each image.

Finally, you use the Picture Package Edit Layout dialog box to manually alter the size and position of your images.

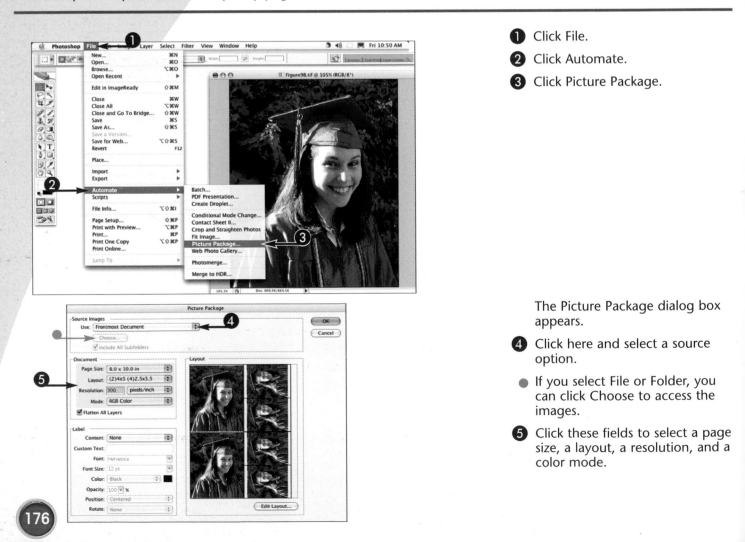

① Click File.

② Click Automate.

③ Click Picture Package.

The Picture Package dialog box appears.

④ Click here and select a source option.

● If you select File or Folder, you can click Choose to access the images.

⑤ Click these fields to select a page size, a layout, a resolution, and a color mode.

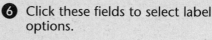

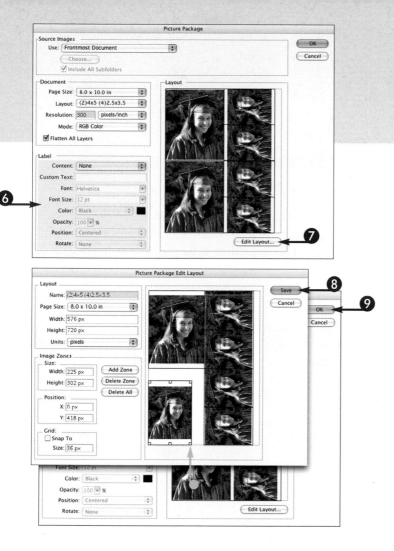

6 Click these fields to select label options.

7 Click Edit Layout.

The Picture Package Edit Layout dialog box appears.

● You can scale an image by dragging on its corner handles, or move it into any position by clicking and dragging the image.

8 Click Save.

Your edits are saved.

9 Click OK in the Picture Package dialog box.

Photoshop creates the Picture Package document ready for printing.

TIPS

Try This!
In the Edit Layout dialog box, you can click Add Zone to add an image to the page; to remove an image, click it and then click Delete Zone.

Did You Know?
You can use the Label option to add a watermark to your images. Use a large font size and type your initials or a simple message. Then set the opacity to a low value. Watermarks dissuade others from using your work without permission.

Try This!
If you do not want to print multiple copies of the same image, you can bypass the Edit Layout dialog box. Click an image in the Layout pane of the Picture Package palette. Immediately a Select an Image File dialog box appears. Find and double-click a substitute file and it replaces the image in the Layout pane.

AUTOMATIONS, WEB PHOTO GALLERY:
Publish Images to the Web

The Web Photo Gallery command allows you to create a simple Web site without having to learn any Web programming language or site authoring programs. Photo Gallery puts together a rudimentary Web site designed to showcase your images. You select a layout from several templates and identify the files you want you display. Photoshop creates an index page, thumbnail views of your images, Web-safe copies of your images, and all the HTML code to create a functional Web site.

The Web Photo Gallery dialog box presents a preview of your Web portfolio. When you choose any style, a Preview thumbnail of the first Web page appears. Just below, you can type your Email address so that a mail link can be added to your page. In the Source

Images pane is the location of your image files, which can be a particular folder or a set of selected files in Bridge. The Destinaltion field identifies the folder where all the necessary Web site elements — pages, images, thumbnails, and so on — will be saved. At this point Photoshop has all that it needs to create a Web site, so you could click OK.

You could, but you might not want to. Additional Options are available to add extras to your site — a Banner, choosing larger images or thumbnails, adding more file information, changing the color of text, links, and backgrounds, and so on. Once you finish selecting options, you can view the Web Photo Gallery in your default browser.

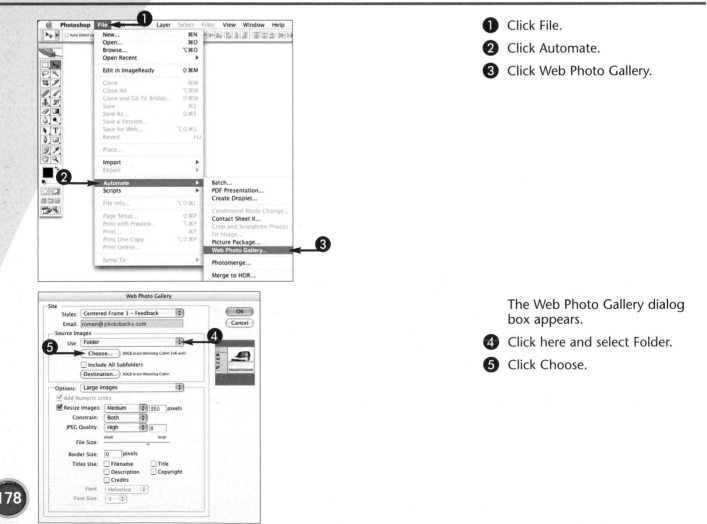

❶ Click File.

❷ Click Automate.

❸ Click Web Photo Gallery.

The Web Photo Gallery dialog box appears.

❹ Click here and select Folder.

❺ Click Choose.

178

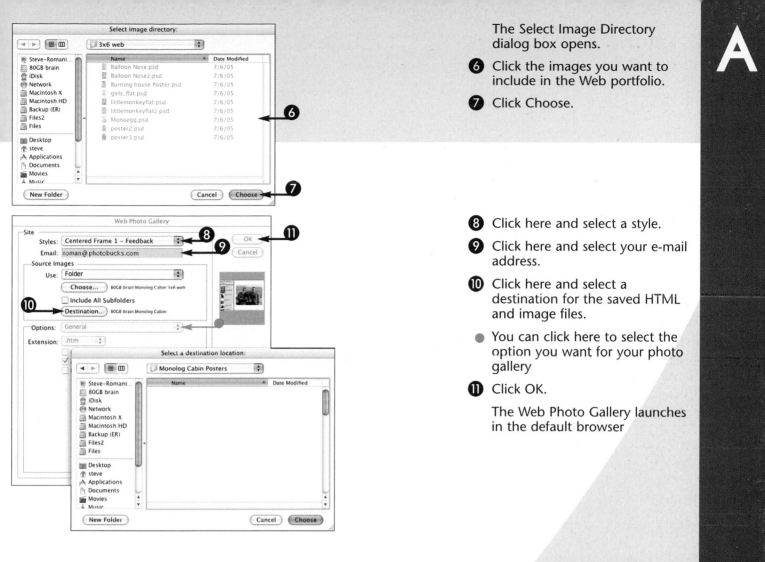

The Select Image Directory dialog box opens.

6 Click the images you want to include in the Web portfolio.

7 Click Choose.

8 Click here and select a style.

9 Click here and select your e-mail address.

10 Click here and select a destination for the saved HTML and image files.

● You can click here to select the option you want for your photo gallery

11 Click OK.

The Web Photo Gallery launches in the default browser

Did You Know?

Every time you select an option from the Options menu, the Options pane changes and prompts you for information and settings appropriate for that option. For example, if your select Large Images, the pane prompts you for size and other characteristics; if you select Custom colors, the pane shows swatches for different elements in a page and clicking a swatch brings up the Color Picker.

Caution!

When the Color Picker appears, make sure that you select the Only Web Colors option (☑ changes to ☐). This ensures, but does not guarantee, that the color you pick is Web-safe — that is it will display as intended regardless of what browser, or platform is being used.

AUTOMATIONS:
Merge to HDR

The Merge To HDR command combines two or more identical photographs taken at different exposures and merges them into one file to capture the full dynamic range of light and shadow. Because most monitors and cameras have a fixed dynamic range, they can only capture and store a limited range of tonal values in one frame. By combining images, Merge to HDR can extract and store different highlight and shadow detail from individual images and create a richer image with high dynamic range.

Because HDR images store much more tonal information, they are much larger in size than other files and can tax your computers memory and disk space. Also, because of the limitations of monitors,

you have fewer commands available for working with HDR images.

You can save an HDR image — a 32-bits per channel image — to 8- or 16-bits per channel; however, you lose the information that only a 32-bits per channel image can store. The success of the Merge to HDR feature depends on the quality and quantity of the photographs you take. You should use a tripod for stability and to ensure the only thing you are changing is the exposure. You should take enough photos to cover the full dynamic range of a scene. The images you merge should have the same pixel dimensions.

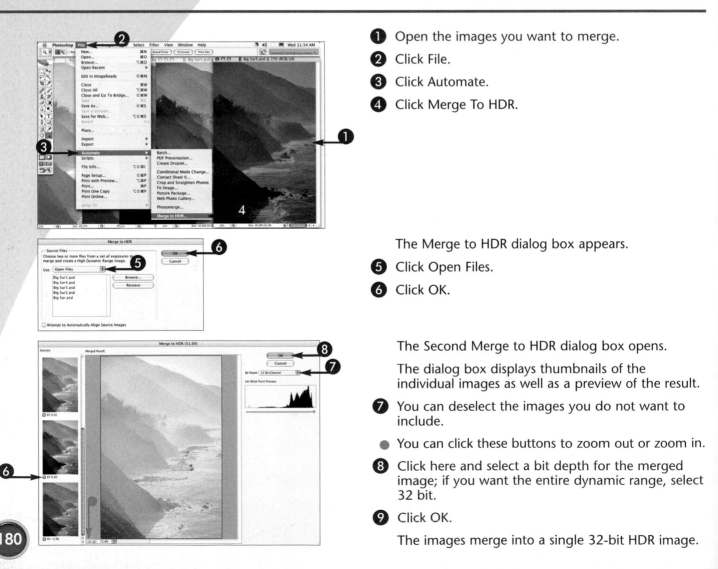

① Open the images you want to merge.

② Click File.

③ Click Automate.

④ Click Merge To HDR.

The Merge to HDR dialog box appears.

⑤ Click Open Files.

⑥ Click OK.

The Second Merge to HDR dialog box opens.

The dialog box displays thumbnails of the individual images as well as a preview of the result.

⑦ You can deselect the images you do not want to include.

● You can click these buttons to zoom out or zoom in.

⑧ Click here and select a bit depth for the merged image; if you want the entire dynamic range, select 32 bit.

⑨ Click OK.

The images merge into a single 32-bit HDR image.

AUTOMATIONS:
Conditional Mode Change

When you run an action that converts RGB to CMYK, if the source is not RGB, an error occurs and the action stops. This is a problem because users of Photoshop often work in RGB mode but need to send CMYK files to printers. If you have many files to convert, having an action to do this is essential.

The Conditional Mode Change command allows you to change the color mode of a file in an action without encountering errors. To use this command you must be in the process of recording an action and must encounter the dialog box where you can

select all, none, or one or more or the following: RGB color, CMYK Color, Grayscale, Lab Color, Duotone Index Color, Multi Channel, and Bitmap.

When you convert an image from RGB to CMYK or Index, you can produce significant color shifts; when you convert to Grayscale, you lose all your color; when you convert from RGB Color to Indexed Color, you remap all of the colors in the document between 2 and 256 colors. Reducing the potential number of colors reduces the file size, but may also affect the image quality.

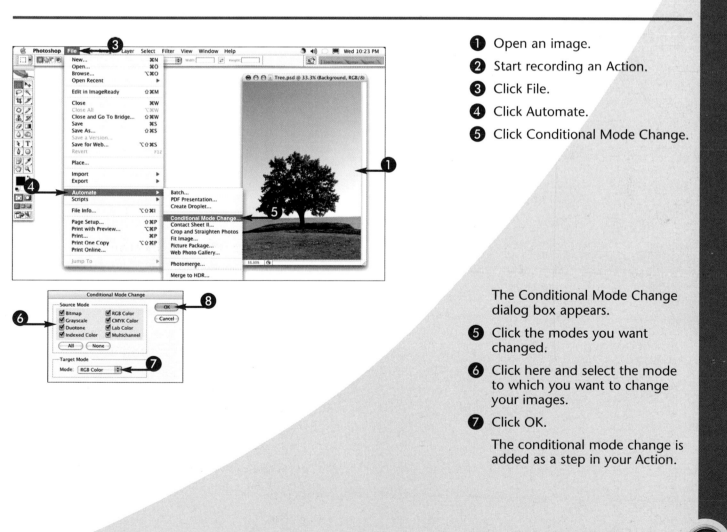

① Open an image.

② Start recording an Action.

③ Click File.

④ Click Automate.

⑤ Click Conditional Mode Change.

The Conditional Mode Change dialog box appears.

⑤ Click the modes you want changed.

⑥ Click here and select the mode to which you want to change your images.

⑦ Click OK.

The conditional mode change is added as a step in your Action.

BIT DEPTH:
Convert an Image from 16 Bits to 8 Bits

If you have a professional camera, which allows you to create 16 bit TIF or RAW images, you can save file space by converting this format to an 8-bit format.

The 16-bit format gives you a smoother transition between colors throughout your image, meaning that one color does not stop at the beginning of another. In addition, shadows or darker areas have more detail. However, you pay dearly for this because 16-bit images contain more color information, thus consuming more disk space. So you gain in latitude, but you lose by producing bigger files that require more computer memory to process.

If you intend to use you image on the Web or onscreen, the 16-bit format gives no advantage because monitor screens have a limited color range, and color depth is lost. Likewise, if you print the images on your home inkjet, you see no discernable improvement in the quality of the images.

The bottom line? Unless you plan to do pretty sophisticated image processing, you are better off with 8-bit image.

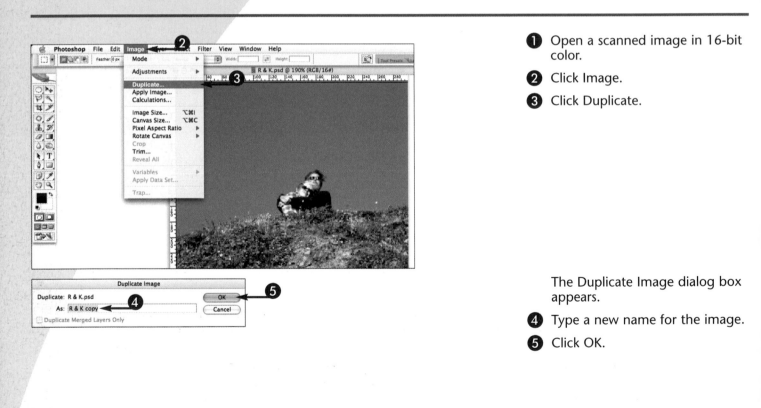

① Open a scanned image in 16-bit color.

② Click Image.

③ Click Duplicate.

The Duplicate Image dialog box appears.

④ Type a new name for the image.

⑤ Click OK.

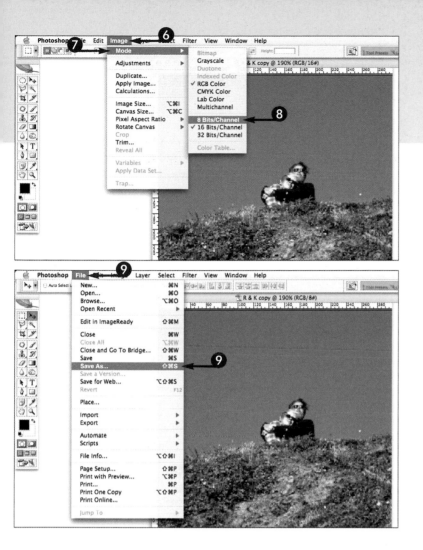

6 Click Image.

7 Click Mode.

8 Click 8 Bits/Channel.

The image converts to 8 bits.

9 Save the image to a location on your hard drive.

Note: You can click File and then Save As to open the Save As dialog box.

Photoshop saves your image in 8-bit color.

You can now print your image without worrying about 16-bit support.

TIPS

Did You Know?

Photoshop supports High Dynamic Range (HDR) images, which are 32-bits /channel files that store the amount of light in each pixel rather that its color. This allows you to brighten or darken an image without detail loss. Photoshop takes advantage of this "exposure" capability and lets you merge two exposures of the same image into one image that takes the best from both.

Did You Know?

Camera Raw images contain unprocessed image data and are the closest equivalent to a film camera's negatives because you can control over exposure, depth of color, and other image quality characteristics. Cameras that support the Raw format provide software to process these files. Currently, there is no standard to which Camera manufactures adhere, so not all graphic programs can process Raw format from all cameras.

BLENDING OPTIONS:
Exclude Colors from a Layer

You can use blending options in Photoshop to combine layers of color and objects to produce interesting and new effects. These options are great for creating a collage or other work of art from you photos.

RGB image are composed of three channels — or specialized "layers" — of red, green, and blue. CMYK, another common color mode, has four channels — cyan, magenta, yellow, and black. In both types of files the colors are a blend of each color channel. You can use these channels to increase, or decrease the intensity of the colors, remove the colors altogether, or watch your image change before your eyes.

The Advanced Blending options allow you to change any channel's color transparency via the Fill Capacity slider. A Knockout option controls which layers "punch through" to reveal content from other layers. These options determine blend's scope and layer style.

The sliders in the Blend It field define a brightness range of pixels as visible or partially visible on the currently targeted layer or the underlying layer. You should start with the Gray option because as a neutral color, you blending any neutral colors so that the other layer colors show through.

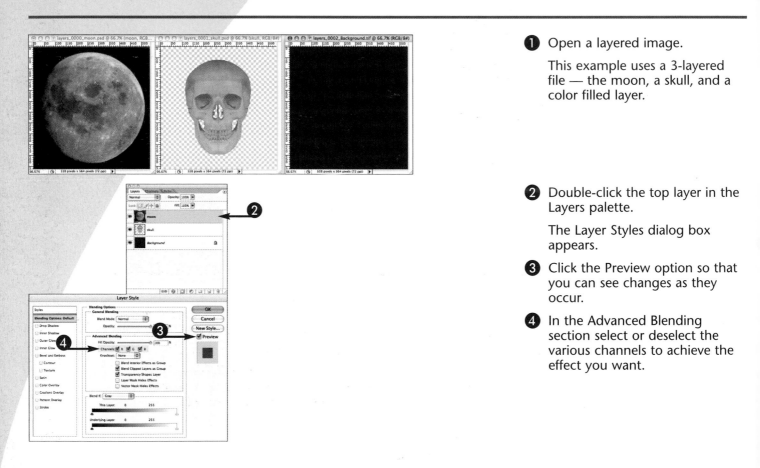

❶ Open a layered image.

   This example uses a 3-layered file — the moon, a skull, and a color filled layer.

❷ Double-click the top layer in the Layers palette.

   The Layer Styles dialog box appears.

❸ Click the Preview option so that you can see changes as they occur.

❹ In the Advanced Blending section select or deselect the various channels to achieve the effect you want.

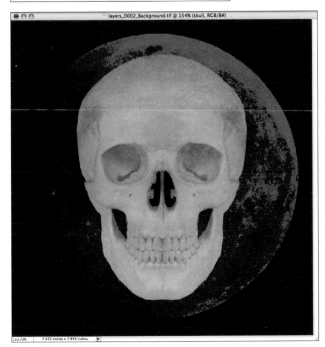

The effects of removing or adding the channel appear in your image.

● You can click here and select a Knockout option.

● You can click here and select other Advanced Blending options.

⑤ Click here and set Blend If mode.

Because gray is a neutral color, it is recommended that you start with the Gray option.

⑥ Click and drag one of the White layer sliders or Black layer sliders inward on the ramp until the lighter or darker pixels disappear.

You can experiment with different colors and slider values.

The result is an interesting intersection of three layers.

TIPS

Try This!
To avoid harsh color transitions and jagged edges, you can adjust the Fuzziness sliders that soften the transition. Press Opt (Alt) as you drag the sliders; half of the slider moves.

Did you know?
If you have an image with a white or a black background, you can make that background transparent. If the background is white, move the white Blend If slider toward the left; if the background is black, move the black Blend If slider toward the right.

Did you know?
If you like the Blend effects you created, you can save those effects to use on another file. On the right side of the Blend dialog box, click the New Style button. The subsequent dialog box asks for a name and gives you the option of saving Layer effects or Blending options, or both.

BLENDING MODES:
Affect Color Relationships Between Stacked Layers

You can produce astounding color effects with blended layers. Blended layers are like having two color transparencies with a colored transparent gel in between them on a light table. The image is a combination of the bottom slide and the top slide affected by the tint of the gel, however, you have the added ability to slide in more complex, specific effects, such as color saturation, color inversion, color darkening, or color bleaching.

Blending modes are preprogrammed effects that determine the color relationships between aligned

pixels on two consecutive layers in the stack. You can assign a blending mode to a layer in the layers palette, or use the Layer Styles dialog box. You can adjust the Opacity slider to strengthen or weaken the effect.

The 23 blending modes in the Layers palette, which affect the layer's color relationship to the layers below it, are divided into seven categories, from top to bottom; normal, darken, lighten, lighting, inverting, and color.

① Open an image with multiple layers.

The example uses four layers.

② Click the layer to which you want to apply a Blending mode.

The Blending mode establishes a relationship between this layer and the one below.

③ Click the Mode menu at the top of the Layers palette directly under the Palette Title tab and select the desired blending option.

Here the Luminosity Blend mode is applied to the layer containing the lower butterfly.

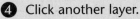

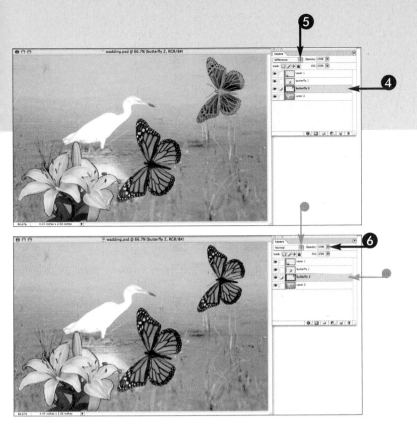

④ **Click another layer.**

In the example, the layer containing the second butterfly is selected.

⑤ **Click the mode menu and select Difference.**

You can experiment with other blending options on your layers.

⑥ **Click and drag the Opacity slider to increase or decrease the effect.**

The example here illustrates Difference at 80%.

● If you do not like any of the effects on one or all of the layers, simply click the layer and return the layer to Normal mode.

Note: Unless you save your file as Photoshop, PDF, or TIFF, you lose your layers and therefore the ability to return layer affects to Normal.

TIPS

Did You Know?

You can use blending modes to increase the saturation and contrast of a layer. After duplicating a layer, move it immediately above the original. Apply a blending mode such as Hard Light. Then click and drag the Opacity slider to control the strength of the adjustment.

Try This!

You can assign blending modes to most painting and editing tools. When you paint with the brush, for example, both the underlying colors and the blending mode you select in the Options bar affect the underlying colors.

Try This!

To correct a dark image, duplicate the image layer. Set the copy Layer Blend mode to Screen. Drag the Opacity slider to control the amount of lightness. Your image lightens without you having to apply more complicated commands.

BRUSHES:
Define and Apply a Custom Brush

You can create a custom brush and make it any shape and size. This is especially useful if you have a specific area over which you consistently apply color or effects, or if you want to apply a specific set of properties with your brush. Once you create your brush, you can easily apply it to any image.

You can create a Photoshop brush any size up to 2500 pixels wide. You can control the angle and softness of a brush directly in the Presets menu located in the Options bar when you select a tool that is applied with a brush.

When you define a custom brush, you use the existing content of an image to define the shape

and texture of your brush tip. A brush tip is a specific shape with several options pertaining to it that affect the way it appears when you apply it with brush strokes. You can easily define custom brush-tip shapes from selected areas of an image or from individual layers.

See also>>

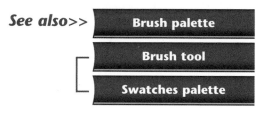

Brush palette

Brush tool

Swatches palette

---

❶ Open a document that contains all or part of an image that you want to make into a brush.

❷ Click the Zoom tool.

❸ Click the image to magnify the area from which you want to create a brush.

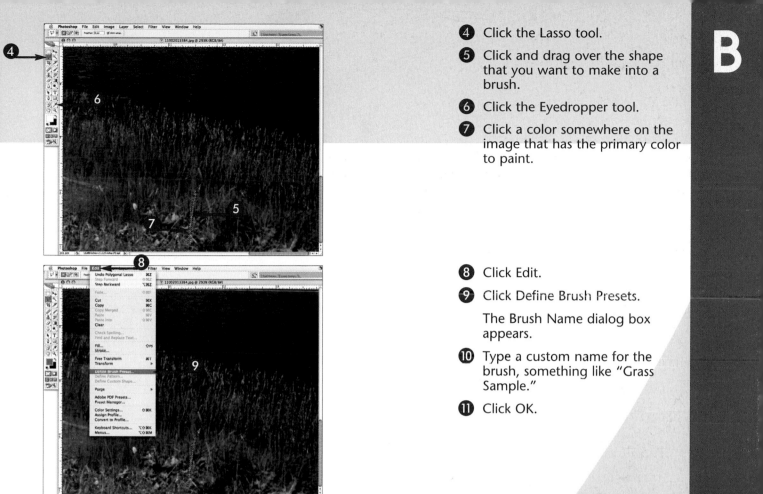

④ Click the Lasso tool.

⑤ Click and drag over the shape that you want to make into a brush.

⑥ Click the Eyedropper tool.

⑦ Click a color somewhere on the image that has the primary color to paint.

⑧ Click Edit.

⑨ Click Define Brush Presets.

The Brush Name dialog box appears.

⑩ Type a custom name for the brush, something like "Grass Sample."

⑪ Click OK.

Warning!

Remember to save your custom brushes! Photoshop does not automatically save the Brushes you create after you name them. Once you exit the current Photoshop session, your Custom Brushes become lost unless you go to the Brushes Palette menu and click Save Brushes. When you do this, Photoshop makes a new set of all the brushes currently in the palette.

BRUSHES:
Define and Apply a Custom Brush (Continued)

Once you create your custom brush, you can apply it to an image as well as change its available options in the Brush palette. These options include scattering, shape, color spacing, angle, transparency variations, color, and size.

Scattering controls how brush marks distribute in a stroke. You select this option to randomly distribute marks horizontally and vertically rather than in a straight line. Shape refers to the amount of roundness and slope of the brush. Color Spacing controls the variations of transparency, hue, and color as you apply strokes. Angle defines the shape

of the tip of the brush and the variation of the applied stroke. For example, you can make the stroke bold and wide at the start and thin and faded at the end. Transparency variation allows you to create a stroke with color that varies in the intensity of the color.

The color and size possibilities of your stroke are endless and include millions of colors and more than a dozen blending mode options. The capabilities of Photoshop's paint engine are only limited by your imagination and the amount of disk and memory available to you.

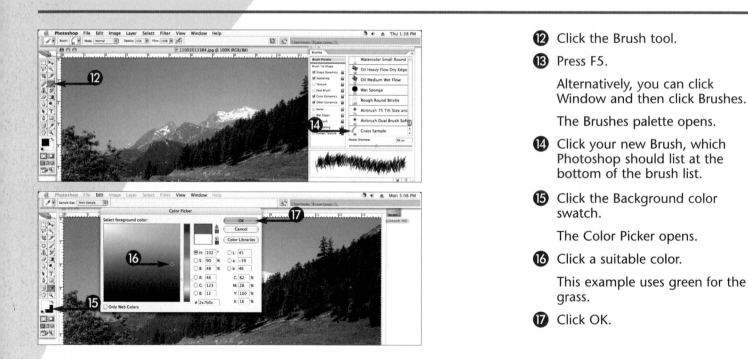

⑫ Click the Brush tool.

⑬ Press F5.

Alternatively, you can click Window and then click Brushes.

The Brushes palette opens.

⑭ Click your new Brush, which Photoshop should list at the bottom of the brush list.

⑮ Click the Background color swatch.

The Color Picker opens.

⑯ Click a suitable color.

This example uses green for the grass.

⑰ Click OK.

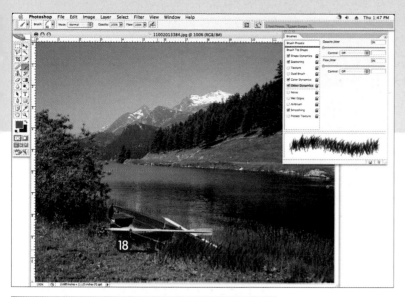

18 Click and drag your brush to paint over the portion of the image that you want to change.

Photoshop changes the image per your custom brush's specifications.

Did You Know?

You can alter the color that is deposited on the surface of the image by selecting a blending mode from the Brush Tool's Options bar. Experiment with different overlay techniques to produce interesting results.

Try This!

You can use any portion of an image as a Custom Brush. For example, if you want to scatter your subject's face throughout an image, select the area containing the face, and then click Define Brush Preset. Remember to give the brush an appropriate name.

CALCULATIONS:
Combine Channels to Create a New File

The Calculations command allows you to take advantage of information stored in two source channels. It calculates the pixel values of each channel and, using internal algorithms plus a blending mode, combines them to create a selection, an Alpha channel, or a new grayscale document. Take, for example, the RGB color model, which is a composite of three channels, Red, Green, and Blue. Each channel is a grayscale duplicate of the others, but differs in the color information it stores. Some channels have better dark/light pixel distribution than others. For example, if your image is particularly dark, you may find that one channel in particular has less tonal variation.

The Calculations command requires that you have the images containing the source channels open and that all images have the same total pixel size. You also must identify the channels to combine.

The Calculations allows you to preview the affect as you apply it. Play with it so that you can understand it better.

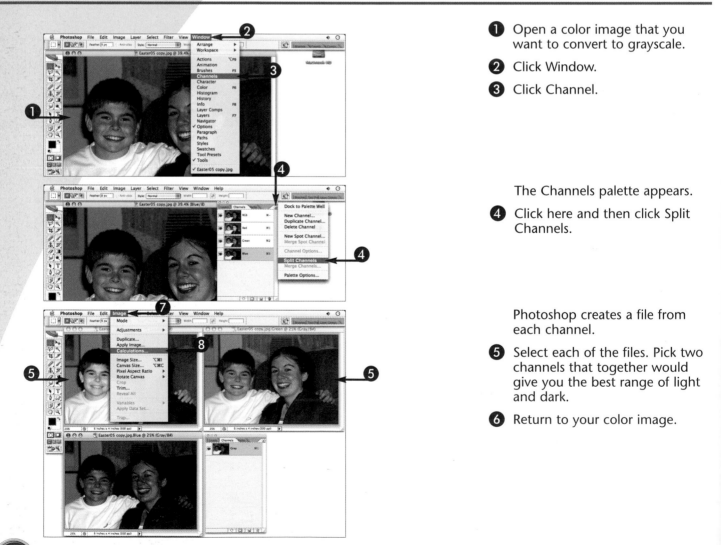

① Open a color image that you want to convert to grayscale.

② Click Window.

③ Click Channel.

The Channels palette appears.

④ Click here and then click Split Channels.

Photoshop creates a file from each channel.

⑤ Select each of the files. Pick two channels that together would give you the best range of light and dark.

⑥ Return to your color image.

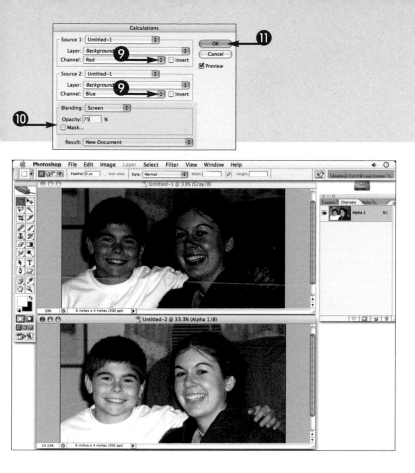

7 Click Image.

8 Click Calculations.

The Calculations dialog box appears.

9 Click here and select channels for Sources 1 and 2.

10 Click to select or type a blending mode, an Opacity value, and where to place the result.

11 Click OK.

The Channels are combined to create a better grayscale image.

TIPS

Try This!

You can display an individual channel on your image window by clicking the thumbnail of the particular channel on the Channels palette. Photoshop makes that channel the only visible channel. If you want to see another, click its thumbnail — now it becomes the only visible channel. To return to the composite view, click the top channel. You can also press Cmd(Ctrl)+"-" to return to the composite view.

Did You Know?

The Add and Subtract blending modes are found only in the Calculations and Apply Image dialog boxes, and not in the Layers palette or Options bar.

CAMERA RAW:
Open and Adjust a Camera Raw File

Photoshop's Camera Raw dialog box allows you to open and process Camera Raw data from digital camera images. Camera Raw files are similar to camera negatives in that no adjustments have been made — all the information captured by the camera sensor is presented. Acting as your darkroom, Photoshop reads this information so you can control all adjustments and settings. You can manipulate the unprocessed files to produce a better JPEG or TIF file.

Not all digital cameras produce Camera Raw data and not all cameras that produce Raw data are compatible with Photoshop Raw plug-ins. However, if yours does, you must specifically select the Camera Raw option per your camera's user manual.

You can open the Camera Raw images in either Photoshop or Adobe Bridge. In the Camera Raw dialog box, you have the Zoom, Hand, Eyedroppers, Crop, and Transform tools, which work like those in Photoshop. In addition, you have several sliders that allow you to adjust color, sharpen details, correct chromatic aberrations, modify a brightness curve, and calibrate the image to a specific profile. You can save the Camera Raw settings and apply them to other images.

① Open an image that has been shot in Camera Raw format.

The Camera Raw interface appears.

② Click here and select Camera Raw Defaults.

The settings revert to the default settings.

③ Click and drag the Temperature slide to adjust the White Balance.

④ Click and drag the Exposure, Shadows, Brightness, Contrast, and Saturation sliders to achieve the effect you want.

⑤ Click the Detail tab.

⑥ Click and drag the Sharpness, Luminance Smoothing, and Color Noise Reduction slider to achieve the effects that you want.

⑦ Click the Lens tab.

⑧ Click and drag the Chromatic Aberration sliders to adjust lens aberrations.

⑨ Click and drag the Vignetting sliders to reduce darkening of your image's corners.

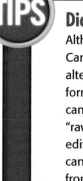

Did You Know?

Although Photoshop cannot save Camera Raw format files, it does offer an alternative — Digital Negative (DNG) format, Adobe's proposed standard for camera raw image files, which preserves "raw" information and serves as an editable backup for raw images. Photoshop can open and process Camera Raw files from many cameras. However, some require you to use proprietary software to process their images.

Did You Know?

Most professional and "prosumer" digital cameras produce Camera Raw images. Photoshop can process raw files from many, but not all, cameras. You can find a list of supported cameras at www.adobe.com.

Did you Know?

Because they contain more information, Camera Raw files are much larger than other common image types, which means they take up more disk and memory space.

CAMERA RAW:
Open and Adjust a Camera Raw File (Continued)

Professional photographers use camera raw files as "digital negatives." The digital negative contains all of the information you need to process the image including controls for white balance, tonal range, contrast, color saturation, and sharpening.

When you open a Camera Raw image, it adjusts the basic image information to optimal levels. It does so based on default settings for specific cameras.

You can make adjustments to your image using the various tabs in the Camera Raw interface. The Adjust tab controls temperature, exposure, shadows, brightness, contrast, and saturation. The Detail tab

lets you adjust sharpness, luminance smoothing, and color noise. The Lens tab lets you reduce chromatic aberrations caused by the inability of the lens to focus the variable color wavelengths in the same spot. The Curve and Calibration tabs help you make small adjustments.

Once you have "developed" a raw image, you can use the settings for other files that came from the same camera. You can save image settings for reuse on other images. In fact you can save those settings as a default for a specific camera.

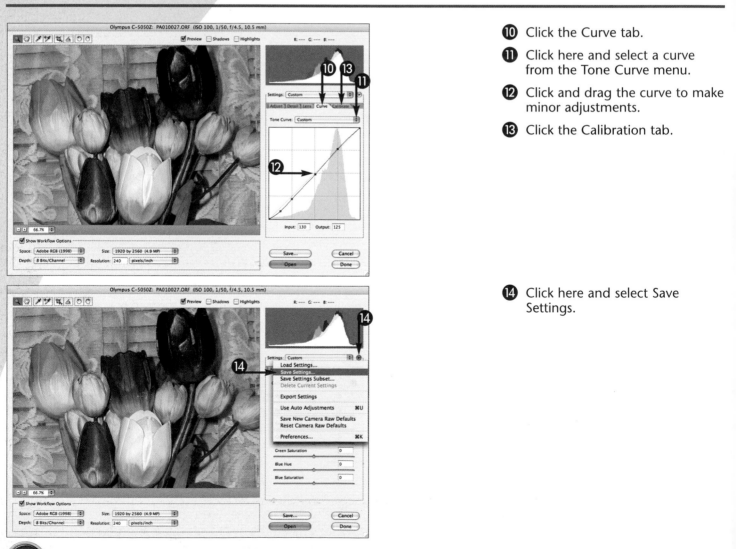

⑩ Click the Curve tab.

⑪ Click here and select a curve from the Tone Curve menu.

⑫ Click and drag the curve to make minor adjustments.

⑬ Click the Calibration tab.

⑭ Click here and select Save Settings.

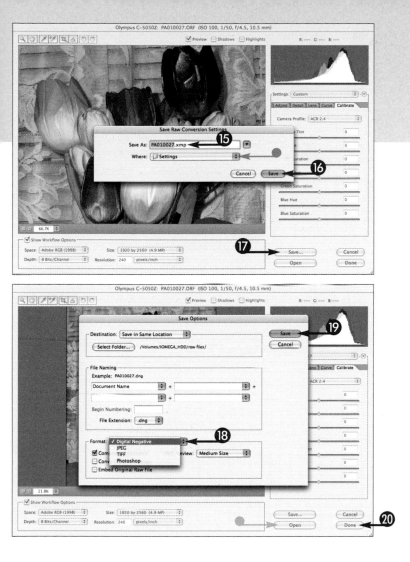

The Save Raw Conversion Settings dialog box.

⑮ Type a name for your settings.

● Photoshop defaults to saving the file in its Settings folder.

⑯ Click Save.

⑰ Click Save.

The Save Options dialog box appears.

⑱ Click here and select Digital Negative.

⑲ Click Save.

You are returned to the Camera Raw dialog box.

● You can click Open to further edit in Photoshop.

⑳ Click Done.

Your settings are saved.

Try This!

You can apply the last settings you created to an image. Click Previous Settings from the Settings dialog box. This is helpful if you are processing a series of images.

Try This!

To observe where the darkest shadows and lightest highlight areas are, click the Shadow Highlight options (☑ changes to ☐) at the top of the interface.

Did You Know?

Photoshop, like most other programs, do not create a thumbnail or preview of raw files. If you want to preview a raw file before you open it, go to Bridge and click the folder where your files are stored. Click Filmstrip View and you can view your images by scrolling through the thumbnails.

CHANNELS, ALPHA:
Save and Load an Alpha Channel

Because making an intricate selection can sometimes be quite labor-intensive, Photoshop lets you save selections as Alpha channels so that you can load and use them again. You should save a selection as an Alpha channel if a selection is complex and you anticipate using it again.

The Save Selection dialog box defaults to saving the selection in your current document. However, you can save it to another document if that document is open and has the exact dimensions as the current document. You can use the Channel field in the Save

Selection dialog box to denote the type of channel you want to create. You select New for a new channel. For an existing channel, you can select the name of the Channel. The Operations options let you create a new selection, add to a selection, subtract from a selection, and intersect with a selection.

You can then save and load your selections.

See also>>   **Tools: Quick mask**

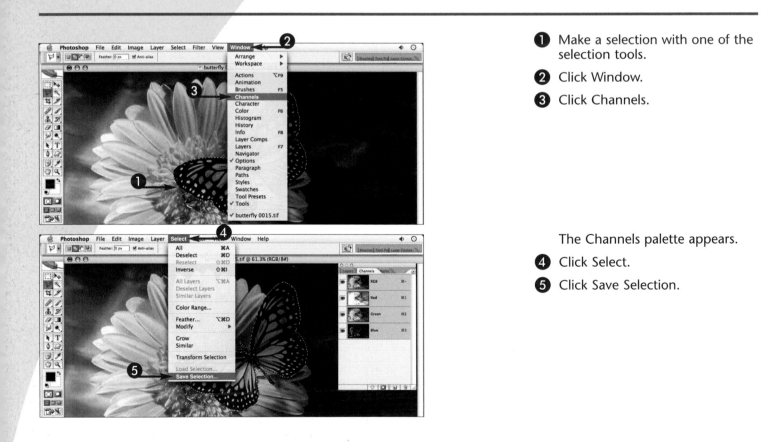

① Make a selection with one of the selection tools.

② Click Window.

③ Click Channels.

The Channels palette appears.

④ Click Select.

⑤ Click Save Selection.

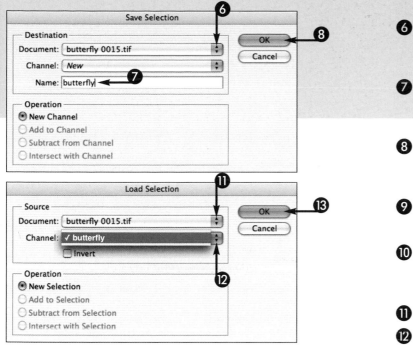

The Save Selection dialog box appears.

6 Click here and select the document where you want to save the selection.

The default is the current open document.

7 Type a name for the new channel.

If you do not name it, it appears in the Channels palette as Alpha 1.

8 Click OK.

The new Alpha channel appears in the Channels palette.

9 Press Cmd+D (Ctrl+D).

The selection is now deselected.

10 Repeat steps **4** and **5**, but click Load Selection in step 5.

The Load Selection dialog box appears.

11 Click here and select a document.

12 Click here and select the channel you created earlier.

13 Click OK.

Photoshop loads your selections.

TIPS

Did You Know?

You can save a selection as a new Alpha channel by clicking the Save Selection As Channel icon. You can also load a selection by clicking the Alpha channel that corresponds to your selection and then clicking the Load Selection icon. Both icons are at the bottom of the Channels palette.

Did You Know?

If you save a selection, you can edit the channel with which it is associated. Just make a selection; click Select and then Save Selection. The Save Selection dialog box appears. Select the name of the Channel from the fly-out menu. At the bottom of the dialog box, you can select one of four options: Replace Channel, Add to Channel, Subtract from Channel, and Intersect with Channel.

CHANNELS, COLOR:
Make a Difficult Selection Using Color Channels

You can use the channels information of an image to isolate and select areas that are difficult to select in the composite channel. For example, an RGB image has three color channels. If you examine each of the channels you find that besides representing different colors, the light/dark values in each of the channels are different. You can exploit this difference in the values and color to make selections. For example, extracting a person from an image with a very complicated background may seem daunting.

However, after examining each of the channels, you may find that in one of the channels the background is nearly obliterated by light. You can use this channel to make a selection.

Once you identify the channel that is most helpful in making the selection, you duplicate it. You then use the copy to create a quick mask. Once you have this general selection, you can use painting tools, color adjustments, and filters to tweak the selection.

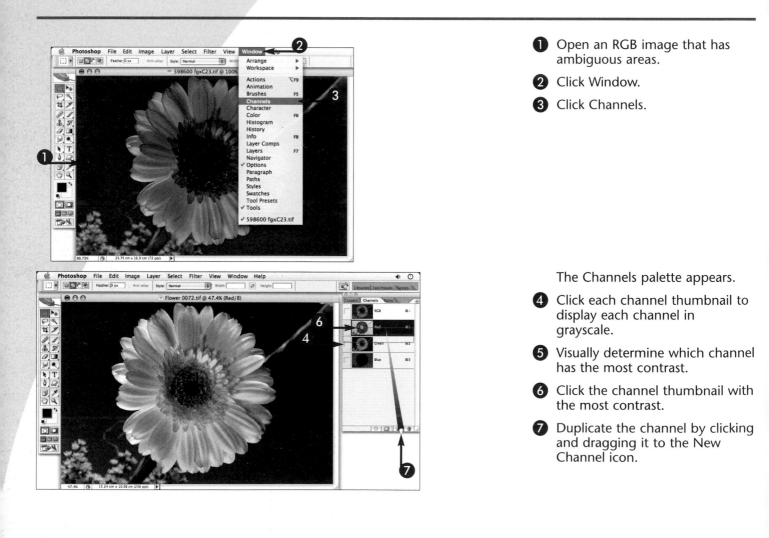

① Open an RGB image that has ambiguous areas.

② Click Window.

③ Click Channels.

The Channels palette appears.

④ Click each channel thumbnail to display each channel in grayscale.

⑤ Visually determine which channel has the most contrast.

⑥ Click the channel thumbnail with the most contrast.

⑦ Duplicate the channel by clicking and dragging it to the New Channel icon.

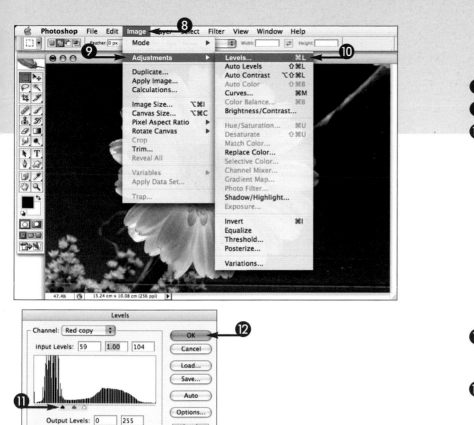

The channel appears in the Channels palette named with the color of the channel and *copy*.

⑧ Click Image.

⑨ Click Adjustments.

⑩ Click Levels.

The Levels dialog box appears.

⑪ Increase the contrast of the channel by dragging the sliders inward.

⑫ Click OK.

Try This!

Another method of selecting difficult areas is by clicking Filter and then Extract. It works well on ambiguous areas, but does not afford the control that the Channels technique offers.

Did You Know?

You can partially select an area within the selection by painting on the Alpha channel with gray.

CHANNELS, COLOR:
Make a Difficult Selection Using Color Channels (Continued)

You can view individual channels to determine which one has more contrast than others. You can then use this channel to make your selection. By applying Levels you can even increase the contrast enough to use the Magic Wand tool. Doing so allows you to make a selection more quickly. In addition, by using the Magic Wand, you can select details, such as hair, feathers, or petals, so that you do not have to spend hours trying to outline the fine details.

When you complete your selection, you can apply it to the image and throw away the new channel. However, if you anticipate using the selection again, you can save the selection as an Alpha channel, which is a channel specifically designed for saving whose functions saving selections.

You may still need to tweak your selection and make it more precise by using the various selection and painting tools that Photoshop has to offer.

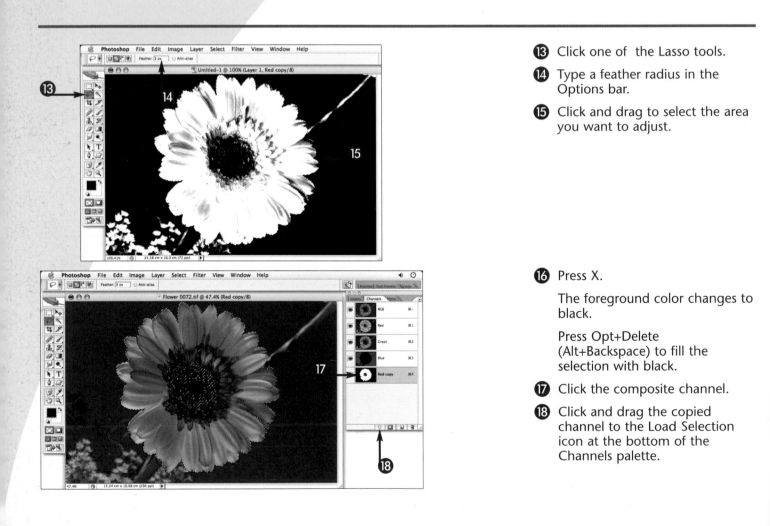

⑬ Click one of the Lasso tools.

⑭ Type a feather radius in the Options bar.

⑮ Click and drag to select the area you want to adjust.

⑯ Press X.

The foreground color changes to black.

Press Opt+Delete (Alt+Backspace) to fill the selection with black.

⑰ Click the composite channel.

⑱ Click and drag the copied channel to the Load Selection icon at the bottom of the Channels palette.

The new Alpha channel loads as a selection.

⑲ Select an operation to apply to the selection, such as adjusting the hue and saturation.

⑳ Press Cmd(Ctrl)+D to deselect.

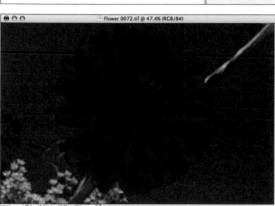

The adjustment is applied to the selection.

TIPS

Did You Know?

The feather radius in step **14** is affected by resolution of the image and determines the amount of the selection that is masked.

Try This!

Do not just use Levels to increase contrast. Try other adjustments, such as Brightness and Contrast, Curves, or Threshold. They may produce better results.

Try This!

The most difficult and critical part of creating a mask is defining a precise edge. Zoom in and carefully paint right up to the edge with a small brush. You can use gray to paint areas that are blending into each other to add opacity for better blending. You can also have one of the Blur filters blur edges and give the selection a slight feather.

CHANNELS, SPOT COLOR:
Add a Spot of Color to Your Image

You can designate solid-color inks to an image with Spot Color channels. Spot colors are additional inks used in a print job other than black or process colors. The inks can be independently printed, or overprinted on top of a grayscale or CMYK image. Each spot color requires a plate of its own. Spot Color channels are independent of the color mode of the image. They are not part of the composite channel in a grayscale, RGB, CMYK, or LAB image. Spot Color channels are also independent of layers.

You can overlay spot colors on top of an image so that they mix with the underlying color and tint it. You can apply it as a solid color or you can knock out the tonal image and replace it with the spot color.

If you do not want your spot color to overprint another spot color or a part of the underlying image, you can create a *knockout*. A knockout prevents ink from printing on part of the image so the spot color can print directly on the paper.

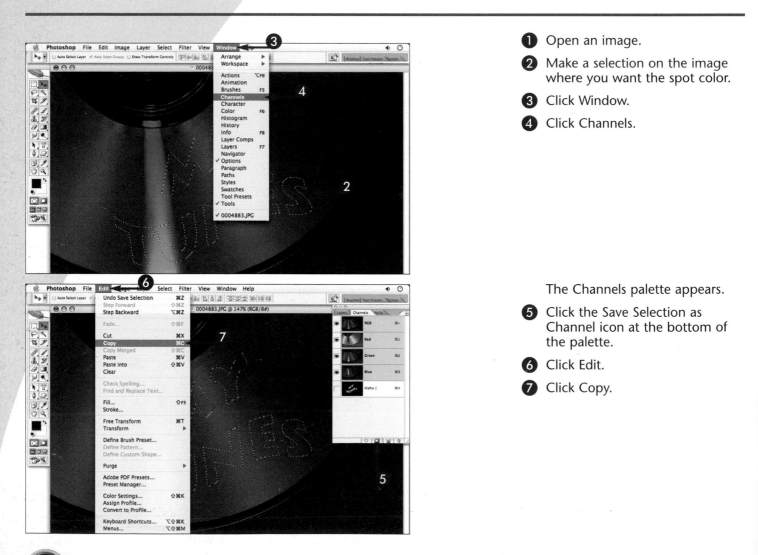

1. Open an image.
2. Make a selection on the image where you want the spot color.
3. Click Window.
4. Click Channels.

The Channels palette appears.

5. Click the Save Selection as Channel icon at the bottom of the palette.
6. Click Edit.
7. Click Copy.

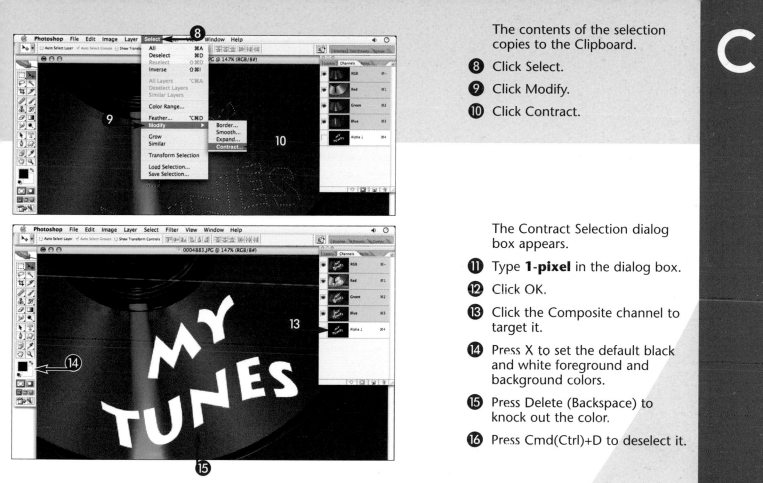

The contents of the selection copies to the Clipboard.

8 Click Select.

9 Click Modify.

10 Click Contract.

The Contract Selection dialog box appears.

11 Type **1-pixel** in the dialog box.

12 Click OK.

13 Click the Composite channel to target it.

14 Press X to set the default black and white foreground and background colors.

15 Press Delete (Backspace) to knock out the color.

16 Press Cmd(Ctrl)+D to deselect it.

TIPS

Tip:
If you want to use and preserve spot channels in an image that you know other programs will use, convert your image to DCS2 Format. InDesign does not recognize spot colors saved in PSD, EPS, or PDF formats.

Caution!
To ensure that your output is consistent, make sure you update your color swatches. What you see on the screen or at your personal printer may not accurately reflect the output received from a printer.

Did You Know?
You can save up to 56 channels in an image. This does not mean that you should, however. Depending on the amount of information stored in each channel, your file size may increase to a point where neither the memory nor disk in your computer can support your image.

CHANNELS, SPOT COLOR:
Add a Spot of Color to Your Image (Continued)

You can also use spot color to create varnish plates. Varnishes are simply translucent inks and, when working in Photoshop, you should treat them as another custom or spot color. They can be applied to highlight parts of an image, or to coat the image with a glossy surface. Sometimes gloss and matte varnishes are used in concert to enhance and emphasize pictures in an image.

You can also use spot color channels to create die cuts. Dies are shaped forms used to cut paper to produce a print job in a particular shape for packaging, for example, or to produce a specifically

shaped hole in a piece of paper — like a stencil. You can create precise shapes by using spot color channels; you can then print those shapes as negatives, which you can then use to create the die. You can also use spot color channels to create embossing dies that can add depth and dimension to a print job.

On higher end print jobs, you often see a spot color added to a CMYK print job to add areas of rich color. These jobs are usually run on printing presses that can print six colors at a time.

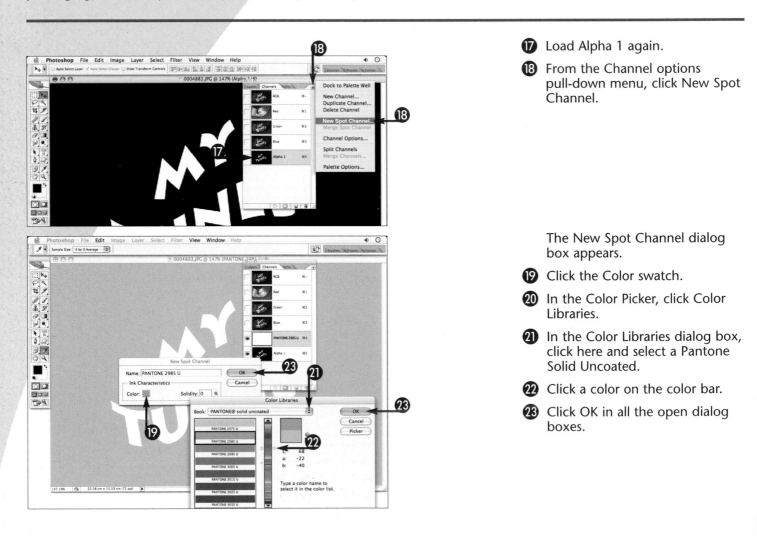

⑰ Load Alpha 1 again.

⑱ From the Channel options pull-down menu, click New Spot Channel.

The New Spot Channel dialog box appears.

⑲ Click the Color swatch.

⑳ In the Color Picker, click Color Libraries.

㉑ In the Color Libraries dialog box, click here and select a Pantone Solid Uncoated.

㉒ Click a color on the color bar.

㉓ Click OK in all the open dialog boxes.

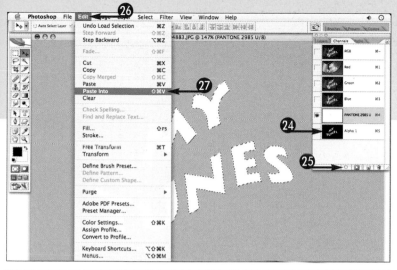

24 Press Cmd (Ctrl) and click the Spot Color channel to select it.

25 Click the Load Channel as Selection icon.

26 Click Edit.

27 Click Paste Into.

The image pastes into the selection.

28 Click the Eye icon next to the Alpha channel to hide it.

29 Click the Composite Channel.

When you print the image, the spot color slightly overlaps the color underneath.

TIPS

Did You Know?

Typing a value in the Solidity box lets you control the viewing density of the Spot Color channel. The Solidity control is for visual reference only. It is there to help you visualize how an ink may appear when printed in a tint value from 0 percent to 100 percent.

Try This!

If you want the spot color ink to print as a solid tint, create a gray selection in the Spot Color channel instead of using black. Spot color inks always print full intensity unless your selection mask in the Spot Color channel itself contains a gradation or tint. Printing inks are usually transparent. When printed over the image, the spot color mixes with colors underneath it.

COLOR MODE:
Bitmap: Convert a Grayscale to a Halftone

You can convert a grayscale image to bitmap, the simplest of all color modes, to reduce an image's colors to two — either 100% black or 100% white. This is perfect when you do not need detail and you have large patches of dark and light. The bit depth of a bitmap image is 1 bit per pixel. Because of this, the file size of bitmap images is much smaller than that of other color modes.

One of the options available under the Convert Grayscale images is the halftone method. Halftone simulates the shading you find in impressionistic

paintings. It converts shaded pixels to black. Then it uses close concentrations of dots for darker areas and more sparse scatterings of dots for lighter areas.

You can use and edit a bitmap image in other applications, such as InDesign and QuarkXpress, because it gives an almost duotone impression without the added file size.

Certain tools are not available in the Bitmap mode, so you may need to convert your image to grayscale if you need to perform edits such as apply Filters or Transform functions.

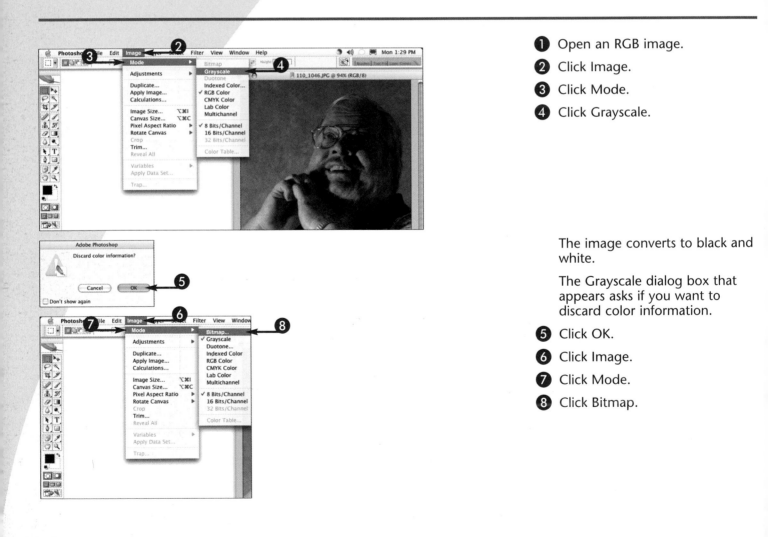

① Open an RGB image.

② Click Image.

③ Click Mode.

④ Click Grayscale.

The image converts to black and white.

The Grayscale dialog box that appears asks if you want to discard color information.

⑤ Click OK.

⑥ Click Image.

⑦ Click Mode.

⑧ Click Bitmap.

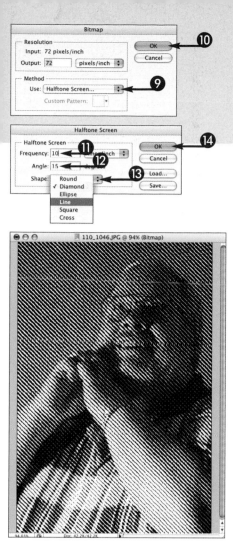

The Bitmap dialog box appears.

9 Click here and select Halftone Screen.

10 Click OK.

The Halftone Screen dialog box appears.

11 Type a frequency.

12 Click here and select an angle.

13 Click here and select a shape.

14 Click OK.

The grayscale is changed to a halftone.

C

TIPS

Did You Know?

Do not confuse Bitmap color mode with the general term *bitmap*, which refers to images that are composed of pixels as opposed to vector-based graphics that use lines and objects to define shapes. Bitmap images are also referred to as Raster images. Also keep in mind that the bitmap file format — .bmp — is only one of several file formats available for saving image files.

Caution!

You cannot convert an image directly from Bitmap mode to any color mode other than grayscale. If you want to add color to a bitmap image, you must first convert it to grayscale. From there you can proceed to any of the other color modes.

COLOR MODE, CMYK:
Convert an RGB Image to CMYK

Because most designers and artists prefer to work in RBG, you find many more Photoshop adjustments and filters available to RGB than to any other. However, most commercial printers use CMYK as a print color mode. This means that, before sending a project to a printer, an artist must convert an RGB to CMYK. CMYK is also referred to as four-color process. This method of defining color involves four channels, one for each of the color inks used: C, Cyan; M, Magenta; Y, Yellow; and K, Black. In contrast, RGB is the color mode used in computer monitors, scanners, and television screens.

CMYK is known as a subtractive process — that is, as the amount of color increases, light is subtracted. In other words, the darker the color desired, the more ink must be used to cover the paper. Full-intensity CMYK creates a dense black. RGB, on the other hand, is an additive process of creating color— the more light you add, the brighter your colors become. Full-intensity RGB equals white light.

See also>> **Techniques: Proof Colors/ Preview CMYK**

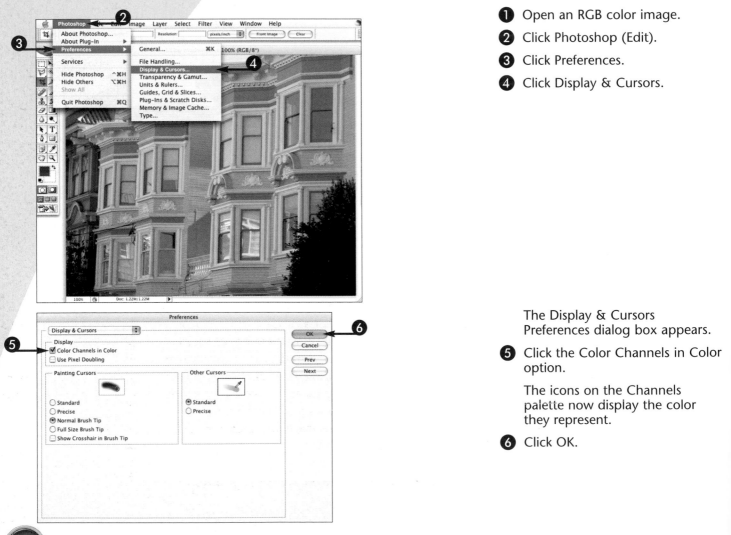

① Open an RGB color image.

② Click Photoshop (Edit).

③ Click Preferences.

④ Click Display & Cursors.

The Display & Cursors Preferences dialog box appears.

⑤ Click the Color Channels in Color option.

The icons on the Channels palette now display the color they represent.

⑥ Click OK.

⑦ Click Image.

⑧ Click Mode.

⑨ Click CMYK Color.

The Channels palette appears and displays channels for Composite, Cyan, Magenta, Yellow, and Black.

⑩ Click each channel's icon, one at a time, to display them individually on the image window.

Each channel represents the separations that are used in printing.

TIPS

Did You Know?

The range of colors a particular color mode can produce is called its *gamut*. RGB color has a wider range — a wider gamut — of colors than CMYK. This means that certain colors you create using RGB mode may not reproduce exactly in CMYK. Use the Gamut warning, which you access by clicking View, and then Gamut Warning, to view the Out-of-Gamut colors.

Try This!

Due to the nature of the color modes, CMYK colors almost always look less brilliant and vivid than RGB colors. Because of this, you may want to keep your images in RGB mode up until the time your document is printed. This way you can keep the brightest colors in your image for needs other than printing.

COLOR MODE DUOTONE:
Convert a Grayscale Image to Duotone

Duotones can help you achieve a wider tonal range than Grayscale or Bitmap mode. When you convert a grayscale image to a Halftone and then print it, the result is only an approximation of gray tones. When a printer prints Halftone it squirts black dots on a page with denser concentrations of dots indicating black, and sparser concentrations white. No matter what the concentration of dots, the printer cannot achieve all 256 levels of gray in the grayscale image. By using more than one shade of ink, you can fill in the gaps.

You can enhance the detail and texture in an image by using duotone. If you print a two-color book with halftones, you can include a second color in the halftones to add an elegant touch. Duotones using dark and metallic ink can impart an opaque, antique quality, while lighter pastel shades may approximate a hand-tinted image.

In Photoshop's Duotone Options dialog box you can apply from one to four colors of ink. By adjusting duotone curves, you can precisely control their distribution.

See also>>　**Adjustments: Curves**

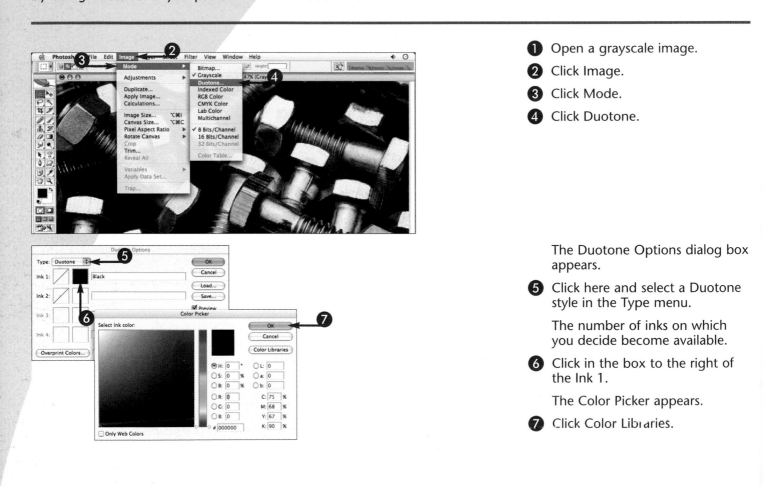

1. Open a grayscale image.
2. Click Image.
3. Click Mode.
4. Click Duotone.

The Duotone Options dialog box appears.

5. Click here and select a Duotone style in the Type menu.

   The number of inks on which you decide become available.

6. Click in the box to the right of the Ink 1.

   The Color Picker appears.

7. Click Color Libraries.

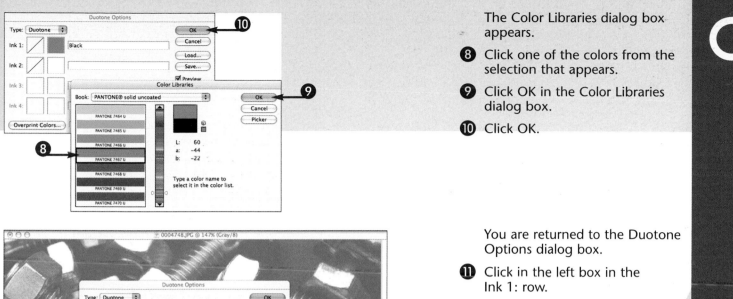

The Color Libraries dialog box appears.

8 Click one of the colors from the selection that appears.

9 Click OK in the Color Libraries dialog box.

10 Click OK.

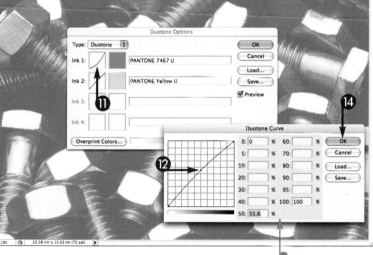

You are returned to the Duotone Options dialog box.

11 Click in the left box in the Ink 1: row.

The Duotone Curve dialog box appears.

12 Click and drag the curve to adjust the ink distribution.

● You can also type alternate values to adjust the ink distribution.

13 Repeat steps **6** to **8** for each additional color.

14 Click OK.

The grayscale image now converts to a duotone.

TIPS

Caution!
Because two or more inks are being superimposed on one another, it is possible to generate too much ink. Improper distribution of ink can saturate the paper and fill in the spaces between the fine halftone dots. Adjust the curves accordingly so that light areas are dominated by light ink, midtone areas are dominated by midcolor ink, and shadows are dominated by dark ink.

Caution!
Because RGB simulations represent solid-color inks, they are often inaccurate. Always look at color chips available for custom colors.

Caution!
Although, metallic inks can create mysterious antique effects that can improve an image's punch, stay away from swaths of solid metallic ink. These inks are generally quite opaque, and are best used in moderation.

COLOR MODE: GRAYSCALE:
Convert a Color Image to Black and White

Because color is not always the most effective way to present an image, you can convert color images to grayscale, what most people call black-and-white images. A grayscale image is composed of one channel with 256 possible shades of gray. Each pixel has a brightness value that can range from 0 (or black) to 255 (white). Sometimes grayscale pixels are measured in percentages of black ink from 0 percent, white, to 100 percent, black. When color images are converted to grayscale, their hue and saturation information is discarded, while *luminosity* values remain intact.

When you convert from color to grayscale, images may lose contrast. You can improve contrast by using any of several adjustment tools, such as Levels and Curves. You can also make adjustments prior to converting by using the Channel Mixer command's Monochrome option.

The best grayscale images have a wide range of values from pure white to absolute black. Depending on how you plan to print these images, you may want to trim the overall range from 5 to 10 percent on either extreme.

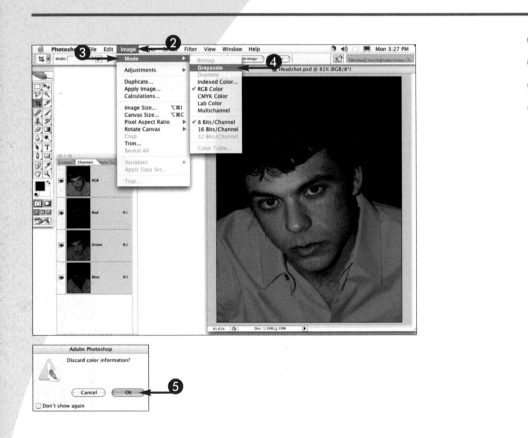

① Open a color image.

② Click Image.

③ Click Mode.

④ Click Grayscale.

The Grayscale dialog box appears.

⑤ Click OK when asked if you want to discard color information.

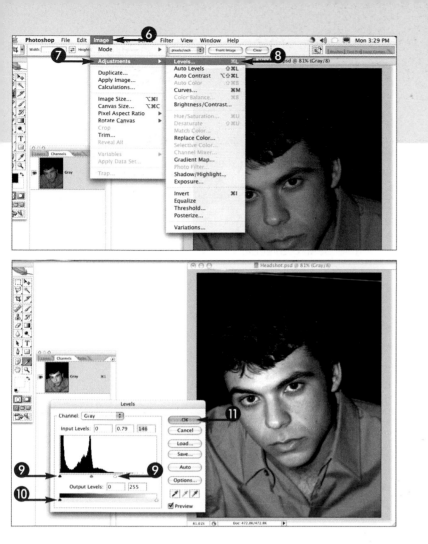

6 Click Image.

7 Click Adjust.

8 Click Levels.

The Levels dialog box appears.

9 Click and drag the Input Levels sliders inward to improve the contrast.

10 Click and drag the Output Levels sliders to darken or brighten the image as needed.

11 Click OK.

The image is converted to black and white.

TIPS

Try This!
You can use the Channel Mixer adjustment to preview and adjust settings prior to converting to grayscale. Start with an RGB image. Click Image, click Adjustments, and then click Channel Mixer. Click the Monochrome option, and click and drag the Color and Constant sliders to balance the tonality. Click OK and then convert to grayscale.

Try This!
Scan in 16-bit grayscale to produce smoother black-and-white transitions. This produces more shades of gray, which makes the image appear to have more depth. The file's size increases, however.

Warning!
When your convert a color image into grayscale, you lose all color information. Once you save and close the image, you cannot undo the operation. Make a backup copy of your color image.

COLOR MODE, INDEX:
Reduce the Number of Colors in an Image for the Web

You can convert your images to Indexed color for publication to the Web. Indexed color mode uses a maximum of 256 colors to display full-color images. However, you can select fewer colors thereby greatly reducing the file size. When you convert an image color to the Indexed mode, Photoshop stores the color information as a color look-up table (CLUT) — that is a swatch library. You can then use a specific palette to display the image to remap the colors as closely as possible to the original. Because they

contains fewer colors, Indexed color files are smaller than other color mode files. An advantage when publishing files to the Web or to multimedia applications.

Indexed color is the default color mode used when saving a file as GIF (Graphic Interchange Format) or as PNG8 (Portable Network Graphic). Your files are automatically converted when you select the Save for Web option.

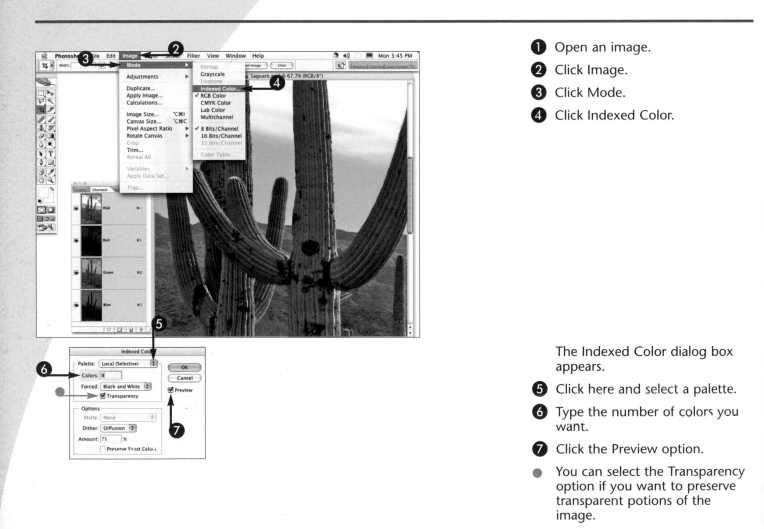

① Open an image.

② Click Image.

③ Click Mode.

④ Click Indexed Color.

The Indexed Color dialog box appears.

⑤ Click here and select a palette.

⑥ Type the number of colors you want.

⑦ Click the Preview option.

● You can select the Transparency option if you want to preserve transparent potions of the image.

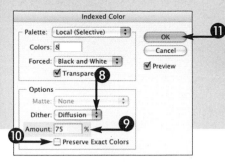

8 Click here and select a dither option.

9 Type a dither amount.

10 Click the Preserve Exact Colors option to avoid remapping colors.

11 Click OK.

The Channels palette displays one indexed channel.

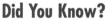

TIPS

Did You Know?

You can perform some of same operations by clicking File and then Save for Web. The Save For Web dialog box actually looks like a trimmed down version of ImageReady. In fact, the dialog box title is "Save for Web – Powered By ImageReady." You can preview different versions of the file, select different optimization options, and access some of the same tools. If you find the interface too limited, you have to click the Edit in Photoshop or Edit in ImageReady icons.

Try This!

View the image as you type the number of colors for your image. The fewer the colors, the smaller the file size, and the faster it loads. A more efficient file may not be the most attractive file. Your mission is to find that optimum point where quantity and quality are evenly balanced.

COLOR MODE, LAB:
Isolate Luminosity Information

You can convert your files to Lab mode to take advantage of the luminosity information. This gives you a wider spectrum of colors from which to choose. The CIE Lab color mode is an international color measurement system developed in 1931 by the International Commission on Illumination (Commission Internacionale de l'Éclairage, or CIE). Lab color consists of three channels — L, a luminance or lightness channel; a, a green-red component; and b, a blue-yellow component.

RGB and CMYK are *device dependent*. The RGB color mode is designed for monitors; CMYK is designed for printers. No matter what approximation the printer or monitor attempt, you experience quality loss. Lab color is *device independent*, with the color model based on the perception of the human eye rather than a mechanical ink or light system. A lab image can go between systems and devices without vibrancy or tonal loss.

To create a Lab color in the Color Picker, specify values from 0 to 100 in the *L* channel to control the lightness or luminosity information, and values from -127 to +128 in the a and b channels to control the color information. With the Lightness channel isolated, you can perform brightness and contrast adjustments without color shifts.

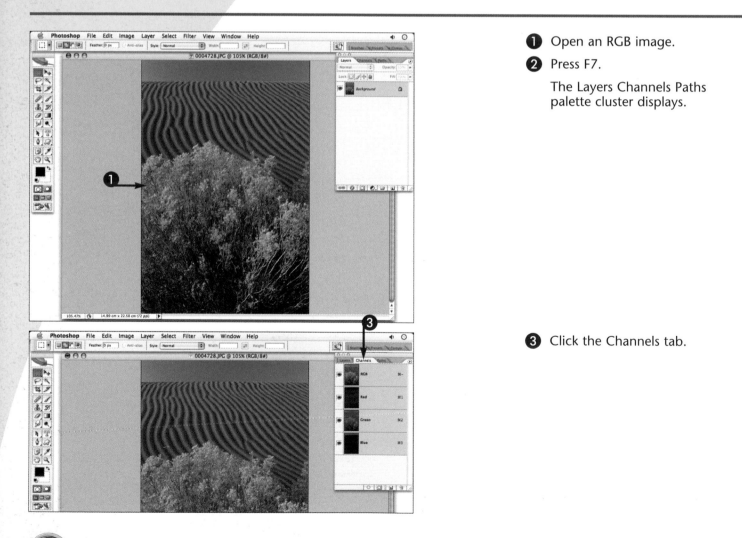

❶ Open an RGB image.

❷ Press F7.

The Layers Channels Paths palette cluster displays.

❸ Click the Channels tab.

218

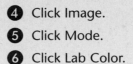

4 Click Image.

5 Click Mode.

6 Click Lab Color.

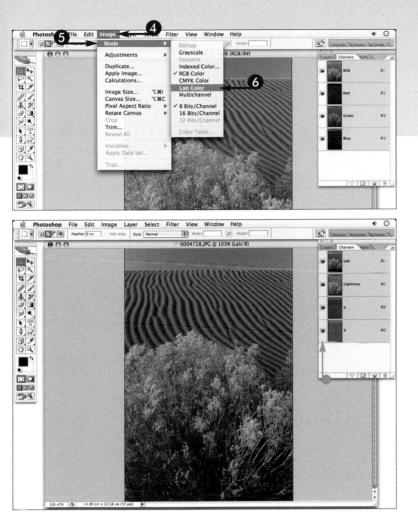

The file is converted to Lab Color.

● In the Channels palette, you can click the Eye icons next to each channel to observe their colors.

TIPS

Try This!
An advantage of editing images in Lab mode is that unlike other color models, you can use sharpening commands without creating artifacts. Because the color information is separate from the brightness information, you can sharpen in the Lightness channel without affecting color.

Try This!
Click Edit, click Preferences, and then click Display & Cursors. Select the Color Channels in Color option. This allows you to see the Lab color content in the Channels palette.

Did You Know?
Lab mode is the intermediate color mode Photoshop uses when it converts from one color mode to another.

COLOR MODE, MULTICHANNEL:
Separate Duotones

You can use Multichannel mode to convert a Duotone image into separate color channels for the purpose of analyzing an image's color information.

The Multichannel mode allows you to view inks you assign to Duotone images by creating a channel for each ink. Unlike the RGB and CMYK color models, which display a separate channel for each of their color components, Duotone shows you only one channel. This makes sense, because Duotones start out as grayscale images, which also have only one channel. To view the Duotone inks you have

assigned, you need to convert your Duotone images to Multichannel mode.

Multichannel mode splits the Duotone, Tritone, or Quadtone into the two, three, or four channel ink colors you have assigned. If you make any changes or adjustments in Multichannel mode, you cannot return to Duotone mode. You can print directly from Multichannel mode. Each channel is treated just like CMYK color separations — a different printing plate for each color. The advantage of using Multichannel is that you can edit the three channels independently.

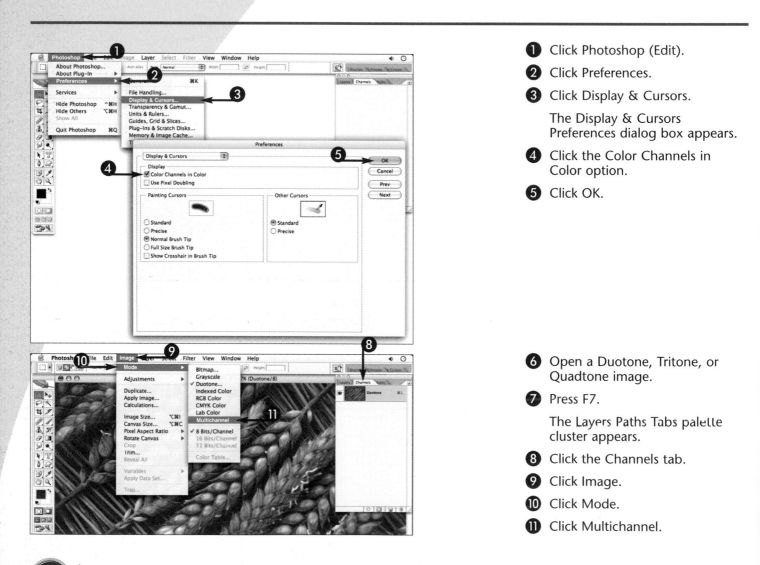

❶ Click Photoshop (Edit).

❷ Click Preferences.

❸ Click Display & Cursors.

The Display & Cursors Preferences dialog box appears.

❹ Click the Color Channels in Color option.

❺ Click OK.

❻ Open a Duotone, Tritone, or Quadtone image.

❼ Press F7.

The Layers Paths Tabs palette cluster appears.

❽ Click the Channels tab.

❾ Click Image.

❿ Click Mode.

⓫ Click Multichannel.

The file is converted to individual color channels.

C

⑫ In the Channels palette, click the Eye icons next to each channel to observe its colors.

You see what colors make up your Duotone image.

COLOR SETTINGS:
Choose a Profile

To ensure consistent color management, Photoshop lets you assign color profiles to each of your devices — monitor, printer, or scanner. You do not need to set these for each document. In fact, unless you change you hardware, you should only have to set profiles when you first install your Adobe software.

The Color Setting dialog box has menus from which you can define settings appropriate to your environment. The Color Settings dialog box controls your Color Working Space and attaches a profile to simulate on-screen how your image looks when you print it to or view it on a particular device. You can also set Color Management Policies that control what happens when Photoshop opens an image that either has no embedded profile or has one that is different from the current color working space.

First, set your Color Settings defaults according to the kind of work you do. If you are unsure, a good place to start is with North American Prepress 2, which includes the Adobe RGB (1998) color space and U.S. Web Coated (SWOP) v2. This is a good space for both RGB and CMYK colors.

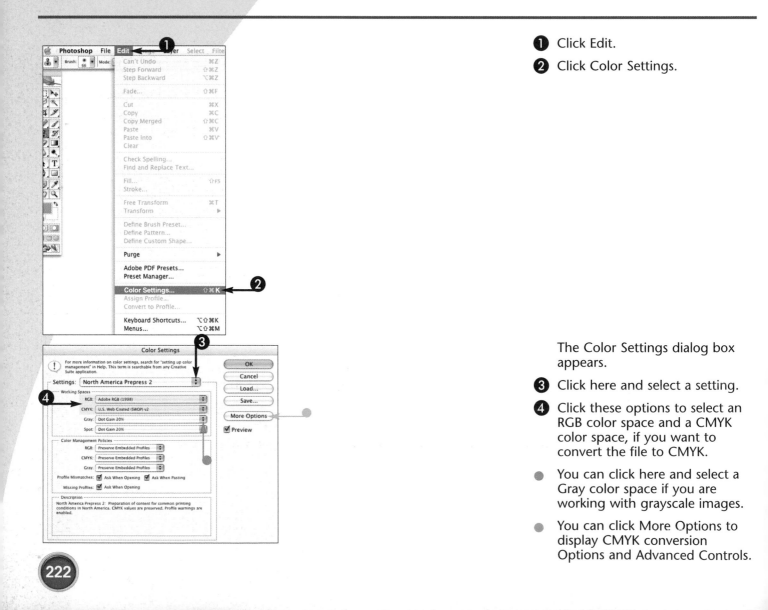

① Click Edit.

② Click Color Settings.

The Color Settings dialog box appears.

③ Click here and select a setting.

④ Click these options to select an RGB color space and a CMYK color space, if you want to convert the file to CMYK.

● You can click here and select a Gray color space if you are working with grayscale images.

● You can click More Options to display CMYK conversion Options and Advanced Controls.

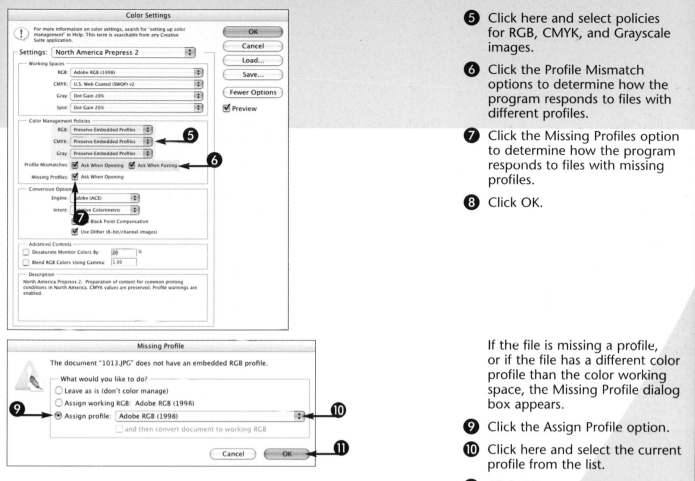

⑤ Click here and select policies for RGB, CMYK, and Grayscale images.

⑥ Click the Profile Mismatch options to determine how the program responds to files with different profiles.

⑦ Click the Missing Profiles option to determine how the program responds to files with missing profiles.

⑧ Click OK.

If the file is missing a profile, or if the file has a different color profile than the color working space, the Missing Profile dialog box appears.

⑨ Click the Assign Profile option.

⑩ Click here and select the current profile from the list.

⑪ Click OK.

The document opens into the current color working space.

TIPS

Did You Know?

Any change to the defaults creates a custom setting. You can save your custom settings with a new name by clicking Save, and your settings remain intact until you change to another setting.

Did You Know?

Color Settings can be difficult to understand. Fortunately, when you place your cursor on a feature, the description at the bottom of the dialog box offers an explanation. For more help, visit the Help menu at the top of the screen.

DESATURATE:
Remove Color from an Image

You can easily convert a color image into a grayscale image. Although there are several ways to remove color from an image or a portion of an image, the Desaturate command is the fastest. No dialog box appears when you use this command; rather, you instantaneously convert an image's pixels to black, white, or shades of gray.

When you use the Desaturate command rather than the Grayscale mode command, the image retains its definition as a color image. This allows you to apply color to the black-and-white image. This is a handy feature if, for example, you wanted to create a sepia tone image of an old photo.

Other features in Photoshop produce the same results — the Saturation slider in the Hue/Saturation dialog box, the Desaturate option of the Sponge tool, and the Gradient Map option. The advantage of using the Desaturation command is that you do not need to provide or know additional information to produce a black and white image.

The example in this section emphasizes the skier in this picture by removing color from the surrounding area.

See also>>

Grayscale

Adjustments:
Channel Mixer

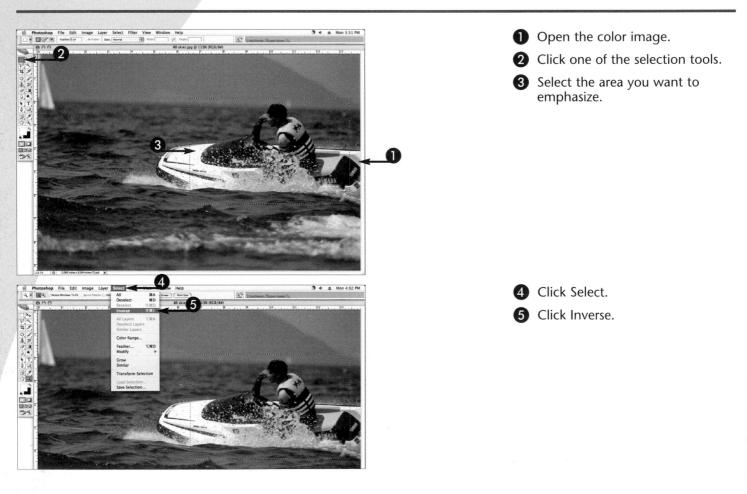

① Open the color image.

② Click one of the selection tools.

③ Select the area you want to emphasize.

④ Click Select.

⑤ Click Inverse.

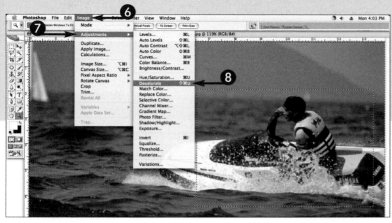

This selects the inverse of the image (the area you want to decolorize).

6 Click Image.

7 Click Adjustments.

8 Click Desaturate.

The area surrounding what you selected in step **3** is now black and white.

TIPS

Did You Know?
When you desaturate an image, you assign equal values to the Red, Green, and Blue pixels thus producing gray. For example, the value of medium gray is 128 Red, 128 Green, and 128 Blue. The disparity in numbers between colors actually creates color because it emphasizes the colors with the highest values.

Try This!
You can press Shift+Cmd+U (Shift+Ctrl+U) for instant desaturation!

DUPLICATE:
Make a Copy of an Image

You can make an exact copy of your image and open it in the workspace. The Duplicate command is an excellent way to create an instant "scratch" image that you can experiment with without fear of damaging the original. You can also use this command to create multiple versions of an image.

You can assign a unique name for your duplicated image in the Duplicate Image dialog box. By default, Photoshop places the original name of the image plus the word "copy" on the duplicate image, but you can change this. Your duplicated image has all of the

characteristics of the original including the height, width, resolution, and color mode plus any layers, channels, paths, or annotations that you may have created. The only thing that is not duplicated is the original image's history.

Duplicating an image does not guarantee that Photoshop automatically saves it, so remember to save the copy of your image before proceeding.

See also>> **Save As**

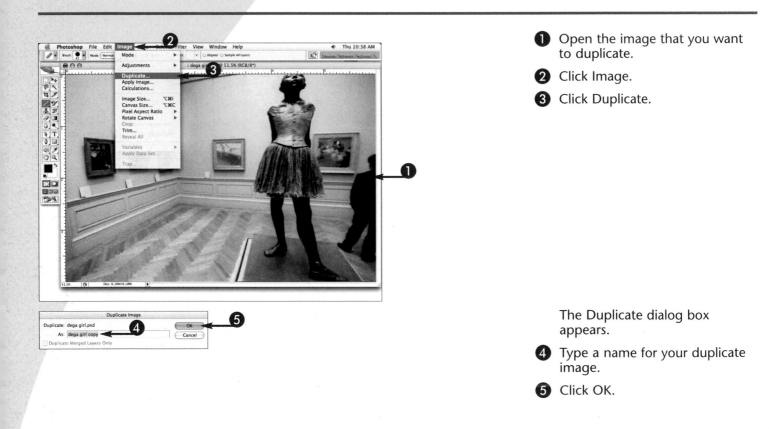

① Open the image that you want to duplicate.

② Click Image.

③ Click Duplicate.

The Duplicate dialog box appears.

④ Type a name for your duplicate image.

⑤ Click OK.

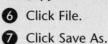

The dialog box opens a second window containing an exact copy with a different name.

6 Click **File**.

7 Click **Save As**.

The Save As dialog box appears.

8 Navigate to the area on your hard drive where you want to save your file.

9 Click **Save**.

Photoshop saves your image.

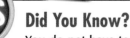

TIPS

Did You Know?
You do not have to add the file extension when you name the document. By default, Photoshop does that for you in both Windows and Macintosh platforms.

Caution!
Be sure to name the document clearly and with a different name than the original. It is very easy to work on the wrong image, especially when you have several images open in the workspace.

Did You Know?
You can create a duplicate of your file in another format. In the Save As dialog box you can select a different format for your file from the Format menu. Choices include TIFF, JPEG, Photoshop, EPS, and others. Photoshop has all these choices because it knows you may want to share an image with someone who requests a specific type of file.

EDIT IN:
Jump to ImageReady

ImageReady is an application bundled with Photoshop that allows you to edit images and create objects intended for use on the Web. ImageReady can optimize images, slice an image to create buttons or other Web objects, create animated clips, and preview images in a default browser. Although it is not as powerful as a dedicated Web authoring program, you can use ImageReady to create impressive Web sites.

ImageReady has many of the features, commands, and options that you find in Photoshop. Although it

acts and feels like a mini Photoshop, ImageReady's main focus is creating optimized images and objects for use on the Web.

You can access ImageReady via the Edit In ImageReady icon at the bottom of the Tools palette. Likewise, ImageReady has an Edit In Photoshop icon so that you can easily toggle back and forth between the two applications. This icon launches ImageReady and opens the current Photoshop image. Once you launch ImageReady, you can easily edit and optimize the image for publication to the Web.

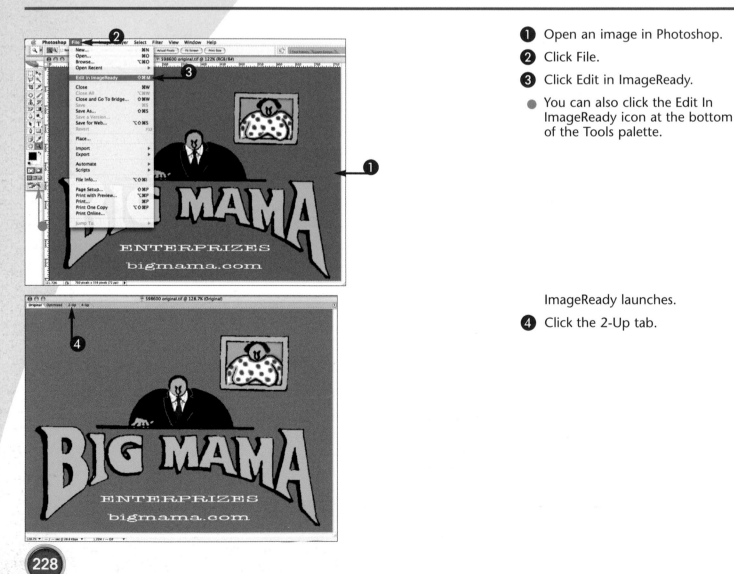

① Open an image in Photoshop.

② Click File.

③ Click Edit in ImageReady.

● You can also click the Edit In ImageReady icon at the bottom of the Tools palette.

ImageReady launches.

④ Click the 2-Up tab.

Two versions of your image appear; one is the original and the second shows what your image looks like when converted to one of the Web-compatible formats.

● The information at the bottom of the second screen shows you the size of the file as well as how long it takes the image to load in a browser.

⑤ Click the Edit in Photoshop icon at the bottom of the Tools palette.

Photoshop becomes active again.

TIPS

Did You Know?
You can toggle between Photoshop and ImageReady by pressing Shift+Cmd+M (Shift+Ctrl+M).

Did You Know?
ImageReady is great for creating fast Web pages with simple interactive elements. If you are looking for more sophisticated software, Dreamweaver and GoLive are excellent tools for building and managing Web sites.

Did You Know?
If you create Web sites on a regular basis, you will find Hypertext Markup Language (HTML) helpful. Programs that produce Web pages usually create what the pros call *heavy code*, or code with extra and unnecessary elements. A basic knowledge of HTML can help you streamline the code that programs like ImageReady generate.

FADE:
Fade an Effect

If after applying a tool, filter, or adjustment you find the result too strong, you can change the opacity or use a blend mode to soften the effect. Both are options you find in the Fade command dialog box. The Fade command adjusts the last effect you applied as if had been applied through an adjustment layer. However, unlike an adjustment layer, the command is only available immediately after you apply the operation to be faded.

The Fade dialog box contains the same basic options that you find in the Layers palette — that is, you can control Opacity from 1 percent to 100 percent and use any of the blending modes, with the exception of Behind and Clear. You can use the Fade command with all of the adjustments, and most of the filters, painting, and editing tools.

The Fade command is a quick alternative to the opacity and blending controls independent of layers. Of course, if you are completely dissatisfied with the effect, you can undo it or undo part of it by use of the History palette, Undo, or Step Back commands.

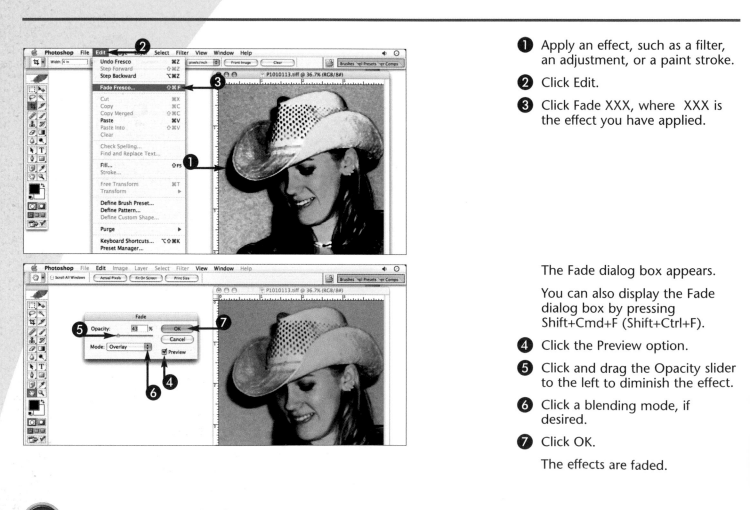

❶ Apply an effect, such as a filter, an adjustment, or a paint stroke.

❷ Click Edit.

❸ Click Fade XXX, where XXX is the effect you have applied.

The Fade dialog box appears.

You can also display the Fade dialog box by pressing Shift+Cmd+F (Shift+Ctrl+F).

❹ Click the Preview option.

❺ Click and drag the Opacity slider to the left to diminish the effect.

❻ Click a blending mode, if desired.

❼ Click OK.

The effects are faded.

FILE INFO:
Attach Data to an Image

You can record and view information about your files using the File Info dialog box. The initial information embedded in files comes from its source — a digital camera, for example — but you can add additional information. You can then use Photoshop, other Adobe products, or other applications that support metadata to view this information. *Metadata* is information about an image, such as copyright, creator, and keywords, which help organize and retrieve a file.

The File Info command can collect and store information in 12 categories. The File Info dialog box displays categories in the left side pane and category specific fields in the right pane.

Categories include Description, Camera Data 1 and 2, Categories, History, IPTC (International Press and Telecommunications Council) Contact, IPTC Content, IPTC Image, IPTC Status, Adobe Stock Photo, Origin, and Advanced. Some fields let you enter information — description, for example — where you can type the title, author, and copyright information. Other fields, such as Camera Data 1 and 2, are not editable because they contain embedded information the image's original source assigns.

See also>>
Techniques, Adobe Bridge

Techniques, History Log

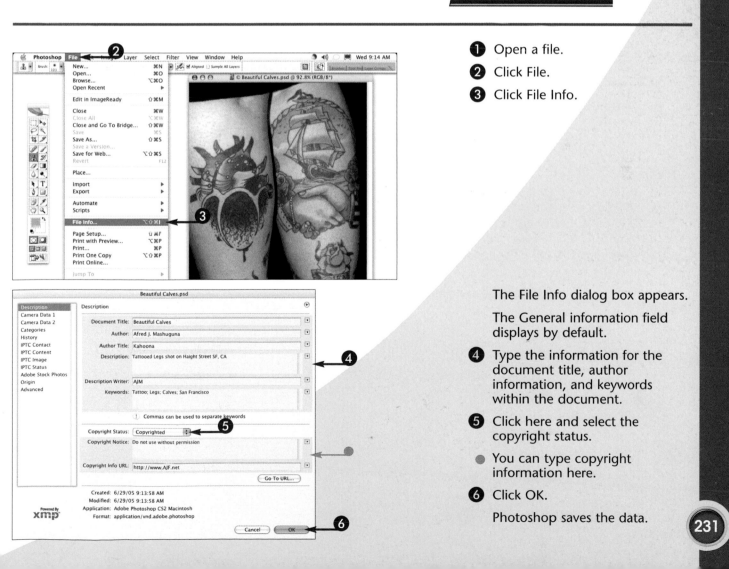

① Open a file.

② Click File.

③ Click File Info.

The File Info dialog box appears.

The General information field displays by default.

④ Type the information for the document title, author information, and keywords within the document.

⑤ Click here and select the copyright status.

● You can type copyright information here.

⑥ Click OK.

Photoshop saves the data.

FILL:
Apply Color to an Area

You can use the Fill Command to change or add color or a pattern to selected pixels. This is useful when you want to apply a color or pattern to a large portion of an image, a task that is tedious when you use a Brush tool. In applying the Fill command, Photoshop provides several ways to adjust the color or pattern.

You can specify the manner in which the Fill command executes by selecting from among several options: Foreground Color fills the selection with the foreground color. Background Color fills the selection

with the current background color. Color displays the Color Picker so that you can select a color. Pattern fills the selection with a pattern from the Pattern menu. History reverts the selection to a targeted state in the History palette. Black fills an RGB value of 0 Red, 0 Green, 0 Blue. 50 percent Gray fills the selection with an RGB value of 128 Red, 128 Green, 128 Blue; White fills the selection with an RGB value of 255 Red, 255 Green, 255 Blue. You can modify all of these options by specifying an Opacity amount and/or a blend mode.

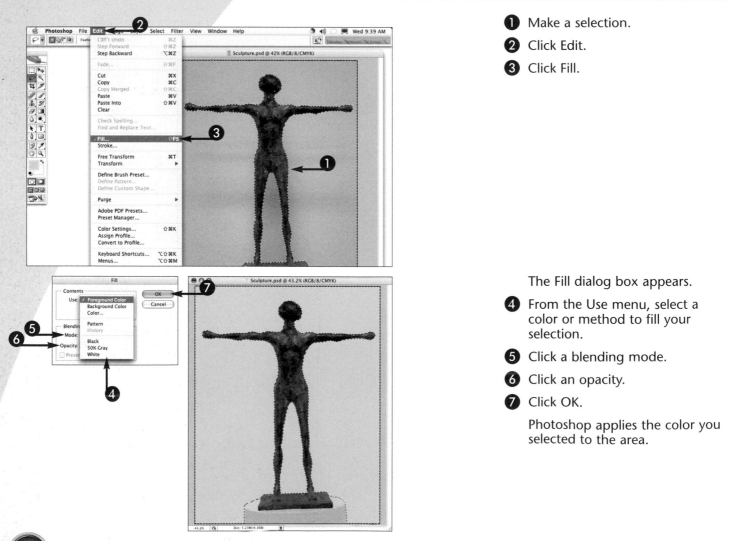

① Make a selection.

② Click Edit.

③ Click Fill.

The Fill dialog box appears.

④ From the Use menu, select a color or method to fill your selection.

⑤ Click a blending mode.

⑥ Click an opacity.

⑦ Click OK.

Photoshop applies the color you selected to the area.

232

FILTER, BLUR:
Blur Parts of an Image

You can soften edges or reduce detail in an image, for example wrinkles, using the 11 individual Blur filters. Average, Blur, and Blur More are fully automated. You select the filter, and Photoshop does the rest without opening dialog boxes. Average fills a selection with the average color of the existing pixels. Blur and Blur More diminish contrast, resulting in softer, smoother edges and transitions. The other eight blur filters present dialog boxes that offer far more control and, with the exception of Radial Blur, a live preview box that lets you view the effect as you apply it.

The Blur dialog boxes contain one or more sliders that let you control the strength, direction, threshold, distance, and so on, depending on the type of blur you select. Sometimes there are also radio buttons or menus that offer a quality setting. The most extensive dialog box is the Lens Blur with several precision controls to produce the effect of depth of field; however, the one probably used most often is the Gaussian Blur filter, which performs overall blurring. It is one simple radius slider that controls the strength of the effect.

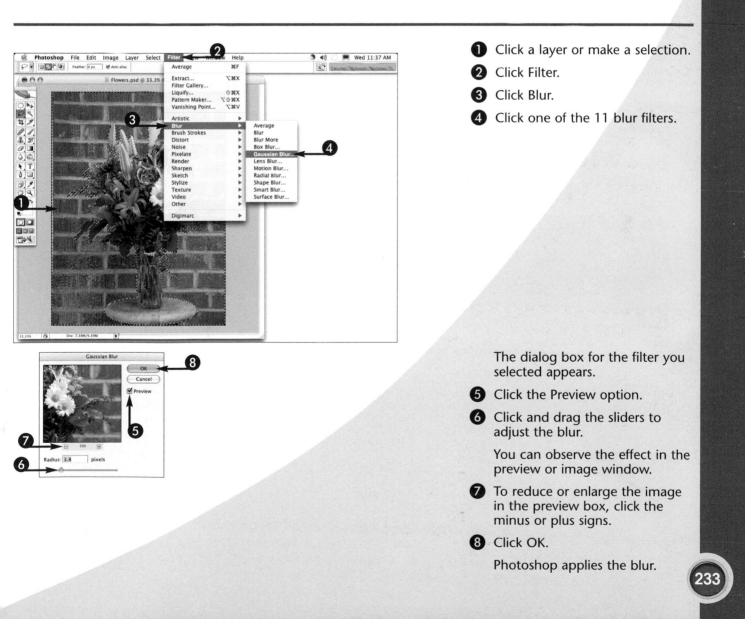

1. Click a layer or make a selection.
2. Click Filter.
3. Click Blur.
4. Click one of the 11 blur filters.

The dialog box for the filter you selected appears.

5. Click the Preview option.
6. Click and drag the sliders to adjust the blur.

   You can observe the effect in the preview or image window.

7. To reduce or enlarge the image in the preview box, click the minus or plus signs.
8. Click OK.

   Photoshop applies the blur.

FILTER, DISTORT:
Pinch an Image

The Distortion filters allow you to rearrange pixels in a image in a variety of creative ways. All distortion filters reshape an image either by pushing pixels in a defined pattern, such as Spherize and Twirl, or by overlaying an effect, such as Glass and Diffusion Glow.

Each of the Distortion filter dialog boxes has a set of controls. Three of the distortion filters — Diffuse Glow, Glass, and Ocean Ripple — use the extensive controls and previews of the Filter gallery. The others have dialog boxes that control the characteristics of the distortion. There is typically a preview of the

image and a set of sliders or buttons that vary the effect.

The most extensive controls are found in the new Lens Correction filter that places the image on a grid in a large preview window and can correct the fisheye distortion inherent in wide-angle lenses. More typical are the Spherize and Pinch filters, with their mode menus and single sliders that weaken or strengthen the effect.

See also>>   **Filter gallery**

Using Filters with Dialog Boxes

❶ Click a layer or make a selection.

❷ Click Filter.

❸ Click Distort.

❹ Click one of the distortion filters.

The dialog box for the filter you selected appears.

Depending on the dialog box, make sure you select the Preview option.

❺ Click and drag the sliders to adjust the effect.

● You can observe the effect in the preview window.

❻ To reduce or enlarge the image in the Preview box, click the minus or plus signs.

❼ Click OK.

Photoshop applies the effect.

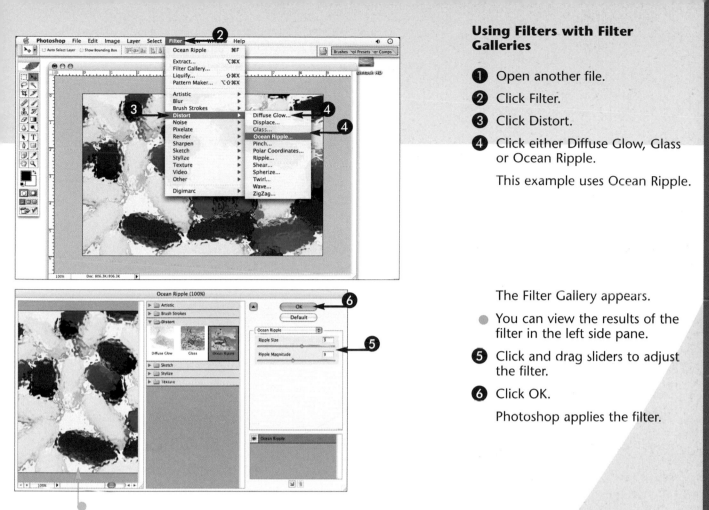

Using Filters with Filter Galleries

1 Open another file.

2 Click Filter.

3 Click Distort.

4 Click either Diffuse Glow, Glass or Ocean Ripple.

This example uses Ocean Ripple.

The Filter Gallery appears.

● You can view the results of the filter in the left side pane.

5 Click and drag sliders to adjust the filter.

6 Click OK.

Photoshop applies the filter.

TIPS

Caution!

The Distort filters are among the most memory-intensive of all Photoshop's operations. To save yourself time watching the progress bar, do your experimenting on a lower-resolution version of your image. When you arrive at the effect you desire, make notes about the settings that produce the effect, and scale up those settings to apply the filter to your high-resolution versions.

Did You Know?

Many of the distortion filters produce different results if the target image is contained within a selection.

Caution!

When you move the pixels of an image by applying one or more of the Distort filters, the pixels become less sharp. This phenomenon increases each time you apply the filter. Instead of applying a filter a little at a time, consider experimenting until you find the level at which you want to finally apply it. You can always apply Undo to return to the original image, and then apply the filter only once.

FILTER, EXTRACT:
Knock Out an Image

You can use the Extract command to isolate a subject in an image and erase the background to transparency. This is helpful when the subject has a complex or indistinct outline, such as fuzz, hair, or feathers, or if its colors are so similar to the background that it melts into it. The Extract filter is a mini-program, complete with preview and edit functions. It lets you define an edge by outlining your subject, and filling the interior of the outline. It then uses the outline to measure the color and brightness of pixels on either side to create a subtle transition area at the edge.

To remove an object from an image, invoke the Extract filter. Once in the Extract dialog, you can create an outline of your subject using the Edge Highlighter tool. You can then fill the area inside the outline. The filled area is what is left after you apply the Extract command. You can preview and edit as many times as you need to perfect the outline of your subject. Once refined, you can extract it. You are then returned to Photoshop where your image contains the extracted object against a transparent background.

Extract the Image

① Open an image that you want to extract.

② Click Filter.

③ Click Extract.

The Extract interface appears.

④ Click the Edge Highlighter tool.

⑤ Click and drag the Brush Size slider to select a brush size, or type a value in pixels.

⑥ Click and drag the Edge Highlighter tool to outline the area you want to extract, making sure that you close the outline.

● If you make a mistake, click the Eraser tool from the dialog box; then click and drag over the highlight.

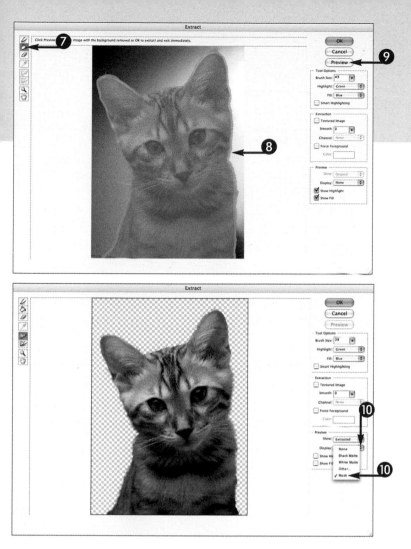

7 Click the Bucket tool.

8 Click within the outline.

The Bucket tool fills the area.

9 Click Preview.

The dialog box displays a preview of the extraction.

10 Click here and select Mask.

TIPS

Try This!
Because, like many filters, the Extract filter is destructive, you should always duplicate your image or at least keep a layer with an intact duplicate.

Try This!
To toggle between the Highlighter and the Eraser while drawing an edge, you can press the Opt or Alt key.

Did You Know?
You can change the color of the highlighted edge and fill used to define the subject you want to extract. The colors you use for this purpose have no effect on the final image. However, it may be useful to change colors if the current colors are too close to your image's colors.

FILTER, EXTRACT:
Knock Out an Image (Continued)

Having outlined and filled your subject, it useful to preview the final product. With the Preview option, you can preview and edit the extracted subject. In preview mode, the background is removed. However, while editing, you may need to see the background so that you can make sure you have not removed part of the subject. Extract allows you to switch between the views of the original image and the extracted object.

The Preview option offers several ways to display your image: grayscale mask or against a white or a black matte; against a colored background; None to

display a transparent background. Several tools are also available to alter the edges and interior of the extracted subject.

The Cleanup tool, the Edge Touchup tool, the Eraser, and the Fill tools are all designed to edit the extraction while in preview mode.

After previewing and editing, you can extract your subject. The final image is the subject surrounded by transparent pixels. If necessary, you can use the History brush or the Background Eraser to touch up stray edge pixels.

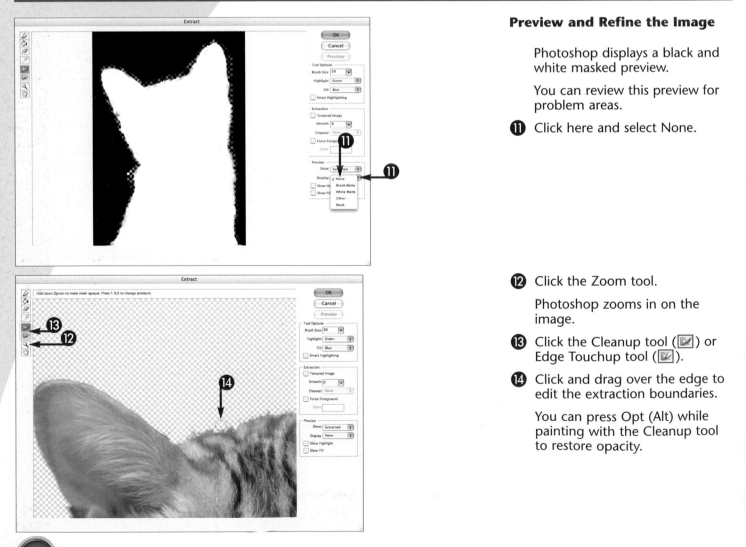

Preview and Refine the Image

Photoshop displays a black and white masked preview.

You can review this preview for problem areas.

⑪ Click here and select None.

⑫ Click the Zoom tool.

Photoshop zooms in on the image.

⑬ Click the Cleanup tool (　) or Edge Touchup tool (　).

⑭ Click and drag over the edge to edit the extraction boundaries.

You can press Opt (Alt) while painting with the Cleanup tool to restore opacity.

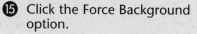

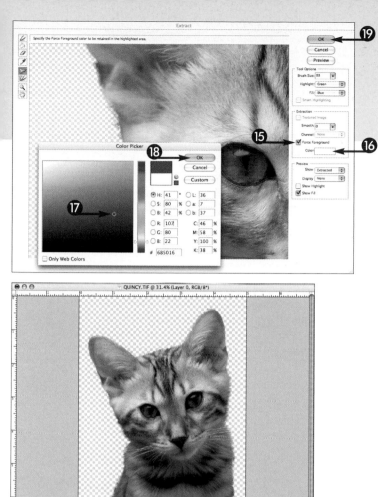

⑮ Click the Force Background option.

Photoshop will retain this color in the highlighted areas.

⑯ Click the Color swatch.

⑰ In the Color Picker, click a color.

⑱ Click OK in the Color Picker.

⑲ Click OK in the extract window.

The final image is extracted.

TIPS

Try This!

To toggle between the Highlighter and the Eraser while drawing an edge, press Opt (Alt). Or you can completely erase the highlight by pressing Opt+Delete (Alt+Backspace).

Try This!

To highlight the entire object, press Cmd+Delete (Ctrl+Backspace) and then select Force Foreground. Use this technique with areas that contain tones of a single color.

Caution!

Your highlighted edge should enclose the subject you want to extract entirely. If there is a gap in your highlighted edge, and you can use the Fill tool to cover the entire image. Undo, Zoom in, and close any gaps.

Caution!

Because of the radical transformation that Extract produces, first duplicate the image or make a snapshot of it.

FILTER, GALLERY:
Apply Artistic Effects

The Filter Gallery lets you select, preview, and apply one or more filters to an image. The Filter Gallery is a convenient way to apply and preview individual effects or several cumulative affects. Many, but not all of Photoshop's filters are included in the Filter Gallery. You can access these through individual commands listed under the Filters command. The Filter Gallery dialog box is organized into three panes: a preview pane on the left; a filter category list in the middle; and a settings and options pane on the right. The settings and options pane changes as you select particular filters. It also contains the OK and Cancel buttons.

The filter categories include Artistic, Brush Strokes, Distort, Sketch, Stylize, and Texture. When you select a folder, a list of filter names appears along with thumbnails that illustrate the filter's effect. The right field activates to display the filter's controls. The image display field on the left now shows the effect on the image of the filter with its current settings.

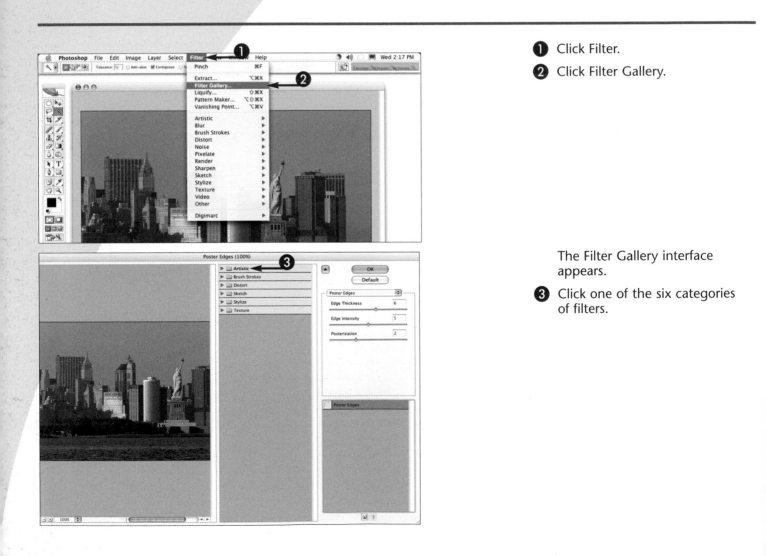

1 Click Filter.

2 Click Filter Gallery.

The Filter Gallery interface appears.

3 Click one of the six categories of filters.

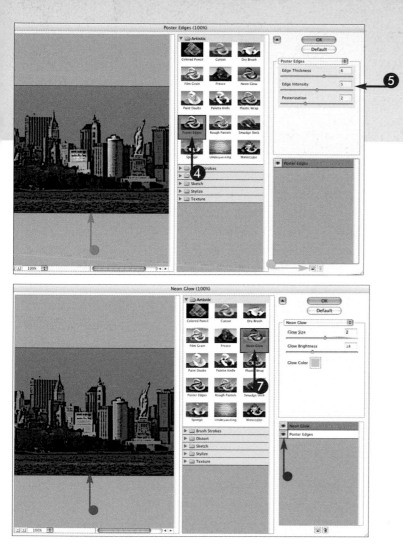

The list of individual filter thumbnails appears.

④ Click one of the thumbnails.

The preview field on the left displays the results of the default filter settings.

⑤ Click and drag the Edge Thickness, Edge Intensity, and the Posterization sliders.

● You can observe the effect in the preview field.

● To add another pass of the same filter, you can click the New Filter icon at the bottom of the palette.

The filter is applied again and its name appears a second time in the list.

⑥ To apply a different filter, click the filter from the middle field.

● You can click the Eye icon next to the filter name to reveal or conceal its effects.

● The preview displays the results.

![TIPS]

Try This?

To increase the size of your preview area, click the Show/Hide button at the top left of the options and settings pane in the Filter Gallery dialog box to hide the filter thumbnails. Hiding the thumbnails expands the preview area.

Try This!

You can apply an artistic filter to a duplicate image on a separate layer and then choose a blending mode or opacity to mitigate the effect.

Caution!

By moving and changing pixels, the application of several filters can degrade the resolution of an image. If you apply more that one filter, and they are available in the Filter Gallery, consider applying them all at once in the Filter Gallery.

FILTER, LIQUIFY:
Sculpt with Pixels

You can use the Liquify filter to distort an image by pushing, pulling, puckering, and bloating any area of an image. The distortions you apply can range from subtle to excessive depending on whether you want to retouch an image or create interesting effects. Therefore, you can use it to remove small bulges and imperfections from a subject or create a caricature.

The Liquify filter contains sophisticated warping and distortion tools that push pixels as if they were clay. It also has a set of masking tools that protect the image from alteration. The reconstruction modes correct unwanted distortions so you can apply a partial or complete reconstruction at will.

An optional mesh grid overlay enables you to gauge the effects of the distortion as you apply it. If desired, you can save the mesh and apply it to an entirely new image regardless of the image's size or resolution.

Previewing capabilities let you experiment before actually applying distortions. You can configure everything exactly the way you want it without the risk of damaging the image.

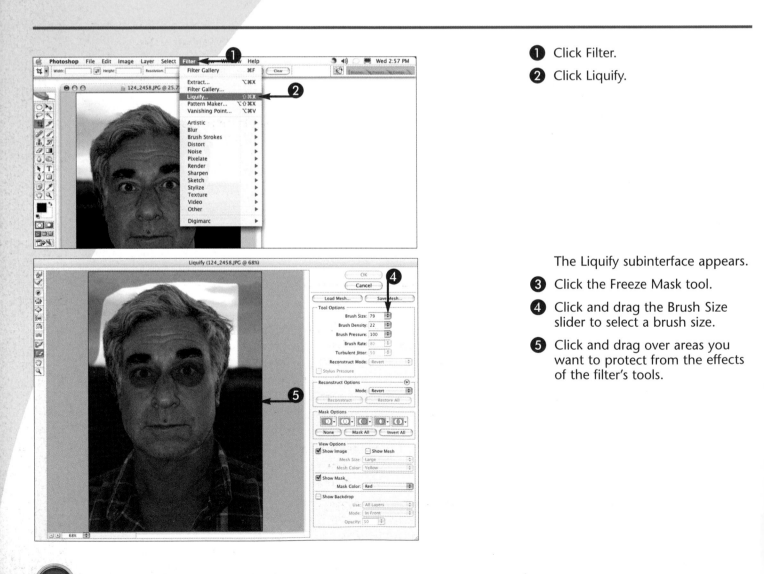

① Click Filter.

② Click Liquify.

The Liquify subinterface appears.

③ Click the Freeze Mask tool.

④ Click and drag the Brush Size slider to select a brush size.

⑤ Click and drag over areas you want to protect from the effects of the filter's tools.

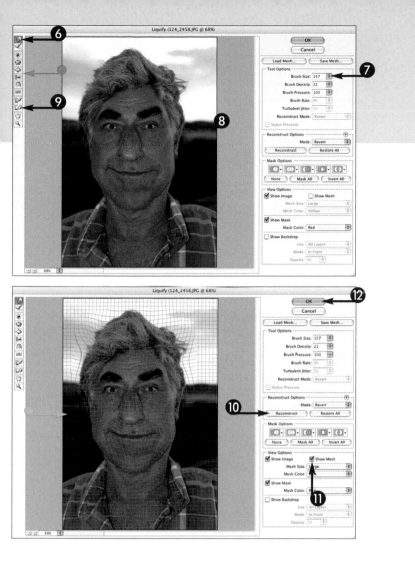

6 Click the Warp tool.

7 Click here and select a brush size.

8 Click and drag the brush over the image.

Photoshop pushes the pixels around.

● You can click the other liquification tools and experiment with some of the other brush characteristics.

9 Click the Thaw Mask tool.

10 To correct unwanted edits, click the Reconstruct tool, and click, and drag over the area you want corrected.

11 Click the Show Mesh option in the View Options field.

● The mesh displays to show the extent of the distortion.

12 Click OK.

Photoshop applies your changes.

TIPS

Did You Know?
The Backdrop feature enables you to superimpose the distortions over the original image for comparison. When you click Backdrop, choose a specific layer or all layers from the drop-down list and adjust the Opacity slider to compare the results.

Caution!
Remember, when using the Liquify filter, that less is usually more. It's real easy to get carried away with this feature and turn your image into a swirling amorphous galaxy of gray mud. With a little restraint and in the spirit of fun you can produce images that defy reality and have your audience wondering "How'd they do that?"

FILTER, NOISE, ADD NOISE:
Add Grain to an Image

You can use the Noise filters to change an image by adding or removing noise, which is randomly distributed pixels of different colors. Depending on the filter you select, you can eliminate dust and scratches from an image or correct images by adding texture to improve blending actions.

In the Add Noise dialog box, the Amount slider controls how far the noise can differ from the existing pixel colors — the higher the number, the greater variation in color of the added noise. Two options are available to define the way noise is distributed across an image. Uniform applies colors randomly throughout the image; otherwise, Photoshop applies the noise in a Gaussian curve, resulting in a more pronounced effect than Uniform delivers. The Monochromatic option distributes noise uniformly across all color channels; otherwise, Add Noise applies its effect randomly to each channel separately, resulting in more color variation. Monochromatic produces grayscale noise. When you work on a grayscale image, the effect is the same whether or not you select this option.

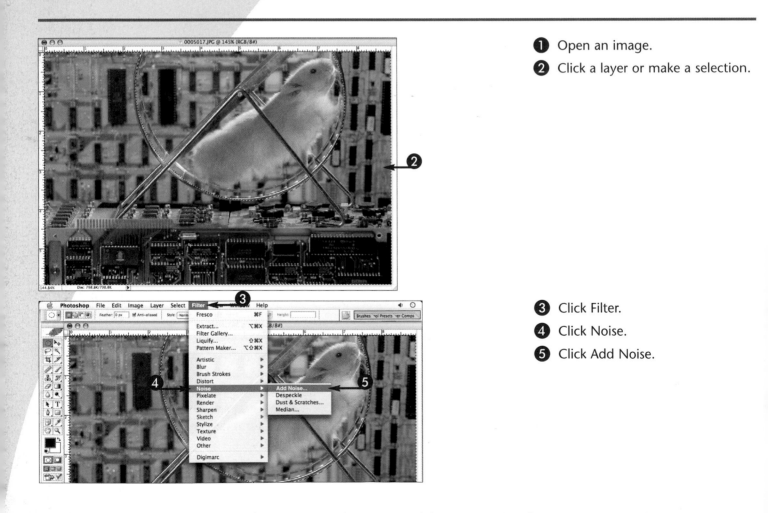

1 Open an image.

2 Click a layer or make a selection.

3 Click Filter.

4 Click Noise.

5 Click Add Noise.

244

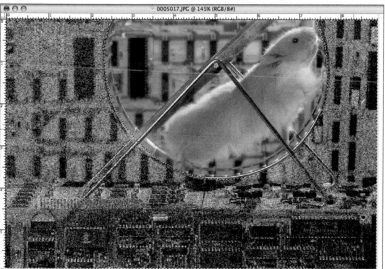

The Add Noise dialog box appears.

6 Click and drag the slider to produce the amount of noise you want.

7 Click OK.

Photoshop adds the amount of noise you selected.

TIPS

Try This!

Apply low amounts of noise to gradient areas to eliminate banding. Add between .10 and .5 percent, depending on the resolution of the image.

Did You Know?

Your camera settings can add noise to your images. This is most noticeable when you shoot pictures in dark settings. Setting your digital camera to high ISO speeds can also cause noise.

Try This!

Noise may affect one channel more than others, so it is a good idea to examine each channel and adjust noise individually. If you select the Reduce Noise filter, you can click Advanced Mode in its dialog box. You can then examine each channel and limit adjustments to the channel with the most pronounced noise problem.

FILTER, NOISE, DESPECKLE, MEDIAN, DUST & SCRATCHES:
Repair Damaged Photographs

You can use the noise removal filters to restore Photographs. Despeckle, Dust & Scratches, and Median all remove noise or artifacts. Despeckle is a blur filter that does its work without benefit of a dialog box; the others offer far more control.

The Median filter is similar to Dust & Scratches, but its dialog box lacks the Threshold slider. Median levels off the noise and eliminates detail. The Dust & Scratches filter was created for the purpose of removing those spots and splotches that many old photos have acquired from years of neglect or abuse.

It has two sliders — Radius, which blurs the selected area; and Threshold, which restores texture. When you use the Dust & Scratches filter it is important to select small areas first. Avoid including any high-contrast details into the selection as those are affected the same as the dust spots and scratch marks.

Apply the minimum amount of the Radius slider you need to blur the contents of the selection; then apply the minimum amount of Threshold to restore the texture.

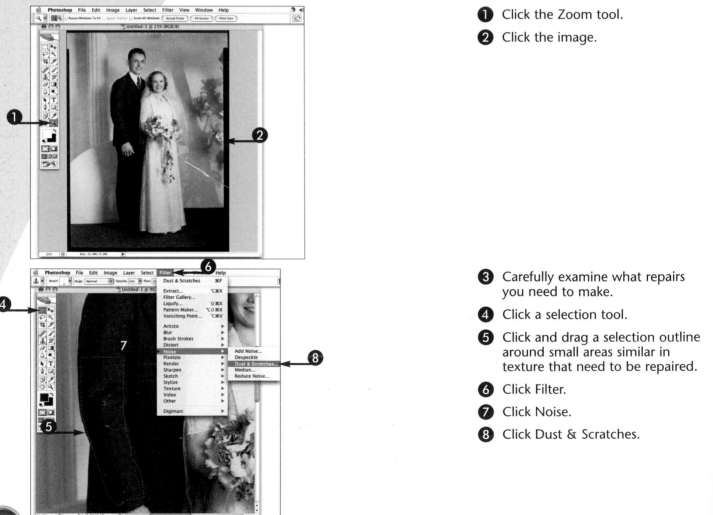

❶ Click the Zoom tool.

❷ Click the image.

❸ Carefully examine what repairs you need to make.

❹ Click a selection tool.

❺ Click and drag a selection outline around small areas similar in texture that need to be repaired.

❻ Click Filter.

❼ Click Noise.

❽ Click Dust & Scratches.

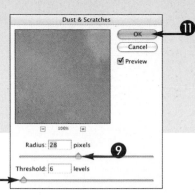

The Dust & Scratches dialog box appears.

9 Click and drag the Radius slider to blur the area within the selection.

10 Click and drag the Threshold slider to restore the texture.

11 Click OK.

Photoshop applies the effect.

You can select another area and repeat the process.

TIPS

Did You Know?

Dust & Scratches, when applied liberally to the entire image, can produce a rather astonishing generalized look to the image resembling an oil painting or color sketch.

Try This!

You may have different areas of an image that require a noise adjustment. After correcting the first problem area, you can select another area and reuse the same filter by pressing Cmd+Opt+F (Ctrl+Alt+F), which applies the effect of the last filter you used.

Did You Know?

Photoshop has a setting that specifically removes JPEG file noise. The Remove JPEG Artifacts option removes blocky image artifacts and halos caused by saving an image using a low JPEG quality setting.

FILTER, NOISE, REDUCE NOISE:
Remove Noise from Your Digital Photographs

You can use the new Reduce Noise filter to improve the quality of images shot in low light or with a high ISO speed, low quality JPEG file, or scanned dark images. You can apply Reduce Noise as an overall correction (Basic) or targeted to a specific color channel (Advanced). Advanced mode allows you not only to select which channels are affected, but also how much of the effect to apply.

The Reduce Noise dialog box has a large preview pane on the left and a setting and options control panel on the right. You can reduce noise globally by using the Basic controls. Included in the Basic controls are sliders with which you can adjust luminosity, amount of detail to preserve, chromatic noise, and sharpening. If you are editing a JPEG image, you can select the Remove Artifacts option to common noise in low-quality JPEG files.

Advanced mode lets you target particular a channel in an image. You select the channels you want to change and then apply a different amount of noise reduction to each channel.

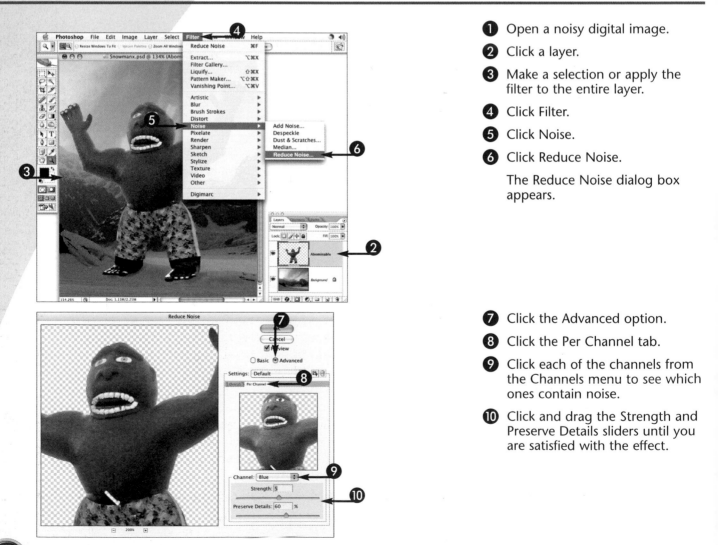

① Open a noisy digital image.

② Click a layer.

③ Make a selection or apply the filter to the entire layer.

④ Click Filter.

⑤ Click Noise.

⑥ Click Reduce Noise.

   The Reduce Noise dialog box appears.

⑦ Click the Advanced option.

⑧ Click the Per Channel tab.

⑨ Click each of the channels from the Channels menu to see which ones contain noise.

⑩ Click and drag the Strength and Preserve Details sliders until you are satisfied with the effect.

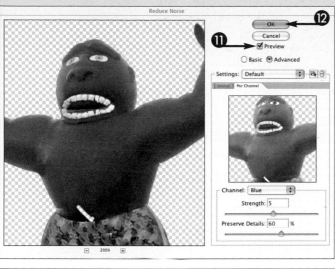

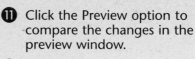

⑪ Click the Preview option to compare the changes in the preview window.

⑫ Click OK.

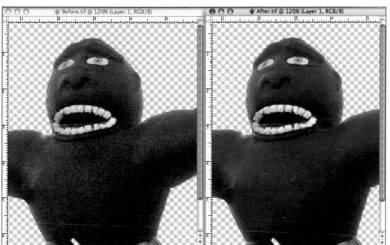

Photoshop reduces the noise in the new version of the digital image.

In the example, the new version of the digital image is on the right side.

TIPS

Did You Know?
Image noise can take two forms: luminance or color. Luminance, or grayscale noise makes an image look grainy or patchy. Color noise adds random pixels of different colors throughout the image. If the problem is luminance noise, look first at the blue channel, where you usually find noise.

Did You Know?
The Reduce Color Noise slider in the Reduce Noise dialog box targets extraneous color pixels. Dragging the slider to the right reduces more random color pixels. Dragging the slider to the left reduces less pixels.

Try This!
To avoid noise altogether, shoot the photograph with enough light to illuminate the image. Also, longer exposures with smaller apertures can help eliminate noise.

FILTER, OTHER, CUSTOM:
Create Your Own Filter

The Custom Filter dialog box lets you design your own filter effect. All of the filters in Photoshop convert the brightness value of pixels in an image. They may also remap the color or location of existing pixels to produce a particular effect. When you create a custom filter, the values you type in the dialog box change the brightness values of each pixel in the image according to a predefined mathematical formula known as *convolution.* Each pixel is reassigned a value based on the values of surrounding pixels. This operation is similar to the Add and Subtract blending, which you use for superimposing images or Alpha channels.

In the Custom dialog box, you can enter values in a grid of rectangular text boxes. You can also enter the values by which you want to multiply brightness from -999 to +999. Negative values darken pixels; positive values brighten them. The preview field and the image window display the results.

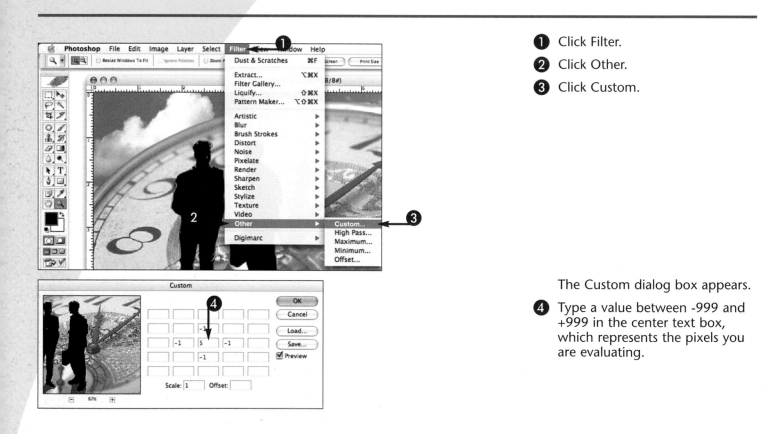

① Click Filter.

② Click Other.

③ Click Custom.

The Custom dialog box appears.

④ Type a value between -999 and +999 in the center text box, which represents the pixels you are evaluating.

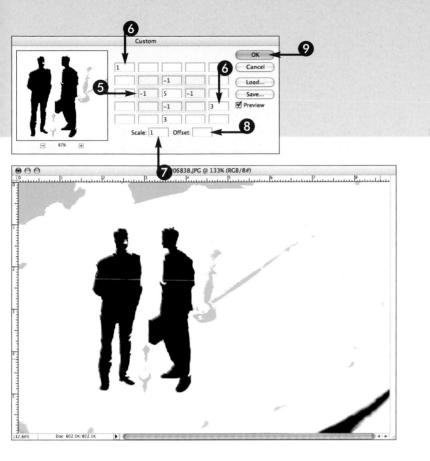

⑤ Type the value in an adjacent text box by which you want the adjacent pixels to be multiplied.

⑥ Type values in other boxes.

You do not have to type values in all the text boxes.

⑦ For Scale, type the value by which to divide the sum of the brightness values of the pixels included in the calculation.

⑧ For Offset, type the value to be added to the result of the scale calculation.

⑨ Click OK.

Photoshop applies the custom filter to each pixel in the image or selection.

TIPS

Try This!

You can click Save to save the custom filters you create and apply them with other Photoshop images.

Did You Know?

You can achieve most of the effects achieved with the Custom filter with the filters that Photoshop provides.

Did You Know?

The Custom filter separates the left brained from the right brained. With instructions like "multiply the brightness value of the pixel to the immediate right of the current pixel by 2, enter 2 in the text box to the immediate right of the center text box..." some of us will run right back to the Filter Gallery.

FILTER, OTHER:
Offset, Move a Layer or a Background

You can use the Offset filter to shift an image, layer, or selection vertically or horizontally. The Offset filter dialog box allows you to move the image or selection by a precise number of pixels. You enter values in the Horizontal and Vertical fields to determine the distance and location to which your pixels will move. Positive numbers move the image to the right or down. Negative numbers move the image to the left or up.

You can make the same precise moves with the arrow keys in conjunction with the Move tool;

however, the difference lies in the fact that Offset determines what happens to the unselected areas by allowing you to select one of three options. Set To Background fills the emptied area with the current background color. If the image you want to move is on a layer, the Set To Background option changes to Set To Transparent and the emptied area becomes transparent. Repeat Edge Pixels fills the area with duplicates of the pixels at the edge of the selection; Wrap Around takes pixels from the opposite side of the selection and duplicates them.

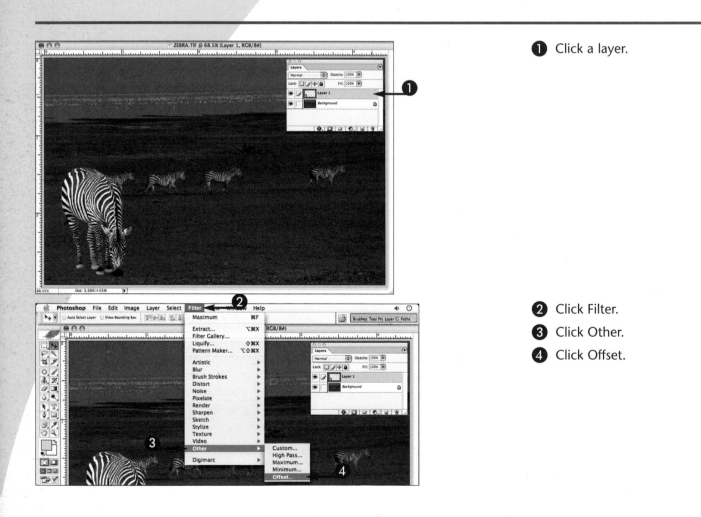

① Click a layer.

② Click Filter.

③ Click Other.

④ Click Offset.

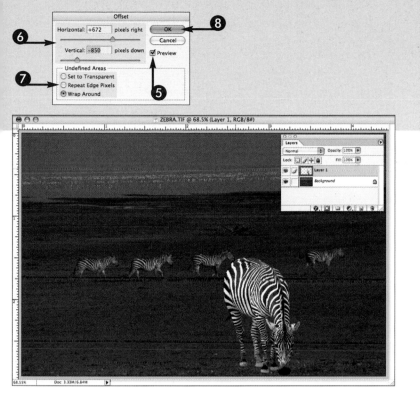

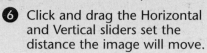

The Offset dialog box appears.

⑤ Click the Preview option.

⑥ Click and drag the Horizontal and Vertical sliders set the distance the image will move.

⑦ Click one of the Undefined area options.

⑧ Click OK.

The results of the move appear in the image window.

Did You Know?

The Horizontal and Vertical sliders display maximum distances for the width and height of the image or selection in pixels. By typing maximum values, you can drag the image completely off the page or out of the selection marquee.

Try This!

Because you cannot move a Background with the Move tool, use the Offset filter instead.

Try This!

You can use the Offset filter to create an animation that mimics a banner marquee with a repeating message. Type your message, duplicate the layer, and then use the Offset filter to move the text. Keep duplicating and offsetting the last layer until you see the text wrap around.

FILTER, HIGH PASS, MINIMUM, MAXIMUM:
Create Traps, Enhance Color

You can use the High Pass filter to find and isolate areas of high contrast. The filter retains edge details in the areas where sharp color transitions occur and suppresses the rest of the image. This filter is better for individual channels because it creates excellent black and white, or limited color images. Applying it to an entire image results in dull, gray colors. You control contrast with the High Pass's Radius slider, which ranges from 0.01 to 250 pixels. Lower values create a flat, gray image while higher values create high-contrast areas that show through lighter gray.

Because the Maximum filter decreases, while the Minimum filter increases, the expanse of a mask, these filters are perfect for spot color printing. A spot color is a custom color that you use instead of or in addition to CMYK colors. This color requires a separate printing plate and therefore separate channel in Photoshop. To accommodate the spot color a hole, or knockout, is cut through the CMYK color.

See also>> **Channels, Spot color**

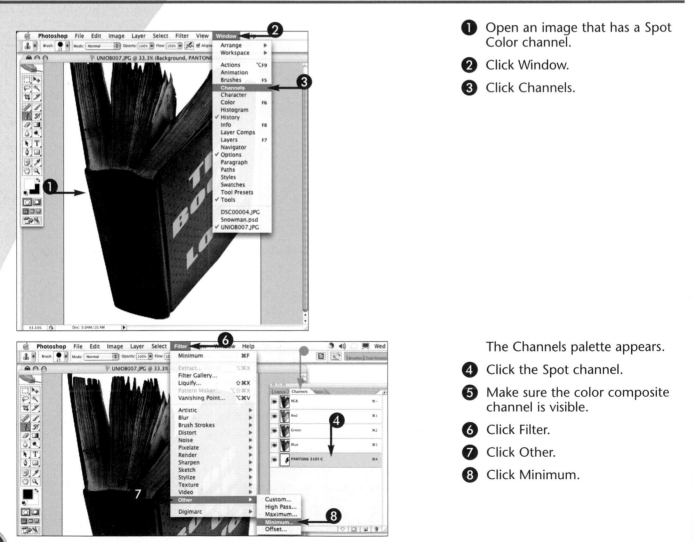

❶ Open an image that has a Spot Color channel.

❷ Click Window.

❸ Click Channels.

The Channels palette appears.

❹ Click the Spot channel.

❺ Make sure the color composite channel is visible.

❻ Click Filter.

❼ Click Other.

❽ Click Minimum.

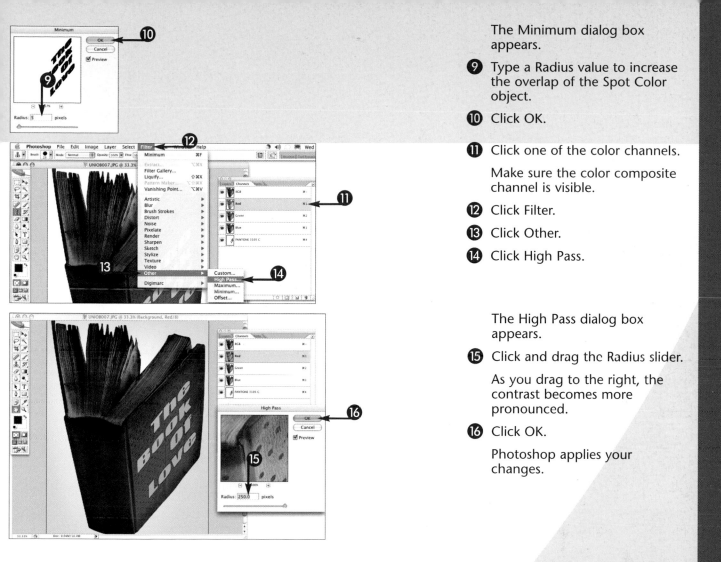

The Minimum dialog box appears.

9 Type a Radius value to increase the overlap of the Spot Color object.

10 Click OK.

11 Click one of the color channels.

Make sure the color composite channel is visible.

12 Click Filter.

13 Click Other.

14 Click High Pass.

The High Pass dialog box appears.

15 Click and drag the Radius slider.

As you drag to the right, the contrast becomes more pronounced.

16 Click OK.

Photoshop applies your changes.

Did You Know?

Traps are usually very small — 1 to 3 pixels — depending on the resolution of the document and type of printing press in use.

Did You Know?

You can use the Maximum filter to create a stroke around an image surrounded by transparency on an individual layer.

Caution!

In printing, if plates are not aligned perfectly, part of the spot color may not fit exactly into the knockout area and show through the ink. You resolve with a trap, or overlap area. You decrease the knockout size with the Minimum filter and increase the spot color spread with Maximum filter. Talk with your print service provider to determine if you need a trap, and if you do, what values to use.

FILTER, PATTERN MAKER:
Create a Random Pattern

You can make and apply a Pattern to an image with the Pattern Maker filter. You use this filter to generate a repeating tile pattern from a selection, a layer, or an entire image. The Pattern Maker dialog box has the familiar Marquee, Zoom, and Hand tools at the top-left of the window to help you create a pattern. The Marquee lets you select an area of the image from which to generate patterns. You can select the Clipboard contents, the entire image, or an area you define with the Marquee tool. The Width and Height input fields determine the size and shape of the tile.

After you determine the source and the size and shape of your tile, you can generate a preview of your pattern. You can generate up to 20 patterns in one session. You can view each of the tiles you generate in the Tile History pane. The pane shows the current generated sample, but you can view the rest using the next or previous arrows just beneath the tile preview.

1 Open an image.

2 Click Filter.

3 Click Pattern Maker.

The Pattern Maker dialog box appears.

4 Click the Rectangular Marquee tool.

5 Click and drag a marquee on the preview to define a pattern area.

6 Click Generate.

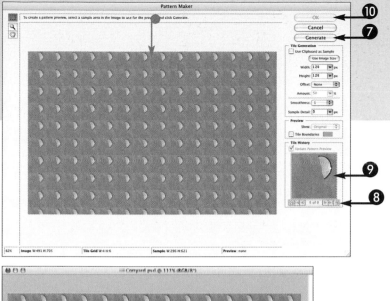

A pattern is generated and appears in the preview window.

7 Click Generate again.

● Another pattern appears.

You can continue clicking Generate until you are satisfied with the pattern.

8 In the Tile History box, click the arrows to review the generated patterns.

9 Click a pattern from the History.

10 Click OK.

Photoshop applies the pattern to your image.

TIPS

Try This!

By clicking the arrow buttons at the bottom of the Tile History area, you can view each set of tiles sequentially. To save a tile, click the disk icon to the left. A dialog box appears that shows you the pattern and allows you to name it. Photoshop saves your new pattern in its list of pattern presets.

Did You Know?

In the Control panel, you can offset the spacing of your tiles horizontally or vertically and specify an Offset amount. Changing the Smoothness settings to 1, 2, or 3 can enhance blending of the edges of your tiles. Increasing the Sample Detail allows greater precision in the formation of your sample.

FILTER, PIXELATE:
Create Impressionist Effects

You can use the Pixelate filters to break up and rearrange your image into variously shaped groups of pixels. Neither Facet nor Fragment offers a dialog box; they simply apply their effects. Of the two, Facet has a more pleasing, irregular, sort of hand-colored effect. Color Halftone's controls include a Radius input, and four screen angles boxes. Crystallize, Mosaic, and Pointillize all offer a Cell Size slider in their dialog boxes that let you designate how many pixels are used to create a cell or clump of grouped color. Larger values result in big groupings

of pixels that rob your image of detail. Smaller values can create more interesting artistic effects, mainly by increasing color contrast from cell to cell.

The Mezzotint filter offers several ways of adding largely uncontrollable noise to your image in the form of dots, lines, or strokes. Mezzotint turns grayscale images black and white, and RGB images are reduced to six colors (red, green, and blue, and their complements cyan, magenta, and yellow) plus black and white.

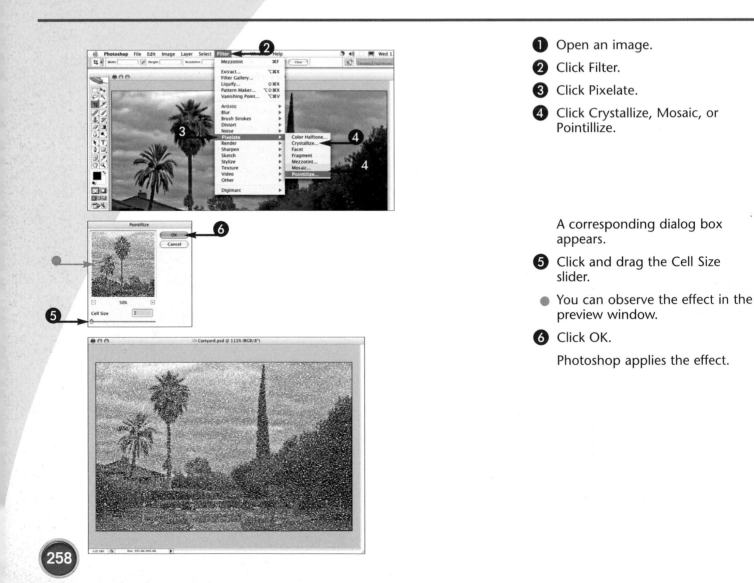

① Open an image.

② Click Filter.

③ Click Pixelate.

④ Click Crystallize, Mosaic, or Pointillize.

A corresponding dialog box appears.

⑤ Click and drag the Cell Size slider.

● You can observe the effect in the preview window.

⑥ Click OK.

Photoshop applies the effect.

FILTER, RENDER, CLOUDS:
Create Sky Patterns

You can use the Cloud filters to create cloudlike colored splotches that you can use along with other filters or adjustments to produce interesting textures. Clouds utilizes the foreground and background colors to create the sky/cloud effect. Difference Clouds uses the opposite colors of the foreground and background colors.

When you apply either of these filters to your image, a hazy mixture of foreground and background colors fills your selection. As you reapply the filter, the cloud pattern changes and shifts. You can use keyboard commands to create a more pronounced effect. Difference Clouds

works in the same way as Clouds, but swaps the colors — if Clouds creates a blue sky and white clouds, Difference Clouds generates an orange sky with black clouds. The swapping of colors refers to the position of colors on a color wheel. Apply the filter again and your colors change back to blue and white.

See also>>

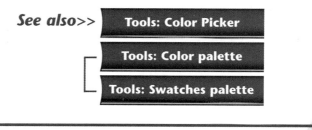

Tools: Color Picker

Tools: Color palette

Tools: Swatches palette

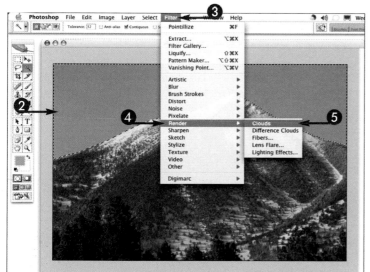

① Click a foreground and background color from the Swatches palette, the Color palette, or the Color Picker.

② Make a selection or target a layer.

③ Click Filter.

④ Click Render.

⑤ Click Clouds.

The image or selection changes to clouds colored with the foreground and background color.

You can press Cmd+F (Ctrl+F) to reapply the filter until you see the clouds you want.

You can press Cmd+Opt+F (Ctrl+Alt+F) to create clouds with more contrast.

FILTER, RENDER, FIBERS:
Make Fibrous Textures

The Fibers filter simulates the look of woven fibers. It uses the foreground and background colors to produce the effect. The Variance slider controls how the colors vary. Low values create longer streaks of color; high values produce short fibers with more distribution of color. The Strength slider controls the thickness of the fibers. Low values create thicker fibers; high settings produce short, stringy fibers. The Randomize button changes how the pattern is generated. As you click it, the fibrous pattern changes. You cannot apply fibers to an empty layer;

the layer must have content. The Fibers filter applies a fibrous pattern to an image on the layer and is contained by the pixels, but does not affect the transparent part of the layer.

If you want to apply the Fibers filter to a surface, duplicate the layer, apply the Fibers filter to it, and use a blending mode to blend the new layer with the original layer.

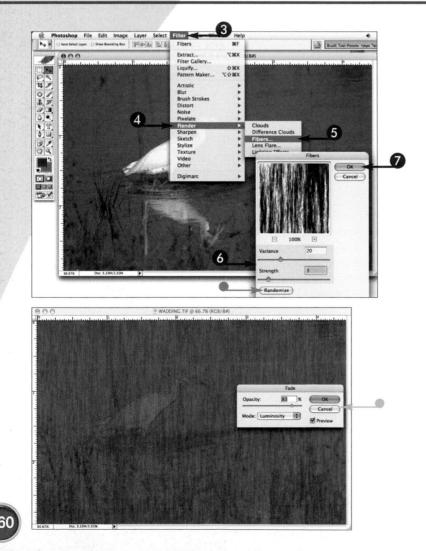

① Click a foreground and background color from the Swatches palette, the Color palette or the Color Picker.

② In the Layers palette, click a layer.

③ Click Filter.

④ Click Render.

⑤ Click Fibers.

The Fibers dialog box appears.

⑥ Click and drag the Variance and Strength slider until you get the desired results.

● You can click Randomize to see more variations.

⑦ Click OK.

● You can press Shift+Cmd(Ctrl)+F make the Fade dialog box appear and fade the affect by clicking and dragging the Opacity slider, selecting a blending mode and clicking OK.

Photoshop applies the filter to the layer.

FILTER, RENDER, LENS FLARE AND LIGHTING EFFECTS:
Create Dramatic Lighting

You can use the Lighting Effects filter and the Lens Flare filter to add interesting lighting effects to an image. Lens Flare produces a simple lighting effect. A preview box shows a replica of your image where you can move the pointer to specify your flare center. The Brightness slider allows you to adjust brightness from 10 percent to 300 percent. Four lens shapes are offered: 50–300mm Zoom, 55mm Prime, 105mm Prime, and Movie Prime. The result is a reflection, like light glinted back off a distant object.

The Lighting Effects dialog box offers several settings and options for simulating the play of spotlights or floodlights over your image. Imagine you are hanging lights in a gallery, shining a flashlight into a dark cave, or driving down a wooded road at night. You can duplicate any of these lighting situations with these versatile options. At the top of the dialog box, the Style menu provides a wide array of lighting styles. Adjust the specific characteristics of your lighting in the Light Type area. You can then save the effects to the Style list.

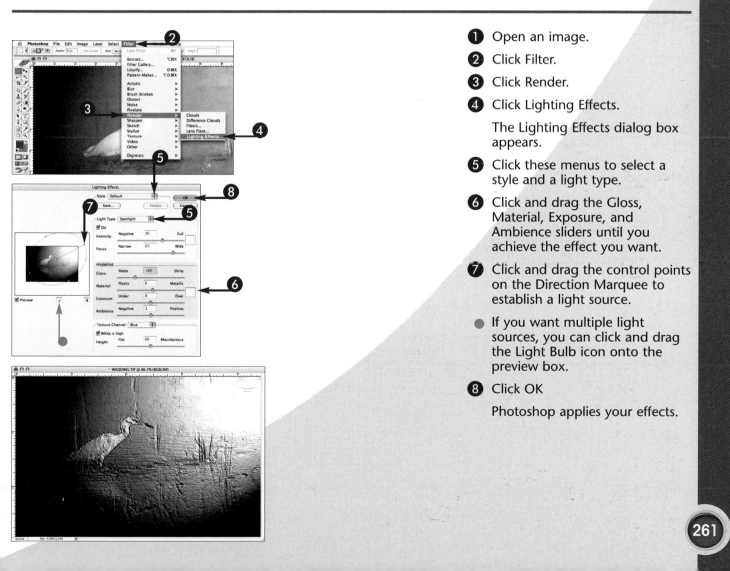

① Open an image.

② Click Filter.

③ Click Render.

④ Click Lighting Effects.

The Lighting Effects dialog box appears.

⑤ Click these menus to select a style and a light type.

⑥ Click and drag the Gloss, Material, Exposure, and Ambience sliders until you achieve the effect you want.

⑦ Click and drag the control points on the Direction Marquee to establish a light source.

● If you want multiple light sources, you can click and drag the Light Bulb icon onto the preview box.

⑧ Click OK

Photoshop applies your effects.

FILTER, SHARPEN, SMART SHARPEN:
Reduce Blur

You can set the Smart Sharpen command to control the amount of sharpening effects in shadow and highlight areas. This level of control is not available in the Unsharp Mask filter. The Smart Sharpen dialog box has an extensive set of controls.

The Amount slider controls the strength of the effect. A higher value increases the contrast between edge pixels, creating the sharper focus. The Radius slider determines the number of pixels surrounding the edge pixels that are sharpened. Larger radius values produce a thicker edge, and a more pronounced sharpening.

The Remove menu sets the type of sharpening. Gaussian Blur is similar to the Unsharp Mask filter. Lens Blur produces finer sharpening of detail and reduces halos. Motion Blur reduces the effects of the blur caused by camera or subject movement. If you choose Motion Blur, set an angle to counteract the direction of the blur.

Select the More Accurate check box to process the file longer for a more accurate blur removal.

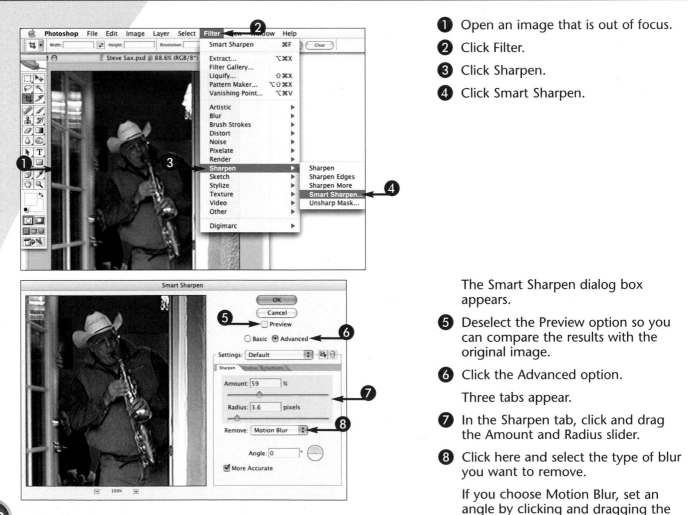

❶ Open an image that is out of focus.

❷ Click Filter.

❸ Click Sharpen.

❹ Click Smart Sharpen.

The Smart Sharpen dialog box appears.

❺ Deselect the Preview option so you can compare the results with the original image.

❻ Click the Advanced option.

Three tabs appear.

❼ In the Sharpen tab, click and drag the Amount and Radius slider.

❽ Click here and select the type of blur you want to remove.

If you choose Motion Blur, set an angle by clicking and dragging the Angle control.

9 Click the Shadow tab.

10 Click and drag the Fade, Tonal Width and the Radius sliders.

The sliders refine the details of the sharpening and eliminate halos.

● You can observe the effects of the filter in the preview box.

11 Click OK.

Photoshop applies your effects.

Did You Know?

Large-format images such as images printed to billboards and banners usually require more sharpening because of the distance and changing lighting conditions in which they are seen.

Caution!

Do not oversharpen an image! It is easy to get carried away with these filters. Sharpen just enough to make the image pop. Remember, you can sharpen your entire image or just a portion defined by making a selection or creating a mask.

Caution!

Sharpen filters affect only the current layer. If you want to apply them to the entire image you may need to merge layers or flatten your image.

FILTER, SHARPEN, UNSHARP MASK:
Sharpen for Print

You can use the Sharpen filters to simulate focus and enhance contras. The Sharpen group contains five filters — Sharpen, Sharpen Edges, Sharpen More, Smart Sharpen, and Unsharp Mask. The first three of these are fully automated. Sharpen increases overall contrast, Sharpen More has a stronger effect, and Sharpen Edges focuses on the areas of highest contrast.

More powerful than any of these are the Smart Sharpen and Unsharp Mask filters. The Unsharp Mask dialog box has three sets of sliders. You can enter a value of 1 percent to 500 percent in the Amount field to define the degree of sharpening — the higher the value, the greater the effect. The Radius slider determines the thickness — from 0.1 to 250 pixels — of an edge. Lower values produce crisp, sharp edges; higher values define edges as thicker and generate greater overall contrast throughout an image.

The Threshold slider, which has a value from 0 to 255, determines the difference in brightness values necessary to recognize an edge. Lower numbers include more pixels; higher numbers exclude pixels.

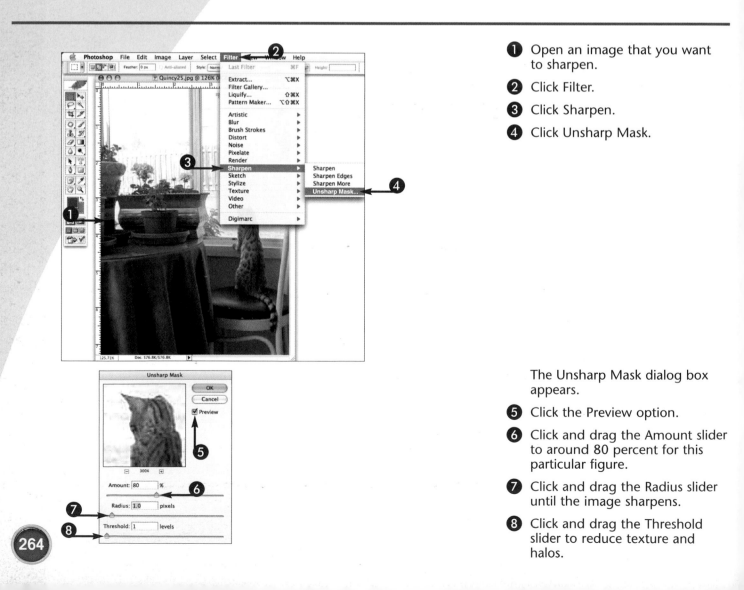

① Open an image that you want to sharpen.

② Click Filter.

③ Click Sharpen.

④ Click Unsharp Mask.

The Unsharp Mask dialog box appears.

⑤ Click the Preview option.

⑥ Click and drag the Amount slider to around 80 percent for this particular figure.

⑦ Click and drag the Radius slider until the image sharpens.

⑧ Click and drag the Threshold slider to reduce texture and halos.

264

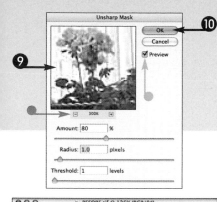

9 Click and drag in the preview field to see different areas of the image.

● You can also click the plus and minus signs to zoom in and out of a particular area.

● You can select and deselect the Preview option to compare results in the image window.

10 Click OK.

Photoshop applies your effects.

TIPS

Did You Know?
Sometimes repeated applications of a lower Amount setting can produce better results than a single application at a higher setting.

Did You Know?
When identifying edges, Unsharp Mask uses the Radius setting as its criteria. The effectiveness of this setting depends upon the resolution of the image. Screen images and Web graphics require a much lower setting than high-resolution images intended for fine printing.

Caution!
Sharpening can produce color shifts. To avoid this problem, duplicate the layer. Place the new layer immediately above the original layer in the stack. Select Luminosity as a blending mode and apply the Unsharp Mask to the luminosity layer.

FILTER, STYLIZE:
Use Edges to Create Graphic Effects

You can apply an interesting group of effects with the Stylize filters. Some filters in the Stylize submenu affect the edges of your image and others map image pixels into geometric shapes. All but two — Solarize and Find Edges — have dialog boxes.

Applying Solarize is similar to combining a photographic negative with a positive. Tiles and Extrude are the two Stylize filters that map to shapes. Tiles breaks your image up into squares. The Extrude filter is similar to Tiles, except that the mapping does not stay in two dimensions. Glowing

Edges uses the filter gallery controls and produces the most dramatic effects. Find Edges and Trace Contour all provide ways of getting a color outline of your image. Diffuse works in a manner similar to the Dissolve Blending mode in that it diffuses the edges of your layer or selection. The Wind filter offers three levels of wind blowing from either left or right. The Emboss filter, with its Angle, Height, and Amount options, produces a smooth gray image with subtle highlight and shadow relief.

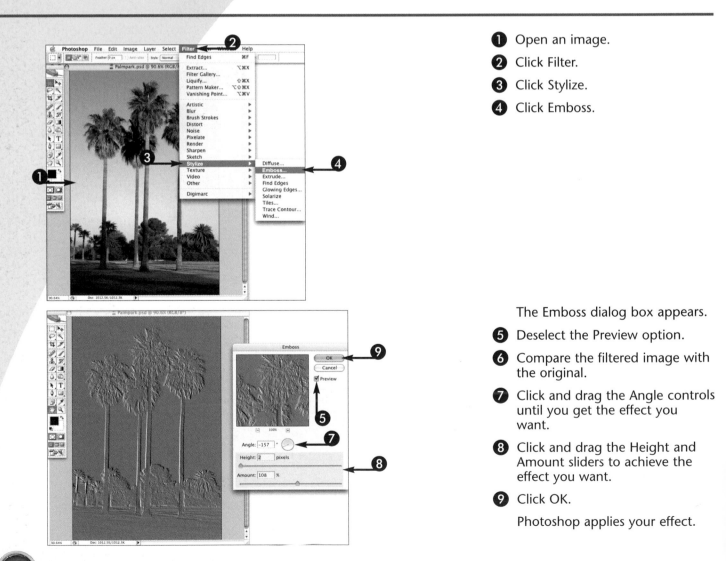

① Open an image.

② Click Filter.

③ Click Stylize.

④ Click Emboss.

The Emboss dialog box appears.

⑤ Deselect the Preview option.

⑥ Compare the filtered image with the original.

⑦ Click and drag the Angle controls until you get the effect you want.

⑧ Click and drag the Height and Amount sliders to achieve the effect you want.

⑨ Click OK.

Photoshop applies your effect.

FILTER, TEXTURE:
Apply Texture

The Texture filters let you apply realistic surfaces to a layer or selection. Texture filters apply a simulated surface to the image. You can access these filters through the Filter Gallery. The texture filters include Craquelure, an irregular broken stone look; Grain, a noisy surface; Mosaic Tile, similar to Craquelure but more regular; Stained Glass, a flat surface of faceted shapes; Patchwork, a three-dimensional system of squares; and the Texturizer, with its four surface variations. Each has a set of controls that lets you regulate the

unique characteristics of the surface texture.

The Texturizer is particularly useful for creating the effect that the image is painted on a surface. You can choose from a list of surfaces including Brick, Burlap, Canvas, and Sandstone. The sliders let you control the scale, relief, and the direction of the light source, and you can invert the effect.

See also>> **Techniques: Filter Gallery**

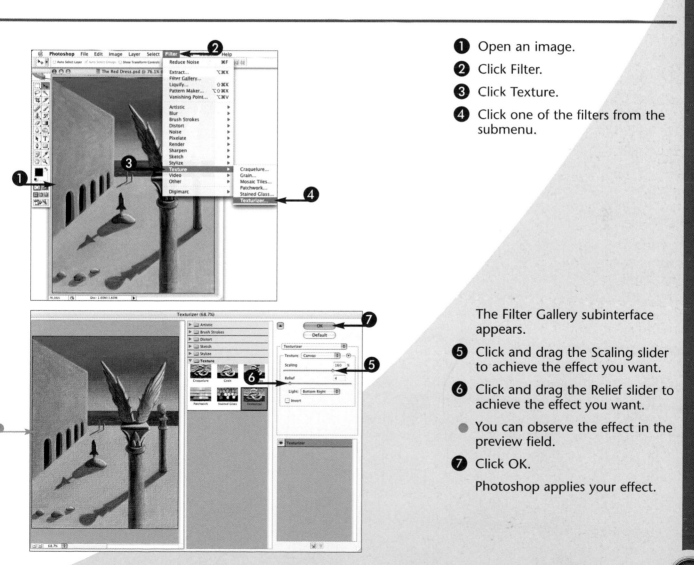

① Open an image.

② Click Filter.

③ Click Texture.

④ Click one of the filters from the submenu.

The Filter Gallery subinterface appears.

⑤ Click and drag the Scaling slider to achieve the effect you want.

⑥ Click and drag the Relief slider to achieve the effect you want.

● You can observe the effect in the preview field.

⑦ Click OK.

Photoshop applies your effect.

FILTER, VANISHING POINT:
Create Perspective

You can correct perspective with the new Vanishing Point filter. For example, if you add a design element to the side of an architectural structure, you can create perspective in the design element so that your image looks more realistic. You use the Vanishing Point filter to specify perspective planes and then apply edits that conform to the converging lines of the plane. Vanishing Point filter produces more realistic composites because when you retouch, add, or remove content in an image, the content orients and scales to the perspective planes.

The Vanishing Point dialog box lets you work directly on a large image preview. The interface contains a

tool for defining the perspective plane, selection tools, and editing tools that perform painting and cloning operations.

To add perspective to your image, first, define the perspective grid on the preview image. You can refine the plane after you draw with the Edit Plane tool. You can then paint, clone, copy, paste, and transform content in the plane. The additional tools — the Marquee, Clone Stamp, Brush, and more — are similar to their counterparts in the main Photoshop toolbox with an Options bar that lets you set specifications.

① Open two images.

② Click Select.

③ Click All.

You can also press Cmd+A (Ctrl+A) to select the images.

④ Click Edit.

⑤ Click Copy.

You can also press Cmd+C (Ctrl+C) to copy your selected images.

Photoshop copies the contents of the image that you want to composite to the perspective grid.

6 Activate the destination image.

7 Click Filter.

8 Click Vanishing Point.

The Vanishing Point dialog box opens.

9 Click the Create Planes tool.

10 Click a point on the image preview, then release the mouse and drag to a new point.

11 Click the mouse again to deposit another point.

Repeat the process until you have a four-point perspective grid.

TIPS

Try This!

To place the results of your Vanishing Point work in a separate layer, first create a new layer before selecting the Vanishing Point command. Creating a new layer each time you use Vanishing Point places the results on a separate layer. This keeps the results editable and makes use of layer features such as opacity, layer styles, and blending modes. Placing the Vanishing Point results in a separate layer and also preserves your original image.

Try This!

To confine the Vanishing Point results to specific areas of your image, either make a selection or add a mask to your image before choosing the Vanishing Point command.

FILTER, VANISHING POINT:
Create Perspective (Continued)

Vanishing Point offers the capability to superimpose an image onto a predefined perspective grid. You can paste an image into the perspective, or you can paint with sampled pixels onto the grid. The cloned image orients to the perspective of the plane in which you are painting. The Stamp tool is useful for tasks such as blending and retouching image areas, cloning portions of a surface to "paint out" an object, or cloning an image area to duplicate an object or

extend a texture or pattern. With an image containing perspective planes open in Vanishing Point, select the Stamp tool.

The Vanishing Point Clone stamp is similar to the Clone stamp in the Tools palette. When you select it, you can set behavior in the Options bar. You then need to set a sampling point by selecting it in the image. Wherever you sample from conforms to the perspective grid.

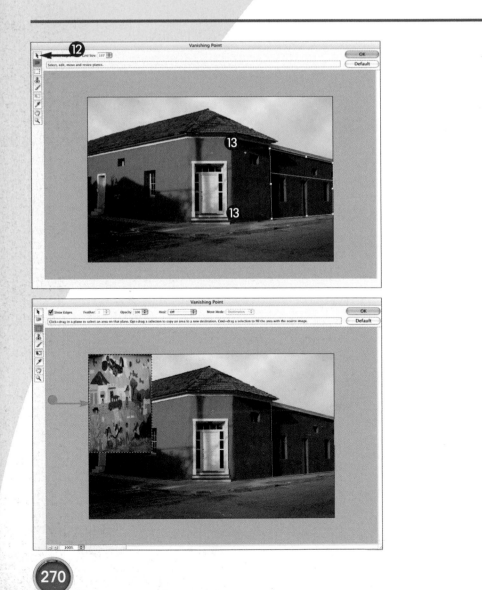

⑫ Click the Edit Plane tool.

⑬ Drag on the corner points to refine the perspective grid.

⑭ Press Cmd(Ctrl)+V

● The contents of the Clipboard pastes into the perspective grid.

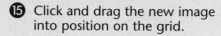

15 Click and drag the new image into position on the grid.

16 Click the Transform tool.

● Click and drag the image by its corner handles to fit into the perspective grid.

17 Click the Marquee tool.

You can type a value to adjust the opacity of the selection.

18 Click OK.

● The image reflects a scaled change.

TIPS

Caution!
This filter can take a lot of time to process images. Experiment on low-resolution images first.

Did You Know?
You can save a lot of processing time if you resize the source image to a rough fit before you paste it into the Vanishing Point filter interface.

Try This!
You can create a new layer each time you use Vanishing Point. Before clicking the Vanishing point filter, create an empty layer. Photoshop stores any results from the filter in the layer. This allows you to edit the results separate from the image. It also gives you access to opacity settings, layer styles, and blending modes. Placing the Vanishing Point results in a separate layer also preserves your original image.

GRADIENT EDITOR:
Make a Custom Gradient

The Gradient Editor allows you to create new gradients or to edit existing ones so you can save gradients and store them for later use. You access the Gradient Editor via the Gradient swatch in the Options bar, which presents a preset list.

The Gradient Editor has a preview bar that displays the proportional distribution of the gradient's colors and the position of any transparency — both of which you can change.

Color stops, the house-shaped sliders at the bottom of the color bar at each end of the preview bar, determine the beginning and end of the colors that

make up the gradient. You can assign a color to a stop by either sampling a color from the image, selecting it from the color picker, or sampling it from the swatches palette. By adjusting a stop's location, you can change the range of a color relative to the other color.

When you select any of the stops, a small diamond marks the midpoint of the transition between the two blended colors. You can adjust this midpoint to redistribute the relative color proportions of the gradient.

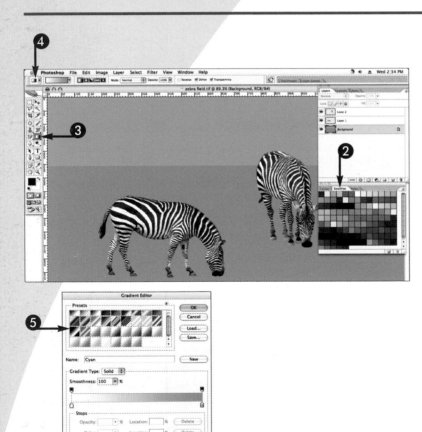

Edit a Gradient

1. With an image open, press F6.

   The Color, Swatches, Styles palette cluster appears.

2. Click the Swatches tab.

3. Click the Gradient tool.

4. Click the gradient swatch on the Options bar.

   The Gradient Editor appears.

5. Double-click a preset gradient at the top of the Editor.

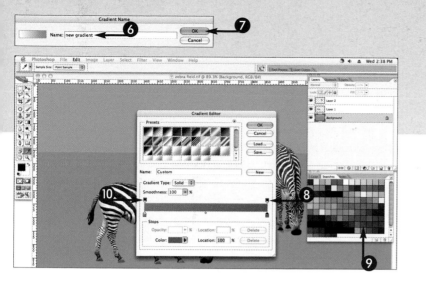

The Gradient Name dialog box appears.

6 Type a new name.

7 Click OK.

8 Click right color stop.

9 Click a swatch in the Swatches palette.

10 Repeat step **8** and **9** for the left color stop.

Photoshop creates your custom gradient.

TIPS

Warning!

To permanently keep and use your custom gradient, you must save it to the default swatch palette by clicking Save in the Gradient Editor. Failing to do so means loss of the gradient if Photoshop preferences are reset.

Did You Know?

Gradients can contain more than two colors. Simply add colors to the preview bar by clicking a Stop and holding the Opt (ALT) key as you drag.

Try This!

You can create a spotlight effect for specific elements. Create a new empty layer on top of the image. Set the Layer Blending mode to Luminosity. Select the Gradient tool. On the Options bar, select a black to white gradient and set the type to Radial gradient. Now click and drag outward on the area you want to highlight.

GRADIENT EDITOR:
Make a Custom Gradient (Continued)

The Gradient editor lets you create gradients with as many colors as you desire. Each time you add a stop under the gradient ramp and assign a color to it, you add new dimensions to the gradient. You can also adjust the transparency of the gradient by adding a stop on top of the ramp; then in the Opacity field, specify a percentage to modify the colors transparency. When you apply the gradient with the Gradient tool on a layer or background, the pixels underneath that color show through. When you add

transparency, you can modify the distribution of the gradient by repositioning the gradient stops or the midpoint diamond on the ramp.

Gradients produce smooth transitions from one color to another. For some wild, grainy effects, try creating a noise gradient, which you can apply via the Type menu and adjusting the color sliders to produce the gradient you want. You can also use the Randomize button to see variations of the gradient.

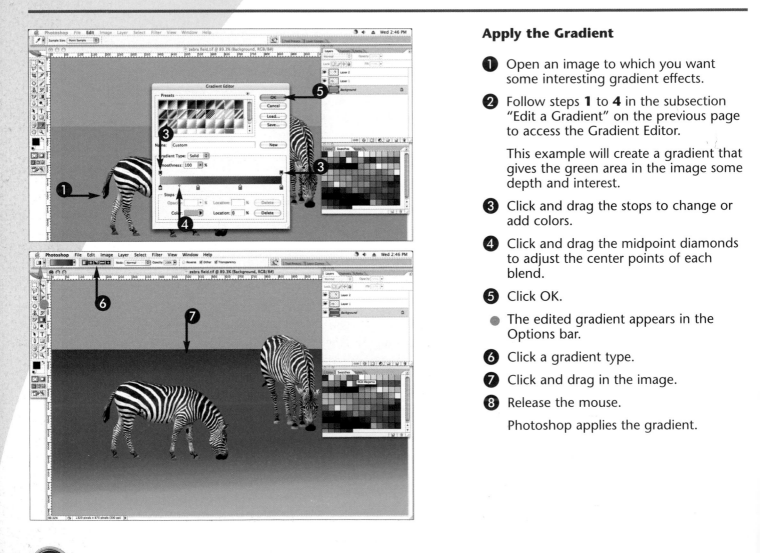

Apply the Gradient

① Open an image to which you want some interesting gradient effects.

② Follow steps **1** to **4** in the subsection "Edit a Gradient" on the previous page to access the Gradient Editor.

This example will create a gradient that gives the green area in the image some depth and interest.

③ Click and drag the stops to change or add colors.

④ Click and drag the midpoint diamonds to adjust the center points of each blend.

⑤ Click OK.

● The edited gradient appears in the Options bar.

⑥ Click a gradient type.

⑦ Click and drag in the image.

⑧ Release the mouse.

Photoshop applies the gradient.

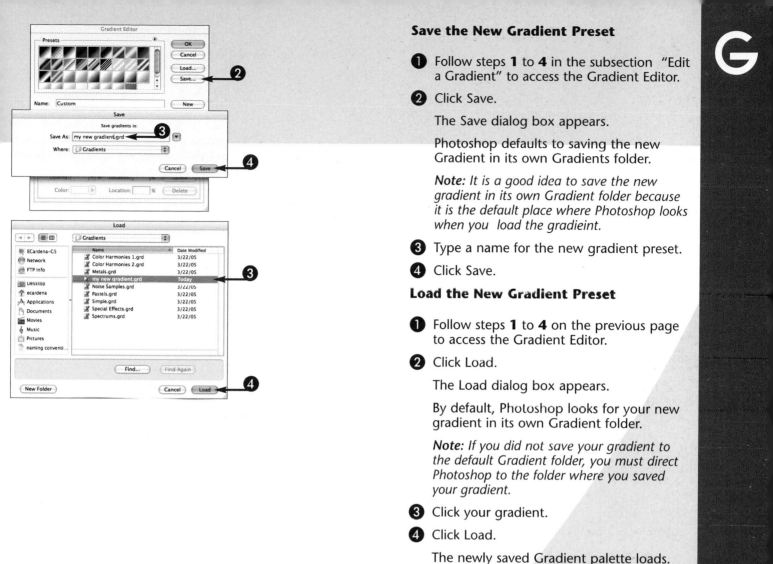

Save the New Gradient Preset

1 Follow steps **1** to **4** in the subsection "Edit a Gradient" to access the Gradient Editor.

2 Click Save.

The Save dialog box appears.

Photoshop defaults to saving the new Gradient in its own Gradients folder.

Note: It is a good idea to save the new gradient in its own Gradient folder because it is the default place where Photoshop looks when you load the gradieint.

3 Type a name for the new gradient preset.

4 Click Save.

Load the New Gradient Preset

1 Follow steps **1** to **4** on the previous page to access the Gradient Editor.

2 Click Load.

The Load dialog box appears.

By default, Photoshop looks for your new gradient in its own Gradient folder.

Note: If you did not save your gradient to the default Gradient folder, you must direct Photoshop to the folder where you saved your gradient.

3 Click your gradient.

4 Click Load.

The newly saved Gradient palette loads.

Try This!

You can create a horizon where a gradient disappears into nothing rather than to white or another color by clicking one of the stops above the color bar. Click and drag the Opacity slider to adjust this value to less than 100%. Adjust the opacity to 0 for total transparency.

Try This!

To generate unique effects, use the Noise Gradients, which give very distinct color bands that begin and end abruptly. In the Gradient Editor, click Type and then click Noise. Click and drag the color sliders to produce the gradient. To experiment further, click Randomize.

HISTORY LOG:
Save a Written History Record

To keep track of what you have done to an image, you can save a record of the tasks that you performed as a History log.

You have three options for saving a History Log. You can save your history as Metadata — the information that is embedded within each image and viewable via the Adobe Bridge Metadata tab; you can save your history as a text file readable by any word processing or text program; or you can do both. If you save a text log file, a Save dialog box lets you specify the name and location of the History log. Thereafter, Photoshop assumes that name and location until you change preferences again. While the Metadata is specific to each document, the Text log accumulates data for all files that Photoshop processes.

After you decide on one of the three options, the Edit Log Items menu lets you determine the amount of information to save. The Sessions Only option only records the time and date that a file was opened; the Concise log records an abbreviated list of the commands and operations you used; the *Detailed* option records a detailed list of the history states, actions, commands, and the specifications of each command, tool, or process.

See also>>

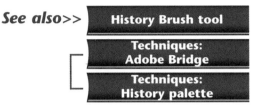

History Brush tool

Techniques: Adobe Bridge

Techniques: History palette

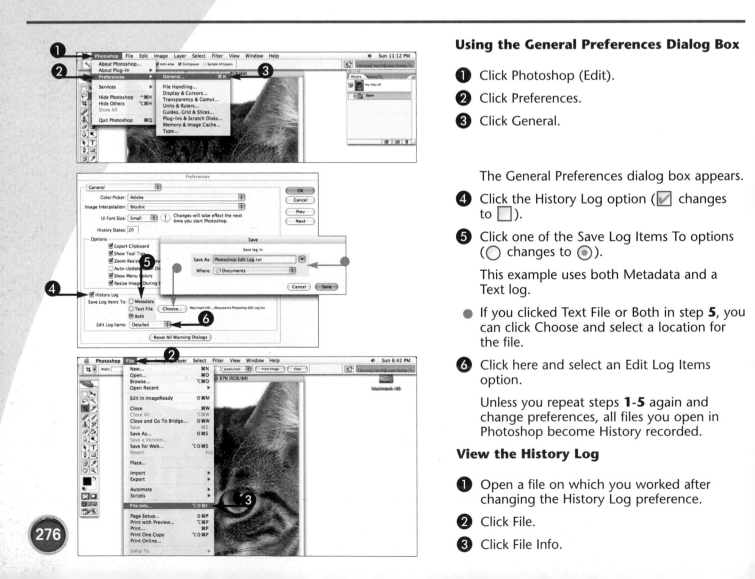

Using the General Preferences Dialog Box

❶ Click Photoshop (Edit).

❷ Click Preferences.

❸ Click General.

The General Preferences dialog box appears.

❹ Click the History Log option (☑ changes to ☐).

❺ Click one of the Save Log Items To options (○ changes to ◉).

This example uses both Metadata and a Text log.

● If you clicked Text File or Both in step **5**, you can click Choose and select a location for the file.

❻ Click here and select an Edit Log Items option.

Unless you repeat steps **1-5** again and change preferences, all files you open in Photoshop become History recorded.

View the History Log

❶ Open a file on which you worked after changing the History Log preference.

❷ Click File.

❸ Click File Info.

276

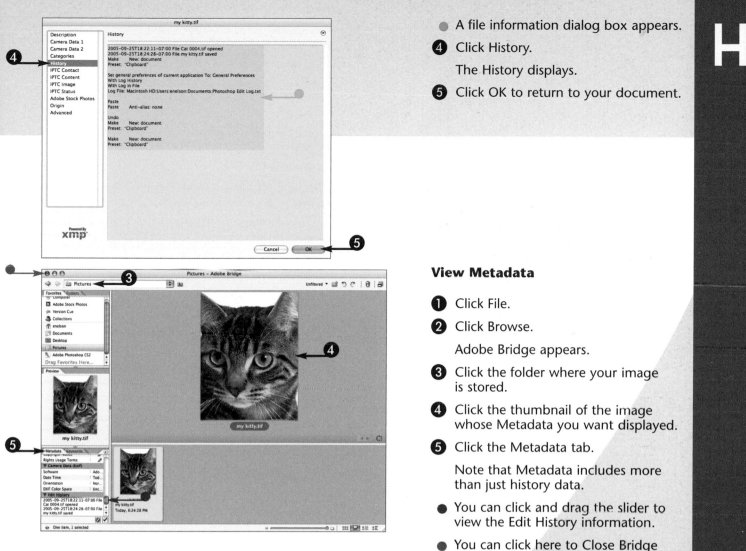

● A file information dialog box appears.

④ Click History.

The History displays.

⑤ Click OK to return to your document.

View Metadata

① Click File.

② Click Browse.

Adobe Bridge appears.

③ Click the folder where your image is stored.

④ Click the thumbnail of the image whose Metadata you want displayed.

⑤ Click the Metadata tab.

Note that Metadata includes more than just history data.

● You can click and drag the slider to view the Edit History information.

● You can click here to Close Bridge and return to Photoshop.

TIPS

Did You Know?

Saving a History Log as detailed text or as a metadata file lets you see all of the specifications of the history so that you can apply the same techniques to other images.

Warning!

Saving History Log Metadata increases the size of a file. The longer you work on a file, the larger your History log becomes and the longer it takes to open and save the file.

Did You Know?

You can use the History Log file to keep track of work you do for a client. Just be sure to change your Photoshop History Log preferences so that Photoshop creates and adds a separate log file for each client.

HISTORY PALETTE:
Create a History State, Save a Snapshot, Save a State as a Document

As you work on an image, the History palette keeps track of each change to the file as a state. You can move backward and forward through these states to undo or redo changes to your file. By default Photoshop keeps track of the last 20 states — deleting the earliest state as it adds new ones. You can increase this number via Photoshop's General Preferences.

An image's history is simply a sequential record of the work that you performed on it. Photoshop automatically records every edit, operation, or technique that you apply to an image. As you work, each event, called a *state* is listed in the History palette. You can select a specific state in the palette

and display it in the image window. You can freely move through the history of the document, alter states, and in so doing affect the outcome of the final image.

Each History state is a record of how the image appears after you apply a specific tool or operation to it and only applies to the current work session. After you close the image, the history is, well, history. When you reopen the document, the history begins again.

See also>>
History Brush tool

History log

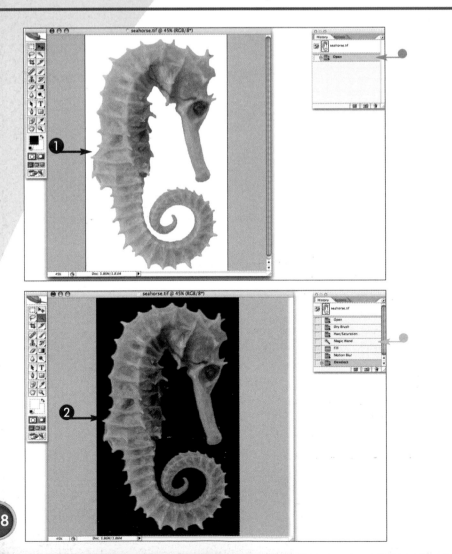

1 Open an image.

The History palette appears by default when the program launches.

● The first state listed in the History palette is the Open state.

If the palette fails to open, you can click Window, and then History.

2 Perform a task on the image, such as making a selection, filling or painting, applying a color adjustment, or using a filter.

● Each task automatically appears in the History palette as you work.

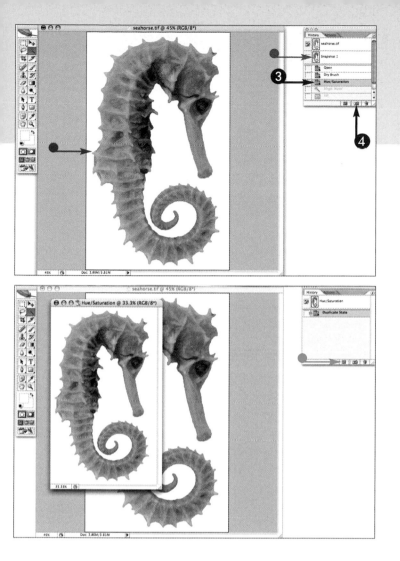

3 Click one of the states.

● The state appears in the image window.

4 Click the Create New Snapshot icon.

● The state is recorded as a new snapshot.

● You can click the Create New Document From Current State icon to duplicate the state into a new document with a new history.

TIPS

Try This!

By default, you can record up to 20 states, after 20 Photoshop deletes the oldest state. You can increase the number of history states, but be aware that this consumes memory. To access the General Preferences dialog box, click Photoshop (Edit), click Preferences, and then click General. A better method is to make frequent snapshots of key history states.

Caution!

If you want to undo several steps, you can click the state in the History list, which contains the last state you want to revert to and resume working. By default, Photoshop deselects all of the history states performed after the selected state. These states do not affect the image, but you can recall them. However, if you *delete* a state, Photoshop cannot recall subsequent states.

IMAGE SIZE:
Change the Size and Resolution of an Image

You can adjust the size and/or resolution of a file (resampling) via the Image Size command. The Image Size dialog box lets you adjust the pixel dimension, print dimension, and the resolution of an image. Depending on the options you check, Photoshop will also apply algorithms to produce a better resized image. Whether increasing or decreasing the size of a file, there is usually some loss in quality when you resample, so the first decision you must make is whether to use an algorithm or not

If you want to use one of Photoshop's several resampling algorithms, click on the Resample Image button. You then have access to a fly out menu from which you can choose one of several interpolation methods—that is formulas which calculate which pixels are added or deleted in an image. The five choices include Nearest Neighbor, Bilinear, Bicubic, Bicubic Smoother, an Bicubic Sharper. Based on these choices Photoshop will apply the appropriate calculation for adding or deleting pixels.

If you choose not to resample, you can simply enter one of the values—width, height, resolution.

Photoshop then redistributes pixels and recalculates the other values. If your image has objects that have Styles applied to them, you can choose to have Photoshop scale the styles proportionally by checking the Scale Styles button.

Whether you choose to resample or not you have a Constrains Proportions on/off button. For good reason the default is to have this button in the "on" position. If the button is deselected, you will probably end up with a stretched or squeezed image, as Photoshop will apply the pixel increase/decrease adjustment only to the field in which you entered a value. For example if you have a 4x5 image and you change the width to 6, the height will remain. Your image will then have a stretched look. There are times when you may want to do this—like when you want to correct the dimensions of a distorted image or when you want that affect for the sake of art.

See also>> `Techniques: Resample`

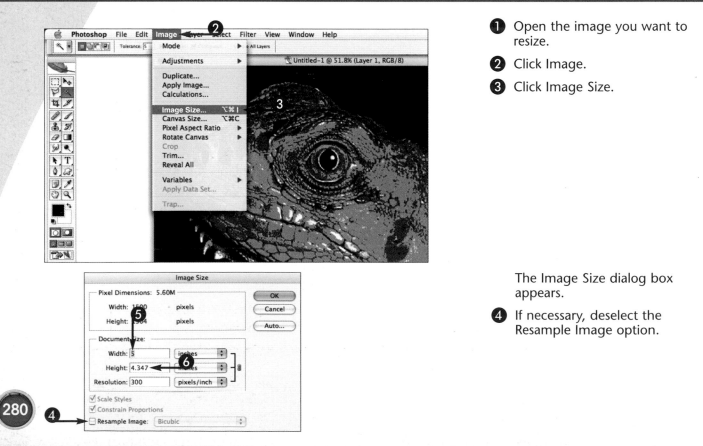

1 Open the image you want to resize.

2 Click Image.

3 Click Image Size.

The Image Size dialog box appears.

4 If necessary, deselect the Resample Image option.

5 Type a new document width.

● The resolution automatically changes to accommodate the new size, but the file size remains the same.

6 Click OK.

● No changes are visible onscreen but if you look at the bottom-left corner of the image window, Photoshop displays its new size.

TIPS

Try This!

You can have Photoshop calculate the best size for an image depending on the image's final use. That is the job of the interactive Resize Image Wizard found under the Help command. Through a series of screens, it asks: how will the image be output — for print or online; what is the desired output size; what is the halftone frequency (PPI) of the printer — several common choices are offered as well as an Other field where you can enter a value. It then presents you with a slider which you drag left (lower quality) or right (higher quality). Photoshop then resizes the image and duplicates the file so that the original remains intact.

Caution!

If you use the services of a commercial printer, always ask the printer what resolution and file format they need. Using standard calculations may be a costly mistake.

IMPORT:
Scan an Image Directly Into Photoshop

You can open a scanned image via Adobe Bridge or the Import command. You can also scan an image directly into Photoshop. The Import submenu offers direct access to the software that drives any installed scanners. You must make sure you turn on the scanner, and select the scanner type for the scanner software to launch.

The software for your scanner may look different from the example displayed here, but most scanner control software lets you define the file size, the resolution, and the input file type— such as line art,

grayscale, or color. You can also specify the output file's bit depth of the scan — 8, 16, or 32 bits per pixel — and choose to de-screen printed images. In addition, you can specify file format. Depending on the sophistication of your scanner, you may also have various other adjustments controls and options— brightness and contrast, a Preview mode, transform tools, and so on.

See also>> **Techniques: Image size**

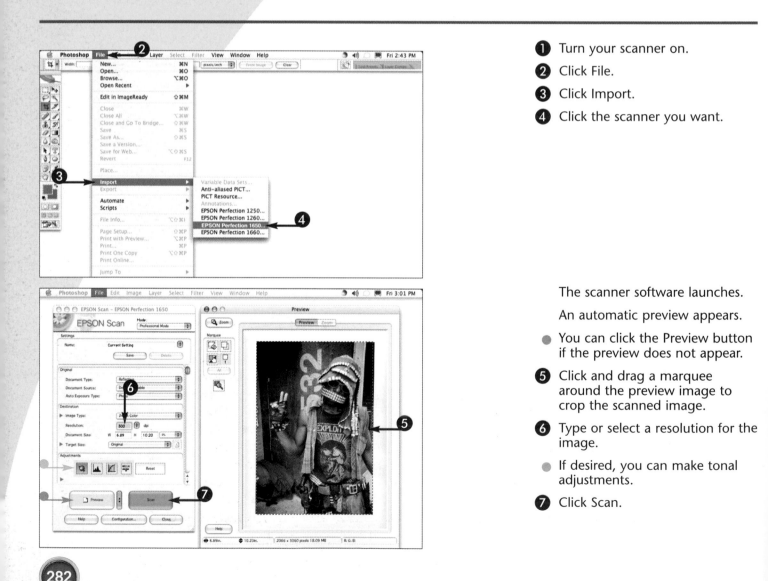

① Turn your scanner on.

② Click File.

③ Click Import.

④ Click the scanner you want.

The scanner software launches.

An automatic preview appears.

● You can click the Preview button if the preview does not appear.

⑤ Click and drag a marquee around the preview image to crop the scanned image.

⑥ Type or select a resolution for the image.

● If desired, you can make tonal adjustments.

⑦ Click Scan.

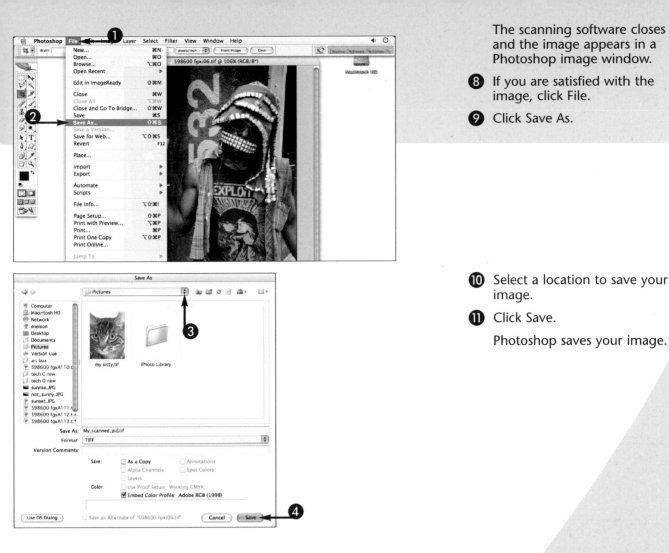

The scanning software closes and the image appears in a Photoshop image window.

8 If you are satisfied with the image, click File.

9 Click Save As.

10 Select a location to save your image.

11 Click Save.

Photoshop saves your image.

TIPS

Did You Know?

It may be better to make brightness and contrast adjustments in Photoshop rather than in the scanning software. Photoshop has a sophisticated set of adjustment tools that most scanner software can't match. The one thing left to the scanner, though, is scanning at an appropriate resolution rather than resizing in Photoshop.

Warning!

To maintain quality, avoid exceeding the optical resolution of the scanner. This means that a factor of size and resolution combined should determine the PPI. For example, if your scanner has an optical resolution of 1200 ppi, you can scan an image at 300 ppi at 400 percent. Exceeding the optical resolution adds pixels using interpolation algorithms that can reduce contrast and sharpness.

IMAGEREADY:
Launch ImageReady, Create an Image Slice and a Rollover

You can use ImageReady to create a rudimentary Web site without having to learn HTML or other Web authoring programs. You will find that ImageReady is in some ways a mini Photoshop. It uses many of the same tools, filters, commands, and palettes to create and edit images. It is the additional Web-related capabilities that separate ImageReady from Photoshop. Some of its capabilities include palettes and commands which help you create web content such as: rollovers — that is areas change color as you hover the mouse over them; image slice

to identify sections of a page, links to e-mail or other web sites or page; and preview a browser in a browser so that you can test your page.

One of ImageReady's key features is helping you optimize your web page. Because users of the internet have various types of computers, monitors, connection types, and connection speeds, among other things, it is always hard to determine the optimal size and type of file to use. ImageReady helps choose the best file by letting you preview an image under different scenarios.

Create an Image Slice

1 In Photoshop, open an image that you want to use as a web page.

2 Click on the Text tool.

3 Click somewhere on the image and type text which you will use as a link.

● Photoshop creates a new text layer.

4 Click on the layer name and change the name to "Rollover".

5 Press Cmd+J (Ctrl+J) to duplicate the layer you just created.

6 Click on the layer name and change the name to "Normal".

7 With the Text tool selected double click on the text.

8 Click here and choose a new color for the text.

9 Click the Jump to ImageReady icon at the bottom of the Tools palette.

The image opens in ImageReady.

10 Click on the Normal layer to make it active.

11 Click Layer.

12 Click New Layer Based Slice.

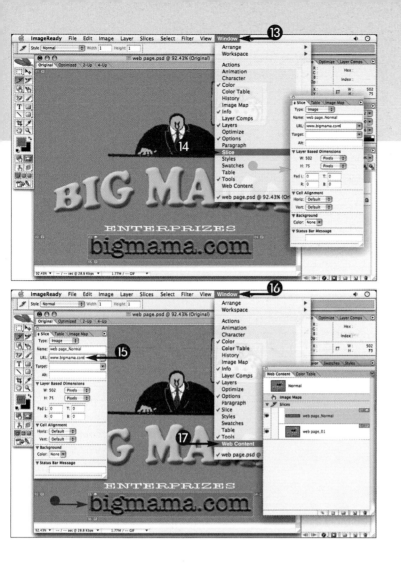

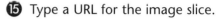

ImageReady creates a slice from layer content.

⑬ Click Window.

⑭ Click Slice.

● The Slice palette appears.

⑮ Type a URL for the image slice.

● This identifies the page to which users will navigate when they click on this slice.

⑯ Click Window.

⑰ Click Web Content.

The Web Content palette appears.

TIPS

Caution!

Before you save an optimized version of a Web page, save the document. Click File, and then Save As and save the file as a PSD. You can then reopen it in ImageReady at any time to rework it. You cannot open the optimized version of the page in ImageReady because it is no longer a single document. Various folders and files are created — HTML documents, image slices, thumbnails, and so on.

Try This!

Take a look at the HTML code—the programming language driving your Web page—produced by ImageReady. It is a text file, so you can open it in any text editor. You'll find that the programming steps are pretty easy to follow. You may even find that, without even trying, you can teach yourself a little HTML programming.

IMAGEREADY:
Launch ImageReady, Create an Image Slice and a Rollover (Continued)

You are probably familiar with Web pages that have "hot" spots—that is, areas that change color as your mouse hovers over them or you click on them. These hot spots are called rollovers—they react to movements of your mouse or other pointing device.

Rollovers are used to alert a user that something will happen if you click on the area — that something is usually navigating the user to a different Web page or creating an e-mail message. If you are going to use a rollover as a link, you should first define a

piece of the Web as an image slice — that is an object to which you can assigned attributes or functions — like assigning a URL (Web address) so you can surf to another page A Rollover also requires you to define two states: Normal or Over. The Over state is what happens when the mouse or other pointer is "over" the area; the Normal state is when it is not. Commonly, the two states are represented by almost identical images—except for color.

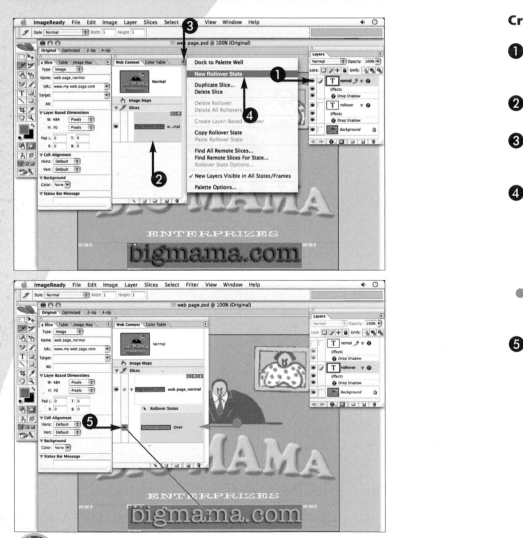

Create A rollover

① Click on eye icon to the left of the Normal Layer in the Layers palette to hide the layer.

② Click here to make the slice you created active.

③ In the Web Content palette click on the triangle on upper right corner.

④ Click New Rollover State.

● ImageReady creates an Over entry in the Web Content palette.

⑤ Click here and drag to the targeted rollover content.

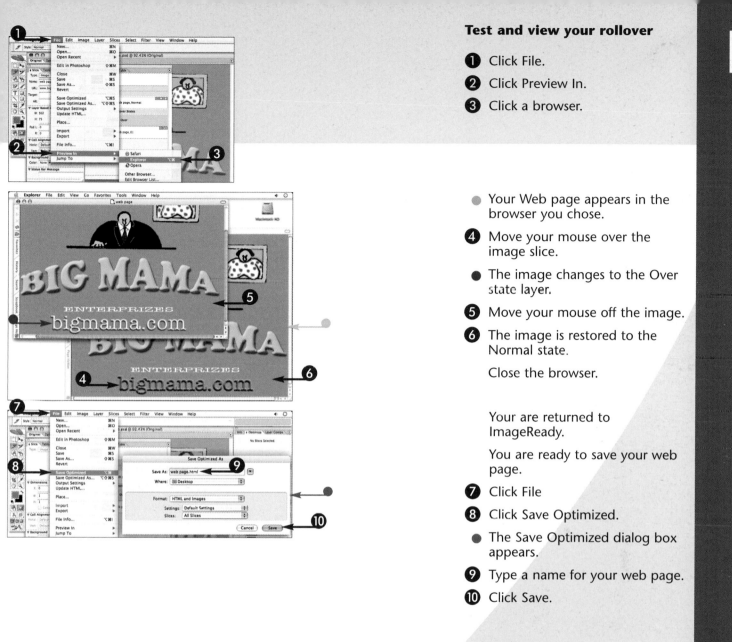

Test and view your rollover

1 Click File.

2 Click Preview In.

3 Click a browser.

● Your Web page appears in the browser you chose.

4 Move your mouse over the image slice.

● The image changes to the Over state layer.

5 Move your mouse off the image.

6 The image is restored to the Normal state.

Close the browser.

Your are returned to ImageReady.

You are ready to save your web page.

7 Click File

8 Click Save Optimized.

● The Save Optimized dialog box appears.

9 Type a name for your web page.

10 Click Save.

Did You Know?

You can program other states into a rollover and create additional rollover frames. Click the Options menu in the Web Content palette and choose the rollover options you want.

Did You Know?

Image maps can be made as a circle shape or a polygon. These tools help more precisely define the image map area.

INFO:
Determine the Numerical Value of Pixels

The Info palette lets you accurately measure the color value of a single pixel or the average of a group of pixels. You can use the measured areas as markers when you make adjustments to the image. By default, the Info palette displays the Actual Color information, the current color mode in the upper-left field. The CMYK equivalents display in the upper-right field. Below the Actual Color field are the x and y coordinates of the position of the cursor. To the right of the Actual Color field are width and height fields of the current selection outline. Document file size and brief instructions for the current tool also appear.

As you drag over the image, the numeric values for the pixel or group of pixels under the cursor appear. You can select one of the eyedroppers in the palette to display an options menu. You can configure the options to display Actual Color, Proof Color, Grayscale CMYK, RGB Color, HSB Color, Lab Color, Total Ink, Opacity, and the bit depth information (8 bit, 16 bit, and 32 bit).

See also>> **Color Sampler tool**

① Press F8.

Alternatively you can Click Window and then Info.

● The Info palette appears.

② Click one of the Eyedropper icons on the Info palette.

③ Click here and select a color mode or model from the menu that displays.

④ Click and drag the cursor across an image.

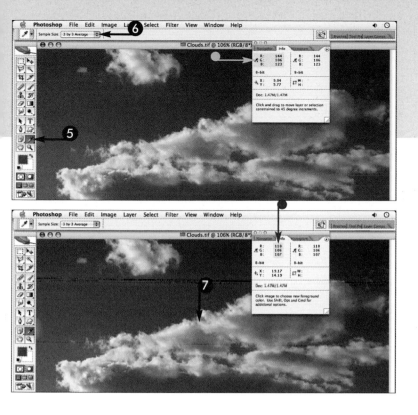

- The numbers change to display the color information.

5 Click the Eyedropper tool in the Tools palette.

6 Click here and select a sample size in the Options bar.

You can select Point Sample, 3 by 3 Average (9 pixels), or 5 by 5 Average (25 pixels).

7 Drag across the image again.

- The values display.

I

TIPS

Did You Know?

When you sample a point in an image, by default the values displayed in the Info palette pertain to the actual information in the image—that is the numbers listed for an RGB file would be RGB values. However, you may want to know what the values would be if the image were to be converted to CMYK. Click on one of the Eyedroppers at the top of the Info palette, a menu appears and you can choose to display CMYK (or other color model) values instead. The Info palette displays the values in italics to distinguish them from actual color numbers.

Try It!

Selecting Palette Options from the Info Palette options menu gives you several options that increase the type of information displayed in the Info palette—like what the current tool is, the document dimension, different measuring devices, and so on.

Did You Know?

You can take readings for 8-, 16-, and 32-bit images at the bottom of the Info palette Eyedropper menus. Pick the bit depth for any of the color modes.

LAYERS, ADJUSTMENT:
Attach a Color Correction to a Layer

Photoshop's Adjustment layers let you apply effects to an image without changing the image itself. The adjustment is done via a layer directly above the image.

You can apply adjustments such as Levels, Curves, or Hue/Saturation to an image by using adjustment commands. However, if you apply the same affect by using Adjustment layers you not only leave your image intact, but you have more control over the intensity of the affects and have the additional options accessed through the Layers Styles dialog box.

By default, an Adjustment layer affects all of the layers below it in the layer stack. You can, however, designate an Adjustment layer to affect only the layer immediately below it.

With Adjustment layers you can selectively apply an adjustment to a specific area of the image. By default, an Adjustment layer has a layer mask attached to it. You can also use Adjustment layers in combination with blending modes and opacity to produce the exact effect you want.

See also>>

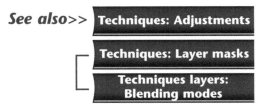

Techniques: Adjustments

Techniques: Layer masks

Techniques layers:
Blending modes

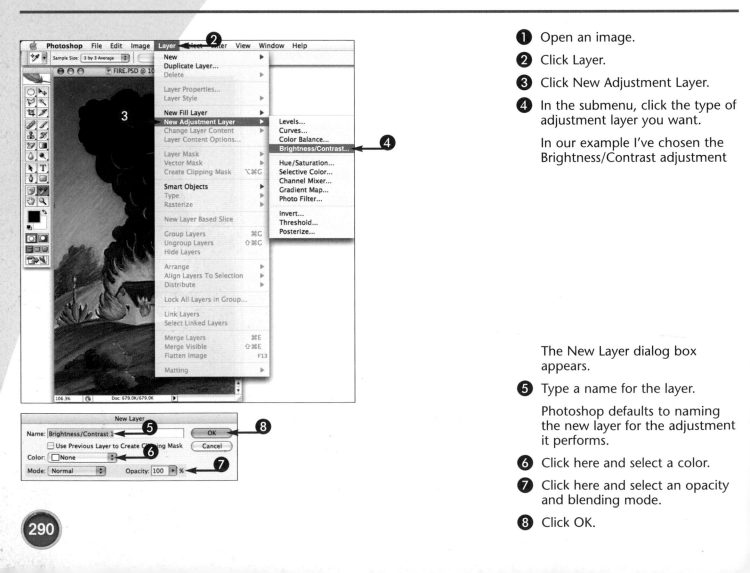

① Open an image.

② Click Layer.

③ Click New Adjustment Layer.

④ In the submenu, click the type of adjustment layer you want.

   In our example I've chosen the Brightness/Contrast adjustment

The New Layer dialog box appears.

⑤ Type a name for the layer.

   Photoshop defaults to naming the new layer for the adjustment it performs.

⑥ Click here and select a color.

⑦ Click here and select an opacity and blending mode.

⑧ Click OK.

Brightness/Contrast

Brightness: 15

Contrast: 5

OK

Cancel

☑ Preview

9

10

FIRE.PSD @ 106% (Brightness/Contrast 1, Layer...

106.3%   Doc: 679.0K/679.0K

The dialog box for the adjustment type you selected appears.

In this example, the Brightness/Contrast dialog box was selected.

⑨ Click and drag the sliders or click the various options until you achieve the desired results.

⑩ Click OK.

You see the affects of adjustments in the image and a new layer appears in the Layers palette.

L

TIPS

Did You Know?

Although, by default, an Adjustment layer affects all of the layers below it in the layer stack, you can designate it to only affect the layer immediately below it. To do so, press Opt+click (Alt + click) the line between the Adjustment layer and the layer below it. The grouped layer indents, indicating that the two layers are now grouped. You ungroup an Adjustment layer in the same way.

Did You Know?

You can group a layer by clicking the Use Previous Layer to Create Clipping Mask option (☐ changes to ☑) in the New Layer dialog box.

Try This!

Click the Eye icon to the right of the new adjustment layer. Your image is intact! Turning the Adjustment on and off allows you to have two versions of the image in one file.

LAYERS, CLIPPING MASK:
Paint a Surface Onto a Layer

When you group layers together, you can perform some very interesting visual tricks. You can literally "tattoo" one image onto the other. With the help of layer masks, layer opacity, and blending modes, you can mold and model an image into a superbly realistic surface.

When you clip a layer, the top layer is cut, or "clipped" in the shape of the layer content immediately below it. The clipping mask is surrounded by transparency or the content of any layers beneath it in the stack.

To join two layers into a clipping group, you must surround the image on the bottom layer by transparency. The layer you want to clip appears one step higher in the stack. When you clip a layer, it fills the shape of the image on the layer below it. The bottom layer serves as a mask to clip the layer immediately above it.

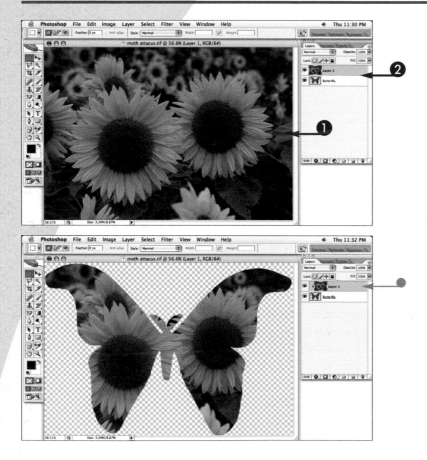

Create a Clipping Mask

1 Open an image that contains at least two layers, one of which contains an object surrounded by transparency.

The top layer contains the surface; the lower layer is an element surrounded by transparency.

2 Press Opt (Alt) and click between the two layers in the Layers palette.

● The top layer is clipped to the lower layer.

The result is that the shape of the object in the lower level is filled with the contents of the top layer.

Apply a Blending mode to the Mask

① Click the top layer.

② Click here to select from a list of blending modes.

This example uses Hard Light.

● Click and drag the Opacity slider to soften the blend affect

The image displays a more interesting pattern.

Did You Know?

You can control the opacity of the brush as you paint by typing a number. If you type **2**, the opacity changes to 20%. If you want to type a value of **61%** for the opacity, do so quickly. You type **6** and then **1** very quickly or you may end up with 60% and then 10%.

Did You Know!

You cannot make the Background layer transparent. If you want to set the Background layer as the bottom portion of your clipping group, you must redefine it as a "regular" layer. You can do this simply by renaming the layer to something other than "Background."

LAYERS, FILL LAYERS:
Apply a Gradient and Pattern

You can fill an area with color, a gradient, or a pattern using a Fill layer. The use of Fill layers gives you more flexibility than other methods of filling areas of color. Fill layers combine the ease of the Fill command with the power of adjustment layer options.

The New Fill Layer submenu of the Layer menu has three options: Solid Color, Gradient, or Pattern. When you select any of these options the New Layer dialog box appears. The New Layer dialog box, allows you to name your layer, to select a blending mode, or to

type an opacity percent. Depending on the type of fill you select, the next dialog box gives you additional options.

See also>>

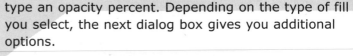

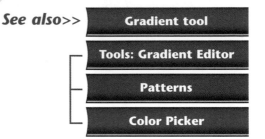

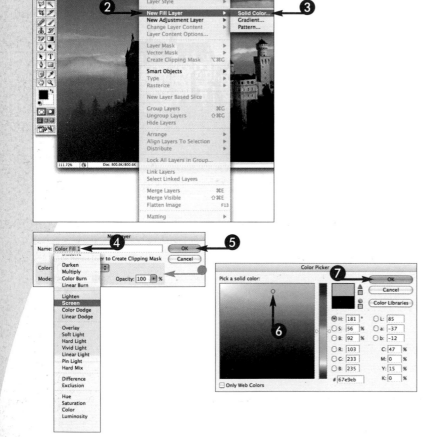

Fill the Layer with a Color

① Click Layer.

② Click New Fill Layer.

③ Click Solid Color.

The New Layer dialog box appears.

④ Type a name for the new fill layer.

● You can select other options from the dialog box.

⑤ Click OK.

The Color Picker dialog box appears.

⑥ Select a color.

⑦ Click OK.

The new Solid Color Fill layer appears in the Layers palette.

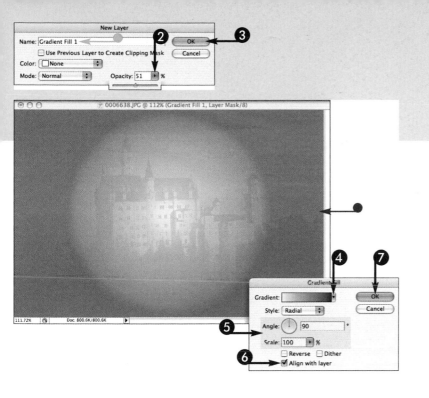

Fill a Layer with a Gradient

① Follow steps **1** to **3** on the previous page, but click Gradient for step **3**.

● The New Layer dialog box appears again and the name of the new layer defaults to Gradient Fill 1.

② Click here and change the opacity.

This example uses 51%.

③ Click OK.

The Gradient Fill dialog box appears.

④ Click here and select a gradient pattern and style.

⑤ Type a scale and angle here.

⑥ Click the Align with layer option.

⑦ Click OK.

● Photoshop fills your image with gradient.

TIPS

Did You Know?

If you make a selection prior to creating a Fill layer, the new Fill layer only fills the selected area and creates a layer mask that conceals the unselected areas. The layer mask thumbnail that appears in the Layers palette displays the revealed area as a white shape and the masked area as a black border.

Try This!

If you want a gradient other than the one presented, click the down arrow to the right of the gradient swatch to select a saved gradient, or click the swatch itself to display the Gradient Editor and create a new one.

LAYERS, FILL LAYERS:
Apply a Gradient and Pattern (Continued)

You can fill a layer with a pattern. As with any layer, you can clip the pattern filled layer to a layer immediately above it. You can also change the opacity setting and select a blending mode.

You can also apply a layer mask to a Fill layer. You may find a pattern fill too busy or overwhelming. A

layer mask solves this problem because it allow you to limit the area(s) that you want to fill with a pattern.

At any point in the editing process you can change the pattern fill in the Layers palette.

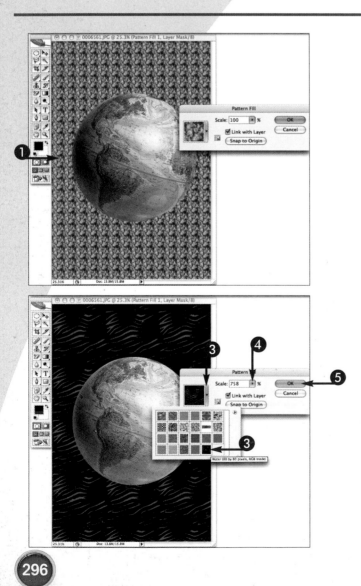

Fill a Layer with a Pattern

1 Select a section of an image to which you want to apply a pattern fill.

2 Follow steps **1** to **5** in the subsection "Fill the Layer with a Color" on the previous page, but in step **3**, click Pattern.

The Pattern Fill dialog box appears.

You see a preview of the pattern, and, because you created a selection, it is only applied to the selected area.

3 Click here and select a pattern.

4 Click here to set the scale.

5 Click OK.

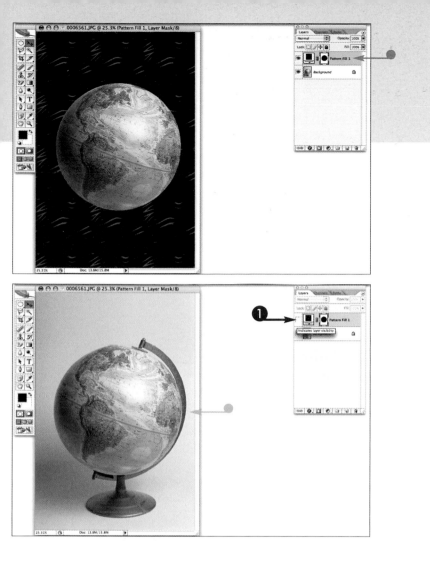

The new layer thumbnails show you not only that Photoshop has applied a pattern, but also that it created a mask.

Return the Image to its Original State

1 Click on the eye icon to the left of the Pattern Fill layer.

● Your original image is intact.

TIPS

Did You Know?
You can edit Color Fill, Gradient Fill, and Pattern Fill layers by double-clicking their thumbnails in the Layers palette to reveal the Color Picker, the Gradient Fill, or the Pattern Fill dialog box.

Try This!
You can move a pattern by targeting the Pattern layer and then clicking and dragging your cursor on the image window.

LAYERS, GROUPS:
Organize Layers Into Folders

Because a single Photoshop file may contain a virtually unlimited number of layers, the potential to produce enormous files makes layer-management absolutely necessary. This is particularly important not just because of the number of layers, but also because the layers have a very complex relationship of adjustments and blends.

Layer Groups provide a way to organize layers by storing them in folders. You can then apply affects or actions to the folder as if it were one layer. For example, you can reveal or conceal the layer group via the visibility icon, reposition the entire group in the stacking order, or transform the group using any of the transform features.

You have several ways to create a layer group: via the Layer menu, the Layer palette menu, or by using the Layer Group icon in the Layers palette. These three options create an empty layer into which you can move layers. Yet another method is to duplicate a group layer.

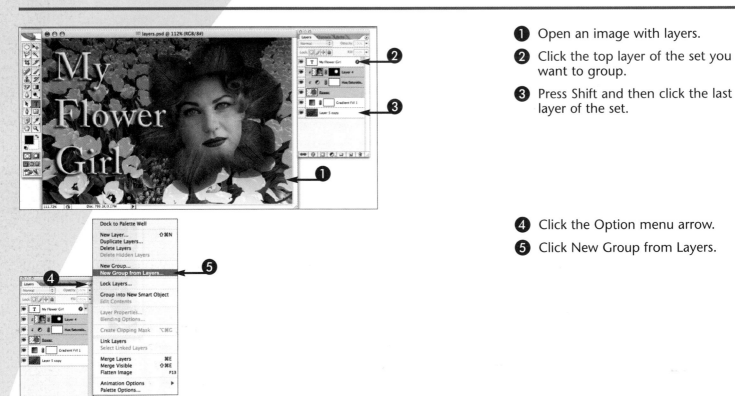

① Open an image with layers.

② Click the top layer of the set you want to group.

③ Press Shift and then click the last layer of the set.

④ Click the Option menu arrow.

⑤ Click New Group from Layers.

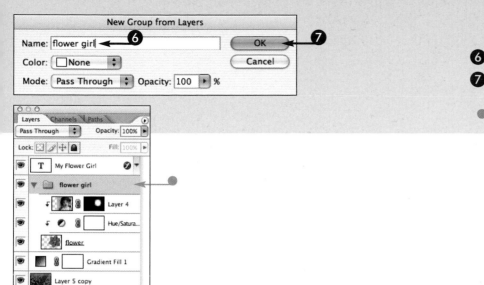

The New Group from Layers dialog box appears.

6 Type a name for the group.

7 Click OK.

● The Layers assemble into a labeled folder.

Did You Know?

The only limitation to how many layers a file contains is the amount of random access memory (RAM) installed in your computer and the amount of disk space available to store it.

Try This!

You can quickly brighten an image by duplicating it as layer — Cmd+J(Ctrl+J) — and then changing the blending mode to Screen. This lightens the pixels of a layer below without tone and hue loss.

Try This!

If your file is so big that it taxes the memory or disk space of your computer, reduce the file size by flattening a group of layers into a single layer. Simply click Layer and then Merge Group.

LAYERS, LINK:
Transform Multiple Layers

You can size, rotate, move, and otherwise transform two or more layers simultaneously by *linking* them. For example, if you have two elements of a logo on separate layers, and you are satisfied with their visual relationship but want to change the size and move them, you can link them so that you can perform these operations on both layers. The advantage of linking layers is that if you know that the layers should always be transformed together, linking them saves you the trouble of remembering that fact.

Photoshop CS2 does allows you to select and transform two or more layers without linking them. However, if you have a complex file with many layers, it doesn't hurt to take advantage of the Link command.

See also>>

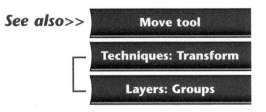

Move tool

Techniques: Transform

Layers: Groups

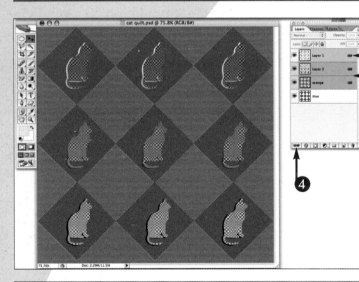

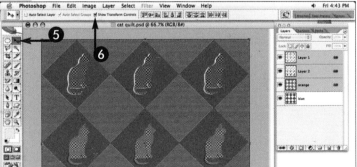

1. Open a layered document.
2. In the Layers palette, click a layer.
3. Press the Cmd(Ctrl) and click additional layers.
4. Click the Link icon at the bottom of the layers palette.

5. Click the Move tool.
6. Click the Show Transform Controls box in the Options bar.

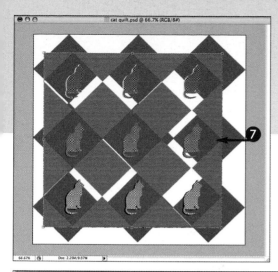

A bounding box is displayed that contains all of the linked elements.

⑦ Click and drag the bounding box to move the layer content, or perform another transformation.

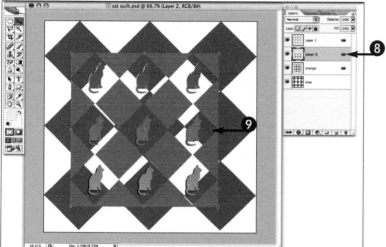

⑧ Click just one of the linked layers.

⑨ Click and drag the bounding box to reduce the size of the selection.

The transformation is applied to all the linked layers even though you selected only one of the linked layers.

TIPS

Did You Know?

You can separate linked layers and they still retain their link to each other. For example, you can move one of three linked layers to group A. The remaining layers can reside outside of the group — making it seem like they are no longer together. If you click on the layers and execute a transform command, all three layers are still transformed.

Did You Know?

You can apply blend modes and adjustments to a layer that is part of a linked group without affecting the other layers. The relationship of linked layers is limited to transform commands — that is, rotate, skew, flip, scale, and so on.

Did You Know?

If you delete a layer that is linked to other layers, the remaining layers are still linked.

LAYERS, LOCKS:
Protect Layer Content

You can lock your layer to prevent any change, or to prevent changes to only a part of your image. Photoshop provides four methods to lock layers, each with its own level of protection. Photoshop indicates these four methods with four *lock icons* in the Layers palette. The lock icons act as toggles to turn the lock on or off.

Lock Transparent Pixels protects transparent areas of a layer. If you attempt to paint or fill the transparent area of a layer, Photoshop does not respond. In a sense, locking transparency works like a mask; only the areas that have pixels responds to Photoshop action.

Lock Image Pixels protects the layer content from painting, color adjustments, or filters. Basically, the entire layer is protected from actions and adjustments other than transform commands. If you to apply a command or action, you see the universal circle with a line through it and the message, "Could not use the xxxx because the layer is locked."

Lock Position prevents you from moving a targeted layer or applying Transform operations such as Scale or Distort.

Lock All protects a layer from all editing functions.

See also>> **Color swatch**

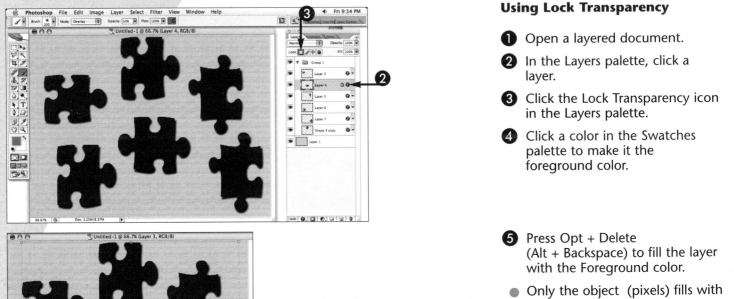

Using Lock Transparency

❶ Open a layered document.

❷ In the Layers palette, click a layer.

❸ Click the Lock Transparency icon in the Layers palette.

❹ Click a color in the Swatches palette to make it the foreground color.

❺ Press Opt + Delete (Alt + Backspace) to fill the layer with the Foreground color.

● Only the object (pixels) fills with color; the transparent area remains unaffected.

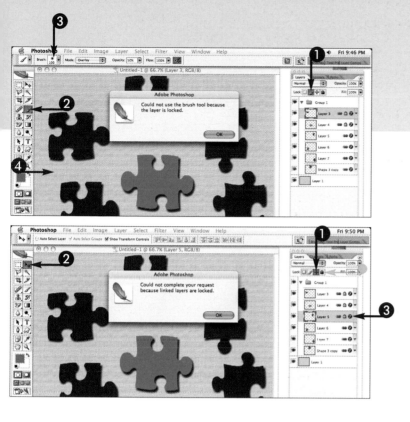

Using Lock Image Pixels

① Click the Lock Image pixels icon.

② Click the Brush tool in the Tools palette.

③ Click a brush from the Brush presets in the Options bar.

④ Drag the brush across the image window.

A circle with a line through it along with a warning box appears.

Using Lock Position

① Click the Lock Position icon.

● You can click the Lock All option to protect the image from all editing.

② Click the Move tool.

③ Click and drag the layer contents.

A dialog box appears warning that the layer is locked.

TIPS

Did You Know?

You know a layer is locked when it displays a lock icon to the right of its name. However, you do not know what kind of lock it is until you click the layer and the appropriate lock icon at the top of the Layers palette darkens.

Did You Know?

Photoshop applies Lock transparency and Lock image by default to layers that contain type. To disable these locks, you must convert type to objects — at which point you lose any type editing functions.

Try This!

You can lock several layers at once by selecting all the layers — click+Shift — and then clicking the Lock Layers or Lock All layers icon from the Layers palette menu.

LAYER MASK:
Conceal and Reveal Layer Content

You can use a layer mask to show or diminish applied adjustments or actions to a layer or sections of a layer. The one requirement is that the layer is not the Background layer. Although you can use a Layer Mask just like a regular mask, it is specifically designed to hide or lessen effects or adjustments applied to pixels in a layer.

When you apply a layer mask, you have two options: Reveal All or Hide All. Reveal All only sets up the environment for you to apply a mask with a brush. To finish the process, you need a brush tool and a

black or white Foreground color swatch to finish the process. For example, to lessen the effects of two blended layers, you can set the Foreground color swatch to black, and apply brush strokes, with the correct softness, size, opacity, and flow.

The Hide All option applies a mask to the entire layer. You then use a paint brush, this time applied with the Foreground swatch set to white, to reveal all or portions of a layer Again, the brush options determine the intensity of the affect.

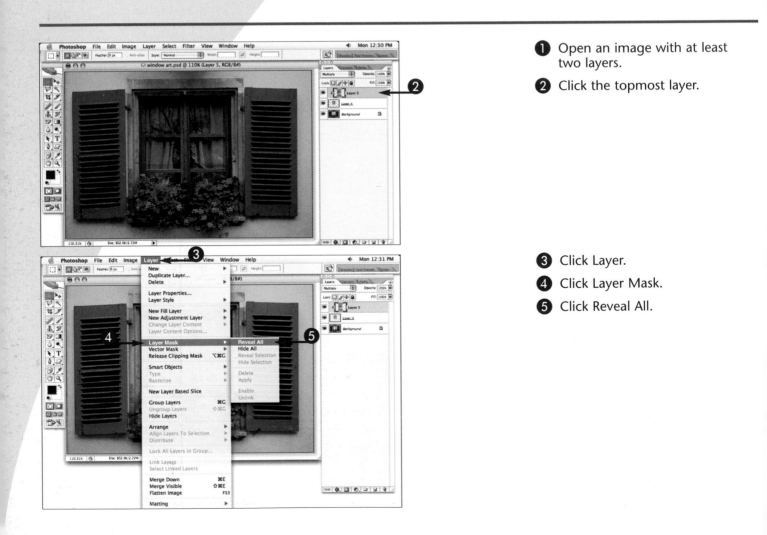

1. Open an image with at least two layers.

2. Click the topmost layer.

3. Click Layer.

4. Click Layer Mask.

5. Click Reveal All.

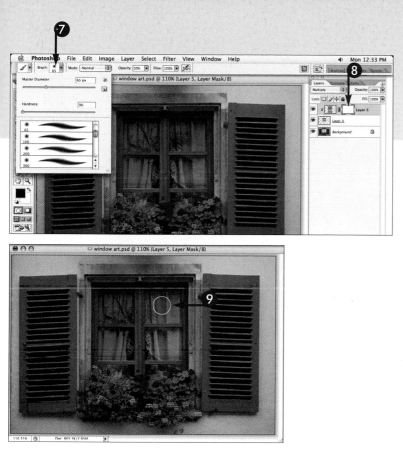

A layer mask appears in the Layers palette.

6 Click a Brush tool.

7 Click here and select a brush size from the presets in the Options bar.

8 Click the Layer mask in the Layers palette.

9 Click the image an start painting.

As you paint, the blending effect diminishes.

If you make a mistake you can repaint the effect by pressing X to change the foreground color to white.

Try This!

You can Shift + click the layer mask to turn it on or off, or click Layer, Layer Mask, and then Enable or Disable Layer Mask. You can Opt + click (Alt + click) the mask thumbnail to view the layer mask in the image window. When you Cmd + click (Ctrl +click) the layer mask, it generates a selection outline.

Try This!

To remove a layer mask, drag the Layer Mask icon to the Trash icon on the Layers palette. The Delete Layer Mask dialog box appears and asks if you want to apply the mask before you discard it.

LAYER, MERGE/FLATTEN:
Combine Layer Content

You can merge or flatten layers to increase your computer's efficiency. Although, in theory, you can create as many layers as you want, in practice, the amount of memory and disk space your computer has limits you. Adding layers increases your file size and memory requirements possibly causing Photoshop to become sluggish.

You can either merge several layers into one or simply flatten the whole image.

To merge layers, select the layers that you want to merge and then, turn the visibility of all other layers off using the eye icon and then use the Merge Visible

command. Alternatively, you can merge two adjacent layers by applying the Merge Down command after selecting the top layer of the two you want to merge.

A final choice is to simply merge all layers by applying the Flatten Image command. Keep in mind that if you flatten an image and then save and close it, there is no way to retrieve the layers. If you want to keep your layers, create a copy of your layered image as backup and work on the merged file.

See also>> **Duplicate an image**

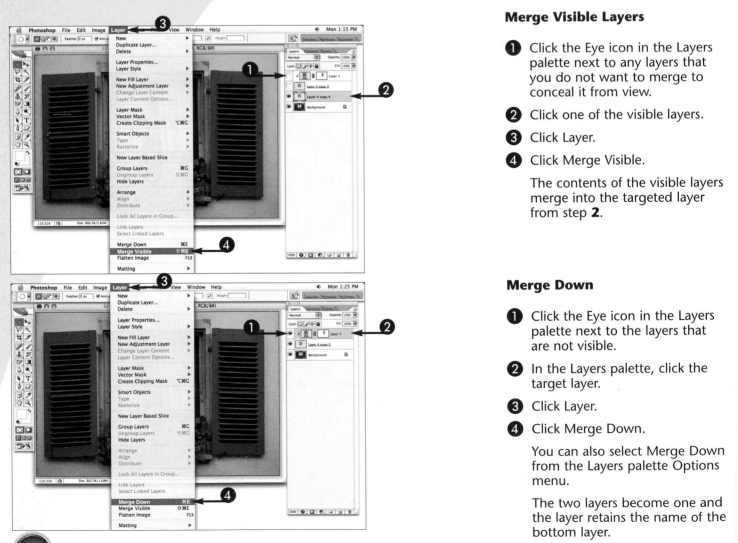

Merge Visible Layers

1. Click the Eye icon in the Layers palette next to any layers that you do not want to merge to conceal it from view.

2. Click one of the visible layers.

3. Click Layer.

4. Click Merge Visible.

   The contents of the visible layers merge into the targeted layer from step **2**.

Merge Down

1. Click the Eye icon in the Layers palette next to the layers that are not visible.

2. In the Layers palette, click the target layer.

3. Click Layer.

4. Click Merge Down.

   You can also select Merge Down from the Layers palette Options menu.

   The two layers become one and the layer retains the name of the bottom layer.

Flatten All Layers

1 Click Layer.

2 Click Flatten Image.

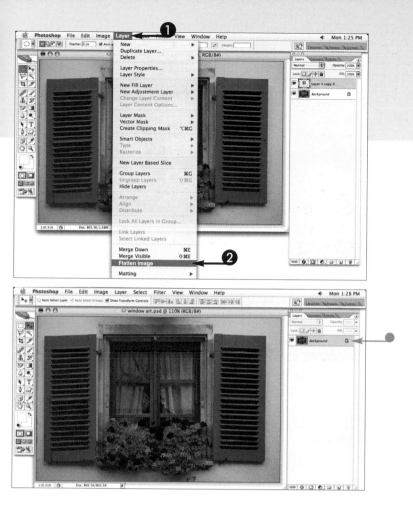

● Photoshop flattens the layers of the image and the remaining layer becomes Background.

TIPS

Try This!
To discard layers whose content you do not want included in the final image, click the Eye icon of each layer to conceal it before clicking Flatten Image. A dialog box appears to confirm that you want to discard the hidden layers. Click Yes to click Cancel to cancel flattening them. The final flattened image will not include the content of those layers.

Did You Know?
You can duplicate a flattened version of the contents of two or more layers to create a new layer. Press and hold the Opt (Alt) key and select a Merge function from the Palette menu. This merges the content of the layers into the targeted layer, but does not delete the original layers.

LAYERS, PALETTE:
Change the Stacking Order

You can control how layers interact with one another by changing their stacking order. By default a Photoshop image contains at least one layer. As you add layers, Photoshop stacks them on top of this layer. The Photoshop image window displays layers in order from bottom to top. That is the object(s) on the topmost layer overlay those behind it.

The Background layer is locked and cannot be transformed or placed in a different position in a layer stack. However, you can unlock the Background by simply renaming the layer to something other than Background. When you flatten an image, the remaining layer becomes the Background layer.

Each layer's row includes a thumbnail of the layer's contents, the layer's name, and icons representing layer styles, masks, or locks you have applied to that layer. An Eye icon toggles on or off to hide or reveal layers. The Layers Palette also displays several layer options. At the very top is a button which lists blending options; to its right is a slider which controls transparency. Just below are lock options and a fill value option.

In addition, the Layers palette has its own menu that you access via the small triangular button on the top-right.

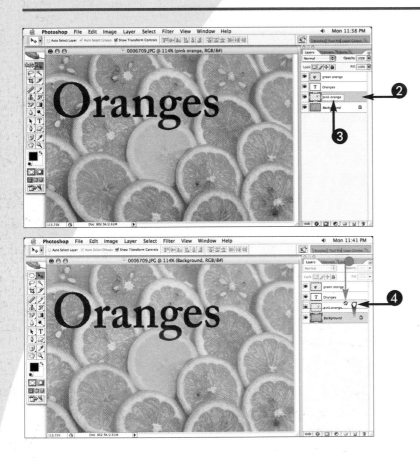

Name Layers

① Open a document containing multiple layers and a background.

② Double-click a layer's name.

③ Type a name for the layer.

You can repeat steps **2** and **3** for all the layers down the stack in numerical sequence.

④ Click and drag the background upward.

● A circle with a line through it appears, indicating that the background cannot be moved.

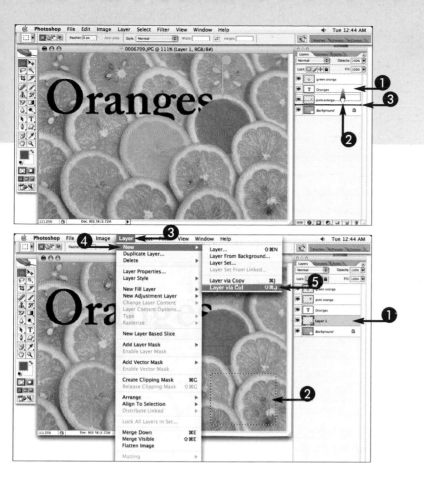

Move Layers in the Stack

1️⃣ Click a layer.

2️⃣ Drag the layer to the layer below it in the stack.

3️⃣ When you see the top-most separation line thicken, release the mouse.

The layer has changed position.

⬤ In this example the pink orange now overlays the "s."

Create a Layer by Copying or Cutting Content

1️⃣ Click a layer.

2️⃣ Make a selection.

3️⃣ Click Layer.

4️⃣ Click New.

5️⃣ Click either Layer Via Copy or Layer Via Cut.

Look at the layer thumbnails.

In the example the New Layer Via Cut command created a new layer, which contains the selection.

The layer below it shows a blank shape where the selection came from.

L

TIPS

Try This!

Press the Opt (Alt) key as you click and drag a layer. Photoshop duplicates the layer. You can also use this technique to duplicate several layers. Shift-click (or Cmd(Ctrl)+click if the layers are not contiguous) to select all the layers you want to duplicate; press Opt (Alt) as you click on any of the selected layers and drag.

Did You Know?

You can change the Background layer to a regular layer by double-clicking on the thumbnail. The layer is given the name "Layer 0" and you can change it like any other layer.

Try This!

Discard a layer by dragging it to the Trash icon at the bottom the Layers palette. You can also discard several layers at once by selecting those layers and then clicking the Trash icon.

LAYERS:
Opacity, Make Areas Transparent or Opaque

Photoshop allows you to control the transparency — or opacity — of layers in an image. The Opacity slider is an option on the Layers palette which enables you to adjust the level of transparency of each layer. By varying the opacity of a layer you can create interesting blending effects between layers. You can also use the opacity control to reduce layer adjustment effects.

If you move the Opacity slider all the way to the left, the layer becomes invisible (represented by a gray checkerboard); if you slide it all the way to the right, the layer is completely opaque. Any value in between gives the layer varying degrees of visibility/transparency. The layer that you cannot make transparent is the Photoshop Background layer. You can rename this layer to something other than Background and apply any effects or adjustments that you want to a regular layer.

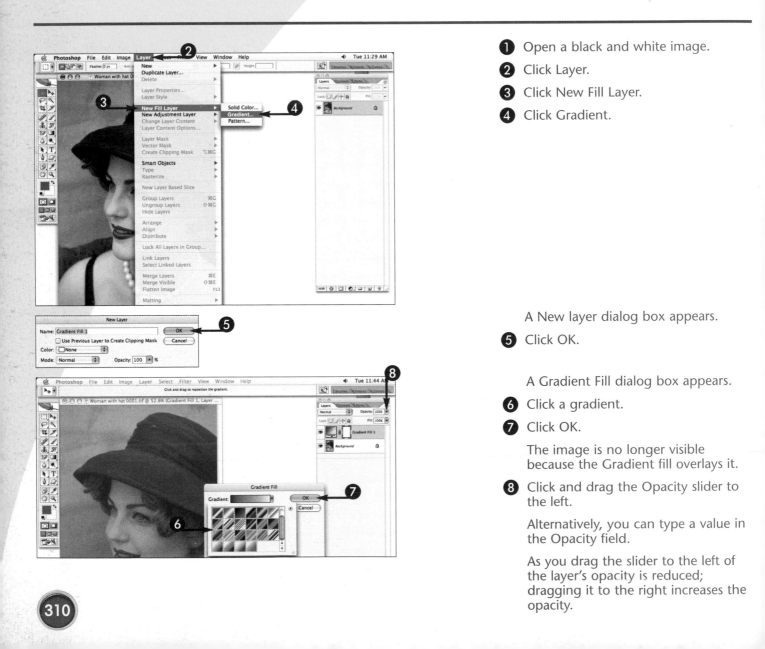

① Open a black and white image.

② Click Layer.

③ Click New Fill Layer.

④ Click Gradient.

A New layer dialog box appears.

⑤ Click OK.

A Gradient Fill dialog box appears.

⑥ Click a gradient.

⑦ Click OK.

The image is no longer visible because the Gradient fill overlays it.

⑧ Click and drag the Opacity slider to the left.

Alternatively, you can type a value in the Opacity field.

As you drag the slider to the left of the layer's opacity is reduced; dragging it to the right increases the opacity.

LAYERS, STYLES:
Jazz Up Your Layer Content

Layer styles can add dazzling effects to your images with enhancements such as drop shadows, neon glowing edges, and deep embossing. When you apply a style to a layer, an italic *f* icon appears to the right of the layer's name in the Layers palette.

To create, define, or edit a layer style, you use the Layer Style dialog box. You can access this box via the layer's thumbnail, via the small F icon

at the bottom of the Layers palette, or via the Blending options command in the Layers palette menu. In addition to the numerous styles offered, each style has many options. The options multiply the number of adjustments you can apply to a layer.

As with other adjustments, you cannot apply layer styles to the Background layer. Nor can layer styles be applied to more than one layer at a time.

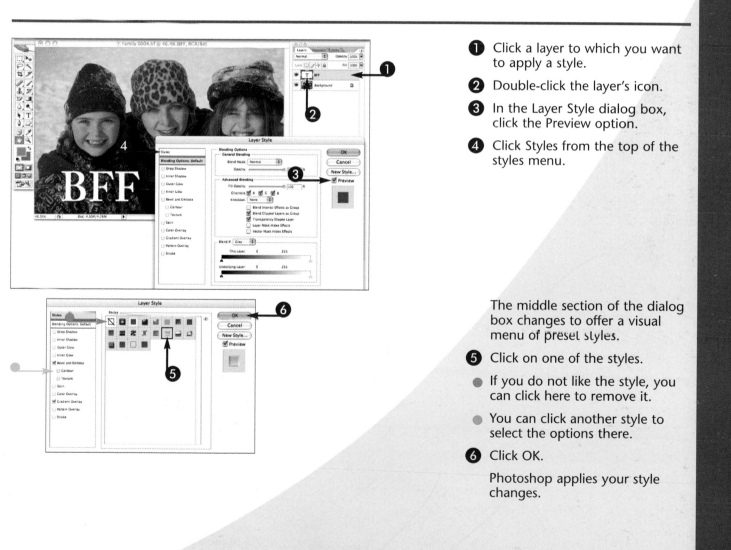

① Click a layer to which you want to apply a style.

② Double-click the layer's icon.

③ In the Layer Style dialog box, click the Preview option.

④ Click Styles from the top of the styles menu.

The middle section of the dialog box changes to offer a visual menu of preset styles.

⑤ Click on one of the styles.

● If you do not like the style, you can click here to remove it.

● You can click another style to select the options there.

⑥ Click OK.

Photoshop applies your style changes.

MATTING:
Eliminate an Unwanted Edge

You can eliminate an unwanted edge with Photoshop's Matting command. This command blends the fringe pixels with pixels of your background.

Because Photoshop is a raster-based graphic application, it sees an image as a collection of square or rectangle pixels and has no clear way of creating smooth curved lines. Therefore, when you select a portion of a curved image, the selection's edge contains some of the stair-step pixels from its background. When you copy or paste your curved selection into another image or layer, the curved edge appears as a fringe in the new image.

To use the Matting command, you must paste the selection into a transparent layer and you must have

the new background directly beneath this new layer. Photoshop offers three Matting options. Defringe eliminates edge pixels depending on the number of pixels you specify for the edge. With this option, Photoshop "blurs" the edge so that the new sections blend in with their new background. The Remove White Matte or Remove Black Matte options do exactly as they say. These options work for selections that you have extracted from white or black backgrounds.

See also>>

Layers, Palette: Change the Stacking Order

Zoom Tool: Take a Close Look at the Image

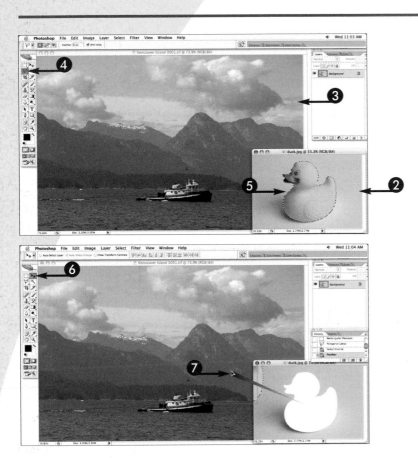

❶ Press F7.

The Layers palette is displayed.

❷ Open a source image from which you can make a selection to drag to another image.

❸ Open a destination image.

❹ Click a selection tool.

❺ Create a selection in the source image.

❻ Click the Move tool.

❼ Click and drag the selection from the source image to the destination image and then release the mouse.

A new layer appears in the destination image's Layers palette.

8 Zoom in on an area of the new layer to see the results of the Matting command.

● Note that the transferred image's edge has fringe pixels.

9 Click the layer containing the selection.

10 Click Layer.

11 Click Matting.

12 Click Defringe.

The Defringe dialog box appears.

13 Type a value in pixels that you want to affect.

14 Click OK.

The edge disappears.

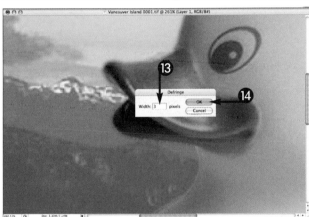

TIPS

Try This!

If none of the matting options works to your satisfaction, you can perform a neat workaround by selecting the image pixels on the layer (press Cmd (Ctrl)) and clicking the layer thumbnail. Click Select, Modify, and then Contract, and type an amount (in pixels) to contract the selection so that it is well within the edge. Click Select, and then click Inverse. You can press Delete (Backspace) to delete the edge.

Did You Know?

You can remove fringe areas using the Advanced Blending sliders in the Layer Styles dialog box. These sliders remove or make pixels transparent. You can preview as you make changes. For added control, you can separate the sliders by pressing Option+Click (Alt+Click).

MEMORY:
Assign Memory to Photoshop

You can assign more memory to Photoshop if you need it. The answer to the frequently asked question "How much RAM should I install to run Photoshop?" is answered by another question: "How much RAM can I afford?"

The Cache settings determine how many copies of your image Photoshop stores in memory to update the screen more quickly at reduced view sizes. The Memory Usage field displays the system's available RAM, the percentage of available RAM allocated to Photoshop, and the same amount in kilobytes. The

default setting of 50 percent is a good beginning to operating the software.

During a Photoshop work session, you can check the Efficiency setting in the status bar at the bottom of the image window. A setting of below 100 percent means that your system is performing less than efficiently. For example, 80 percent means that 20 percent of the operations are being performed in virtual memory. You can increase the percentage of memory by 10 percent increments until the efficiency remains at the maximum 100 percent.

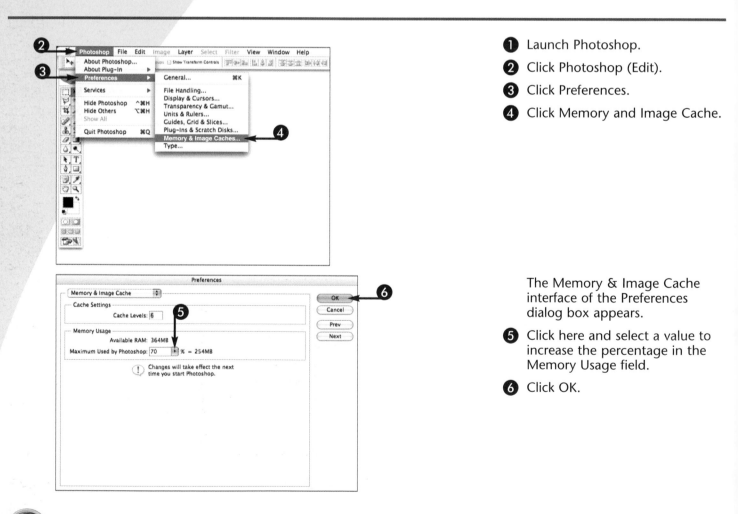

① Launch Photoshop.

② Click Photoshop (Edit).

③ Click Preferences.

④ Click Memory and Image Cache.

The Memory & Image Cache interface of the Preferences dialog box appears.

⑤ Click here and select a value to increase the percentage in the Memory Usage field.

⑥ Click OK.

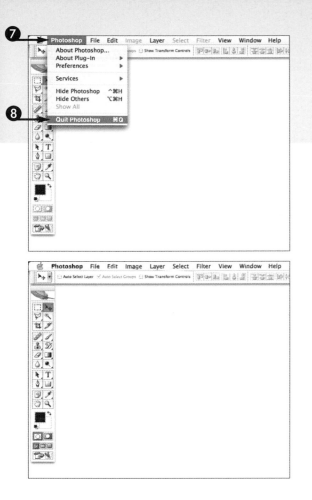

7 Click Photoshop (Edit).

8 Click Quit Photoshop.

9 Relaunch Photoshop.

The new setting takes effect and you are ready to take full advantage of your memory.

TIPS

Caution!

Never allocate all your memory to Photoshop. Your operating system requires some of the memory to perform necessary functions and you may need or want to run other applications at the same time that you have Photoshop open. Take a look at our your operating system manual to determine how much memory is needed to maintain basic computer functions. If you find that you are constantly "running on empty," it may be time to invest in more memory!

NAVIGATOR:
Find Your Way

As its name implies, the Navigator allows you to move around an image. No matter what portion of your image is displayed in the Photoshop window, the Navigator always displays the entire image. It provides you with a viewer (a red rectangle), which can be used to navigate around your image and zoom in and out of portions or your entire image.

As you zoom in to work on portions of your image, the Photoshop window will display only a portion of your image and you may loose track of where you are relative to the whole image. This is where the Navigator is most helpful. The full image is always displayed in the Navigator palette. Also, a moving rectangle surrounds the area of the image which is currently displayed in your Photoshop window.

By default, the Navigator palette is not displayed on your Photoshop screen. Because it is a very helpful tool, you may want it to be displayed automatically. Just go to the Window menu and click Navigator.

As you work, the Navigator allows you to zoom in and out of an image without changing tools. When you move the slider at the bottom of the Navigator palette to the right, you zoom in; move the slider to the left, you zoom out. You can also move to a different section on the image by placing the cursor within the red rectangle and dragging the mouse.

See also>>   **Zoom tool**

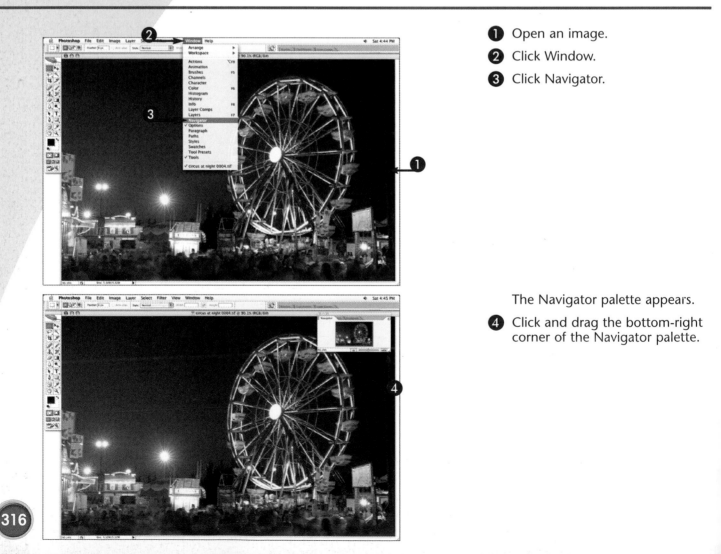

① Open an image.

② Click Window.

③ Click Navigator.

The Navigator palette appears.

④ Click and drag the bottom-right corner of the Navigator palette.

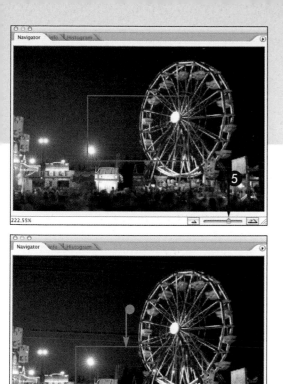

The palette size increases.

5 Click and drag the Navigator palette slider to the right.

● A red rectangle within the viewer changes size as you zoom in and out of your image.

This gives you a reference point so that you know in what part of the image you are located.

You can place the cursor inside the red rectangle, and click and drag to view different parts of the image. See how you can move to any area!

TIPS

Try This!

You can click the percentage field in the lower-left corner of the Navigator palette and type a percentage value between .10% and 1600%. When you press Enter to commit your changes, the image in the Photoshop window magnifies or reduces to the percent value you typed.

Try This!

If you click the small triangle to the right of the Navigator tab, a menu appears from which you can select Palette Options. You can then change the color of the Navigator rectangle from red to another color. If the rectangle is too close to the color of your image and too hard to see, it is a good idea to change the color of the rectangle to distinguish it from its surroundings.

NEW:
Create a New Document

Although you may think of Photoshop as software that modifies images from a scanner or digital camera, you can also create new artwork in Photoshop from scratch. You can start creating new artwork by first creating a new document via the Document dialog box, which allows you to name your document as well as to set its dimensions, file type, color mode, and other characteristics.

Although you have the option to do so, you do not always have to define characteristics for a new document because Photoshop provides a list of Preset types and sizes. For example, you can select

4 by 6 in the preset list to create a document for a standard postcard or photograph.

If you do create a newly defined type of document and you intend to create several such documents with the same characteristics, you can easily save the characteristics as a Preset. Photoshop includes the named Preset in the Preset list in the New dialog box.

See also>>

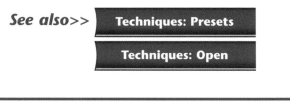

Create a New Document

❶ Click File.

❷ Click New.

The New dialog box appears.

❸ Click here and select a size from the Preset menu.

● Alternatively, you can type a height, width, and resolution, and select a color mode in the Preset.

❹ Click here and select a background type.

● If you change any of the options in the dialog box after selecting a Preset, Photoshop activates Save Preset.

Create a Preset

⑤ Click Save Preset.

The New Document Preset dialog box appears.

⑥ Click the options that you want to include in your new document.

⑦ Click OK.

⑧ Click OK in the New dialog box.

The new document appears in the workspace.

TIPS

Try This!
Try displaying a file in Photoshop while you have the History palette open. Now, apply a blending mode or filter to your image. When you click the Create new document button, Photoshop creates a new document for you.

Did You Know?
You do not have to draw and paint to create a new document. You can copy and paste sections of other images to create a collage. You can also layer images and apply layer styles to create an interesting work of art.

Did You know?
You can create new files from layers in one image. Photoshop provides a script called "Export Layers to Files," which you can find by clicking Photoshop and then clicking Scripts.

OPEN:
Open a Document

You can open a document to work on it in Photoshop using the Open command. Most of the files that you work with in Photoshop are scanned images or digital camera photographs. Using the Open dialog box, you can quickly and easily select the file or files you are after and open it.

The Open dialog box allows you to search for files using the drive and folder Icons. Depending on what type of computer and Operating System (OS) you have, you may have additional searches and options. For more on these additional features, see your OS documentation, as Photoshop is using a utility of that system.

You can specify the type of file you want to open. The Enable option in the Open dialog box gives you a list of the types of files you want to see listed. For example, most digital cameras default to creating JPEG files, so you can limit the Open dialog list to JPEG files. If you do not find a file you expect to have on your disk, simply change the Enable option to All Readable Documents.

See also>> **Techniques: Adobe Bridge**

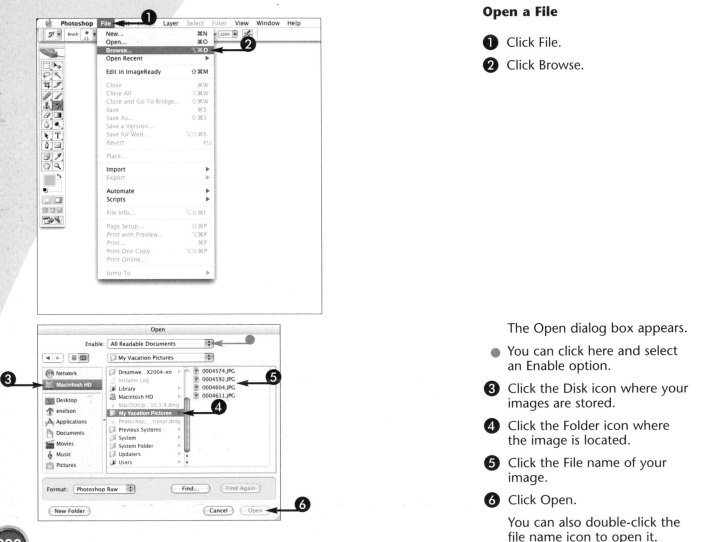

Open a File

1 Click File.

2 Click Browse.

The Open dialog box appears.

● You can click here and select an Enable option.

3 Click the Disk icon where your images are stored.

4 Click the Folder icon where the image is located.

5 Click the File name of your image.

6 Click Open.

You can also double-click the file name icon to open it.

The file opens in the Photoshop window.

Open a Recent File

1. Click File.
2. Click Open Recent.
3. Click the file name of your recently opened file.

   Photoshop opens your file.

TIPS

Did You Know?

There are two different kinds of Open file dialog boxes available: the OS dialog (the traditional Mac OS or Windows dialog box) and the new Adobe dialog. To Access the new Adobe dialog box, you must first click the Enable Version Cue Workgroup File Management option (☑ changes to ☐) in Photoshop Preferences.

Did You Know?

If you are part of a workgroup and various people work on the same file, Version Cue keeps track of who and when last changed a file. By selecting the Adobe dialog in the Open dialog box, you are availing yourself of this type of information, plus a preview of the image you want to open. You can switch to this view by clicking the Use Adobe Dialog button in the lower-left corner of the Open dialog box.

PALETTES:
Show, Move Cluster, Collapse, Dock Palettes

You can reorganize the palettes on your workspace to fit your individual needs. Palettes give you easy access to commands and features located in the main command menu, which allows you to navigate through several steps of menus and submenus.

Photoshop palettes "float," which means that you can place them anywhere on your screen, or toggle them on or off at will. You can also invoke palettes through function keys.

By default, palettes are organized into related clusters. The swatch palette, for example, is grouped with the color and styles palettes. If you want, you can organize them into groups that make more sense to you. You also can collapse them or dock them to the Palette Dock in the Options bar to save space on the workspace. You can also attach a palette to another palette, which lets you to drag them as a visible unit.

See also>> **Techniques: Workspace**

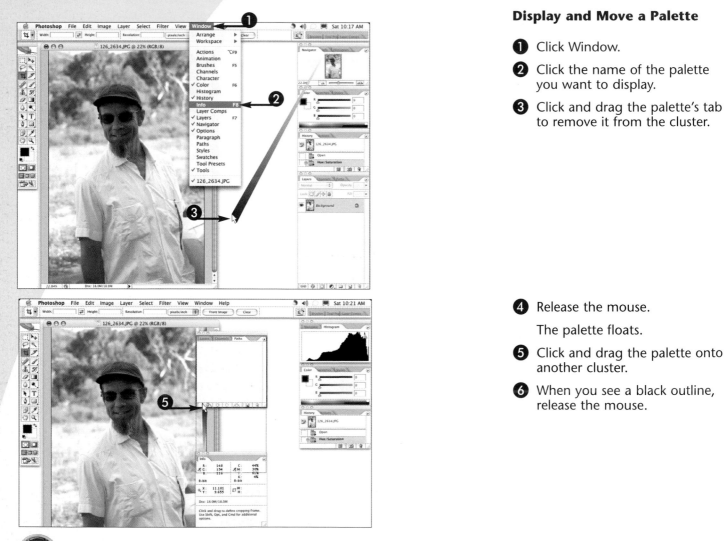

Display and Move a Palette

① Click Window.

② Click the name of the palette you want to display.

③ Click and drag the palette's tab to remove it from the cluster.

④ Release the mouse.

The palette floats.

⑤ Click and drag the palette onto another cluster.

⑥ When you see a black outline, release the mouse.

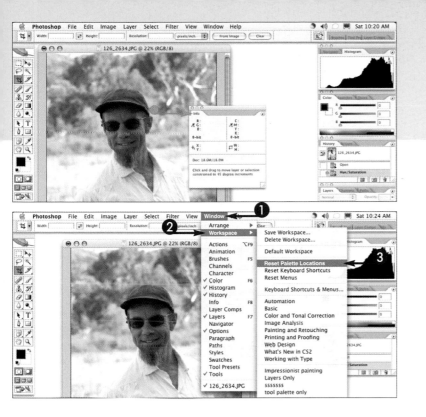

The palette is now a part of another cluster.

● You can double-click the palette's tab to collapse or expand it.

You can click the palette's tab and drag it to the Palette Dock in the Options bar to dock it.

Reset a Palette's Location

① Click Window.

② Click Workspace.

③ Click Reset Palette Locations.

The palettes are restored to their default locations.

TIPS

Try This!

You can save the location of your palettes. Arrange them in the way that works best for you and then click Windows, click Workspace, and then click Save Workspace. When the Save Workspace dialog box appears, type a name and click the Capture Locations option.

Shortcuts!

To display or hide a palette, click Window, and then the palette name. To hide or display all of the active palettes on the desktop, press Tab. Press Shift+Tab to hide all palettes except for the Tools palette. To quickly find shortcut keys to open palettes, click Edit and then click the Keyboard Shortcuts command.

PASTE, PASTE INTO:
Paste Content Into a Selection

You can paste an image or part of an image into a selection. For example, if you want to place a face that looks into a room from a window, you can copy the face, make a selection of just the window panes, and then paste the image into the window. Photoshop creates a Layer Mask, which you can edit.

When you paste your image, Photoshop creates a new layer that has an attached Layer Mask. The Layer Mask is in the shape of the selection so that it conceals the portion of the pasted image that is outside the selection outline. This produces the effect that the image is actually behind the destination area.

If you do not anticipate needing to adjust the paste into result, you can optimize your file by flattening the layers. You can also merge the mask layer with the underlying layer.

See also>>

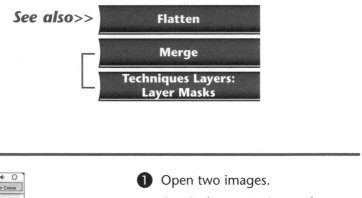

Flatten

Merge

Techniques Layers:
Layer Masks

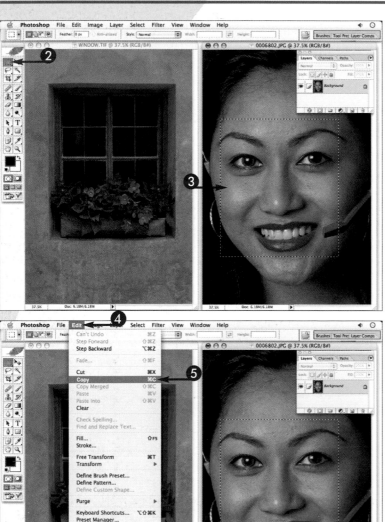

① Open two images.

One is the source image from which you copy, and the other is the destination image to which you paste.

② Click a selection tool.

③ Click and drag a selection outline around the area you want to copy.

④ Click Edit.

⑤ Click Copy.

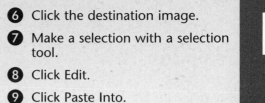

6 Click the destination image.

7 Make a selection with a selection tool.

8 Click Edit.

9 Click Paste Into.

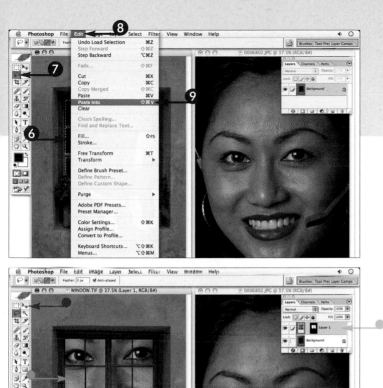

● The image is pasted into the selection.

● A new layer is created with a layer mask attached.

● You can click the Move tool and then click and drag the pasted image into the desired position.

TIPS

Did You Know?

After you paste the image, you can nudge the image with the up, down, left, and right arrows.

Did You Know?

You can resize the image with the Move tool.

Caution!

When you paste a selection or layer from another document, and that document is of a different resolution, the pasted selection retains the pixel dimensions of its source. The result is that the pasted selection becomes out of proportion with your target document. Also, if the two documents' color profiles are different, you will need to choose which color model or profile to use.

PATH, CLIPPING PATH:
Create a Knockout

You can create a clipping path to reveal only a section of an image. You can think of a mask in terms of rolled out dough that you cut with a cookie cutter. What you create is a knockout with the dough is the mask; the hole is the knockout. The function of a clipping path and a knockout is the same except in the type of data they affect; a knockout works with raster data while a clipping path works with vector data.

You can export a knockout you create in Photoshop as a clipping path to other programs. A clipping path is most useful when you surround the image with transparent space. Unfortunately, when another

program, such as Adobe Illustrator, InDesign, or QuarkXpress, uses that file, instead of being surrounded by "nothing" it is now surrounded by white because Photoshop exports the outline of your object as a clipping path, which is really a selection (knockout) translated into a Beziér curves — or, vector shapes. Any area contained within the path is visible. Areas outside the path are transparent when viewed in the destination program.

See also>>

Pen Tool

Techniques; Work path

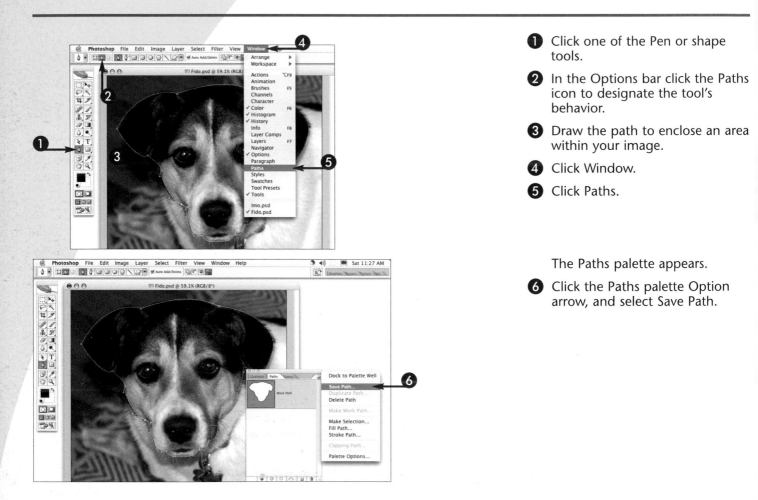

❶ Click one of the Pen or shape tools.

❷ In the Options bar click the Paths icon to designate the tool's behavior.

❸ Draw the path to enclose an area within your image.

❹ Click Window.

❺ Click Paths.

The Paths palette appears.

❻ Click the Paths palette Option arrow, and select Save Path.

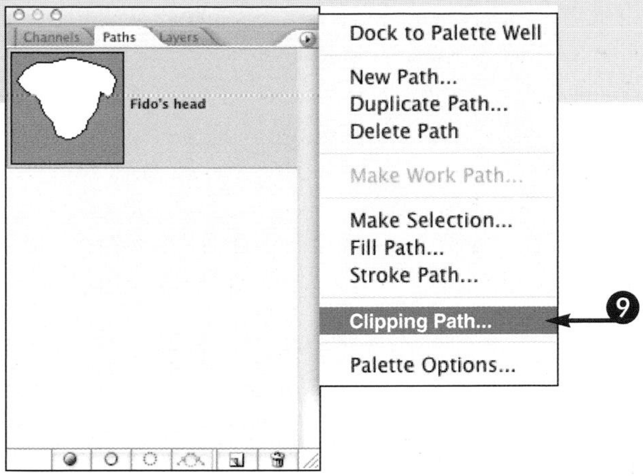

Save Path

Name: Fido's head ⑦

OK ⑧

Cancel

Channels | **Paths** | Layers

Fido's head

Dock to Palette Well

New Path...
Duplicate Path...
Delete Path

Make Work Path...

Make Selection...
Fill Path...
Stroke Path...

Clipping Path... ⑨

Palette Options...

The Save Path dialog box appears.

⑦ Type a new name for the path.

⑧ Click OK.

⑨ Click the Paths palette Options arrow, and select Clipping Path.

P

TIPS

Try This!

You can place a clipping path into a desktop publishing or vector illustration program and then wrap type around its shape.

Caution!

You can soften and feather Photoshop selections and masks, which is ideal for capturing the shape of a fuzzy object. On the other hand, vector-based curves (clipping paths) are smooth, and hard edged objects. This means that you cannot preserve the softness of an indistinct edge when you export clipping paths.

PATH, CLIPPING PATH:
Create a Knockout (Continued)

To create a clipping path in Photoshop you begin with either a path you created with the Pen tool or basic shapes tool, or you make a path from a selection. Either way, the next step is to save the path. If you do not save it, Photoshop considers it a temporary work path. After saving the path, you can designate it as a clipping path via the Paths palette or Photoshop Layers command.

To preserve clipping paths, you must save your document as a Photoshop (PSD), PDF, EPS, or TIFF

format document. Because both PSD and TIFF files support layers and channels (paths are saved in channels) they are an appropriate choice. EPS files are the choice file format for vector-based programs and are a standard format that most programs support. EPS files are also universally trusted as a reliable format across platforms and can contain both vector and bitmap data. EPS also supports transparency. Photoshop can now export transparencies directly to EPS by creating the clipping paths for you.

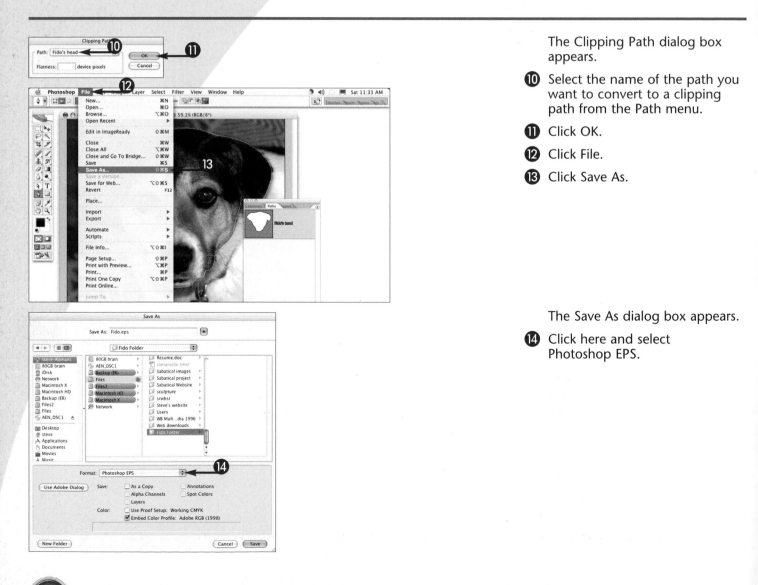

The Clipping Path dialog box appears.

⑩ Select the name of the path you want to convert to a clipping path from the Path menu.

⑪ Click OK.

⑫ Click File.

⑬ Click Save As.

The Save As dialog box appears.

⑭ Click here and select Photoshop EPS.

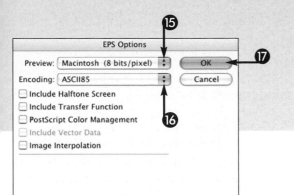

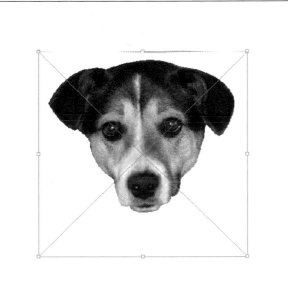

The EPS Options dialog box appears.

⑮ Click here and select a preview option, depending on the type of computer and the platform you are using.

⑯ For the Encoding type, click Binary.

⑰ Click OK.

⑱ Open a document in a desktop publishing program or vector-drawing program, and place the EPS image.

The clipping path masks out everything outside the path.

TIPS

Did You Know?
A clipping path always has a hard edge, and you cannot feather it, so sometimes your image may look a little rough around the edges. You can remedy this problem to some degree by selecting a color similar to the background of the target destination document and feathering your image into it. Then create the clipping path slightly larger than the image to include some of the background.

Did You Know!
EPS files can preserve type so that it is editable. The good news is that you do not have to retype text every time you changed it. The bad news is that, you do have to have the associated font(s) to edit and resave.

PATH PALETTE:
Create a Work Path

You can control path operations via the Paths palette. A path is listed in the Path palette the same way that channels and layers are listed in their appropriate palette. Once you save it, you can load, edit, export it to other programs.

When you draw a path with the Pen tool, it appears as a thumbnail in the Paths palette, and is named Work Path. The work path is a temporary element that records changes as you draw new sections of the path. If you complete a path on an image, you

can use the Pen tool to draw another path. What you draw appears on the same Work Path thumbnail as the first path. To create separate additional paths, you must save the work path via the Save Path command in the Palette menu.

See also>>

| Pen Tool |
| Shape Tools |
| Techniques: Paths, Clipping Paths |

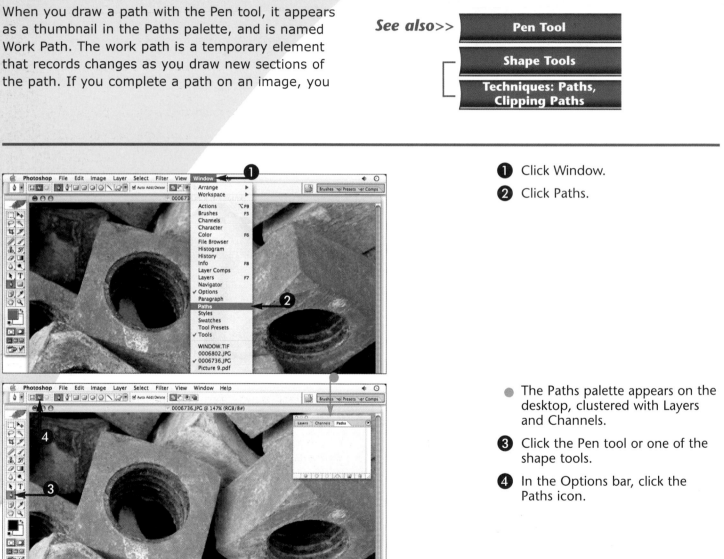

① Click Window.

② Click Paths.

● The Paths palette appears on the desktop, clustered with Layers and Channels.

③ Click the Pen tool or one of the shape tools.

④ In the Options bar, click the Paths icon.

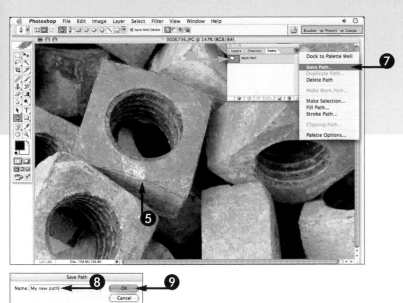

5 Click the image to draw a path.

● The work path thumbnail appears in the Paths palette.

6 Continue to draw the path.

The thumbnail takes on the appearance of the path as you draw.

7 When you finish drawing the path, click Save Path from the Palette Options menu.

The Save Path dialog box appears.

8 Type a name for the path.

9 Click OK.

Photoshop saves your path.

You can load your path and use it later.

![TIPS]

Try This!
You can also save a path by dragging the work path to the New Path icon at the bottom of the palette.

Did You Know?
The Paths palette lists saved paths from top to bottom in the order in which they were created. You can reorganize the paths within the list by clicking the path's name or thumbnail and then dragging it to the desired location.

Try This!
You can increase or decrease the size of the Paths palette thumbnails or turn them off by clicking Palette Options from the Palette fly-out menu and selecting the option (◯ changes to ◉) next to the desired thumbnail size.

PATH: STROKE/FILL:
Paint a Border and a Colored Shape

You can stroke a path to create a line that has a definable color and width. This is an important operation in Photoshop because it is really the only way to create smooth curved lines precisely. To stroke a path, you draw a path or load a saved path from the Paths palette. You then select a color from the Foreground, Background, Color Picker, or either black or white. The painting tool you select determines the texture and shape of the path. All these options are offered in the Stroke Path dialog box.

Photoshop strokes the path with the characteristics of the chosen tool as defined in the Options bar.

To fill the area within a path, you draw an open or closed path or display an existing path from the Paths palette. You then select a foreground color and open the Fill Path dialog box. In the additional Rendering field, this dialog box has a feather radius option, for feathering the edges of the path, and an Anti-aliased option.

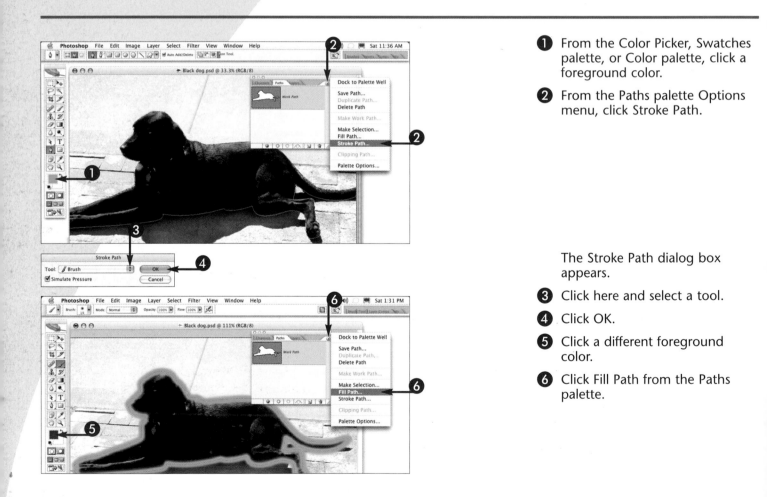

① From the Color Picker, Swatches palette, or Color palette, click a foreground color.

② From the Paths palette Options menu, click Stroke Path.

The Stroke Path dialog box appears.

③ Click here and select a tool.

④ Click OK.

⑤ Click a different foreground color.

⑥ Click Fill Path from the Paths palette.

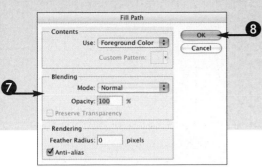

The Fill Path dialog box appears.

⑦ In the Fill Path dialog box, click or type the specifications for the fill.

⑧ Click OK.

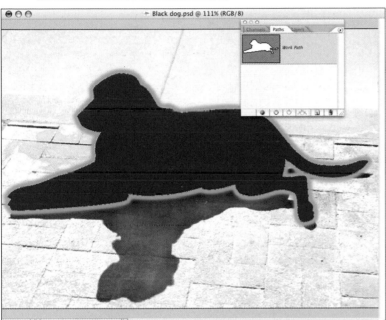

Your path is filled.

TIPS

Try This!

Click the Stroke Path button at the bottom of the Paths Palette to increase the opacity of a stroke. Each click makes the path darker, making it look thicker.

Caution!

You cannot stroke a path if a Layer Mask or text layer is active. Make sure that the layer on which you have a path is the active layer by clicking on it first.

Try This!

You can fill a path with the current Fill Path dialog box settings by clicking the Fill Path icon at the bottom of the Paths palette.

PATTERN:
Create a Pattern

To create interesting textures, you can fill a selection with a pattern. You can make the pattern one large tile or multiple duplicate tiles. You can make the pattern out of any image so long as the image is contained within a rectangle, or *tile*, that defines its top, bottom, left, and right edges. You can also use patterns provided by Photoshop.

You use the Rectangular Marquee to select your tile. The Rectangular Marquee must have a feather radius of 0 pixels; in other words, you cannot make a feathered selection. Next, you define the pattern and then place it in the Preset Manager so that you can select it from the list of patterns. If you look in any of the tools or techniques that support patterns, you find your pattern there, too, in the tool's pattern list.

You can apply patterns to the image with the Pattern Stamp, the Fill command, the Paint Bucket tool, the Healing Brush tool, the Patch tool, or as a Pattern Fill layer.

After you create the pattern, if you want to change it, make changes to the original source file and then resave it as a pattern preset.

See also>>

Healing Brush Tool

Paint Bucket Tool

Patch Tool

Pattern Stamp Tool

Techniques: Fill

Techniques: Layers, Fill Layers

Techniques: Filter, Patternmaker

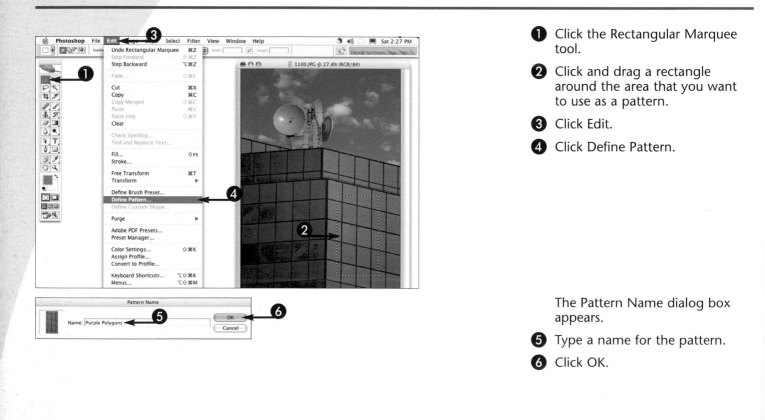

① Click the Rectangular Marquee tool.

② Click and drag a rectangle around the area that you want to use as a pattern.

③ Click Edit.

④ Click Define Pattern.

The Pattern Name dialog box appears.

⑤ Type a name for the pattern.

⑥ Click OK.

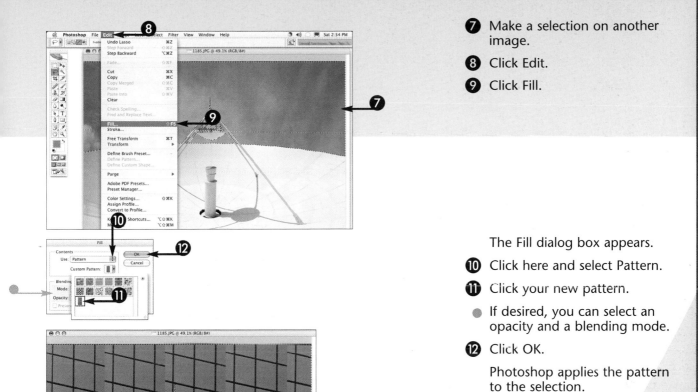

7 Make a selection on another image.

8 Click Edit.

9 Click Fill.

The Fill dialog box appears.

10 Click here and select Pattern.

11 Click your new pattern.

● If desired, you can select an opacity and a blending mode.

12 Click OK.

Photoshop applies the pattern to the selection.

TIPS

Caution!
If you select an area on the image and you find that the Define Pattern command is grayed out in the Edit menu, check the Rectangular Marquee's Options bar to be sure that the Feather Radius reads 0 px.

Try This!
For even more control over the application of the pattern, make a Pattern Fill layer.

Did You Know?
If you want to change the pattern, keep in mind that you cannot edit it directly. You must edit the source image and then resave the pattern.

PREFERENCES:
Restore Factory Defaults

You can restore your preferences with a simple keyboard command. Preferences control the behavior and appearance of Photoshop. If Photoshop behaves unpredictably or frequently shuts down, it may indicate that the preferences are damaged. You should restore your preferences to the originally installed default settings. Re-creating your preferences file resets Photoshop to its original defaults.

When you modify any setting and quit the program, the information is saved to these files.

A set of *preferences* is created when you first launch Photoshop. These are the factory default settings. Any changes you make to the program are recorded in the preferences file. When you quit the program after a work session, these preferences are stored so that the next time you launch the program, the position of the palettes, tool settings, color of the guides or grid, and any other changes you make remain the same.

See also>>   **Workspace**

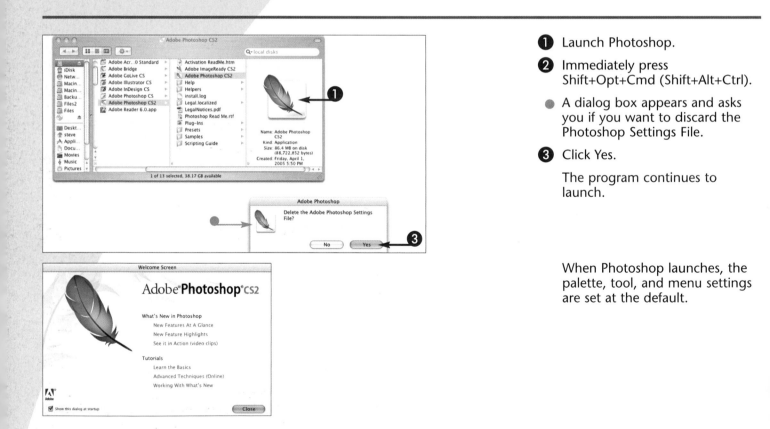

① Launch Photoshop.

② Immediately press Shift+Opt+Cmd (Shift+Alt+Ctrl).

● A dialog box appears and asks you if you want to discard the Photoshop Settings File.

③ Click Yes.

The program continues to launch.

When Photoshop launches, the palette, tool, and menu settings are set at the default.

PRESET MANAGER:
Save Tools and Palettes

In Photoshop, you can use the Preset Manager to manage several libraries from a single window. The Preset Manager is a library that stores tools and palettes that you have saved.

As you add or delete items from the palettes, such as swatches or styles, for example, the currently loaded palette in the Preset Manager displays the changes. You can save the new palette and load any of the palettes on the system.

The Preset Manager list divides its menu into three groups of commands. The top group includes a list of display options for the items within the palette, which let you display the items as thumbnails or by their names. The second field lets you restore the current palette to the default or replace it with a previously saved palette. The third group lists additional palettes that you can readily access.

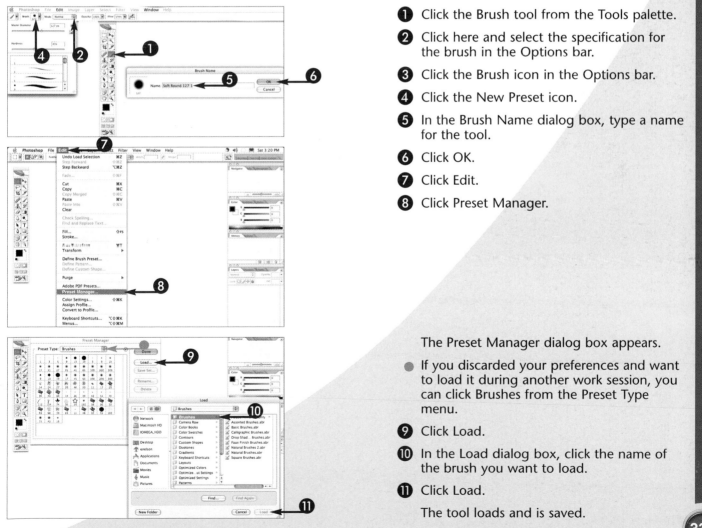

1. Click the Brush tool from the Tools palette.

2. Click here and select the specification for the brush in the Options bar.

3. Click the Brush icon in the Options bar.

4. Click the New Preset icon.

5. In the Brush Name dialog box, type a name for the tool.

6. Click OK.

7. Click Edit.

8. Click Preset Manager.

The Preset Manager dialog box appears.

● If you discarded your preferences and want to load it during another work session, you can click Brushes from the Preset Type menu.

9. Click Load.

10. In the Load dialog box, click the name of the brush you want to load.

11. Click Load.

The tool loads and is saved.

PRINT WITH PREVIEW:
Print Your Document

You can use Photoshop's Print with Preview menu to control how your document prints. The preview image on the left side of the Preview dialog box displays the image's size in relation to the paper chosen in the Page Setup dialog box.

Other options also aid in printing your document. The Position field gives the location of the printed image on the current paper size. The Center option centers the image on the paper. Scaled Print Size lets you scale the image size while maintaining the image's constrained proportions. The Scale To Fit Media option sizes the image to fit the paper. With the

Show Bounding Box option, you can manually scale and reposition the image. If you have an active selection, you can then print only that part of the image with the Print Selected Area option.

Before you print, the current printer's interface opens. Here, you can select the Show More Options option to expand the dialog box. The expanded area offers two sets of settings. Output allows you to select the method and add options based on the type of printer. Color Management settings determine the output quality and the color profile.

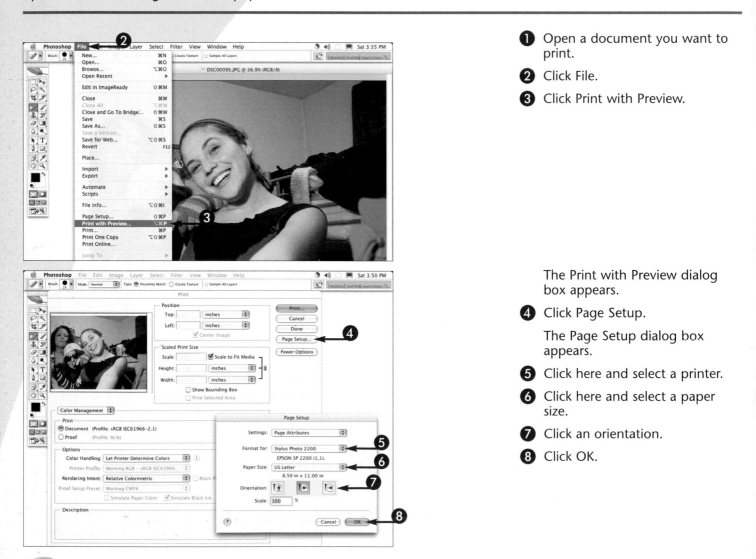

① Open a document you want to print.

② Click File.

③ Click Print with Preview.

The Print with Preview dialog box appears.

④ Click Page Setup.

The Page Setup dialog box appears.

⑤ Click here and select a printer.

⑥ Click here and select a paper size.

⑦ Click an orientation.

⑧ Click OK.

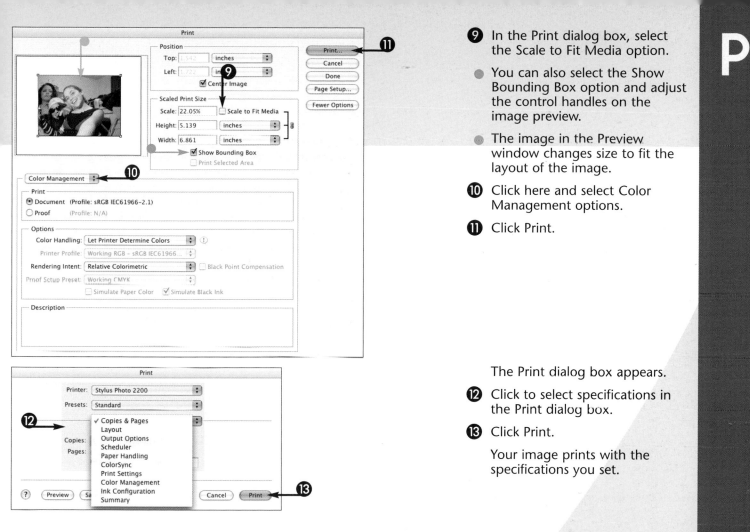

9 In the Print dialog box, select the Scale to Fit Media option.

● You can also select the Show Bounding Box option and adjust the control handles on the image preview.

● The image in the Preview window changes size to fit the layout of the image.

10 Click here and select Color Management options.

11 Click Print.

The Print dialog box appears.

12 Click to select specifications in the Print dialog box.

13 Click Print.

Your image prints with the specifications you set.

Try This!

The page specifications in the Page Setup dialog box include selecting a printer, paper size, scale, and orientation.

Try This!

If you have a document that is much larger than the paper you have available and you want to see it in full scale, print it in sections. Make a selection, and then click File, click Print with Preview, and then click Print Selected Area.

Try This!

If you get a warning that your image is larger than the paper's printable area, you can click File, click Print with Preview, and then click Scale to Fit Media. Also, make sure that you have selected the right page orientation for your document.

PURGE:
Clear Memory

If you run out of memory while working on an image, Photoshop lets you purge the caches reserved for Undos, Copy and Paste, and History. You generally discover that you have run out of memory when you try to save an image only to have a dialog box appear telling you that you cannot complete a task because the scratch disk is full. Instead of quitting the program and losing all that hard work, you can control what data you want to delete. You can free up the Undo, the Clipboard, and the History memories individually, or dump the content of all of these features.

Purging the memory cache can help you proceed with your work, but it is advisable at this point that you save, quit the program, and free up space on your hard drive by discarding unneeded documents. You can also choose another or an additional scratch disk in order to purge material.

Please note that purging memory is an operation that you cannot undo, so make sure that you want to free up Undo, the Clipboard, and the History memories before you perform these steps.

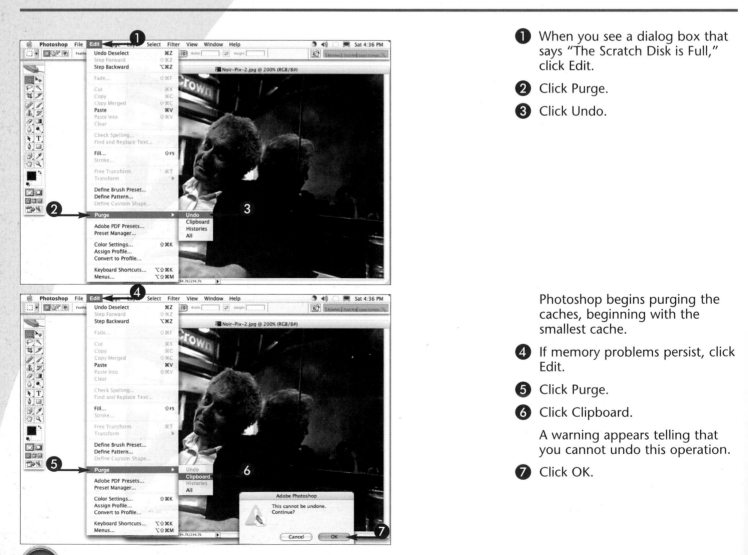

① When you see a dialog box that says "The Scratch Disk is Full," click Edit.

② Click Purge.

③ Click Undo.

Photoshop begins purging the caches, beginning with the smallest cache.

④ If memory problems persist, click Edit.

⑤ Click Purge.

⑥ Click Clipboard.

A warning appears telling that you cannot undo this operation.

⑦ Click OK.

Photoshop purges your Clipboard.

8 If memory problems still continue, click Edit.

9 Click Purge.

10 Click Histories.

A warning appears telling that you cannot undo this operation.

11 Click OK

Photoshop purges your history.

12 If you need to free additional memory, click Purge.

13 Click All.

A warning appears telling you this can't be undone.

14 Click OK.

Your memory is purged.

TIPS

Try This!

Allocate memory to Photoshop by clicking Memory and Image Cache from the Preferences menu. The default is 50 percent and you can add more if you need it, but never exceed the amount you need to run the system software and any other programs you may need.

Did You Know?

Make sure you install adequate memory to maximize performance in Photoshop. How much is enough? As much as you can afford!

Caution!

You should not assign as scratch disks any disks that are not local drives. Assigning scratch disks to either results in poor or unreliable memory use.

QUICK MASK:
Make a Selection with the Paint Tools

Quick Mask allows you to quickly isolate a selected area of an image. This allows you to make more precise selections.

After you select an area of an image with any of the selection tools, you can use the Edit in Quick Mask mode button in the tools palette. Quick Mask overlays a red, translucent color over the area outside of the selected section. By using a painting tool you can increase or decrease this translucent color mask. To increase the size of the mask, make sure the Foreground color swatch is black, and paint additional pixels; to decrease the size of the mask, make sure the Foreground color is white, and paint over the masked area.

Note that because you want to make the mask as precise as possible, you may need to zoom in on an area where you need to refine the mask.

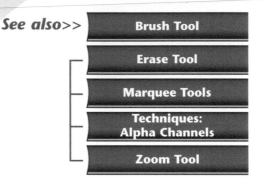

See also>>

- Brush Tool
- Erase Tool
- Marquee Tools
- Techniques: Alpha Channels
- Zoom Tool

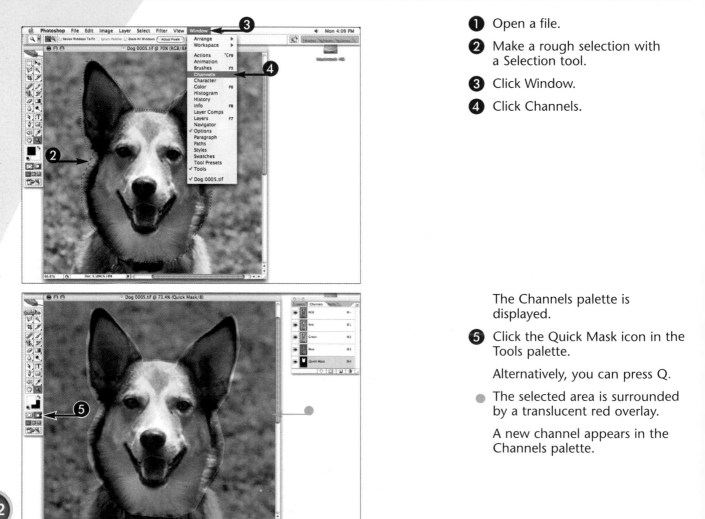

① Open a file.

② Make a rough selection with a Selection tool.

③ Click Window.

④ Click Channels.

The Channels palette is displayed.

⑤ Click the Quick Mask icon in the Tools palette.

Alternatively, you can press Q.

● The selected area is surrounded by a translucent red overlay.

A new channel appears in the Channels palette.

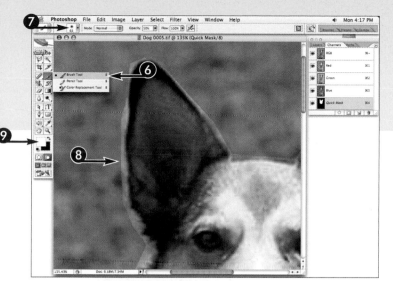

6 Click the Brush tool from the Tools palette.

7 Click a brush from the Brush presets in the Options bar.

8 Click and drag to paint the areas where you want to extend the mask.

Although the Foreground swatch color is black, the Paint tool deposits the translucent red mask color.

You can use the Erase tool to erase some of the mask.

9 Click here to change the Foreground color to white.

Alternatively you can press X.

10 Drag the brush over the area where you want to remove the mask.

TIPS

Did You Know!

You can display the Quick Mask as grayscale by turning off the Eye icon on two of the color channels in the Channels palette. Viewing the image in grayscale may help you to correct the Quick Mask more precisely by allowing you to see the image without any color that may blend with the mask.

Try This!

You can change the color and opacity percent of the Quick Mask. Double-click the Quick Mask Channel. A Quick Mask Options dialog box appears. Pick the color and type the percent value. Click OK.

QUICK MASK:
Make a Selection with the Paint Tools (Continued)

You can make your Quick Mask more precise by changing the attributes of the brush. By selecting a softer, larger, or textured brush, you can create a unique mask. This is particularly helpful if your selection contains an object with hair, for example. A hard, square brush makes the selection look like a cut-out; a soft, textured brush captures a more realistic selection. You can also modify your brush

and its effects by changing the Opacity, Flow, or Mode from the Options bar.

If you want to save a complicated selection for future use, you can convert a Quick Mask into a selection and then store it as an Alpha channel. Alternatively, you can save the selection for later recall via the Select and then Save Selection menu options.

Your selection is improved.

⑩ Select a brush with texture from the Options bar.

The example uses a "chalk" like brush to better select the hair area of the dog.

⑪ Drag the brush over a new area.

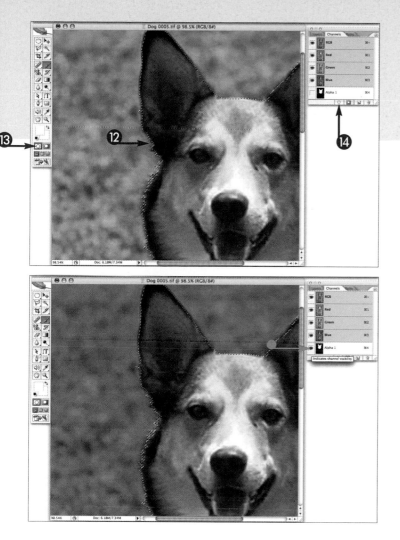

⑫ Click the Edit In Standard Mode icon on the Tools palette.

Alternatively, you can press Q.

● Your selection is now perfectly outlined.

⑬ Click the Save Selection as an Alpha Channel icon at the bottom of the Channels palette.

The Quick Mask is saved as Alpha channel.

⑭ To view your saved Channel, you can click the square to the left of your Alpha channel name.

TIPS

Warning!

To ensure that all of your area is completely masked, you can set the Opacity slider in the Options bar to 100 percent. The default setting of 50 percent opacity means that you are painting with a translucent color. Although, this is helpful because you want to see the image through the mask as you paint, the result may be that the painted area is not completely masked.

Try This!

Press X to toggle the Foreground swatch from black to white. When the Foreground swatch is white, the paintbrush acts like an eraser and deletes pixels from the mask; when the Foreground swatch is black, the paintbrush adds more pixels to the mask.

RASTERIZE:
Change Vector Objects to Bitmap Objects

You can convert vector (resolution independent) objects to bitmap (pixel defined) objects using Raster commands. Vector objects include paths, shapes, shape layers, fill layers, vector masks, Smart Objects, and type. All other objects in Photoshop are Bitmap objects.

Vector objects are mathematically defined curves in contrast to objects defined by a pixel grid. These curves, called Beziér curves, require a different set of tools from pixel objects. For example, you cannot select and modify a Beziér curve with the selection tools like the Marquee and Lasso tools, or the Magic Wand. Instead, you use the Path selection tools or

the Path Editing tools. Furthermore, you cannot apply pixel-based operations such as filters or color adjustments to vector objects. You must first rasterize the objects or convert them to pixels.

You can select the type of object you want to rasterize, including Type, Fill Content, Vector Mask, Shape, Smart Object, Layer, or All Layers. After you rasterize, you cannot edit type on the layer. Furthermore, you cannot edit the other objects with the pixel editing tools and commands.

See also>>

| Techniques: Paths |
| Tools: Shapes |

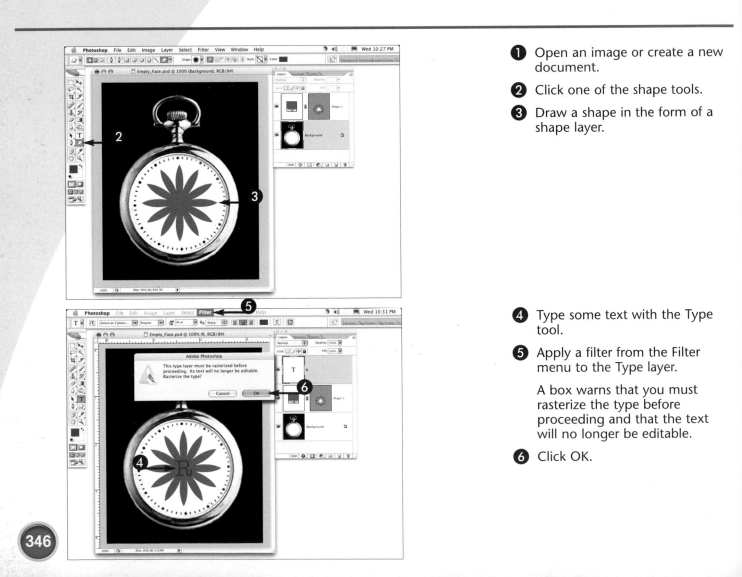

❶ Open an image or create a new document.

❷ Click one of the shape tools.

❸ Draw a shape in the form of a shape layer.

❹ Type some text with the Type tool.

❺ Apply a filter from the Filter menu to the Type layer.

A box warns that you must rasterize the type before proceeding and that the text will no longer be editable.

❻ Click OK.

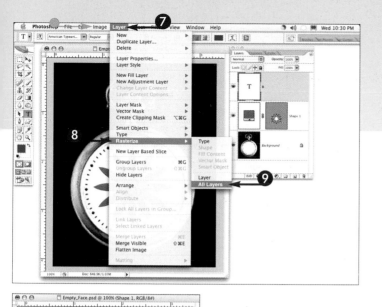

Photoshop rasterizes and applies the type.

● If you click the shape layer, then click Image, and then Adjustments, the adjustment choices are grayed out.

⑦ Click Layer.

⑧ Click Rasterize.

⑨ Click All Layers.

The vector objects on all the layers become bitmap.

When you apply an adjustment to the shape layer, the adjustment takes place.

TIPS

Did You Know?

Vector objects are resolution independent. You can increase them in size without loss of sharpness. You can also print them crisply on any printer regardless of the resolution image's resolution.

Did You Know?

Photoshop is designed to work with bitmap images, therefore there are more effects and adjustments that you can apply to pixels than to vectors. You can apply layer styles to vectors, but filters and color adjustments do not affect them. Illustrator, which is designed to create and modify vector images, has a variety of effects and filters you can apply to vectors. Because the most recent versions of Photoshop can now handle vectors, you can create elements in Illustrator and then drag and drop them into Photoshop.

RESAMPLE:
Increase or Decrease the Size of an Image

You can increase or decrease the size of your image by resampling. Resampling changes the image resolution and or the physical size by adding or deleting pixels. When you resample down, you discard pixels. When you resample up, you create new pixels.

You can select a resampling type by selecting it from Photoshop's Preferences dialog box, so that Photoshop applies the type to all transformed images. Alternatively, you can use the Image Size dialog box to apply resampling to individual files. Either way, you are offered five resampling (interpolation) algorithms from the fly-out menu.

The algorithms determine how Photoshop adds or removes pixels from your image. Nearest Neighbor adds pixels by evaluating each adjacent pixel — it is a fast but imprecise method that works best with images with more abrupt color changes; Bilinear adds pixels by averaging the value of surrounding pixels; Bicubic, which is slower, evaluates the values of surrounding pixels and uses complex calculations to add pixels to produces better results than Nearest neighbor or Bilinear; Bicubic Smoother slightly blurs the edges of areas to produce the most contrast when it adds pixels for a more sublimated continuous-tone look; Bicubic Sharper adds an additional sharpen algorithm to better enhance edge contrast.

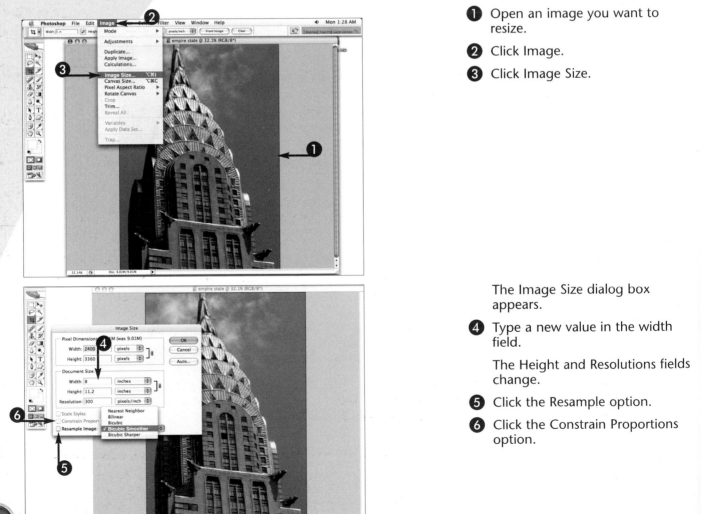

① Open an image you want to resize.

② Click Image.

③ Click Image Size.

The Image Size dialog box appears.

④ Type a new value in the width field.

The Height and Resolutions fields change.

⑤ Click the Resample option.

⑥ Click the Constrain Proportions option.

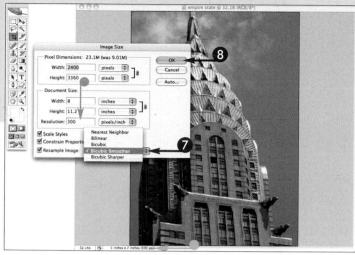

- If you type a value in the resolution field, this time the other fields do not change.

7 Click here and select a method from the Interpolation menu.

- Note the size of the image at the bottom of the screen.

8 Click OK.

- The information at the bottom of the images shows that the size of the image has changed.

TIPS

Try This!
For best results, experiment and compare interpolation algorithms. Usually Bicubic, Buicubic Sharper, and Bicubic Smoother produce the best results for photographs, while Nearest Neighbor produces the best results for line art and desktop icons.

Caution!
Avoid resampling an image to increase its size. Resampling up can seriously compromise the quality of the image by softening the edges and diminishing the contrast.

Did You Know?
You set resampling interpolation settings for transformation commands, several of the distortion filters, and the Crop tool in the General Preferences dialog box. You access this dialog box by clicking Photoshop (Edit), Preferences, and then General.

RETOUCHING TECHNIQUES:
Retouch an Old Photograph

Photoshop has many tools that can restore old photos damaged by dust, scratches, abrasions, mold, that are faded, or have areas missing. You can combine several tools and techniques to correct these problems.

To preserve as much detail as you can from the photograph, scan the photo at least 300 ppi at 100 percent for print output. For smaller images that you want to enlarge, scan the image at a higher resolution to compensate for the increase in size. Scan images that you intend to keep black and white in grayscale. This creates a smaller file size, and may result in loss of some flaws, such as discoloration and stains.

The tools and filters you most commonly use for retouching are the Clone tool, the Healing Brushes, the Patch tools, and the Dust and Scratches filters. After you remove flaws and artifacts, most restored

black-and-white photos generally require a contrast adjustment. Color images usually require a color adjustment.

Photo restoration can be extremely labor-intensive. Some images are simply beyond repair. Experience helps you determine which images you can restore and which are not worth the effort.

See also>>

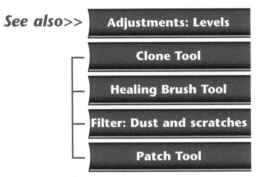

Adjustments: Levels

Clone Tool

Healing Brush Tool

Filter: Dust and scratches

Patch Tool

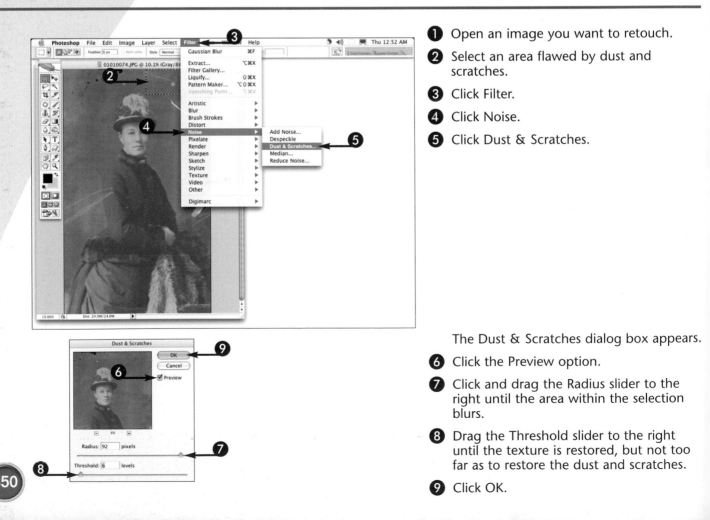

① Open an image you want to retouch.

② Select an area flawed by dust and scratches.

③ Click Filter.

④ Click Noise.

⑤ Click Dust & Scratches.

The Dust & Scratches dialog box appears.

⑥ Click the Preview option.

⑦ Click and drag the Radius slider to the right until the area within the selection blurs.

⑧ Drag the Threshold slider to the right until the texture is restored, but not too far as to restore the dust and scratches.

⑨ Click OK.

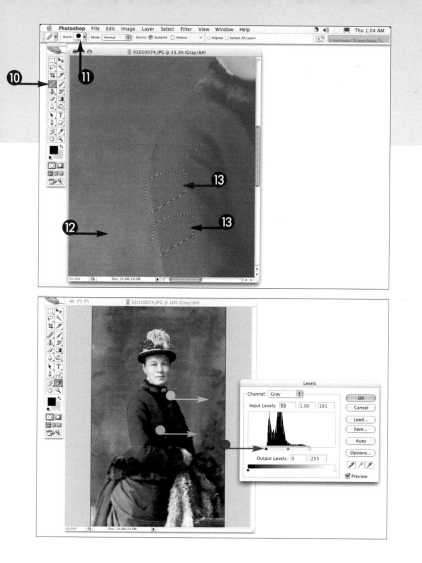

⑩ Click the Healing Brush tool.

⑪ Click here and select a brush size from the Options bar.

⑫ Sample an area of similar tonality by pressing Opt (Alt) and clicking the mouse.

⑬ Click and drag over the scratch.

The sampled area is cloned and blended with the surrounding pixels.

● You can use the Patch tool to restore missing texture.

● You can use the Clone tool with a soft brush to repair large rips in the image.

● You can use the white and black Input silders in the Levels dialog box to adjust the contrast or to darken or brighten an image.

TIPS

Try This!
Often, you may need to apply the Dust & Scratches filter more than once or to more than one area. You can reapply the current settings of a filter by pressing Cmd+F (Ctrl+F). You can redisplay the dialog box by pressing Cmd+Opt+F (Ctrl+Alt+F).

Did You Know?
Whenever possible select the area you want to repair before using the Clone tool. This prevents the Clone tool from accidentally "repairing" areas that you meant to keep intact.

Try This!
If you have to retouch anything larger than just a small spot and you are working with the Healing Brush too or the Clone Stamp tool, work slowly and reset your sampling point frequently; otherwise, the repair will not look seamless.

SAVE:
Save Your Files

You can save your files to preserve your work and prevent data loss. You can also use the Save command to create duplicates of original files before you make extensive changes. Photoshop has several variations of the Save command. The Save As command allows you save your document with a new name in the same location or to a different location. As you save you can also select a different format for your file.

By selecting or deselecting the options in the Save field of the Save As dialog box, you assign different characteristics to your document. The As Copy option creates a new, identical document that is automatically renamed with the current document's

name plus the word *copy*. The document does not open in the current image window.

If your document has Alpha channels, layers, annotations, or spot colors, there are options that let you save or discard these elements. The Use Proof Colors option embeds the current proof setup and the Embed Color Profile option embeds the document's color working space.

Saving a document automatically updates the changes to the current document.

See also>>

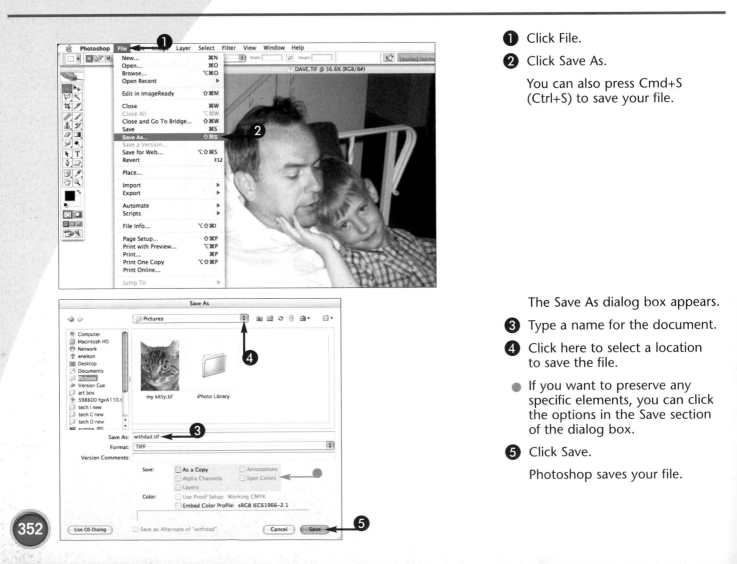

❶ Click File.

❷ Click Save As.

You can also press Cmd+S (Ctrl+S) to save your file.

The Save As dialog box appears.

❸ Type a name for the document.

❹ Click here to select a location to save the file.

● If you want to preserve any specific elements, you can click the options in the Save section of the dialog box.

❺ Click Save.

Photoshop saves your file.

SCRATCH DISK:
Change Your Virtual Memory Disk

In addition to the default working disk, you can assign up to three additional Scratch Disks to better manage Photoshop's efficiency. You can identify these via Photoshop's Plug-Ins & Scratch Disks section of Preferences. When a Photoshop work session exceeds the amount of allocated memory (RAM), it uses your hard disk space as virtual memory extension — Adobe calls this a Scratch Disk. If your hard drive is not partitioned or you do not have additional hard drives installed, the only space Photoshop can use as a scratch disk is your sole drive.

By default, the primary scratch disk is the startup disk, but you can reassign it to your fastest hard

drive or the one with the most unused space. If you have additional hard drives, you can select a second, third, and fourth drive on which to allocate space. When the primary scratch disk is full, the second one kicks in, then the third, and so on. You should avoid working on removable media disks because they are usually less stable and much slower than hard drives. After you designate a new primary scratch disk, quit Photoshop and relaunch it.

See also>>   **Techniques: Memory**

**Techniques:
Purge Memory**

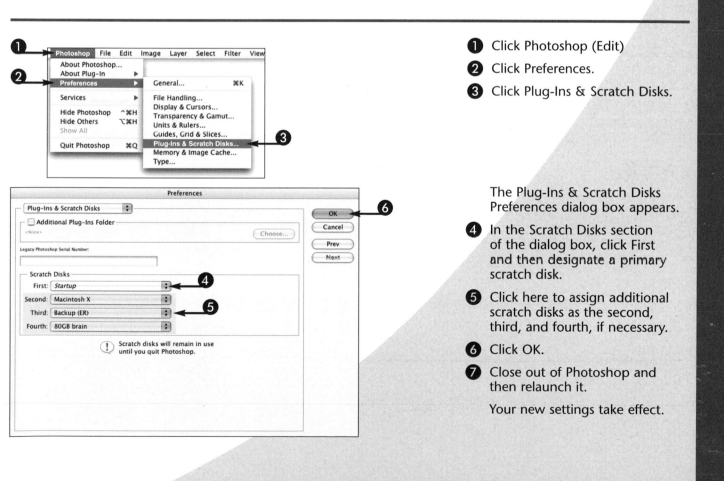

① Click Photoshop (Edit)

② Click Preferences.

③ Click Plug-Ins & Scratch Disks.

The Plug-Ins & Scratch Disks Preferences dialog box appears.

④ In the Scratch Disks section of the dialog box, click First and then designate a primary scratch disk.

⑤ Click here to assign additional scratch disks as the second, third, and fourth, if necessary.

⑥ Click OK.

⑦ Close out of Photoshop and then relaunch it.

Your new settings take effect.

SELECT, ANTI-ALIAS:
Create a Transition Zone

When you select the anti-aliased option, you produce a selection whose edge is soft to better blend with surrounding pixels. This feature allows you to apply adjustment to an area of an image without seeming to be a patch. The anti-alias effect produces a small pixel border around the edge that blends into the adjacent color to create a transition zone.

Without the anti-aliased edge, any selection based adjustment to an image appears aliased — that is, you see a stair-step, jagged affect where the selection ends and the rest of the image begins.

Anti-aliasing is different from feathering, which creates a blurred edge. Feathering sometimes gives a selection a halo-like look while anti-aliasing blends with adjacent pixels.

You can create a collage by combining several selections from various sources. Using the anti-alias option when creating these selections makes the composite — that is, the new image from multiple sections — look more like a seamless whole rather than a patch quilt.

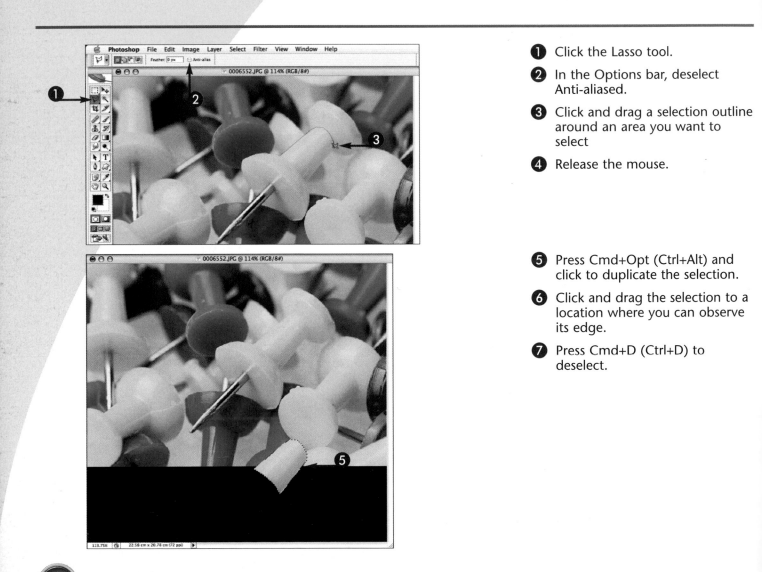

1 Click the Lasso tool.

2 In the Options bar, deselect Anti-aliased.

3 Click and drag a selection outline around an area you want to select

4 Release the mouse.

5 Press Cmd+Opt (Ctrl+Alt) and click to duplicate the selection.

6 Click and drag the selection to a location where you can observe its edge.

7 Press Cmd+D (Ctrl+D) to deselect.

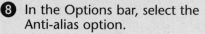

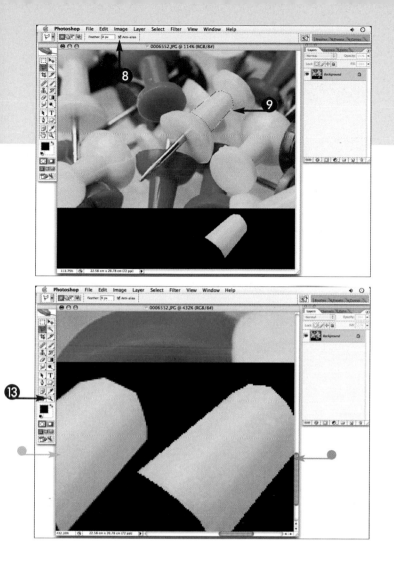

⑧ In the Options bar, select the Anti-alias option.

⑨ Click and drag a selection outline around an area you want to select; then release the mouse.

⑩ Press Cmd+Opt (Ctrl+Alt) and click to duplicate the selection.

⑪ Drag the selection to a location where you can compare the edges.

⑫ Press Cmd+H (Ctrl+H) to hide the edges of the selection.

⑬ Click the Zoom tool and then click the area until you can see the edges of the composites.

● The aliased edge is now a hard edge.

● The anti-aliased edge has a small semitransparent transition zone of a few pixels.

TIPS

Try This!

You add to a selection by pressing and holding Shift as you click and drag with the Selection tool. You can subtract from a selection by pressing and holding Opt (Alt) as you click and drag with the Selection tool. You can intersect selections by pressing Shift+Opt (Shift+Alt) as you click and drag the Selection tool.

Caution!

You can apply anti-aliasing to type so that it blends in with the background. However, be careful when you apply anti-aliasing to small type in low resolution images. The affect may make the type fuzzier and less readable.

SELECT, COLOR RANGE:
Select by Color

You can use the Color Range command to select areas of similar color. Color Range identifies pixels of similar color to create a selection. This command is ideal when you need to apply an adjustment, such as color replacement, to several areas of similar color throughout the image.

By default the Color Range command begins by applying a mask to the entire image. The Select menu in the Color Range dialog box gives you several options for selecting color: by sampling with the Eyedropper tool; by selecting specific colors, such as reds, yellows, blues, magentas, greens, or cyans; by selecting tonal values, such as Highlights, Midtones,

or Shadows; or Out-of-Gamut colors — colors out of the range of the current color model.

For more control, you can select the Sampled Colors default from the menu. You can use one of the eyedroppers and then drag over the image to select a single color. The Plus Eyedropper increases the range of colors, while the Minus Eyedropper decreases the range. The Fuzziness slider also extends the range of selection into adjacent pixels. The mask reveals what is being included in the selection as you drag. You can use the Invert option to invert the selection.

See also>> **Techniques: Adjustments**
Replace Color

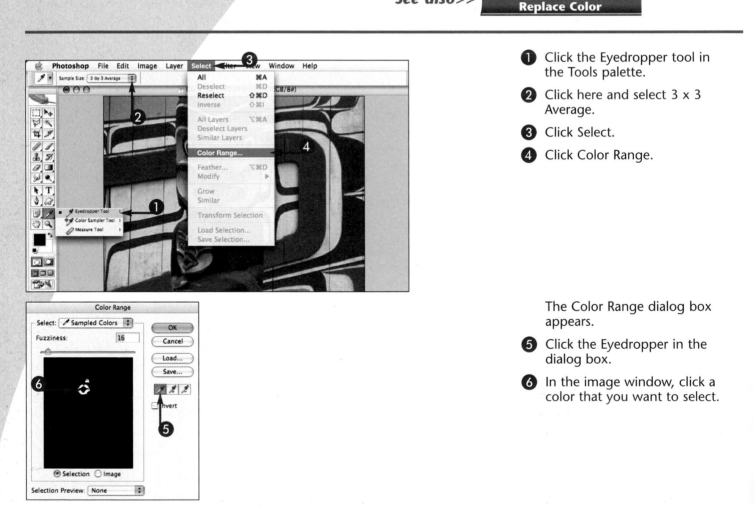

① Click the Eyedropper tool in the Tools palette.

② Click here and select 3 x 3 Average.

③ Click Select.

④ Click Color Range.

The Color Range dialog box appears.

⑤ Click the Eyedropper in the dialog box.

⑥ In the image window, click a color that you want to select.

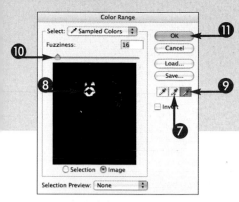

7 Click the Plus Eyedropper.

8 Click and drag over additional areas to add color.

9 Repeat steps **7** and **8** with the Minus Eyedropper, clicking and dragging over the areas you do not want to include in the selection.

10 When the areas you want are sampled, click and drag the Fuzziness slider to the right to include adjacent areas in the selection or to the left to exclude them.

11 Click OK.

● On the image, the areas you included in the mask are surrounded by the marching ants of the selection marquee.

If necessary, you can deselect parts of the image that you do not want to include.

TIPS

Did You Know?
The Selection Preview menu lets you select from Grayscale, White Matte, Black Matte, Quick Mask, or None modes in which to view the mask in the image window. These preview modes help you identify the areas of the image to include in the selection.

Did You Know?
You can limit what Color Range samples by first selecting an area on the image with a selection tool and then clicking Select, and then Color Range. The mask displays the selected area.

Try This!
You can change the setting in the Eyedropper tool Options bar to 3 by 3 Average for low-resolution images, and 5 by 5 for high-resolution images to sample an average of a group of pixels.

SELECT, FEATHER:
Make a Seamless Composite

You can use feathering to create a gradual transition between the inside and the outside of the selection border. When you apply an effect to a feathered selection, its edges soften and become more transparent. Feathering increases the credibility of your composites by gradually blending colored pixels into each other and eliminating any evidence of a hard edge.

You can preprogram a selection tool before you use it to produce a soft-edged selection. You can do this by entering a numerical value for the feather radius in the Feather field of the tool's Options bar. You can

also apply feathering after you make a selection via the Feather command in the Select menu. This produces a dialog box where you can specify a value in the Feather Radius field.

The Feather Radius's value extends the specified number of pixels outside the selection outline, where it becomes increasingly more transparent, and inside the selection border, where it becomes increasingly more opaque. For example, if you type a value of **10**, the distance of the feather is **20** pixels from the opaque pixels inside the selection border to absolute transparency outside the selection border.

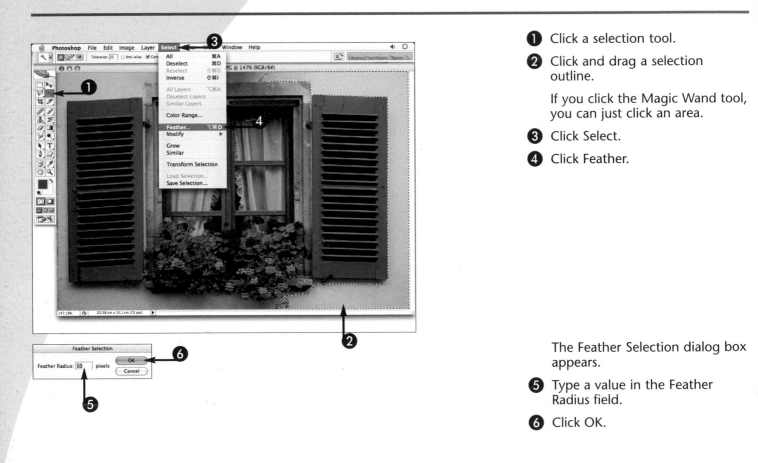

① Click a selection tool.

② Click and drag a selection outline.

If you click the Magic Wand tool, you can just click an area.

③ Click Select.

④ Click Feather.

The Feather Selection dialog box appears.

⑤ Type a value in the Feather Radius field.

⑥ Click OK.

7 Apply an adjustment or other operation to the selection.

The feathered edge of the adjustment blends into its surroundings.

You can repeat steps **1** to **7** again to produce a feathered selection with produces seamlessly blended edges.

TIPS

Did You Know?

When you apply feathering to a selection, the selection becomes less precise and changes shape. This is because Photoshop blurs the edges of the selection in order to create a transparent transitional area. This causes any effect or adjustment to fade as it approaches the edge of the selection.

Tip:

To view the effect of feathering, press Q to toggle into Quick Mask mode. The mask reveals the gradual transition of the selection edge. Before applying an effect, toggle out of Quick Mask by pressing Q again.

SELECT, MODIFY:
Alter a Selection

After you make a selection, you can change its edge by using any of four Modify subcommands — Border, Expand, Smooth, and Contract. Each command changes the selection outline thereby changing its size.

Expand increases the size of a selection; Contract reduces it. Each command allows you to change the size of a selection by adding or subtracting pixels from the edge of a selection — you can add/subtract fro 1 to 100 pixels.

Border frames a selection by creating a new selection of pixels starting at the edge of the old selection and

moving inward by a specified number of pixels. The Border dialog box allows you to create a frame whose thickness can vary from 1 to 200 pixels.

Smooth rounds sharp corners of a selection, eliminating protrusions and stair-stepped areas of the selection border. You can use the Smooth dialog box to enter a sample radius value between 1 and 100 pixels. Larger values increase the effect.

See also>>

Alter the Edge of a Selection

① Click a selection tool.

② Select an area of the image.

③ Click Select.

④ Click Modify.

⑤ Click Contract.

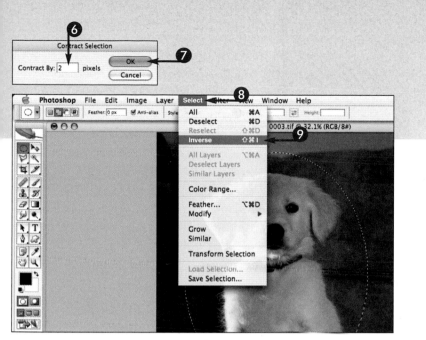

The Contract Selection dialog box appears.

6 Type a value in pixels.

7 Click OK.

8 Click Select.

9 Click Inverse.

The selection inverts.

TIPS

Did You Know!

Although the Border command does create a "frame" by selecting edge pixels, it is not really intended to be a frame like one into which you might place a picture. You can fill the Border selection and create a soft frame, but there is a more direct way if a frame is your ultimate goal. You can click Edit and then Stroke. You can then define the color and width of the stroke at the onset.

Did You Know?

When you transform a selection, the small icon in the center of the transformation box represents the point of origin. You can move this icon prior to scaling or rotating the selection to change the point from which the selection transforms. When you want to move the box, place your cursor anywhere in the selection except on the icon.

SELECT, MODIFY:
Alter a Selection (Continued)

Because you are unlikely to produce a perfect selection every time, Photoshop offers several methods to modify a selection. You can expand it, contract it, modify the border, and smooth it. You can also it conceal it, transform it, add to it, subtract from it, or eliminate it entirely. These commands are important because they facilitate the process of selecting an area or creating a mask. If your selection is not perfect, you may be tempted to recreate it. However, a better idea is to learn to use the selection editing command.

To use the editing commands, you must have an active selection. You can then use the Select menu commands to make modifications. The Grow command increases the size of a selection by the number of pixels you enter in the Tolerance field of the Magic Wand's Options bar. The Similar command selects all pixels within the color range of the pixels within the selected area. The Tolerance setting in the Magic Wand's Options bar controls the amount that you select.

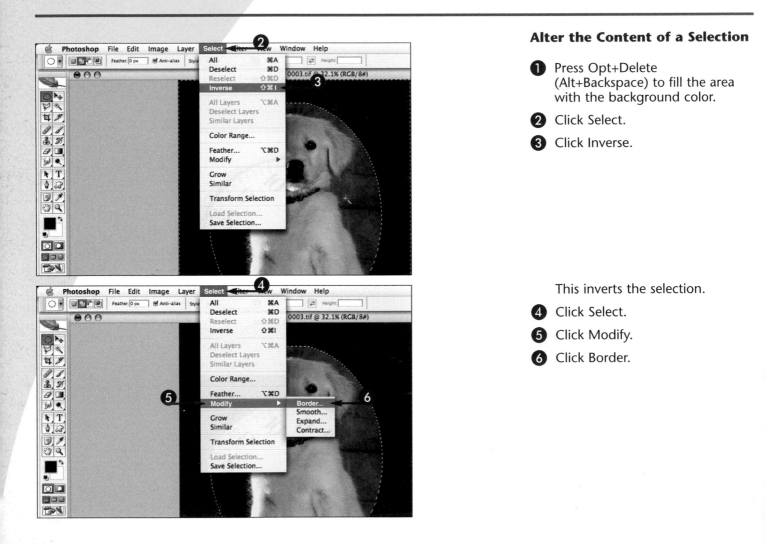

Alter the Content of a Selection

① Press Opt+Delete (Alt+Backspace) to fill the area with the background color.

② Click Select.

③ Click Inverse.

This inverts the selection.

④ Click Select.

⑤ Click Modify.

⑥ Click Border.

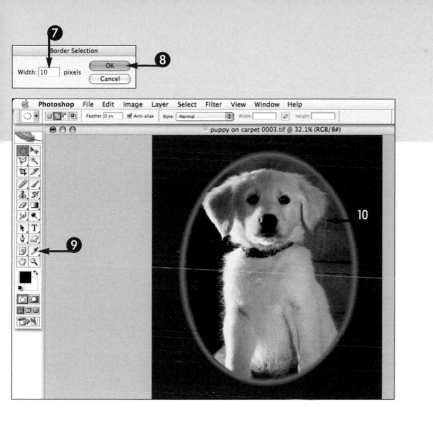

The Border Selection dialog box appears.

7 Type a value in the Width box.

8 Click OK.

9 Click the image with the Eyedropper tool.

10 Click a color on the image to pick up a color for the Foreground swatch.

11 Press Opt+Delete (Alt+Backspace) to fill with the Background swatch color.

The border area fills with the color.

TIPS

Did You Know?
When adding or subtracting from a feathered selection, you should use the same feather and anti-aliasing values you used in the original selection.

Did You Know?
When you select the Border command, the selection is always anti-aliased. It is soft edged so that it can blend with adjacent pixels.

Caution!
When you enter a value in the Feather Radius field make sure you take into account the size of your selection. Adding a large feather radius to a small selection may obliterate it. Photoshop responds with the message that no pixels are selected. Either increase the size of your selection or reduce the feather radius.

SMART OBJECTS:
Define a Smart Object

You can embed Smart Objects, which are vector objects, into Photoshop files without converting them to raster, the native Photoshop format. You can then perform nondestructive transformations — resizing, applying layer styles, moving — to these vector-based objects. The original vector data remains intact. You can create a Smart Object to preserve an original Photoshop document or to embed vector files.

There are several different ways of working with Smart Objects. You can convert one or more layers of a Photoshop document into one Smart Object layer. You can place an existing file inside an existing

Smart Object. You can paste or drag and drop vector graphics from Adobe Illustrator or PDF content into a Smart Object.

You can also duplicate an existing Smart Object to create two versions from the same source image. If you edit one, you update both.

To make a Smart Object, select one or more layers and select the Group into New Smart Object option from the Layer Options menu. The layer displays an icon on its thumbnail to indicate that it is a Smart Object.

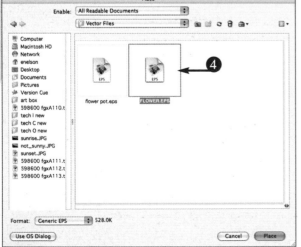

1 Open a Photoshop file.

2 Click File.

3 Click Place.

The Place dialog box appears.

4 Double click a Vector file.

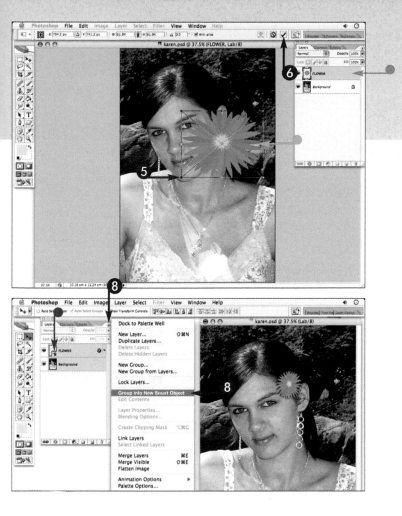

● Photoshop creates a new layer containing the placed file and the layer is given the placed file's name.

● A transformation box surrounds the placed object.

⑤ Click and drag corners to resize the object.

⑥ Click the Commit button in the Options bar when satisfied with size and placement of the object.

● An icon on the layer thumbnail indicates that it is a Smart Object.

⑦ Shift+Click to select each layer of your document.

⑧ From the Layer palettes menu, click Group into New Smart Object.

Your file is "flattened" and smaller, but the Smart Object is retained.

TIPS

Did You Know?
You can identify a smart object thumbnail from a regular layer thumbnail in the Layers palette by the icon in the lower-right corner of the thumbnail.

Try This!
If two or more smart objects use the same source image, you can separate them to work with them independently. Doing so creates an independent copy of the source image.

Click one or more of the smart objects in the Layers palette. Click Layer, click Smart Objects, click New Smart Object Via Copy. A new smart object appears on the Layers palette with the same name as the original and the suffix *copy*.

Smart Objects let you retain the vector data of the original image when you apply transformations. The transformations are non-destructive because they are resolution independent. The vector object's data is embedded in the Photoshop file as a Smart Object. You can place EPS and PDF into a single layer, which you can then modify in the original application such as Adobe Illustrator. You can store the source data as a Smart Object inside a Photoshop document, and work on a composite of that data in the image. The Smart Object renders itself based on the source data.

This process also facilitates compatibility between all Adobe Creative Suite applications.

Smart Objects let you preserve data that Adobe Photoshop does not ordinarily handle by automatically transforming the data into a recognizable object. You import symbols from Adobe Illustrator and other third-party applications such as Flash and you can apply transforms, layer styles, opacity, blend modes, and mesh distortions within Smart Objects. Following an edit, the Smart Object layer is updated with the edited content.

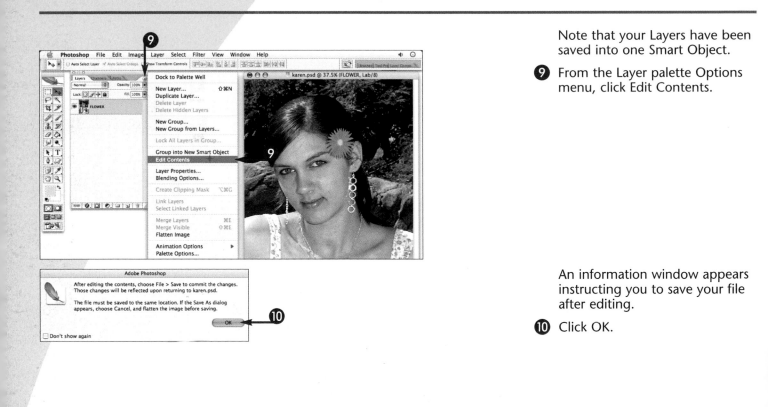

Note that your Layers have been saved into one Smart Object.

⑨ From the Layer palette Options menu, click Edit Contents.

An information window appears instructing you to save your file after editing.

⑩ Click OK.

A new window appears containing your image.

- The top of the window identifies the file, which has the same name as the placed vector file, but with the PSB extension.

- The layers palette now shows the original 2 layers.

⑪ Make a layer adjustment to smart object.

⑫ Press Cmd(Ctrl)+S.

Photoshop saves the file.

Note: If this is the first time saving the object, the Save as dialog box appears. Click Save.

⑬ Press Cmd(Ctrl)+W.

The files closes and Photoshop returns to your original document.

After a few seconds, your document changes to reflect the modifcations you made to the Large Format File.

You can resave your document.

TIPS

Did You Know?
Because Smart Objects are on layers, you can apply layer styles to them. This enables you to combine the versatility of an Illustrator vector graphic with eye-popping Photoshop effects.

Did You Know?
Smart Objects can be scaled to any size without losing their quality because they are vector objects and are resolution independent.

STROKE:
Create a Colored Border

You can apply a colored border around an active selection with the Stroke command. Strokes can vary in characteristics, depending on how you configure them. In the Stroke dialog box, you can enter a value in pixels between 1 and 250 for the stroke width. You can select a color from the Color Picker as well as a location for the stroke — Inside, which places the stroke on the inside of the selection outline; Center, which centers the stroke between the inside and the outside of the selection outline; or Outside, which places the stroke on the outside of the selection outline.

Next, you can select a blending mode from the menu to affect the relationship of the color that is being applied over the colors on the image. Set the opacity from 1 percent to 100 percent. If the image is on a layer surrounded by transparency, you can click the Preserve Transparency check box to prevent the transparent area from being stroked.

See also>> **Techniques, Paths: Fill and Stroke a Path**

① Press Cmd(Ctrl)+A to select the entire image.

● Alternatively, you can make a selection or any shape or size with one of the selection tools.

② Click Edit.

③ Click Stroke.

The Stroke dialog box appears.

④ Type a value in pixels for the width.

⑤ Click the color swatch.

The Color Picker appears.

6 Click a color.

7 Click OK to close the Color Picker.

8 Click OK to close the Stroke dialog box.

Photoshop adds a stroke to your image.

Caution!
Depending on selection and stroke location, if you place the stroke outside of a selection on a transparent layer, you may not see any results.

Try This!
Another method of applying a stroke is to use the Layer Styles Stroke option. You can stroke any layer content as long as it is surrounded by transparency, but you cannot stroke active selections.

Did You Know?
You can add a stroke to type. However, you should not follow steps **1** and **2** in this section or you cannot use it as text. Instead, double-click the text layer and apply a stroke via the Layer Style menu.

TRANSFORM:
Flip, Resize, Rotate, or Distort an Image

You can stretch, squeeze, rotate, and distort an image and otherwise transform layer content and selections. You can apply any of the transform features to a selection or to an independent layer or to a group of layers and to linked layers.

Photoshop has five transform options: Scale, Rotate, Skew, Perspective, and Distort. With each, you are presented with a bounding box that you can alter via its handles. When you activate the Warp option, a grid with nine cells appears. Repositioning the anchor points or the grid lines alters the image. You can select the Flip Vertical and Flip Horizontal options to flip the image into a mirror reflection.

If you select any of the manual transformation operations, the Options bar changes to display default numerical values for the position, size, angle of rotation, and vertical and horizontal angle of skew. You can type values to more accurately transform layer content or selected areas.

See also>>

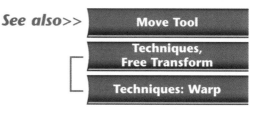

Transform the Image

① Open an image that has layer content, or select an area with one of the selection tools.

② Click Edit.

③ Click Transform.

④ Click either Scale, Rotate, Skew, Distort, or Perspective.

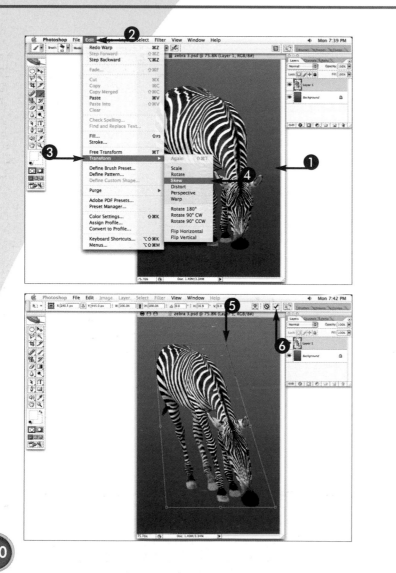

A bounding box appears, complete with anchor points, line segments, and pull handles.

⑤ Click and drag at least one of the corner points of the bounding box.

The image transforms.

⑥ Click the Commit button or press Enter.

Rotate or Flip the Image

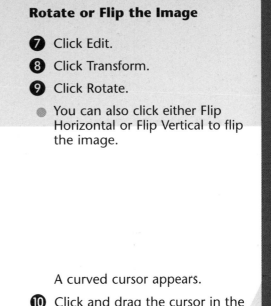

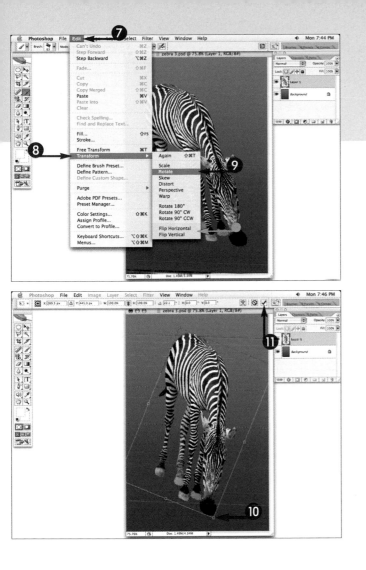

⑦ Click Edit.

⑧ Click Transform.

⑨ Click Rotate.

● You can also click either Flip Horizontal or Flip Vertical to flip the image.

A curved cursor appears.

⑩ Click and drag the cursor in the direction you want to rotate the element.

⑪ Click the Commit button or press Enter.

Note: *You do not have to click the Commit button or press Enter to accept the Flip Horizontal or Flip Vertical commands.*

TIPS

Caution!

Scale, Distort, and Perspective use global interpolation algorithms to resample the element that is being transformed. Increasing the size of an element can seriously affect its quality.

Did You Know?

You can use the Move tool with the Show Transformation Controls option selected in the Options bar (✓ changes to ☐) to perform some of the same functions.

Try This!

You can press Cmd(Ctrl)+T to invoke Free Transform. A Bounding box appears that allows you to scale, reposition, and rotate the object. You also have access to the Options bar to do more precise transformation of the object. When you are done, either click the Commit button or simply Press Enter.

TRIM:
Eliminate Border Pixels

The Trim command reduces the size of an image by eliminating all pixels surrounding an object that meets particular conditions. The default condition is that Photoshop trims away all transparent pixels at the edge of an object thereby leaving the smallest image containing at least one non-transparent pixel on each side.

The Trim dialog box offers you variants on this action. You can remove all pixels of the same color as either the top left or bottom right pixel surrounding an image. You can also trim only the

top, bottom, left, or right edged pixels. By selecting or deselecting these options in the Trim dialog box, you determine how much of the image Photoshop trims away.

The Trim tool, in effect, crops your image to the smallest dimensions possible by trimming away unnecessary edge pixels without cutting off an object or objects in an image.

See also>>    **Crop Tool**

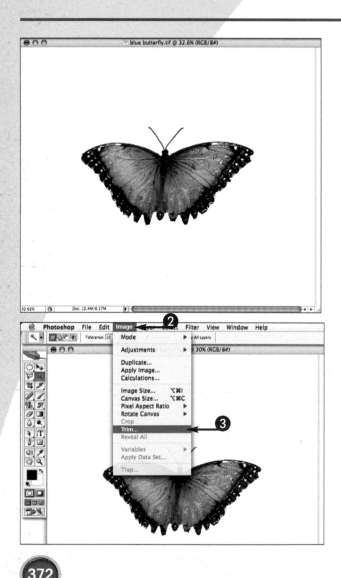

① Open an image in which an object or objects are surrounded by either a solid color not found on the objects edge pixels or by transparent pixels.

② Click Image.

③ Click Trim.

The Trim dialog box appears.

④ In the Based On section of the dialog box, select either Top Left Pixel Color or Bottom Right Pixel Color (○ changes to ⊙).

⑤ In the Trim Away section of the dialog box, Photoshop defaults to selecting all sides, but you can deselect options (☑ changes to ☐).

⑥ Click OK.

Photoshop trims the image to its new size.

TIPS

Try This!

If you do not have a uniform border of pixels, you can still trim an image — although, you must use the Crop command. Select a rectangular area. Next, click Image, and then click Crop to eliminate the areas outside the selection outline.

Did You Know?

One advantage of using the Crop tool rather than the Trim command is that you can set a specific size for your cropped image — both in dimension and in resolution. This is especially important if you want to set a uniform size for your images. When you use the Trim command, the resolution remains the same, but Photoshop automatically changes the dimensions.

TYPE MASK TOOL, HORIZONTAL/VERTICAL:
Create a Character-Shaped Marquee with a Pasted Image

You can generate type vertically or horizontally as a selection marquee. You can then paste an image in the marquee that you have created. The result is a mask shaped into letters through which you can see your image.

The default Horizontal Type Mask tool generates horizontally oriented text on a mask. Likewise, the Vertical Type tool generates a column of vertical characters. When you type text with this tool, a pink mask surrounds the type on a path. You can edit the

text and modify its characteristics or run a spell check on it. You can also move or transform the text using its bounding box.

Once you accept your changes, the type converts to a selection marquee that you can fill with color or another image. The Type Mask tool Options bar displays the same type characteristics as the Type tool with the exception of the Color option, where the swatch is gray, but the tool produces colored fill.

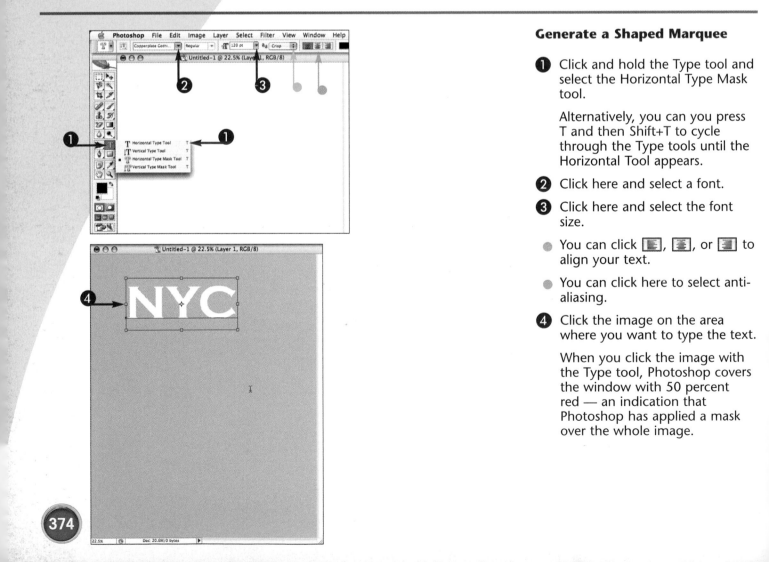

Generate a Shaped Marquee

1 Click and hold the Type tool and select the Horizontal Type Mask tool.

Alternatively, you can you press T and then Shift+T to cycle through the Type tools until the Horizontal Tool appears.

2 Click here and select a font.

3 Click here and select the font size.

● You can click ▤, ▤, or ▤ to align your text.

● You can click here to select anti-aliasing.

4 Click the image on the area where you want to type the text.

When you click the image with the Type tool, Photoshop covers the window with 50 percent red — an indication that Photoshop has applied a mask over the whole image.

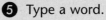

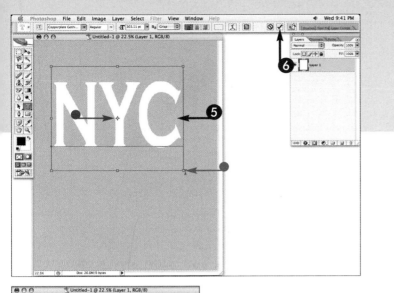

⑤ Type a word.

As you type letters the mask is removed from the letter shapes.

To reposition or transform the type without exiting the Type mode, press and hold the Cmd (Ctrl) key until a Transform box surrounds the type.

● To move text, you can press and hold Cmd (Ctrl) and place your cursor inside this box and drag in any direction.

● To resize type, you can press and hold Cmd (Ctrl) and drag a corner or side of the bounding box.

⑥ Click the Commit button.

The type becomes a selection marquee into which you can copy another image.

TIPS

Caution!

When you move text with the Type Mask tools, do not use the Move tool. Selecting the Move tool converts the text to an outline so that you can no longer edit it. Instead, while still in the Type Mask tool, place the cursor under the type path, click and drag the type path into position.

Did You Know?

To generate a Type mask on a curved path, draw the path with the Pen tool, select the Type Mask tool, and click the path.

TYPE MASK TOOL, HORIZONTAL/VERTICAL:
Create a Character-Shaped Marquee with a Pasted Image (Continued)

After you create your mask, you can paste an image into the text. Once pasted, you can size, reposition, and otherwise transform the image. The Paste Into command generates a new layer with a Layer Mask. You see a Layer Mask thumbnail in the Layers palette to the right of the image. The white areas on the thumbnail are revealed, while the black areas are masked layer content. In this case the Layer Mask is in the shape of the text characters.

You can use the Move tool with its transformation operations or the features in the Transform commands on the Edit menu to scale, rotate, distort, change perspective, or warp the layer content for a perfect fit inside of the character shapes. In addition you can apply layer styles like drop shadows, inner and outer glows, beveling, embossing, satin, and pattern fills to the layer content to produce outstanding effects.

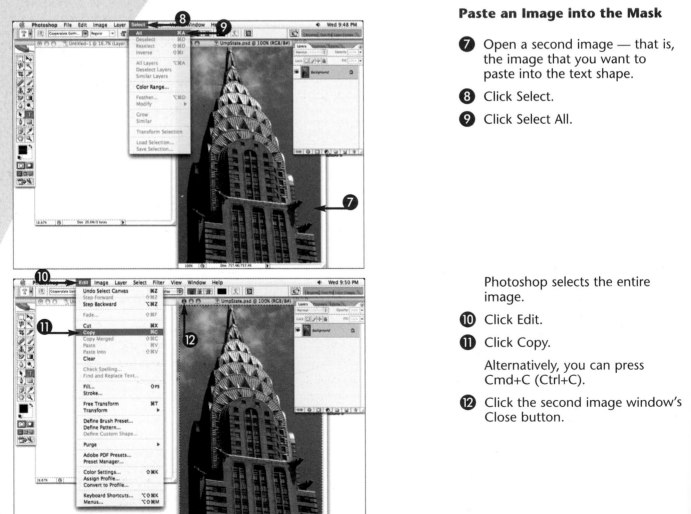

Paste an Image into the Mask

⑦ Open a second image — that is, the image that you want to paste into the text shape.

⑧ Click Select.

⑨ Click Select All.

Photoshop selects the entire image.

⑩ Click Edit.

⑪ Click Copy.

Alternatively, you can press Cmd+C (Ctrl+C).

⑫ Click the second image window's Close button.

When you close the second file, the original image becomes active.

⑬ Click Edit.

⑭ Click Paste Into.

Alternatively, you can press Shift+Cmd+V (Shift+Ctrl+V).

● The image appears in the text.

● You can reposition the image in the text by clicking the Move tool, clicking Show Transform Controls in the Option bar, and then clicking and dragging the image to better position it within the text.

● You can also resize the image by dragging any of the side or corner handles.

TIPS

Caution!

Once you click the Commit button, the text that you produced with the Type Mask tool is no longer "text." The text becomes just a shape and you cannot edit the words or phrases with the type tool.

Did You Know?

When you generate a type mask, the resolution of the text is the same as the resolution of the document. Note that the edges of the letters in low resolution documents may be jagged.

Try This!

You can apply the text you generate with the Type Mask tool to any layer. Select the layer before filling and the selection becomes active on the target layer.

TYPE, FIND AND REPLACE:
Locate and Change Text

The Find and Replace Text command enables you to quickly locate and change editable text. Using the Find and Replace Text dialog box, you can enter text for which you want to search and, if you want, text with which to replace it.

You can either globally find and replace all instances of a word or words with another word or words — that is, change all instances at once; or you can manually find an instance of a word, replace it, and then find the next instance, and so on. To globally find and replace, you use the Change All option. To

manually change words, you use the Find Next option and select the Change/Find option to find the next instance.

You have several options with the Find and Replace Text command. Search All Layers searches all text in any visible layers. Forward moves forward through the document when you select Find Next. Case Sensitive selects words that match not only the letters but also case. Whole Word Only finds and changes an entire word — not text that may contain fragment.

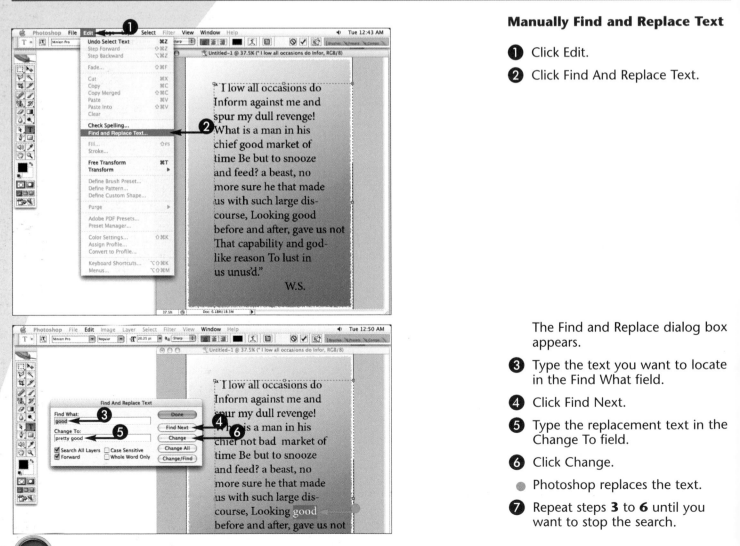

Manually Find and Replace Text

❶ Click Edit.

❷ Click Find And Replace Text.

The Find and Replace dialog box appears.

❸ Type the text you want to locate in the Find What field.

❹ Click Find Next.

❺ Type the replacement text in the Change To field.

❻ Click Change.

● Photoshop replaces the text.

❼ Repeat steps **3** to **6** until you want to stop the search.

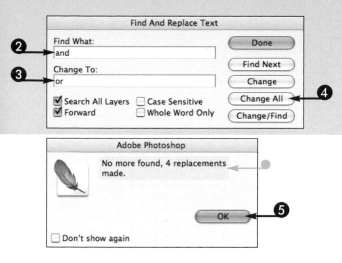

① Follow steps **1** to **3** in the section "Manually Find and Replace Text" on the previous page to open the Find and Replace Text dialog box.

② Type text to be found in the Find What field.

③ Type replacement text in the Change to field.

④ Click Change All.

● An information box appears telling you how many instances were replaced.

Photoshop replaces all instances of the specified text with the replacement text.

⑤ Click OK.

The Information box and the Find and Replace Text dialog box closes.

TIPS

Try This!

You can use the Find and Replace command to locate and replace punctuation marks, numbers, and even letter and word spaces.

Did You Know?

If you click Find Next and there are no remaining instances of the text you are searching for, a dialog box appears saying "No more found, (number) replacement made."

Warning!

If you select the Forward option (☑ changes to ☐) in the Find and Replace dialog box, make sure your cursor is at the beginning of your text. If the cursor is not at the beginning, you may be fooled into thinking that Photoshop did not find a particular word or text in your text box. Better yet, just deselect the Forward option (☐ changes to ☑) until you really need it.

TYPE, PARAGRAPH:
Generate Type in a Box

You can create type to label and add interest and information to your image. You have three ways to create type in Photoshop: from a point, on a vector path, or within a bounding box. Due to its lack of formatting, point text is best for only a word or two while a vector path, which follows the outline of a shape, is better for small amounts of decorative text. Text in a bounding box, shown in this technique, is best for large amounts of text because you can easily control text.

As you type in the bounding box, the text automatically wraps to the next line. You can then use the box's anchor points to resize the box and

reflow the text. You can also change the text's alignment, indentation, paragraph spacing, font, font size, scaling and letter spacing in the Paragraph and Character palettes, or in the Option bar. You can also use the Move tool and the Show Transformation Controls option in the Options bar to transform text.

See also>>

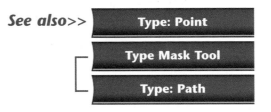

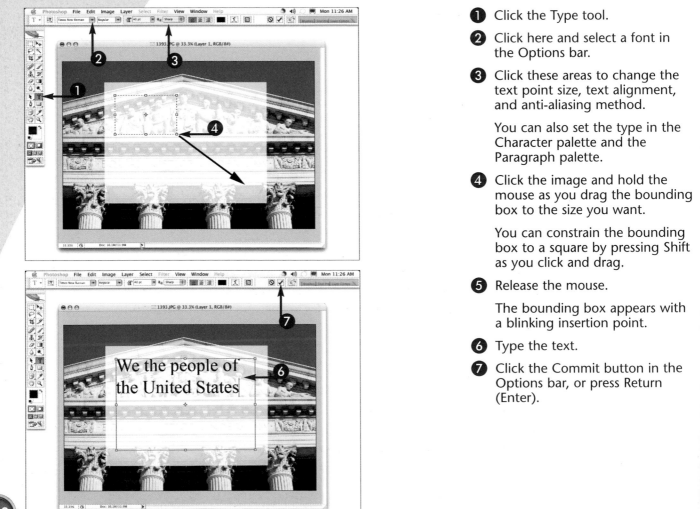

① Click the Type tool.

② Click here and select a font in the Options bar.

③ Click these areas to change the text point size, text alignment, and anti-aliasing method.

You can also set the type in the Character palette and the Paragraph palette.

④ Click the image and hold the mouse as you drag the bounding box to the size you want.

You can constrain the bounding box to a square by pressing Shift as you click and drag.

⑤ Release the mouse.

The bounding box appears with a blinking insertion point.

⑥ Type the text.

⑦ Click the Commit button in the Options bar, or press Return (Enter).

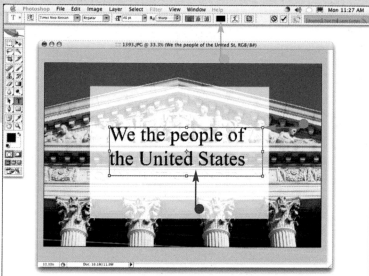

- You can re-adjust the size of the bounding box by clicking and dragging any of the corner or side points.

- You can click here to change the color of the text.

- You can place your cursor inside the bounding box and then click and drag the box to move your text.

Photoshop displays your text in the box reflecting your specifications.

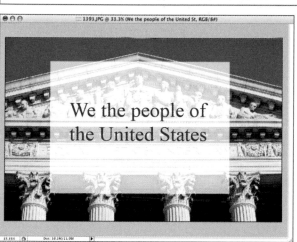

Did You Know?

To better control your point type, you can convert it to paragraph type text. Select the type layer, then click Layer, click Type, click Convert Point, and then click Convert Paragraph Text.

Try This!

You can transform your text by selecting its layer and pressing Cmd(Ctrl)+T. Clicking and dragging the handles of the bounding box transforms the text.

Try This!

You can convert type into paths or outlines of the letters by selecting the Type layer and then clicking Layer, Type, Convert to Work Path, or Convert to Shape. Work Path creates a path in the shape of your characters and the text retains its properties. Convert to Shape converts the text into an outline, which you can no longer edit.

TYPE, PATH:
Generate Type on a Curved Path

Text as an important design element is the basis for most graphic design. It is not surprising then, that Photoshop allows you to "play" with text by providing a way to flow text on or inside a shape or along an open path.

You first draw a path with the Pen tool or create a Vector shape with one of the Basic Shape tools. You then apply the Type tool to the path or the edge of the shape and flow the text as you type. Depending on the Type tool — Horizontal or Vertical — the text flows perpendicular or parallel to the baseline.

Once text is on a path you can edit it in various ways. You can select the shape or path containing the text with the Path Selection tool and move and transform it as with any other Photoshop object.

You can also change various characteristic of the text via the Options bar — things like alignment, orientation, font size, and color. You can also use the Character and Paragraph palettes to change characteristics of the type.

See also>>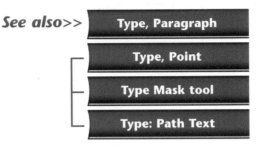

Type, Paragraph

Type, Point

Type Mask tool

Type: Path Text

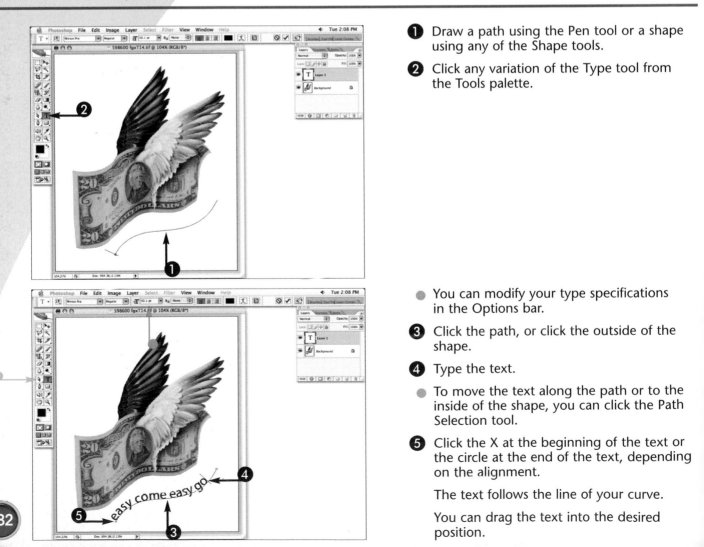

① Draw a path using the Pen tool or a shape using any of the Shape tools.

② Click any variation of the Type tool from the Tools palette.

● You can modify your type specifications in the Options bar.

③ Click the path, or click the outside of the shape.

④ Type the text.

● To move the text along the path or to the inside of the shape, you can click the Path Selection tool.

⑤ Click the X at the beginning of the text or the circle at the end of the text, depending on the alignment.

The text follows the line of your curve.

You can drag the text into the desired position.

TYPE, POINT:
Generate Type from a Point

You can type text in Photoshop by simply clicking anywhere on the surface of an image. Photoshop defines this as point type. Because the text you enter does not have a right or left limit, you must control its size manually. Alignment for point type works like a rectangle around the text. The left side aligns with the insertion point, the right aligns with the end of longest line of text, the top aligns with the first line of text and the bottom aligns with the last line of text. Flush left aligns text to the insertion point; flush right moves the rectangle so that the right side locates itself at the insertion point; center moves the rectangle so that its center is located at the insertion point.

Justification is not available for point type because — invisible rectangle aside — technically there are no right, left, top or bottom limits for point type and you cannot space the text into infinity. To justify the text, you must convert it to paragraph type.

See also>>

| Type, Paragraph |
| Type Mask Tool |
| Type, Path |

① Click the Type tool.

② Click here and select a font in the Options bar.

③ Click here and select a font point size.

④ Click a justification icon.

⑤ Click your image.

A blinking insertion point appears.

⑥ Type the text.

If your text comes to the end of the line, you must press Return (Enter).

⑦ Click the Commit button.

Your text appears on your image.

TYPE, CHECK SPELLING:
Assure Proper Spelling

The Check Spelling features allow you to checks for spelling accuracy to produce a more professional document. The feature checks your document against Photoshop's dictionary and displays the words that do not match. If know you spelled the word correctly, you can add it to the dictionary.

If you misspelled the word, by default, Check Spelling assesses the word in all unlocked and visible Type layers. To check only one layer, select the layer and deselect the Check All Layers option in the Check Spelling dialog box.

Check Spelling displays all misspelled or unfamiliar words in the Not In Dictionary field and offers the word's closest approximation in the Change To field. It also lists alternate substitute words.

As Check Spelling scans through the entire document, you can select from several actions: you can ignore one or all instances of the word; you can change one or every instance of the word; or you can add the word to Photoshop's default dictionary so that Check Spell does not flag the word as misspelled again.

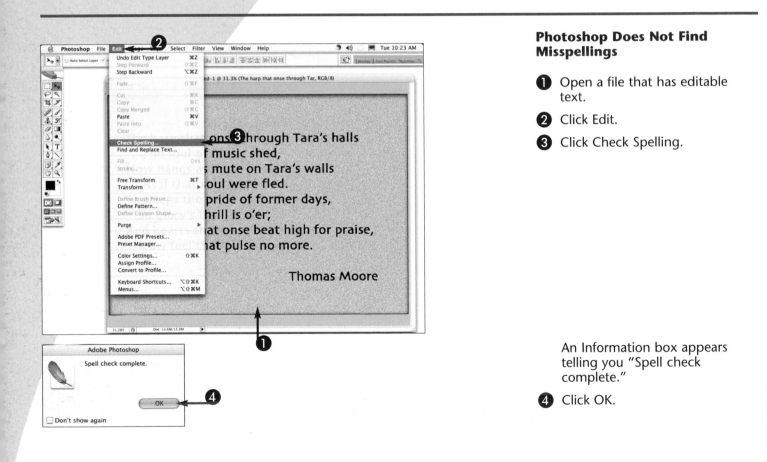

Photoshop Does Not Find Misspellings

① Open a file that has editable text.

② Click Edit.

③ Click Check Spelling.

An Information box appears telling you "Spell check complete."

④ Click OK.

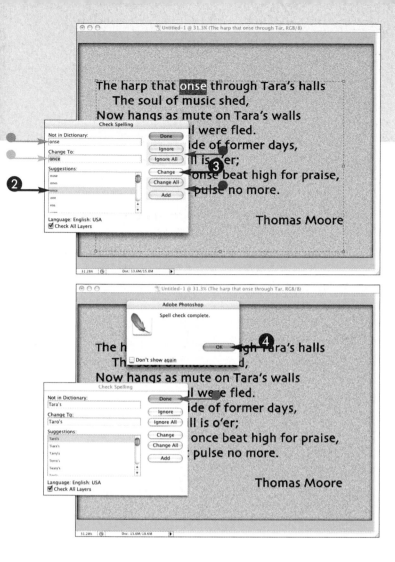

Photoshop Finds Misspellings

① Follow steps **1** and **2** on the previous page.

● The Check Spelling dialog box appears and displays the first unrecognized word.

② Click the correct spelling in the Suggestions field.

● Alternatively, you can type an alternate spelling or a substitute word in the Change To field.

③ Click Change.

● Alternatively you can click Ignore, Ignore All, Change All, or Add.

● You can click Done to exit Check Spelling at any time.

Check Spelling continues to display each unfamiliar word in the Check Spelling dialog box.

When Check Spelling finishes, a prompt displays telling you that the Spell check is complete.

④ Click OK.

TIPS

Try This!
To check the spelling of a single word, click the Type tool and then right-click the word. A menu appears from which you can select Check Spelling. If the word is not in its default dictionary, Photoshop displays the Check Spelling dialog box; if the word is in its dictionary, the information box announces that the check spelling is complete.

Did You Know!
You can specify the language dictionary that you want to use. At the bottom-right corner of the Character palette you find a fly-out menu from which you can select from 23 dictionaries.

Warning!
The Check Spelling command is not a substitute for proofreading. It simply flags words it does not recognize. It does not correct grammatical errors, misused words, or alternate spellings.

VECTOR MASKS:
Use a Path to Knockout an Area

You can protect or hide a section of an image by creating a mask that overlays that section. Photoshop converts any path that you draw with the Pen tool or any of the Basic Shape tools into a *Vector Mask*, which is fully editable with the Pen and Path Selection tools. This means you can add, delete, or modify the shape of the mask to produce very precise knockouts. Photoshop assumes that the interior of the shape is the visible portion of the image while the exterior of the shape is the mask.

Vector Masks are similar in function to Layer Masks, except that Vector Mask shapes are composed of Beziér curves — very precise, smooth lines, which

are unaffected by the size or number of pixels in an image. For less abrupt edges, you must use selection or drawing tools that do not create Beziér curves — the marquee tool for example. Then you can add feathering or some other softening technique.

Vector Masks appear as thumbnails in the Layers palette. The white portions of the thumbnail show the image, and the gray portions conceal the image.

See also>>

| Techniques: Paths |

| Techniques: Layer masks |

① Open an image.

② Click a shape tool or the Pen tool from the Tools palette.

③ Click the Paths icon in the Options bar.

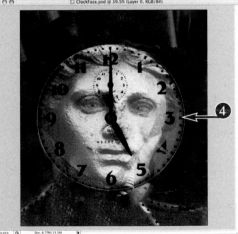

④ Draw a path around an area on the image that you want to isolate.

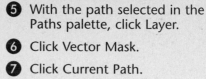

⑤ With the path selected in the Paths palette, click Layer.

⑥ Click Vector Mask.

⑦ Click Current Path.

● The path outline clips out anything outside the path, making it invisible and letting any layer beneath show through.

V

TIPS

Try This!
Click off the Vector Mask path in the Paths palette, deselect it, and hide the path outline. You can edit it at any time by selecting it again.

Try This!
You can apply layer styles to a vector mask layer. Double-click the layer and the Layers style dialog box appears. Add a drop shadow or any other style that appeals to you.

Did You Know?
You can create vector masks from the custom shapes that Photoshop provides. The palette of custom shapes is available when you select the Basic Shapes tool and click the Shape option on the Options bar. You can select from the default palette that is presented or load additional palettes that contain animal shapes, music notes, ornaments, and more.

VIDEO:
Prepare an Image for a Digital Video

Photoshop is not just a graphic tool for print and Web images. You can use Photoshop to create or modify images for use by a dedicated video application, and for post production.

Pixels are the foundation of the digital image. In Photoshop, you can vary the resolution of an image, and affect its size and quality. In the digital video realm, however, the size of an image is constrained by a constant resolution of 72 dpi and a fixed pixel *aspect ratio*, which is the relationship between the width and height of an image and which affects the actual shape of pixels. Video pixels can have two

shapes. In Photoshop and standard digital video digitized from analog, the pixels are square. In digital video created with a digital video camera, the pixels are rectangular.

A pixel's shape is an important characteristic of video frames. Not taking this into account may cause Photoshop to crop, stretch, or squeeze your images into a video frame. When you want to create an image for use in a video application, Photoshop helps you define the proper aspect ratio by providing preset sizes for different video formats.

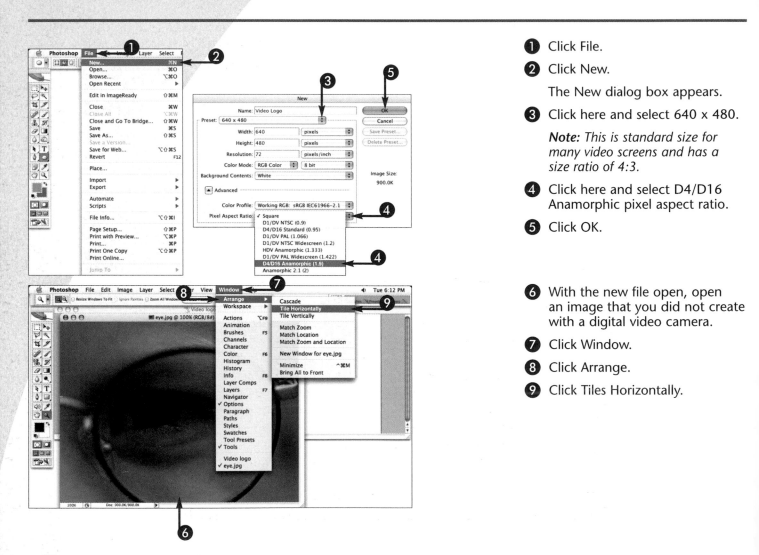

① Click File.

② Click New.

The New dialog box appears.

③ Click here and select 640 x 480.

Note: This is standard size for many video screens and has a size ratio of 4:3.

④ Click here and select D4/D16 Anamorphic pixel aspect ratio.

⑤ Click OK.

⑥ With the new file open, open an image that you did not create with a digital video camera.

⑦ Click Window.

⑧ Click Arrange.

⑨ Click Tiles Horizontally.

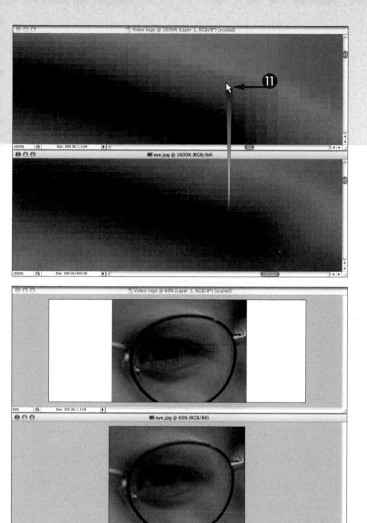

Photoshop positions the two files so that you can see both at once.

⑩ Zoom in on a section of the digital video camera image.

Note that the pixels are square.

⑪ Click and drag the current image into the file you created in steps **1** to **5**.

If you zoom in on a section of this file now, you will see that the pixels are not square.

⑫ Zoom the images until you can see them.

Note the difference between the two images.

⑬ Save the new file as a Photoshop file.

The image is ready for import into a video application.

TIPS

Did You Know?

You use RGB (Red/Green/Blue) color mode for screen or any other type of digital video output. The colors refer to the three colors of light that create all other visible colors. All images you create for use in a video or a screen must be in RGB mode.

Caution!

An image designed for use in video or screen must never exceed 72 pixels per inch (ppi). Increasing the ppi to 150 or 300 causes trouble because most monitors or other video devices do not support a resolution greater than 72 ppi, which means you actually increase your file's size without benefit.

WARP:
Bend and Twist an Image

Photoshop's new Warp function allows you to bend, stretch, push, or twist any image into an interesting shape. The Warp function superimposes a nine-celled grid over a layer or portion of a layer. You can drag the intersecting points and lines within the grid in any direction and in doing so, you can preview changes in your image as it conforms to the contours of the grid.

If you do not want to create a custom Warp shape, you can select from predefined Warp shapes (Styles) in the menu in the Options bar. Once you select a warp style, you can adjust the grid to customize the style.

The Warp Orientation icon in the Options bar adds another twist to adjust the manipulation of an image by allowing you to adjust the grid's orientation including toggling between a portrait and landscape orientation.

To change the shape of your grid with more precision, you can enter values for the percentage of vertical and horizontal distortion as well as the bend of the grid.

See also>>

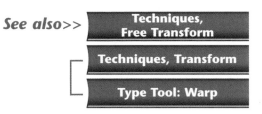

| Techniques, Free Transform |
| Techniques, Transform |
| Type Tool: Warp |

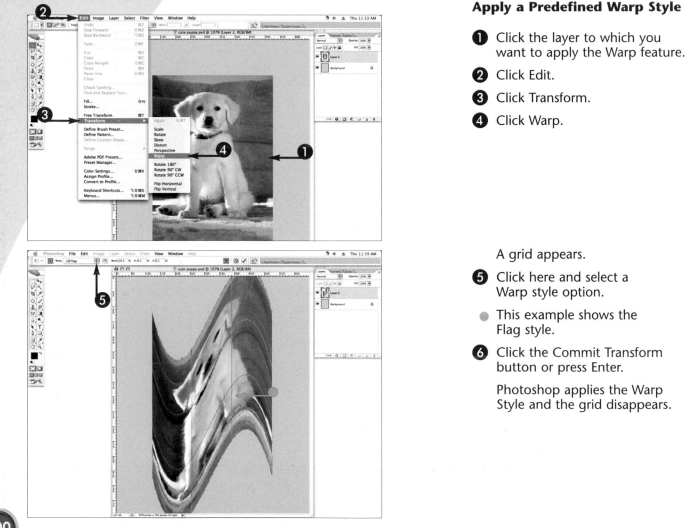

Apply a Predefined Warp Style

1. Click the layer to which you want to apply the Warp feature.
2. Click Edit.
3. Click Transform.
4. Click Warp.

A grid appears.

5. Click here and select a Warp style option.

● This example shows the Flag style.

6. Click the Commit Transform button or press Enter.

Photoshop applies the Warp Style and the grid disappears.

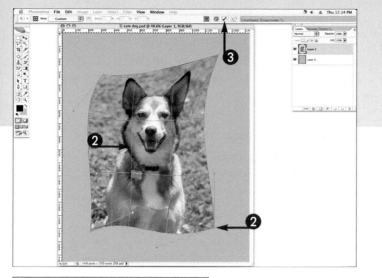

Apply a Custom Grid

① Follow steps **1** to **4** on the previous page.

A grid appears.

② Drag several points and lines of the grid.

Your image distorts.

As you drag the lines of the grid, handles appear.

You can click and drag these handles to make your image distort more.

③ Click the Commit button to implement the warp.

Photoshop applies your changes, and the grid disappears.

Did You Know?

You cannot Warp Text via the Edit command. Text has its own Warp option, which you can access when you select the Text tool.

Caution!

When you use some warp styles, such as Fisheye, the Orientation icon becomes unavailable or grayed out. This is because the shape that the style creates remains the same whether the orientation is portrait or landscape.

Try This!

You can also warp an image by using the Edit, Distort commands. Instead of a grid, a simple rectangle appears. Drag the corners and sides of this rectangle to warp your image.

WEB, ANIMATION:
Create a GIF Using Layers

An animation file displays a sequence of frames in rapid succession so that the eye perceives movement. Photoshop's new Animation palette creates animation files using a series of layers, which generate a sequence of frames for an animation. Although you do not create a movie with Photoshop or ImageReady — there are more appropriate and sophisticated applications out for that — you do create clips, which are short, small files for use on a Web page.

Although you can create a sequence of animation frames, you may find it simpler to transform a single image into an animation file. For example, you can animate an image of a single flower using duplicate layers each of which have small changes in color to create an almost fireworks-like animation. Alternatively, you can create a Tween animation.

Although elementary, the Animation palette offers more advanced options that allow you to control the delay rate and the number of times the animation repeats.

Once you create your animation, you can preview it in Photoshop's image window. You should also save the frames as a GIF file.

See also>>

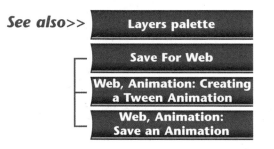

| Layers palette |
| Save For Web |
| Web, Animation: Creating a Tween Animation |
| Web, Animation: Save an Animation |

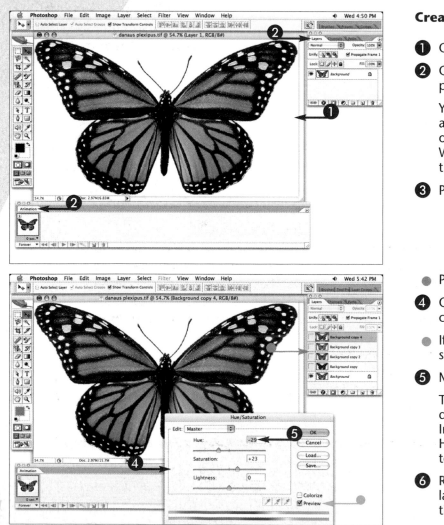

Create the Animation

① Open an image.

② Open the Layers and Animation palettes.

You can click Window and then Layers and Windows and then Animation to open the Layers palette. You can click Window and then Animation to click the Animation palettes.

③ Press Cmd+J (Ctrl+J).

● Photoshop creates a duplicate layer.

④ Open the dialog box or click the tool to change your image.

● If the dialog box has a Preview option, select it to preview your changes.

⑤ Make a change to your image.

This example opens the Hue/Saturation dialog box, which opens by clicking Image, then Adjustments, and then Hue/Saturation, and it makes changes to the image's hue.

⑥ Repeat steps **3** to **5** to create more layers, changing the image slightly each time.

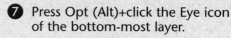

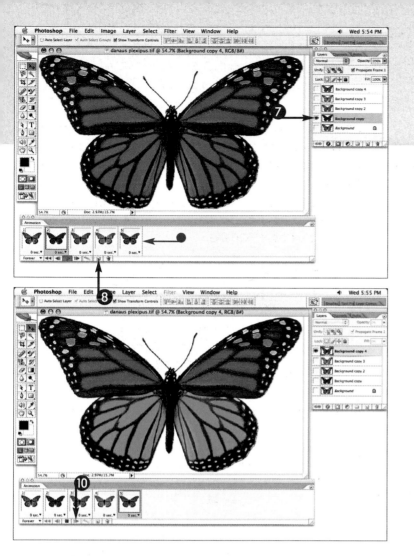

7 Press Opt (Alt)+click the Eye icon of the bottom-most layer.

Only that layer is visible.

8 Click the Duplicates selected Frames button on the Animation palette.

9 Repeat steps **7** and **8** until you reach the top-most layer.

● You have now created an animation frame from each layer.

Play the Animation

10 Click the Play Animation Button on the Animation palette.

The Animation plays in the Photoshop window.

You can now save your animation for the Web and place it on your Web page

You can now add your animation file to your Web page.

TIPS

Try This!

Instead of inventing ways to transition from frame to frame, try the Tweens option (⬚) in the Animation palette. Create an Animation clip with just two frames with the same image in two colors. Click ⬚ and determine how many frames you want to create between the initial two frames. Photoshop varies the opacity as it creates frames to make the transition from the first to the last frame smooth.

Did You Know?

The Save for the Web dialog box contains options for optimizing your files for the Web. You can preview several formats of your image and decide what combination of size and number of colors results in the best Web file.

WEB, ANIMATION:
Create a Tween Animation

Instead of creating an animation by duplicating layers and making small changes to each layer, you can quickly and easily create a Tween animation. The Tween (or between) option is a feature that creates intermediate frames to smooth transitions between or among frames.

The simplest way to create a Tween animation is to create two identical objects and then make a small change to one of the objects. For example, you can create two layers that have the same flower, and then paint the first flower's petals red, and the

second flower's petals blue. You can then apply the Tween option to create the "in between" frames to show a progression of the object. For the flower example, the petals change from red to blue. You control the number of in between frames.

See also>>

Web, Animation: Create an Animation with Layers

Web, Animation: Save an Animation

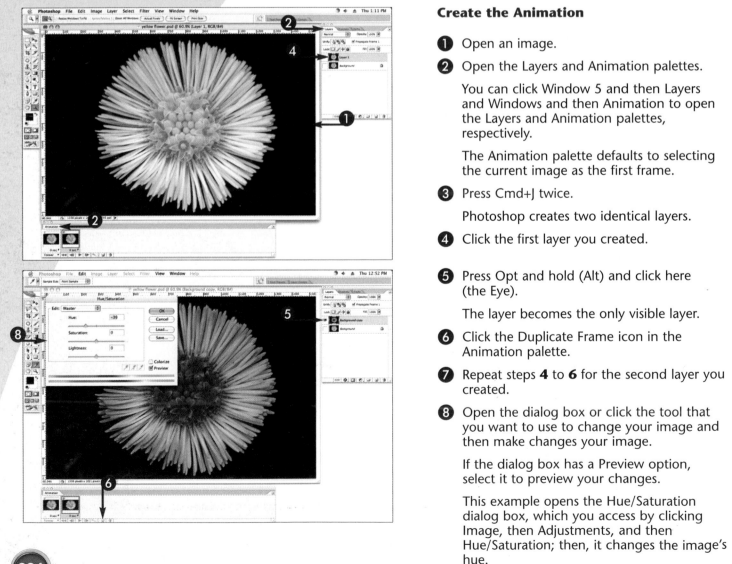

Create the Animation

1. Open an image.

2. Open the Layers and Animation palettes.

   You can click Window 5 and then Layers and Windows and then Animation to open the Layers and Animation palettes, respectively.

   The Animation palette defaults to selecting the current image as the first frame.

3. Press Cmd+J twice.

   Photoshop creates two identical layers.

4. Click the first layer you created.

5. Press Opt and hold (Alt) and click here (the Eye).

   The layer becomes the only visible layer.

6. Click the Duplicate Frame icon in the Animation palette.

7. Repeat steps **4** to **6** for the second layer you created.

8. Open the dialog box or click the tool that you want to use to change your image and then make changes your image.

   If the dialog box has a Preview option, select it to preview your changes.

   This example opens the Hue/Saturation dialog box, which you access by clicking Image, then Adjustments, and then Hue/Saturation; then, it changes the image's hue.

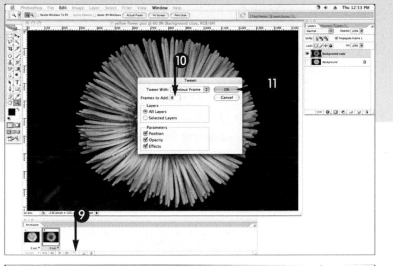

9 Click the Tween Animation Frames button in the Animation palette.

The Tween dialog box appears.

10 Type the number of "in between" frames you want to add.

11 Click OK.

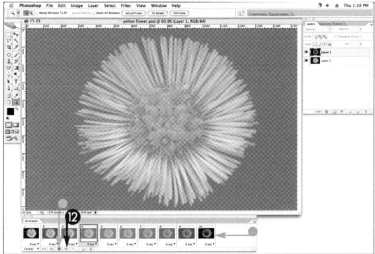

Play the Animation

Photoshop adds the number of frames that you specified in step **10**.

12 Click the Play Animation Button in the Animations palette.

● Photoshop processes each frame and then plays your animation in the Photoshop window.

● You can click the Stop Animation button in the Animation's palette to stop your animation.

TIPS

Try This!

When you optimize colors in an animation, you can use the Adaptive, Perceptual, or Selective palettes, which are color reduction algorithms that decide the optimum number of colors that result in a pleasing but efficient image. Remember that increasing the number of colors in an image increases the file size, which means a longer load time. You are the ultimate judge in balancing color with file size.

Did You Know?

When creating an animation in Photoshop, you can toggle directly to ImageReady. ImageReady gives you even more options designed to optimize and enhance your Animation file for use on the Web.

WEB, ANIMATION:
Save an Animation as a GIF

Once you create an animation file in Photoshop, whether you created it using duplicated layers or the Tweening option, you must save the file as a GIF because this format is what Photoshop and ImageReady recognize as an animation file.

Before you save your image, you must optimize it via the Save for Web dialog box, which controls the file size, number of colors, and preset GIF optimization settings. You first may need to resize the image on the screen because the size that appears when you initially open the dialog box is the size as it will appear on the Web. There is no formula for the optimum settings for your file. You must experiment

with the options, including dithering, transparency, and compression, and decide when your file has achieved the optimum settings. This example gives you an introduction to the possible options that optimize your animation file for the Web.

Once you are satisfied with your image's optimization, you can save your file as a GIF.

See also>> **Web, Animation: Create an Animation with Layers**

Web, Animation: Creating a Tween Animation

Web, Save For: Save Non-Animation Web Files

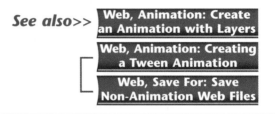

Optimize the Animation

1 Open an animation that you have previously created.

2 Click File.

3 Click Save for Web.

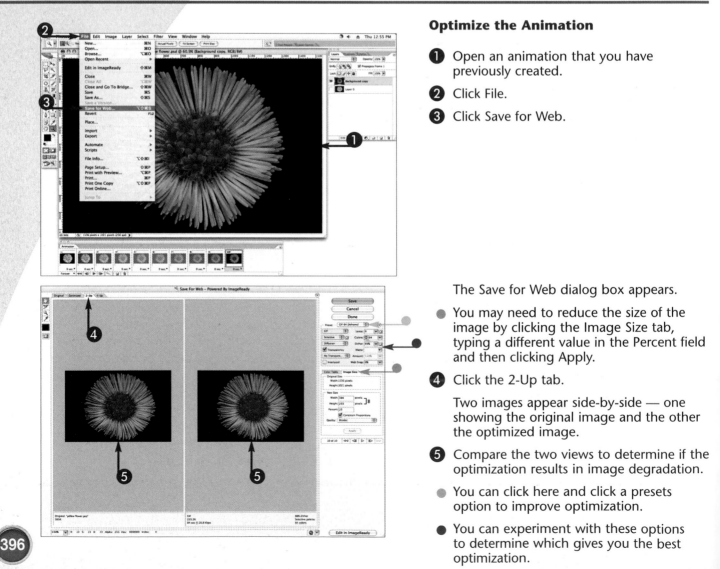

The Save for Web dialog box appears.

● You may need to reduce the size of the image by clicking the Image Size tab, typing a different value in the Percent field and then clicking Apply.

4 Click the 2-Up tab.

Two images appear side-by-side — one showing the original image and the other the optimized image.

5 Compare the two views to determine if the optimization results in image degradation.

● You can click here and click a presets option to improve optimization.

● You can experiment with these options to determine which gives you the best optimization.

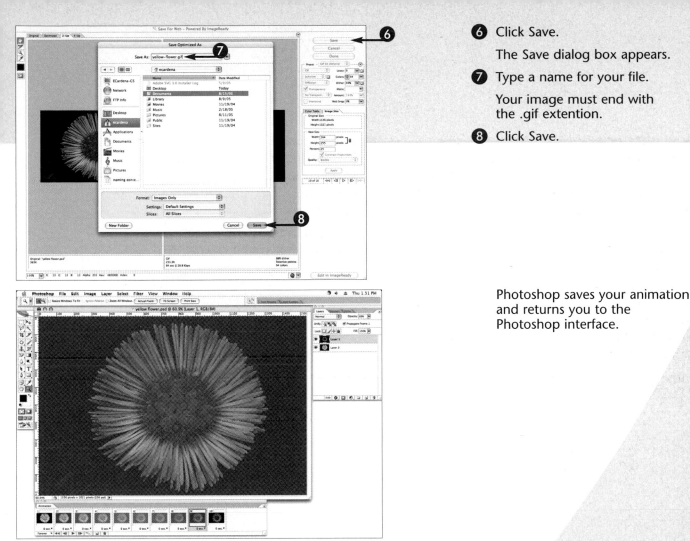

6 Click Save.

The Save dialog box appears.

7 Type a name for your file.

Your image must end with the .gif extention.

8 Click Save.

Photoshop saves your animation and returns you to the Photoshop interface.

TIPS

Try This!

You can establish the speed at which your animation moves from one frame by selecting all the frames and clicking the arrow on the lower right of any frame. A menu appears from which you can select a uniform time delay for your animation. You can also assign a different delay time for each frame.

Try It!

By default you animation is set to play "forever" — that is, it loops through the frame sequence until you or a program stops it. If you include your animation in a Web page, "forever" means that the animation plays from the time a user accesses the Web page until the time that he or she closes the page. If you do not want your animation to run forever, you can change the looping option to play only once or a precise number of times. To do so, click the Selects looping options button at the lower left corner of the Animation palette.

WEB, SAVE FOR:
Save Non-Animation Web Files

You can use the Save for Web command to save several types of Web friendly files. When you select this command instead of the Save or Save as commands, you can access a module of Photoshop that offers various Web optimizing file options.

In the Save for Web dialog box, you can preview and compare various optimization schemes. The Original tab shows the image before any changes; the Optimized tab previews the image with selected optimization features; the 2-Up tab compares the original image to the optimized image; the 4-Up tab shows the original image with three other optimization views. The right side of the dialog box offers file formats, compression options, color palettes, and color controls as well as pre-defined optimization sets.

The Save for Web dialog box works outside of Photoshop to created new and separate files from the one currently in the Photoshop window. Applied options are not reflected when you return to Photoshop. After you close the Save for Web dialog box, you can save the Photoshop image in any desired format.

See also>> **Web, Animation: Save an Animation**

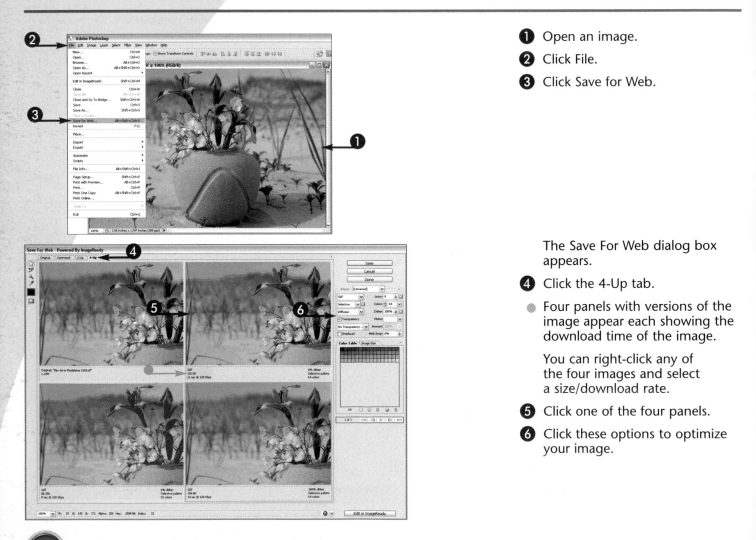

① Open an image.

② Click File.

③ Click Save for Web.

The Save For Web dialog box appears.

④ Click the 4-Up tab.

● Four panels with versions of the image appear each showing the download time of the image.

You can right-click any of the four images and select a size/download rate.

⑤ Click one of the four panels.

⑥ Click these options to optimize your image.

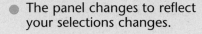

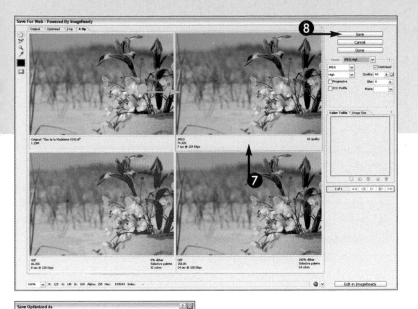

- ● The panel changes to reflect your selections changes.

  You can easily compare various images for quality, file size, and download rate.

7 Click the image you judge as best.

8 Click Save.

The Save dialog box appears.

The new file defaults to the preset type of the panel you selected.

9 Type a name for your file.

10 Click Save.

Photoshop saves your newly optimized file.

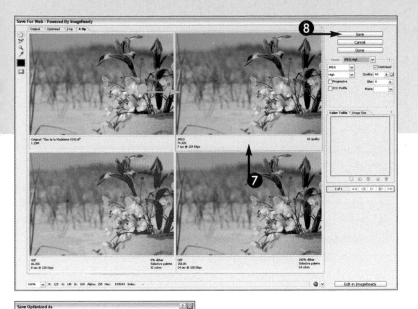

TIPS

Warning!
You determine the best size/download rate by making educated guesses. For example, if most viewers access the Internet with a modem (not DSL or Cable), that optimizes your file to a size/download rate of no more than 56K.

Did You Know?
JPEG, not GIF, is the best choice for uploading a photograph to the Web. GIF files use a discreet number of colors, resulting in abrupt transitions between colors, which give a paint-by-number look.

Did You Know?
You can decrease the download time of larger images by "slicing" them into smaller sections. You can divide an image into two or more sections with the Slice Select tool. Click the Slice Select tool and drag over a selection. You can then optimize each slice as if it were a separate image.

WORKSPACE:
Restore Palettes, Save Workspaces

The Workspace commands under the Window menu let you organize and save a working environment. The Photoshop working environment includes the location of palettes, tool settings, and default dialog box options. Although its most common function is to restore palettes to default settings and locations, you can also use the Workspace commands to reset keyboard commands and menus.

The Workspace command allows you to create custom workspaces for a particular set of actions

you need to perform. For example, if you are working on a set of paintings to which you want to apply uniform actions or techniques, it may be helpful to save the Brushes, Color, Swatches palette locations, attributes, and other settings. You save and then reload all these as needed.

Photoshop also provides a selection of workspaces that you can load and use. When you load a workspace, the relevant palettes are color coded in the Window menu.

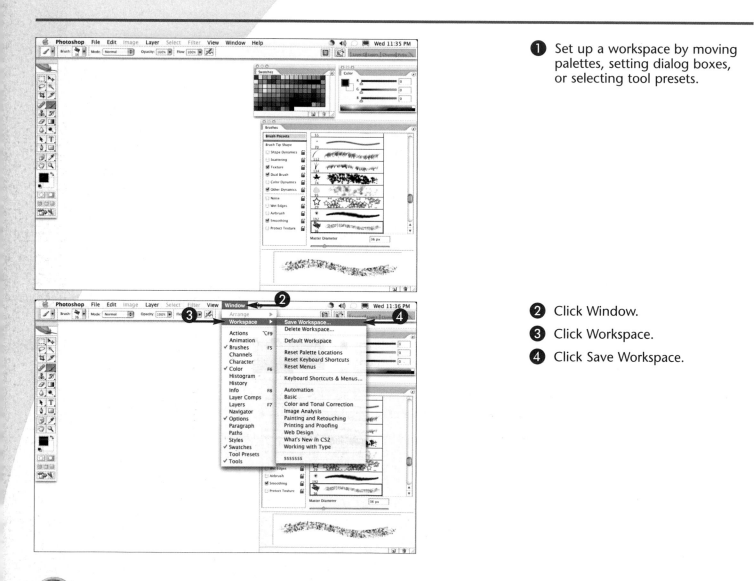

① Set up a workspace by moving palettes, setting dialog boxes, or selecting tool presets.

② Click Window.

③ Click Workspace.

④ Click Save Workspace.

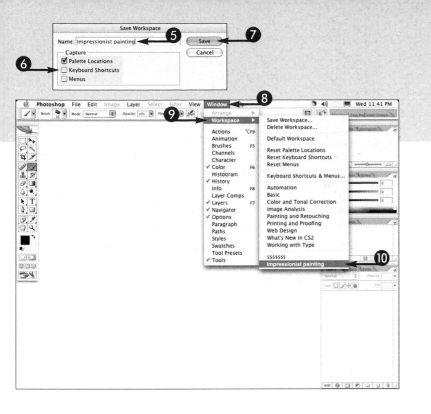

The Save Workspace dialog box appears.

5 Type a name for the workspace.

6 Click options that apply to your situation.

7 Click Save.

8 Click Window.

9 Click Workspace.

10 Click the name of your custom workspace.

The name of the workspace appears on the list in the Workspace submenu.

TIPS

Try This!

To delete a Workspace, click Window, click Workspace, click Delete Workspace. The Delete Workspace dialog box appears and you are presented with a list of available Workspaces. Select the workspace you want to delete, click delete, and then click Yes to confirm the removal of the Workspace.

Index

Numbers

8-bit images *versus* 16-bit, 182–183

A

actions. *See also* automations.
    apply to images, 128–129, 166
    convert color modes, 181
    record, 126–127
Add blending mode, 193
Add Noise filter, 244–245
Add to selection button, 84–85
Adjustment layers, 290–291
adjustments. *See also* Adjustment layers; filters.
    Auto Color command, 129–130
    Auto Contrast command, 129–130
    Auto Levels command, 129–130
    backlit images, 156–157
    balance color brightness, 136
    blending modes, 186–187, 230
    brightness, 130–131
    Channel Mixer, 132
    CMYK color, 158
    color, 129–130
    color balance, 131
    Color Balance command, 131
    color cast, 131, 134–135
    color gradients, 138
    color matching, 148–149
    Color Range command, 154–155
    color replacement, 154–155. *See also* Eyedropper tool;
      hue/saturation adjustments.
    color to grayscale, 132, 138
    contrast
        automatic, 136
        automatically, 129–130
        blending modes, 186–187
        by levels, 143–145
        manually, 130–131
        visually, 160
        white and black points, 144–147
    cool images, 150–151
    curves, 134–135. *See also* Duotone color mode.
    Curves command, 133
    Curves dialog box, 134–135
    darkness, 187
    Equalize command, 136
    exposure, 137, 156–157
    Exposure dialog box, 137
    Gradient map, 138
    grayscale to color, 140–141
    hue, 139
    Hue/Saturation command, 139–141
    Invert command, 142
    Levels command, 143–147
    lightness, 187
    line-art from photographs, 159
    linked layers, 301
    Match Color command, 148–149
    monochrome, 132
    negative images, 142
    opacity, 230
    Photo filter, 150–151

Posterize command, 152–153
Replace Color command, 154–155
saturation, 139
Selective Color command, 158
serigraph effect, 152–153
Shadow Highlight command, 156–157
soften effects, 230
Threshold command, 159
tonal range, 130–131, 133, 134–135
Variations command, 160
warm images, 150–151
Adobe Bridge, 122–125. *See also* File Info command.
Advanced Blending sliders, 313
aliased lines, 76–77
Align command, 161
alignment
    See gridlines
    See guidelines
    See rulers
    See Smart Guides
Alpha channels, 198–199, 352. *See also* Quick Mask.
anchor points
    add, 63
    convert, 63
    delete, 63, 73
    stretch, 64–65
angle gradients, 32–33
Angle option, 190
animation
    banner-like marquee, 253
    for the Web
        GIFs, 392–393, 396–397
        Save for Web command, 398–399
        from single image, 392–393
        tweens, 394–395
annotations
    See also Audio Annotations tool
    See also File Info command
    See also metadata
    See also Notes tool
    clear all, 3, 55
    create, 2–3, 54–55
    delete, 3, 55
    description, 2–3
    save, 352
anti-alias technique, 354–355. *See also* feathered edges.
Apply Image command, 162–163. *See also* Calculations command;
    Layers palette.
Arrange command, 164–165
arrowheads, 101
As Copy option, 352
aspect ratio, 383
Audio Annotations tool, 3. *See also* annotations; Notes tool.
Auto Color command, 129–130
Auto Contrast command, 129–130
Auto Levels command, 129–130
automatic selections, 88–89
Automation Batch command, 166. *See also* Adobe Bridge; Droplets.
automations. *See also* actions.
    batch processes, 166
    color modes, convert, 181
    Conditional Mode Change command, 181
    Contact sheet command, 168–169
    contact sheets, 168–169
    convert to applications, 170–171
    Crop and Straighten command, 167

Index

Index

Index

Index

Index

Index

Index